THE QUEERNESS OF NATIVE AMERICAN LITERATURE

INDIGENOUS AMERICAS

Robert Warrior, Series Editor

Chadwick Allen, *Trans-Indigenous: Methodologies for Global Native Literary Studies*

Raymond D. Austin, *Navajo Courts and Navajo Common Law: A Tradition of Tribal Self-Governance*

Lisa Brooks, *The Common Pot: The Recovery of Native Space in the Northeast*

Kevin Bruyneel, *The Third Space of Sovereignty: The Postcolonial Politics of U.S.–Indigenous Relations*

Glen Sean Coulthard, *Red Skin, White Masks: Rejecting the Colonial Politics of Recognition*

James H. Cox, *The Red Land to the South: American Indian Writers and Indigenous Mexico*

Daniel Heath Justice, *Our Fire Survives the Storm: A Cherokee Literary History*

Brendan Hokowhitu and Vijay Devadas, *The Fourth Eye: Māori Media in Aotearoa New Zealand*

Thomas King, *The Truth about Stories: A Native Narrative*

Scott Richard Lyons, *X-Marks: Native Signatures of Assent*

Jean M. O'Brien, *Firsting and Lasting: Writing Indians Out of Existence in New England*

Paul Chaat Smith, *Everything You Know about Indians Is Wrong*

Lisa Tatonetti, *The Queerness of Native American Literature*

Gerald Vizenor, *Bear Island: The War at Sugar Point*

Robert Warrior, *The People and the Word: Reading Native Nonfiction*

Robert A. Williams Jr., *Like a Loaded Weapon: The Rehnquist Court, Indian Rights, and the Legal History of Racism in America*

The Queerness of Native American Literature

Indigenous Americas

Lisa Tatonetti

MIN
NE
SO
TA

University of Minnesota Press
Minneapolis
London

Portions of the Introduction and chapter 1 were previously published as "Native American Literatures," in *The Cambridge History of Gay and Lesbian Literature,* ed. Ellen McCallum and Mikko Tuhkanen (Cambridge University Press, 2014); copyright 2014 by Cambridge University Press. Portions of chapter 3 were previously published as "From Wallace to Wishkob: Queer Relationships and Two-Spirit Characters in *The Beet Queen, Tales of Burning Love,* and *The Last Report on the Miracles at Little No Horse,*" in *Critical Insights: Louise Erdrich,* ed. P. Jane Hafen (Hackensack, N.J.: Salem Press/Grey House Publishing, 2013), 207–28; reprinted by permission of EBSCO Information Services, Ipswich, Massachusetts. An earlier version of chapter 4 was previously published as "Visible Sexualities and Invisible Nations: *Big Eden, Johnny Greyeyes,* and *The Business of Fancydancing,*" *GLQ: A Journal of Lesbian and Gay Studies* 16, nos. 1–2 (2010): 157–81.

Published by the University of Minnesota Press
111 Third Avenue South, Suite 290
Minneapolis, MN 55401-2520
http://www.upress.umn.edu

Library of Congress Cataloging-in-Publication Data

Tatonetti, Lisa.
The queerness of Native American literature / Lisa Tatonetti.
(Indigenous Americas)
Includes bibliographical references and index.
ISBN 978-0-8166-9278-1 (hc : alk. paper)
ISBN 978-0-8166-9279-8 (pb : alk. paper)
1. American literature—Indian authors—History and criticism. 2. American literature—20th century—History and criticism. 3. Gays' writings, American—History and criticism. 4. Gender identity in literature. 5. Lesbianism in literature. 6. Homosexuality in literature. 7. Indians in literature. I. Title.

PS153.I52T38 2014
810.9'897—dc23 2014002049

Printed in the United States of America on acid-free paper

The University of Minnesota is an equal-opportunity educator and employer.

20 19 18 17 16 15 14 10 9 8 7 6 5 4 3 2 1

For all the Native writers whose work I read, teach, study, and love. Your words change lives, mine among them.

Contents

· INTRODUCTION ·

Two-Spirit Histories

Two-Spirit writers are merging the selves that colonialism splits apart.

—Beth Brant, *Writing as Witness*

THE *QUEERNESS OF NATIVE AMERICAN LITERATURE* is meant to function as both literary map and critical lens. On one hand, its analyses work to expand the archive, while on another, they endeavor to provide new ways of seeing. At its center, this study hinges on links among queerness, Indigeneity, and relationship, whether such affiliations are acknowledged or ignored, (re)claimed or disavowed. Across the course of my investigation, such associations first undergird the construction of a genealogical narrative of a field, showing it to be a map of relationship(s), and then help recover long-forgotten ties between two simultaneous literary renaissances in the 1970s. Building from these archival recoveries, we then resee the unruly articulations of queer relationships in now-canonical Native literature and subsequently analyze how three narrative films deny relationship by representing sexual and national affiliations as opposing "choices" for queer Native people. Finally, these links among queerness, Indigeneity, and relationship coalesce in a queer Indigenous methodology that dares to imagine land, self, and family in the wake of attempted genocide. In each case, whether by undertaking recovery, forwarding textual analysis, or defining Indigenous methodology, this study enters into conversation with—and, I hope, expands—queer Indigenous studies as a discrete field of knowledge with its own histories and its own practices of meaning making.[1]

To set up this claim, I turn first to a brief overview of the nuanced Indigenous histories that, as central points of reference for so many of the queer Native writers analyzed here, necessarily background any attempt to map a genealogy of queer Native literatures. Understandings of gender and sexuality in North American Indigenous communities differed significantly from those of the Spanish, French, and Anglo conquistadores, explorers, missionaries, travelers, settlers, and early anthropologists whose documentations of encounter provide much of the written records of these historical periods. Many Indigenous communities recognized third and fourth genders and acknowledged roles for tribal members whose gender expression existed outside a naturalized male/female binary. Among the Zuni, for example, gender was considered an "acquired rather than an inborn trait. Biological sex did not dictate the roles individuals assumed."[2] These complex gender roles and performances countered dominant European gender ideologies, and thus, at times, explorers and settlers responded to such differences with horrifying violence. In one of the best-known early examples, when Vasco Núñez de Balboa encountered men dressed in women's clothes in Panama in 1513, he stripped the men naked and loosed his dogs to kill them. In 1540, Álvar Núñez Cabeza de Vaca described his time among the Karankawa Indians of Texas, saying, "In the time that I continued among them, I saw a most brutish and beastly custom, to wit, a man who was married to another, and these be certaine effeminate and impotent men who goe clothed and attired like women, and performe the office of a woman."[3] Evidence of the nuanced gender roles that scandalized Cabeza de Vaca does not exist for every Native nation; however, anthropologist Will Roscoe argues, "Alternative gender roles were among the most widely shared features of North American societies," having "been documented in over 155 tribes."[4] The extant eighteenth- and nineteenth-century documentation demonstrates gender variance existed in every region of North America, crossing geographical, national, and linguistic boundaries.[5] These multiple gender roles were as diverse as Native nations themselves. Sue-Ellen Jacobs explains that the definitions of these roles may "encompass cross-sex, same-gender sexual relationships yet . . . may not include same-sex, cross-gender sex. . . . The sexuality of individuals originally classified as 'berdache' . . . turns out to be not exclusively homosexual, nor exclusively transgendered, nor transvestite. Some males were (and still are) classificatory women, and some females were (and still are) classificatory men for life or for shorter, specified periods."[6] Such gender diversity reflects the complexity of Indigenous cosmologies, and the public decline of these complex gender systems relates directly to the sustained settler assault on Indigenous traditions. As a result of physical and psychological pressures from settlers, practices that once had been essential components of daily life transformed into less visible—though still extant—ways of being. Perhaps the best-known contemporary anthropological work on Two-Spirit peoples in North America has been undertaken by Native anthropologists Beatrice

Medicine, Wesley Thomas (Navajo), and, more recently, Brian Joseph Gilley (Chickasaw/Cherokee) and Anglo anthropologists Jacobs, Sabine Lang, Roscoe, and Walter L. Williams.[7]

While Native nations had tribally specific terms for those in gender-variant positions—such as "winkte" among the Lakota and "nàdleehí" among the Navajo—anthropologists historically used the term "berdache," which has connotations of sexual deviance. In 1990, at the third annual Native American/First Nations gay and lesbian conference in Winnipeg, Canada, a group of Indigenous scholars and activists instead coined the term "Two-Spirit." As Jacobs, Thomas, and Lang explain in their landmark collection *Two-Spirit People,* this decision responded to an anthropological history that situates Native people as objects of study and to the troubling etymology of "berdache." More important, though, by coining "Two-Spirit," Indigenous people not only reclaimed the power of self-definition but also created a concept that evoked Indigenous rather than colonial histories and cosmologies.[8] At the same time, the transhistorical, pan-Indian term marked Native American and Aboriginal peoples' desire to distance themselves from non-Native queer peoples. Qwo-Li Driskill (Cherokee), Chris Finley (Confederated Tribes of the Colville Reservation), Gilley, and Scott Lauria Morgensen argue that the "advent of the term *Two-Spirit* began a new era in the study of past and present Native American gender and sexual diversity."[9] While "Two-Spirit" has not been universally embraced, the term indexes an ideological shift that marks the inception of queer Indigenous studies.[10]

Seeing the Split

One of the foremothers of the field, Bay of Quinte Mohawk writer Beth Brant, references the ideological shift in understandings of queerness and Indigeneity when she argues, in the piece from which I take my epigraph, that "Two-Spirit writers are merging the selves . . . colonialism splits apart."[11] Though Brant wrote these words more than twenty years ago, this enforced split between sexual and tribal identities continues to exist today, even as queer Indigenous studies emerges as a scholarly field. Such fissures mark not only the sort of historic violences mapped in the previous section but also, as Mark Rifkin points out in *The Erotics of Sovereignty,* a particular way of seeing queerness, Indigeneity, and Indigenous nationhood.

I was reminded of the persistence of the split, even among well-meaning Native studies scholars, at a recent academic panel I attended. The panel's topic was one of the field's foundational meetings, "Native American Literature: Criticism and Curriculum," which took place in 1977 over the course of a twelve-day seminar in Flagstaff, Arizona. Laguna author Paula Gunn Allen (1939–2008), another major figure in queer Native literature, was the project director of the Flagstaff meeting and edited the influential book that came out of that gathering: *Studies in American Indian Literature: Critical Essays and Course Designs* (1983). With these connections in mind, I asked the panel, "How did discourses of queerness circulate in the 1970s, given Allen and Mohawk poet Maurice Kenny's centrality to these early meetings? Or did such discourses circulate at all?" During the ensuing discussion, a panelist shared a story about attending an early 1980s reading Allen gave at the Newberry Library with her then partner, white lesbian feminist Judy Grahn. The speaker noted that Allen's overt references to lesbian sexuality "made the Indian audience uncomfortable." This observation was followed by the suggestion that much of Allen's acclaim had come from the lesbian, gay, bisexual, transgender, transsexual, intersex, and queer (LGBTIQ) community. In the context of the comment, it was clear that the LGBTIQ community was imagined as necessarily, even inherently, non-Native.

However unintentionally, these statements envision two discrete communities—a heterosexual (or at least heteronormative) Native audience and a non-Native LGBTIQ audience. Relationship between the two is disavowed, and in the process, an implicitly heteronormative narrative of the field's construction is put forth. Although these were off-the-cuff answers to an on-the-spot question, the beliefs that ground this academic exchange speak to the necessity of centering queer texts, images, and methodologies in Indigenous studies. *The Queerness of Native American Literature* moves toward that goal by demonstrating that the field of Native literature was always already queer.

Merging the Selves, Mending the Split

I begin the work of (re)centering queerness in Native literary studies by stating an important but still unrecognized intersectional reality: the study of Native literature as a scholarly field came into being at roughly the same time as the publication of early queer Native literature, and the two bodies of work were, in fact, driven by many of the same queer Indigenous intellectuals. Allen, for example, from the outset of her career, was both a significant creative writer and an important academic voice. Her first poetry collection, *The Blind Lion,* was published in 1974, just a year before she received her doctorate in American studies from the University of New Mexico.[12] During this same period, Allen played a pivotal role in the development of American Indian studies. As Rodney Simard explains in his editorial notes for the 1987 retrospective issue of *Studies in American Indian Literatures (SAIL),* "ASAIL [the Association for the Study of American Indian Literatures] was founded in 1971, . . . in order to raise consciousness and extend 'Red Power,' by a small group of scholars . . . who gathered at MLA for the first time in 1972."[13] This group was "spearheaded by Paula Gunn Allen and Robert W. Ackley of Navajo Community College."[14] The 1977 Flagstaff conference was part of an intentional development of American Indian literary studies, as was the conference's resulting newsletter, which would later become the academic journal *SAIL.* By 1980, the scholarly collective Allen helped found had named the journal's first editorial board, which, today, reads like a veritable who's who in the field: Paula Gunn Allen, Gretchen Bataille, Joe Bruchac, Larry Evers, Vine Deloria, Dell Hymes, Maurice Kenny, and Robert Sayre. Despite the fact that Allen was key to *SAIL*'s development and queer Native writers such as Allen, Kenny, and Brant were crucial to the field's inception as scholars, creative writers, and editors, scholarly conversations about Two-Spirit literature were slow to develop. In fact, The critical reception of Allen's texts can be read as a narrative of a field becoming.

The reception of queer Native literature falls into three distinct phases over the course of *SAIL*'s history. From the journal's inception as the Association for the Study of American Indian Literatures' newsletter in 1973 to the mid-1980s, when *SAIL* had become a full-fledged academic journal, critical conversations about contemporary queer Native *literature* did not yet occur (although *anthropological* discussions of the figure of the "berdache" had by then an already long history). From 1985 to the early 1990s, references to queer Native literatures were veiled, appearing, if at all, in book reviews of texts by writers such as Allen and Brant rather than in full-length critical essays. In 1994, Susan Gardner edited a special issue of *SAIL* titled "Feminist and Postcolonial Approaches," which prefigures the recognizable body of scholarly criticism about queer Native literatures that blossomed in the late 1990s and early 2000s. Upon returning to these early critical pieces for this book, I was struck by a clear commonality: the rise of early scholarship on Two-Spirit literature is marked by essays on the first novel to have an overtly queer protagonist—Allen's 1983 *The Woman Who Owned the Shadows.*[15]

If the response to Allen's fiction drove early criticism on queer Native literature, the responses to Allen's critical writing could be read as a synecdoche for one of the central schisms in the field of Native American and Indigenous studies about the visibility and importance of Indigenous erotics: Is attention to historical traditions of gender variance a distortion of Indigenous political priorities? Is it a settler colonial intrusion into Native American and Aboriginal cultures? And, concomitantly, is queer Indigenous literature simply a distraction from the "real" concerns of Native studies, nations, and peoples? These questions, which mirror the previously referenced conference conversation, can be found in early critical reactions to Allen's theoretical interventions.

One example of such discomfort can be seen in M. Annette Jaimes (Juaneño/Yaqui) and Theresa Halsey's (Hunkpapa Lakota) 1992 collection, *The State of Native America: Genocide, Colonization, and Resistance,* which was published not only on the eve of the Columbus quincentennial but also at a time when many more queer Native writers were coming to press (as chapter 1 will demonstrate). In a discussion of the very real problem of non-Indians legitimating queer identities by portraying Indigenous practices as universal, Jaimes and Halsey argue that Allen "pander[s] to the needs and tastes of non-Indian gay and lesbian organizers."[16] Further, they cite "an Inuit lesbian poet," who argues for a sort of hegemony of queerness: "Now comes this idea, brought in from the outside for reasons that really have nothing to do with us, that Indianness and homosexuality are somehow fused, that you can't 'really' be Indian unless you're gay or lesbian, or at least bisexual. . . . [T]he danger is that it could eventually cause divisions among us Indians that never existed before, and right at the point when we're most in need of unity."[17] Queer Indigeneity functions as a specter of menace here, threatening tribal solidarity and, in the process, feeding the cultural imperialism Jaimes and Halsey critique throughout their work. In this scenario, Allen serves as a lightning rod for anxieties about the imbrication of Indigeneity and queerness that evinced themselves in the early years of the field. Within such fears, the legibility of same-sex Indigenous desire threatens an imagined Indigenous heteronorm and, subsequently, endangers Indigenous coalition and sovereignty. In this equation, heteronormativity *is* Indigeneity.

Writing ten years after Jaimes and Halsey, in *Indigenous American Women: Decolonization, Empowerment, Activism,* Devon Abbott Mihesuah comments on Allen's 1986 *The Sacred Hoop:*

> Personally speaking (and this is what Allen is doing), I have never heard anyone knowledgeable about my tribe's (Oklahoma Choctaw) traditional gender relations speak of such commonplace homosexuality, and neither my husband (Comanche) nor anyone in his family has heard of such things among his tribespeople, either. My Navajo, Apache, and Hopi students (many of whom hail from traditional families), in addition to my Mohawk, Salish-Kootenai, Sioux, Cherokee, and Assinaboine friends and colleagues—both heterosexual and homosexual—also find the notion unsettling. Often discussions about homosexuality (such as this one) reveal that there is a connection between the authors' personal lives and the topic they write about, rendering the issue interesting but subjective.[18]

Mihesuah's remarks, which occur within a discussion of matrilineality and women's social and political power, situate homosexuality in a sort of Indigenous "don't ask, don't tell" space that is specifically set apart from her analysis of women's empowerment. Like Jaimes and Halsey, Mihesuah understands tribalism as inherently heteronormative: the "personal" experience of queerness exists entirely outside the tribal. These regulatory deployments of tradition function much as those critiqued by Diné feminist historian Jennifer Nez Denetdale in her work on the Diné Marriage Act of 2005 and prominent queer Indigenous studies scholars Craig Womack (Muscogee Creek/Cherokee) and Daniel Heath Justice (Cherokee Nation).[19] Denetdale challenges nationalist ideologies that frame Indigenous nationhood and sovereignty within U.S. nation-state models. Such models, she argues, advance American imperialism and "manifest a hatred and intolerance of difference within Navajo society."[20] This post-9/11 "militarized Navajo cultural landscape has led . . . tribal leaders to call for a return to traditional values [that] actually reinscribes patriarchy."[21] Justice terms such deployments of tradition "exclusivist and often very selective" discourses "that are used to exclude queer Indians from the supposedly tribal 'real,' and the complexity of rhetorical (self-)representations of queer Native desire."[22] As examples of how this ideological schism over Native representations manifests in early readings of Allen's work, Jaimes and Halsey cast queerness as divisive, non-Native, and a threat to Indigenous coalition, whereas Mihesuah invokes the weight of tradition to disavow Indigenous histories of gender variance and same-sex erotics.

Though Allen has, at various times, been dismissed as dangerous, essentialist, anachronistic, and as forwarding a "romantic, sentimentalized Euroamerican notion of the Indian," Womack argues, "Allen's critics need to do a better job of analyzing the historical moment that surrounds *The Sacred Hoop* and contributes to her views of women's and Native identities."[23] I would add that, like the regulatory anecdote recounted by the conference panelist, early anxieties about Allen's work speak to larger issues: they show how the split between sexuality and Indigeneity is described and demanded and they depict a field coming into being. In each case, these conversations index how, in the words of queer of color theorist Roderick A. Ferguson, "canonical formations outline trajectories for ethical subject formation; they specify what it means to be a human, a citizen, and a moral being. As champions of normativity, these formations can only be consummated through the regulation of nonheteronormative difference."[24] The critical reception of Allen's fiction and theory therefore provides a window into the ideological tensions that historically accompanied canon formation in queer Native studies. Allen is, then, vital to the historiography of *both* Native studies *and* queer Indigenous studies as well as to our acknowledgement of the imbricated nature of the two; she "merges the split" on multiple levels. Thus the entwined stories of the scholarly reception to Allen's creative and critical writing provide one beginning to *The Queerness of Native American Literature,* the narrative of the (somewhat rocky) road to (something like) a body of critical approaches to a queer Indigenous literary tradition.

The Erotic Imaginary in Indigenous Literature

While the texts and authors addressed in this study are imbricated in an Indigenous intellectual history with roots as deep and ancient as the continent, they also cannot be separated from broader historical events of the 1960s, 1970s, and 1980s, when African American, Chicana/o, Asian American, American Indian, Aboriginal, women's, and gay and lesbian civil rights battles were gaining momentum and press across North America. These rights-based *political* movements of the mid- to late twentieth century in every case had corresponding *literary* movements. Many early queer Native writers came to prominence in the journals and anthologies that arose as part of these important political movements: queer Indigenous writers published both in largely white LGBTIQ venues and in 1980s and 1990s women/queer of color anthologies.[25] In *Methodology of the Oppressed,* Chela Sandoval argues this latter coalition of feminist writers/activists "developed an original form of historical consciousness, the very structure of which lay outside the conditions of possibility that regulated the praxes of 1960s, 1970s, and 1980s U.S. social movements."[26] Ferguson, following Immanuel Wallerstein, discusses this historical period as a point at which "liberal ideology seemed to have flourished globally. . . . Western nations were presumably turning away from their past oppressions and national liberation movements were coming to power throughout the third world."[27] However, the liberal capitalist impetus of this period, as Ferguson shows, carried normative imperatives for gender and sexuality often duplicated in otherwise radical resistance movements like the Black Panther Party and the American Indian Movement. The rise of U.S. third world or women of color/queer of color feminisms countered these normative imperatives. Though not often discussed as such, queer Native writers like Allen, Chrystos (Menominee), Brant, and Midnight Sun (Anishinaabe/Métis) were as much a part of these collaborative women/queer of color movements and anthologies as they were of concurrent Native political movements. Thus another central claim of this book is that queer Native literature comes from a space of *opposition* (to dominant settler norms, to normative neoliberal agendas, to heteronormative resistance movements) *and* a space of *relationship and coalition* (with other Native queers, with other queers of color, with other Indigenous peoples).

A return to Ferguson helps us parse out this delicate balance between coalition and unity, allowing us to remember, as Cherríe Moraga cautions, that while "the danger lies in ranking the oppressions," at the same time, "the danger lies in failing to acknowledge the specificity of the oppressions."[28] Moraga speaks of the difficulty of alliance politics; these difficulties undergird the ways queer Native literature aligns with and differs from queer of color politics. On one hand, as addressed at length in chapter 1, this space of coalition is an important and heretofore overlooked correspondence between Native and non-Native queer of color writers—the history of the field is a map of relationship(s). On the other hand, the critiques of nationalism, so important to the histories that Sandoval and

Ferguson mine, translate poorly, if at all, to Native contexts as Jaimes and Halsey's and Mihesuah's challenges to Allen illustrate—nationalism cannot be (and is not) so definitively rejected by Indigenous writers. And in fact, "nation" is defined differently in various Indigenous contexts.[29] Articulating the black lesbian feminist contribution to a queer of color paradigm, Ferguson maintains, "In terms of black feminism, black lesbians went farthest in retheorizing culture so that it would reflect a gender and sexual disruption to heteropatriarchy and inspire practices and formulations that were alternative to nationalism."[30] Ferguson draws stark distinctions between black nationalist and black lesbian agendas and praxis, locating the disruptive possibilities of black lesbian consciousness as necessarily outside the boundaries of nationhood, which in this equation is envisioned as necessarily limiting to queer writers and thinkers. However, queer Native writers from this same era produce work that often *demands* the acknowledgment of tribal nationalism and sovereignty. As Rifkin notes, "not all nationalisms are equivalent."[31] For this reason, I suggest that while Allen's early critics define Indigeneity as radically outside a queer continuum, queer Native feminists and, subsequently, queer Native literature and theory turn on an understanding of the erotic as not simply tied to but actually *constitutive of* sovereignty and Indigenous nationhood. Thus rather than a point of division from or within Native communities, "the erotic," to use Sharon Patricia Holland's words, functions as "one particular kind of glue."[32]

As well, the erotic is often tied explicitly to a deployment of the term "queer." Womack contends that "behind the use of the term queer is the argument that gay people are not the same as straight people, that a queer frame of reference causes one to see the world differently than a straight frame of reference does."[33] Queer folks, in this book, can be lesbian, gay, bisexual, transgender, transsexual, intersex, Two-Spirit, and even, on occasion, heterosexually identified. Queerness is a social category and therefore a subjectivity (albeit of a fluid nature). Queerness is not, though, simply the opposite of heterosexuality. Instead, queerness, to use Beatrice Medicine's wording, encompasses multiple "facets of action."[34] At its most generous, queerness serves as an umbrella term, and therefore same-sex desire, nondominant gender performances, Two-Spirit community building, nonerotic partnered relationships, and male lactation are all queer practices examined in this book (even though the folks who perform and depict such practices may well term neither these examples nor themselves queer). Transnational queer theorist Jasbir Puar contends, "There is no exact recipe for a queer endeavor, no a priori system that taxonomizes the linkages, disruptions, and contradictions into a tidy vessel."[35] At the same time, queerness, as Puar and Indigenous studies scholars such as Justice, Morgensen, Rifkin, Andrea Smith, and Womack have shown us, provides an analytic, a way of seeing, a path to understanding (some part of) our ever-shifting contexts.[36]

Importantly, queer names a subjectivity or practice that diverges from *dominant* norms. Queer practices or desires and concepts like the heteronorm or queer imaginary necessarily work within and/or against a settler-defined sex/gender dichotomy. What we term, for lack of better words, "gender nonconformity," "gender variance," "homosexuality," or "third or fourth gender practices" would not have been queer in original contexts and may not be queer today in certain Indigenous communities. In fact, the central claim of this book—that Native literature was always already queer—in many ways rests on a faulty premise: in most instances, the *historical* practices invoked to make this claim were *not* originally constituted as queer. Yet I nevertheless continue to forward this statement because the post-1970s Native literary tradition that *The Queerness of Native American Literature* focuses on was created *within* (and most times purposefully *against*) settler understandings of sex and gender. Thus while the term "queer" is inadequate in some contexts, its resilience and resistance speaks to the work of the Native writers in this study, even though it cannot fully describe that writing and cannot always adequately describe the people creating such art.

While the erotic often parallels the term "queer," the two are not interchangeable. The erotic is a theoretical concept that encompasses nonnormative gender practices and, particularly, the experience, articulation, and generative nature of desire. Unlike queer, the erotic is not a subjectivity. The product and process of embodied desire, the erotic is both an active praxis and an analytic. Articulated first by black lesbian feminist Audre Lorde in *Sister Outsider* (1984), the erotic, she tells us, is a "power," a "resource," a "creative energy" that arises from a "depth of feeling."[37] The erotic also forges activist consciousness: "Recognizing the power of the erotic within our lives can give us the energy to pursue genuine change within our world, rather than merely settling for a shift of characters in the same weary drama."[38] Speaking of the same neoliberal capitalist imperatives that Sandoval and Ferguson later examine, Lorde explains that "within living structures defined by profit, by linear power, by institutional dehumanization, our feelings were not meant to survive."[39] The erotic, then, when acknowledged, is a decolonial imperative—to feel, to remember, to act—that is *situated in the body.*

In "Your Skin Is the Map," Osage scholar Robert Warrior articulates the erotic through a reading of Muscogee Creek author Joy Harjo's poetry, likewise reminding us that "theory, however abstract, is something that is done in our bodies."[40] "The erotic," Warrior continues, "thus, is a key to affirming the worth and the wholeness of the self. Its expression is an act of resistance and colors all other such acts."[41] Brant, too, sees physical, psychic, and political power in the erotic: "The use of the erotic in Native lesbian work becomes a tool by which we heal ourselves. . . . But Native lesbian writing is not only about sex and/or sexuality. There is a broader cultural definition of sexuality that is at work here. *Strong bonds to Earth and Her inhabitants serve as a pivotal edge to our most sensuous writing.*"[42] This physical, emotional, sexual, and political relationship to land, which is a key aspect of Indigenous literatures more broadly, permeates the Indigenous concepts of the erotic referenced throughout *The Queerness of Native American Literature.*

As chapter 1 will discuss further, Brant, Driskill, and Deborah A. Miranda (Ohlone/Costanoan-Esselen Nation/Chumash) all posit versions of the erotic that likewise see this embodied experience of desire as endemic to Indigenous histories of resistance. Miranda argues an Indigenous erotic "has a particular context for this particular continent," especially as "both love and the erotic are at odds with the violence and domination that structures any colonizing or patriarchal culture."[43] Thus an Indigenous erotic confronts "five hundred years of colonization" and "historical traumas [that have] directly target[ed] Native women's bodies" and modes of expression.[44] For Indigenous writers, reclaiming the "power," "resource," and "creative energy" of the erotic, to use Driskill's words, "relates our bodies to our nations, traditions, and histories."[45] Rifkin contends these complex articulations of Indigenous erotics represent "alternative visions of peoplehood and sovereignty."[46] This vision of the erotic as tied to land, nationhood, and political and sexual sovereignty is a key distinction between the erotic imaginaries in queer of color and Indigenous literatures and theories. While numerous scholars—including Brant, Driskill, Miranda, Rifkin, Warrior, and Womack—have discussed some version of what Miranda has termed the "Indigenous erotic" and Driskill a "sovereign erotic," I return us briefly to Allen's *The Sacred Hoop* to consider how this foundational text can augment early critical understandings of the erotic in Native studies.

While Allen never explicitly refers to "the erotic" in her critical terminology, she nevertheless deploys the theoretical concept in her early construction of an Indigenous feminist theory. Like Lorde, Allen links the erotic and power and subsequently imagines that assemblage as related to but not defined or contained by desire. To use her words, the erotic is a "sexual connection" or "power that women carry within their bodies."[47] Like Brant's "strong bonds to Earth and Her inhabitants," Allen's feminist imaginary includes an embodied sexual desire that privileges Native people's interactions with land.[48] Moreover, Allen connects erotic power to Indigenous creation stories, citing Pueblo and Cherokee oral traditions. In both cosmologies, Allen notes, a creator figure "made the first food from her own body-seed."[49] The erotic consequently functions as body/land matrix: "By transferring the power she possesses to the corn and tobacco (her flesh and her bones), [the creator] makes certain that the life forms she has vitalized will remain vital. Thus one aspect of her power is embodied in the children, while another aspect is embodied in the corn and tobacco. In their mutual energy transfer, all will live."[50] By enmeshing the erotic in these Indigenous creation stories, Allen imagines a community-centered, landscape-specific, erotic cosmology. The narrative of affiliation and relationship inherent in Allen's early concept of the erotic becomes, as the ensuing chapter will show, a hallmark of queer Native studies. Rifkin makes the astute observation that "starting from an erotics, embodied sensations and sensitivities, yields a different perspective on—a new *metaphor* for—practices and histories of peoplehood."[51] Allen suggests that perhaps this metaphor has been here all along.

Queer Writers and Images in Indigenous Literatures

Sociologist Joane Nagel argues that "national and sexual boundaries are mutually reinforcing" and "implicit in the meaning of national boundaries ('who are we?') are certain prescriptions and proscriptions for sexual crossings."[52] Such prescriptions have had significant consequences in Native literary studies where, as chapter 1 demonstrates, with only a few notable exceptions, analyses of Indigenous texts precluded considerations of sexuality until the late 1990s. *The Queerness of Native American Literature* is part of a recent upsurge of scholarship that addresses this gap. To do so, each chapter turns on a narrative of relationship and a different type of recovery: the genealogical, the archival, the thematic, and the methodological.

Chapter 1 offers a provisional history of the authors, genres, and subjects of queer Native studies, narrating a map of relationship(s) and thereby providing a much-needed genealogy of the field. Chapter 2, a recovery and analysis of Kenny's early poetry from 1970s queer journals, moves from broad canvas to brush stroke, using the historical archive to expand our understanding of the relationship between two concurrent literary renaissances and to challenge heteronormative concepts of the Native 1970s. Chapter 3 stages recovery through a return to the fiction of one of the most prominent writers in Native literature, Louise Erdrich (Anishinaabe). By tracing the queer characters and relationships in more than twenty-five years of Erdrich's texts, this chapter underscores the claim that, in inception, theme, and content, the body of Native literature has always been queer. The subsequent chapter expands the analysis of queer characters and images—a concern that stretches across this book—to perhaps the most readily accessible representations of queer Native people: those in narrative film. Thus chapter 4 examines how the imbricated fields of queerness, Indigeneity, and nationhood circulate in three twenty-first-century narrative films: Thomas Bezucha's *Big Eden* (2000), Jorge Manuel Manzano's *Johnny Greyeyes* (2000), and Spokane/Coeur d'Alene author/filmmaker Sherman Alexie's *The Business of Fancydancing* (2002). Looking at how our imaginative geographies sever sexuality from Indigeneity and nation, thereby *denying* relationship, this chapter argues for the productive possibilities of queer Indigenous studies as a critical lens. Chapter 5 undertakes a final recovery in an analysis of Koyoonk'auwi Maidu writer Janice Gould as an important but understudied poet and further extends the deployment of queer Native studies as analytic. Keeping in mind sociologist Leslie McCall's contention that "different methodologies produce different kinds of substantive knowledge," this chapter reads across Gould's three understudied poetry collections—*Beneath My Heart* (1990), *Earthquake Weather* (1996), and *Doubters and Dreamers* (2011)—to consider how Gould constructs queer diasporic practices, locales, and processes of identification through a methodology I term "Indigenous assemblage."[53] This mobile and generative practice acknowledges the *shifting* nature of events, experiences, and perception, the known *and* unknown. Finally, the conclusion looks toward the future of queer Indigenous studies. As a whole, *The Queerness of Native American Literature* offers both map and compass, considering both the genealogy and geography of queerness in Native literature from the 1970s to the present.

· CHAPTER 1 ·

A Genealogy of Queer Native Literatures

> *Our writers of today are marking new directions on the path that was originally mapped out for us. We are making new signposts. There is a strong movement of Native gay and lesbian poetry and prose. We write honestly about homophobia from our own communities, as well as those outside us. We write about love, about sex, about the history of Two-Spirits. There are more voices coming from the working class and working poor amongst us. Many of us are teachers, continuing the tradition of passing on our history and language. We write about that. We write about being mothers, fathers, maids, teachers, factory workers, healers; we write about being writers, artists.* We write about being human.
>
> —Beth Brant, *Writing as Witness*

THIS CHAPTER steps into a vibrant, ongoing conversation about queer images and texts in Native American and Aboriginal literatures. In some ways, we can read this conversation as having been ongoing since time immemorial—perhaps picking up from the drawings of multiply gendered kachina figures holding both a bow and corn in the Petroglyph National Monument on the outskirts of Albuquerque, New Mexico; from the first time the Diné told the story of Turquoise Boy; from the interview with Osh-Tisch, a Crow boté in 1919; or from the stories of Hastíín Klah, a well-known Navajo nàdleehí, or the Brown Weasel woman, a female Piegan warrior. Histories of gender variance and stories about and by what we might today broadly define as queer Native people have existed in the land now called North America since the first people to live on this land fell from the sky, emerged from below, or migrated here as the glaciers crept forward. The conversation *The Queerness of Native American Literature* enters, then, is ancient and charts the survivance of Indigenous people and traditions from these origin points to the present day.

If the roots of these narratives go back to time immemorial, they also, one could argue, emerge from a post-1970s literary renaissance in which queer Native voices and texts proliferate. As I'll discuss at length in chapter 2, the earliest iterations of overtly queer Native literature occur in the wake of two concurrent political moments rarely spoken of together—the post-Stonewall movement for gay rights and the Red Power era of Native activism. I suggest the Native American and Aboriginal writers publishing from the 1970s to the present offer *another* beginning to *The Queerness of Native American Literature,* one that emerges from the activism and imagination of the late twentieth century.

I speak here about a literary tradition—or more specifically, a genealogy—not in a Western-based, chronological sense that marks time as linear (though I address chronology in this chapter) but in the sense of genealogy as a map of relationship(s), as a way to better see and recognize kinship. The story of queer Native literature—which both explodes into visibility in the past fifteen years and emerges from time immemorial—narrates genealogy *through* the web of such relationships. These relationships, like third and fourth gender roles in Native communities, may at times have been driven underground, overlooked, or even reviled, but the connections between and among queer Indigenous peoples themselves, as well as the webs that tie contemporary Indigenous peoples to earlier Native understandings of sexuality and gender, remain extant. This chapter thus maps a history of queer Native literature and criticism as a way to exhume and invigorate genealogical connections, as a way to demonstrate that the seeming renaissance of the twenty-first century, like all such renaissances, stems, as Robert Warrior might remind us, from deep and abiding roots and long-standing Indigenous intellectual traditions.[1]

Reseeing 1970s Literary Histories

Some of the earliest overtly queer Native literature has been, until recently, relatively unknown. In Native literary studies, this lack of visibility stems from two impulses in the field. The first hinges on a scholarly (and perhaps readerly) preoccupation with full-length fiction: attention was (and still is) paid to full-length fiction at the expense of short stories, memoir, nonfiction, drama, and, most importantly, poetry, which is by far the most common genre in Two-Spirit literature. The second source for this lack of visibility is a (mis)understanding of the Red Power era as inherently heteronormative, a time when, as Craig Womack might say, "men were men and buffalo were scared."[2] Thus despite the establishment of the Gay American Indians (GAI), a political organization cofounded in 1975 by Barbara Cameron (Lakota) and Randy Burns (Paiute) during the Red Power era, queer Native people during this period were often represented as products of settler colonialism—Indigenous queerness was therefore crafted not as historical continuity but as a settler incursion into an imagined Indigenous heteronorm (as seen in the examples that began this book). However, rather than being inherently oppositional, the post-Stonewall movement for gay rights and the Red Power era of Native activism coalesce in the emergence of queer Native literature in the 1970s.

I briefly turn here to Maurice Kenny's 1970s poetry—which I analyze at length in chapter 2—to lay the groundwork for this claim. Though more queer Indigenous texts and authors will undoubtedly be reclaimed as we move further into the twenty-first century, Kenny is currently the first Native American writer to publish literature with overtly queer themes. Born in 1929 in Watertown, New York, he published his first poetry collections in the 1950s and his first work with Two-Spirit themes in the 1970s. *Only as Far as Brooklyn,* the earliest of Kenny's collections to include explicitly queer work, was published in 1979 by Good Gay Poets, a press that arose in the wake of the 1969 Stonewall Rebellion. Good Gay Poets emerged from the flourishing intellectual concerns of the Boston Gay Liberation Front as part of the queer literary renaissance, which included small publications and independent presses aimed at gay and lesbian audiences.

The earliest of Kenny's work from these journals appears in the fall 1974 issue of *Fag Rag,* which contains "A Night, a Bridge, a River: (Beneath Brooklyn Bridge)" and "Greta Garbo." As I show in the next chapter, these poems center queer urbanity and gay male relationships rather than Indigeneity and depict Brooklyn Park, a space known for gay cruising, as a site of queer connection. By contrast, "Apache," which Kenny published in the June 1975 edition of *Mouth of the Dragon,* satirizes stereotypical expectations of Indigeneity. Thus the titular Apache "warrior" rides not a horse but a "Yamaha" motorcycle. Likewise, he "hotel[s]" in "wild Oakland" as opposed to lodging on a reservation, in a tribal village, or in the dusty west of the U.S. popular imagination.[3] Ultimately, Kenny's poems from the gay journals and newspapers of the queer renaissance destabilize dominant representations of Native identities in which Indigenous men are often depicted as hypermasculinized warriors ineluctably bound to the nineteenth century in affect and action. Refutations of such inaccurate images of Native peoples recur from the earliest pieces of Native literature in English to the present. Thus this motif marks the relationality of concerns between and among Native peoples, whether living on reserves, on reservations, or in cities and, importantly to this genealogy, whether identifying as Two-Spirit, queer, or straight.

If Kenny's work, as "Apache" demonstrates, includes themes seen throughout Native literature, it also indexes a concern specific to queer Native literature: the historical existence of same-sex desire in Indigenous cosmologies. The interest in Two-Spirit histories in this era extends into the arena of Indigenous politics, as characterized by the objectives of GAI, the first political organization for queer Native people.[4] Burns explains the organization's goals in an *Advocate* interview: "We are really trying to break down stereotypes in both directions. In the Indian community, we are trying to realign ourselves with the trampled traditions of our people—Gay people were respected parts of the tribes. . . . In the gay community, we're trying to break down the image of the Indian as a macho militant that gay white people have."[5] These distortions and divisions were manifest in the disparate gay and Native journals and newspapers of the 1970s where Kenny's writing functioned as one of the few links between the two concurrent bodies of literature. As such, Kenny's 1970s writing sheds light on (a sometimes concealed) relationality, signaling the possibility of affiliation between and among diverse peoples and politics that have heretofore gone largely unacknowledged in our (re)imaginings of the Native 1970s.

A prime example of Kenny's interest in the historical existence of same-sex desire in Indigenous communities can be seen in his best-known queer-themed poem, "Winkte," which was originally published together with "Loves into Legends" in *ManRoot*'s spring/summer 1977 issue. "Winkte" calls for recognition of the accepted role Two-Spirit people had in their tribal nations. However, while "Winkte" casts queer sexuality and Indigeneity as intimately imbricated—Two-Spirit people, the speaker claims, strengthen rather than threaten their tribal nations—such was not the case in the literary history of the era during which these pieces were published. In fact, Kenny's little-known poetry from 1970s gay journals challenges the markedly heteronormative ethos of the Native newspapers, journals, and literary collections of the Red Power era.[6] I conclude chapter 2 with one such heteronormative response: a 1977 letter written by the editor of the influential Native American journal *Akwesasne Notes* to the editors of the U.S. gay journal *RFD* that characterizes queer Native sexuality as "not normal and a detriment to" Native lifeways.[7] As this refusal of relationality suggests, acknowledging the potential *associations* between the post-Stonewall gay publishing renaissance and the American Indian literary renaissance radically shifts our 1970s imaginary. By drawing such associations, this genealogy enables us to see not something new but that which has always been: like the lived histories of Native peoples, the literary history of Native studies was queer since its inception.

Queer Indigenous Literature Anthologized

While Kenny's post-Stonewall poetry provides an important foundation for lesbian, gay, bisexual, transgender, transsexual, intersex, and queer (LGBTIQ) Native literatures, the best-known early articulation of Two-Spirit concerns can be found in the influential women/queer of color anthologies that emerged in the 1980s. These anthologies were born from the period I discussed in the Introduction, which Leslie McCall terms a "moment of critique, in which hegemonic feminist theorists, poststructuralists, and antiracist theorists almost simultaneously launched assaults on the validity of modern analytical categories."[8] Key among these were "critiques by feminists of color of white feminists' use of *women* and *gender* as unitary and homogenous categories reflecting the common sense of all women."[9] Such critiques were first issued in newsletters and periodicals published by women of color organizations across the country.[10] The year 1974, for example, saw the formation of the Combahee River Collective, which challenged the heteronormative agenda of the National Black Feminist Organization by "construct[ing] a notion of black women that was simultaneously queer, antiracist, feminist, and socialist."[11] That same year, Salsa Soul Sisters Third World Wimmin Inc., a multicultural lesbian organization, was founded and subsequently began publishing *Third World Women's Gay-Zette* in 1976. Out of these political movements came collections of poetry, prose, and essays that challenged the racial bias of white feminism and the heterosexism of many rights-based political groups of color. These women/queer of color anthologies gave queer Native writers a heretofore absent visibility. Yet despite their importance to Native women's and queer Native literature, these anthologies, like the queer journals of the 1970s, have not been discussed as central to the body of Native literature. In fact, the divide between Indigenous literature and theory and women/queer of color literature and theory has, until recently, yawned like a chasm. However, as I'll show here, the two bodies of work are intimately related (though, as in most relationships, intimacy does not necessarily engender understanding). Thus while such anthologies signal a coalitional politics, they also at times threaten to subsume the specific concerns of queer Indigeneity under the rubric of a generic multiculturalism, a monolithic queerness, or, concomitantly, a heteronormative vision of Indigeneity. As this survey will illustrate, then, white feminists are not the only ones to forward the homogenous signifiers McCall invokes. Despite such limitations, an overview of crucial anthologies from the past thirty years points to the key authors and evolving concerns of queer Native literature from the early 1980s to the present day.[12]

Gloria Anzaldúa and Cherríe Moraga's 1981 *This Bridge Called My Back: Writings by Radical Women of Color* is the earliest and best known of such collections. *This Bridge*'s significance stems not only from its status as the first collection of literature by women of color but also from its direct address of the imbricated relationships racism, poverty, and sexism have with homophobia. The anthology includes five queer writers who identify either as Native or as Native and Latina: Barbara Cameron (Lakota), Jo Carrillo, Chrystos, Naomi Littlebear Morena, and Anita Valerio (Blood/Chicana—now Max Wolf Valerio). While these writers share concerns with other women of color, such as that of violence against women, they also powerfully depict issues particular to Indigenous peoples, such as stereotypical expectations about Native identities and the generational trauma of settler colonialism. Thus Chrystos invokes Native peoples' histories in government boarding schools—"In the scars on my knee you can see children torn from their families / bludgeoned into government schools"—while Cameron describes the reservation/nonreservation divide and "the realities of being an Indian in South Dakota," where "Indians were open game for the white people, to kill, maim, beat up, insult, rape, cheat, or whatever atrocity the white people wanted to play with."[13] In addition, the Native writers in *This Bridge* confront subjects in which queer Indigenous peoples hold vested interests, such as Valerio's contention that "lesbianism" can function as "a barrier" to tribal affiliation.[14] *This Bridge,* then, maps the connections and disjunctions between Native women and other women of color, whose calls for coalition often failed to recognize the specificity of tribal nationhood as well as those between

Two-Spirit and more canonical Native literature from this period, the latter of which did not overtly engage same-sex concerns.[15]

In terms of thinking genealogically, the groundbreaking collections from this period of literary history hinge on relationships: personal (the relationships between and among women of color as friends), activist (the relationships between and among people of color, especially women, as social change agents), and systemic (the relationships between people of color, especially women, and the settler state logics of oppression that attempt to restrain and contain them). Beth Brant's important 1984 collection, *A Gathering of Spirit: A Collection of Writing and Art by North American Indian Women,* for example, stems from her friendship with Michelle Cliff and Adrienne Rich, then editors of the multicultural lesbian literature and arts journal *Sinister Wisdom.* With Cliff and Rich's encouragement, Brant began soliciting work for the first anthology of Native women's writing edited by a Native woman. Brant's *A Gathering of Spirit,* which first appeared as a 1983 special issue of *Sinister Wisdom,* included among its sixty-plus contributors twelve women who identified as Native lesbians.[16] Brant's collection centers on relationships across affiliations of ethnicity, gender, sexuality, and experience as the words of established writers intermingle with those of women who are poor, imprisoned, and unknown in the literary world. Brant explains, "I wrote everywhere I thought there was a story to tell. I wanted to hear from the women yet unheard. I wanted voices traditionally silenced to be a part of this collection. So I wrote to prison organizations in the U.S. and Canada. I made contact with the anti-psychiatry network, Native women's health projects. I sent to everyone I could possibly think of and then looked for more."[17] As a result, *A Gathering of Spirit* powerfully illustrates how the realities of class, sexual violence, and incarceration imbricate any understanding of Indigenous sexualities. Thus while the writers in Brant's collection address themes vital to Native literature, they also more overtly engage the relationship between and among settler colonial policies, the prison industrial system, and Indigenous peoples and communities than did *This Bridge* or any previous collection of Native literature. Looking back at her experience with *A Gathering of Spirit,* Brant comments, "Perhaps there is a lesson here. When Natives have the opportunities to do *our own* editing and writing, a remarkable thing can happen. This thing is called *telling the truth for ourselves*—a novel idea to be sure and one that is essential to the nurturance of new voices in our communities."[18]

As *A Gathering of Spirit* underscores, a pivotal aspect of the genealogy I chart here is its transnational—or what Chadwick Allen would term "trans-Indigenous"—nature: texts, themes, and authors in this queer Native literary history traverse the U.S.–Canadian border.[19] Sharon Patricia Holland cites Anzaldúa's *Borderlands/La Frontera* (1987) as an important precursor to "the turn to the transnational in queer theory"; a look back at early collections of Native literature show the centrality of these same crossings in Indigenous work and marks queer Native literature as offering further and even earlier articulations of transnationalism.[20] In fact, in queer Native 1980s literature, settler borders, which at times cross tribal land to split reservation from reserve and Native American nations from Aboriginal, are consistently figured as figments of settler imagination. In the introduction to "Native Women," the 1986 special issue of the Canadian feminist quarterly *Fireweed,* Ivy Chaske and Connie Fife (Cree), who edited the issue together with lesbian feminist Midnight Sun, speak to the ideology inherent in such spatial divisions, explaining,

> Initially we were asked to focus on Native Women in Canada. After opening to submissions from all Native Women on the continent, we went back to *Fireweed* to educate them on the issue of imposed boundaries. We informed them that as Women of sovereign nations we would not recognize these infringements on the submissions of Native Women. We will not allow ourselves to be divided for we share common ground and solidarity. The submissions of our sisters to the south reaffirms that their struggle is our struggle; just as our struggle is theirs.[21]

The completed special issue of "Native Women" included thirty Native American and Aboriginal writers, four of whom identified as queer: Brant, Chrystos, Gould, and Midnight Sun. Importantly, the transnational ethos—or "common ground"—the editors cite crosses not just settler borders but also the borders of literature and politics in Native communities: just as collections of Indigenous writing like *Living the Spirit* and the special issue of *Fireweed* traverse settler borders, so too were organizations like the U.S.-based Gay American Indians paralleled by and in conversation with Aboriginal Two-Spirit groups.[22]

Urban centers in both the United States and Canada saw the rise of a queer Native presence in the 1970s and 1980s: the Greater Vancouver

Native Cultural Society began in the mid-1970s, while the mid-1980s saw the inception of the first queer Aboriginal political group, Winnipeg's Nichiwakan Native Gay and Lesbian Society, founded after the 1986 suicides of two young First Nations men. In 1987, Native peoples attending the Gay and Lesbian March on Washington organized the "Basket and the Bow: A Gathering of Lesbian and Gay Native Americans." The Minneapolis gathering, which was held the subsequent year, broadened participants to include Aboriginal peoples.[23] As Albert McLeod, the codirector of Two-Spirited People of Manitoba, explains, "Eleven delegates from Winnipeg attended this inaugural event, which was captured in [Dakota filmmaker] Mona Smith's 1990 video, *Honored by the Moon*."[24] These meetings became the International Two-Spirit Gathering, which is held annually at alternating sites in Canada and the United States and from which emerged the historical term "Two-Spirit" as well as the influential collection *Two-Spirit People*. Such collaborative, transnational practices continue to inform queer Indigenous organizing and literary production, further underlining the inherently relational rather than chronological nature of Indigenous knowledges, peoples, and literatures. In many ways, then, collections like *Living the Spirit* and the special issue of *Fireweed* evidenced a transnational feminist critical consciousness that has continued to drive Indigenous activism and theory in the United States and Canada (as seen most recently in the worldwide support of the Aboriginal political movement Idle No More).

A landmark in the history of queer Native literature was the 1988 publication of the first anthology to focus solely on Two-Spirit texts: *Living the Spirit: A Gay American Indian Anthology*. *Living the Spirit* was compiled by the GAI in collaboration with the white anthropologist Will Roscoe. Roscoe served as administrator, while all "decisions regarding contents, format, and publication arrangements were made by the GAI's board of directors."[25] Like Brant's *A Gathering of Spirit*, *Living the Spirit*, too, carefully distinguished Indigenous concerns both from those of other people of color and from those of a white-identified queer community. For example, Burns's preface begins by differentiating queer Indigenous history from U.S. settler history: "When the U.S. Supreme Court cited 'millennia of moral teaching' in support of Georgia's sodomy law and when the Vatican declared homosexuality 'intrinsically evil,' they must not have been thinking of American history and American morals. Because, throughout America, for centuries before and after the arrival of Europeans, gay and lesbian American Indians were recognized and valued members of tribal communities. As Mohawk author Maurice Kenny declares, 'We were special!'"[26] Comprised of fiction, poetry, memoir, interview, essay, photography, painting, and drawing, the anthology evidences both the GAI's growth as an organization and the talent of the many queer Native writers and artists of the period.[27] The collection ranges from Kenny's and Midnight Sun's insightful essays on Two-Spirit histories, to Chrystos's meditations on the psychic cost of racism, to Seminole/Muscogee/Diné visual artist Hulleah Tsinhnahjinnie's parody of a Lone Ranger and Tonto cartoon. Morgensen contends the book "frame[s] Native writers . . . not as icons of gay nature but as historical actors seeking a place within contemporary Native communities."[28] I would add that through these varied media and voices, *Living the Spirit* creates a continuum in which contemporary Indigenous artists build on the legacies of Native people who occupied diverse genders and sexualities to craft specifically Indigenous understandings of what it means to be queer and Native in the late twentieth century.

The power of coalition—whether between and among Two-Spirit people (*Living the Spirit*), Native women (*A Gathering of Spirit*), or women of color more generally (*This Bridge*)—undergirds many 1980s and early 1990s collections. In *Making Face, Making Soul* (1990), Anzaldúa continues this tradition with her second anthology by women of color writers. Her introduction cites the importance of such coalitions, which function, she explains, as "the very spaces and places where our multiple-surfaced, colored, racially gendered bodies intersect and interconnect."[29] At the same time, however, the introduction also demonstrates the potential limits of such intersectional visions by omitting reference to Indigenous languages in a section titled "In Which Voice/With Which Voice," where Anzaldúa states that "women-of-color in the U.S. must not only transform silence into our native speech, but as immigrants, Chicanas/Latinas and speakers of Black or different varieties of Asian English as well as other dialects, we must learn a foreign tongue—standard American English."[30] Likewise, when discussing the "difference between appropriation and proliferation," Anzaldúa cites non-Native novelist Tony Hillerman as "an example of a white man who . . . widens our knowledge of the Hopi and Navajo cultures."[31] Thus while six Native women are published in *Making Face, Making Soul*—Allen, Brant, Chrystos, Harjo, Gould, and Anne Waters (Seminole/Choctaw/Chickasaw/Cherokee)—the efficacy of these intersections for Native women is questionable.[32]

The centrality of women of color feminist texts to the history of queer Native literature continues with Jamaican Canadian writer Makeda Silvera's 1991 *Piece of My Heart,* the first North American anthology specifically devoted to creative work by queer women of color.[33] In her introduction, Silvera discusses the anthology's history, explaining that though the first submissions call went out in the mid-1980s, the project took five years to gain momentum. Silvera suggests that perhaps lesbians of color "were not ready to put [their] lives on the line. . . . not ready to come out, leave family—leave home in search of another home and family."[34] The rhetoric positing queerness as a barrier to familial connection, common for the time, is both reflected (as seen in Valerio's work) and resisted by Two-Spirit writers. Rather than seeking a new home in non-Native queer communities, Native writers often address the need for retaining and/or reinvigorating ties to Indigenous kinship networks. The differences between queer of color and queer Indigenous ideologies, such as those addressed in the introduction, are therefore highlighted by these 1980s and early 1990s anthologies. In Silvera's collection, for example, the necessity of cultural/familial affiliation informs Brant's short story "Home Coming," while Eastern Cherokee author Victoria Lena Manyarrows's poem "The Drum Beats" suggests that Native lesbians become "whole and wise" only through acts of cultural affirmation tied to Indigeneity.[35]

Like the aforementioned women of color anthologies, collections of Native women's writing continue to serve as vehicles for queer Native writers from *Living the Spirit* to the present; however, not all of these collections directly engage Two-Spirit identities or same-sex desire, showing that, just as in the Red Power era, later Native-specific venues were not necessarily more reflective of Two-Spirit concerns than mainstream queer or queer of color coalitions. In fact, influential anthologies like Cherokee writer Rayna Green's *That's What She Said: Contemporary Poetry and Fiction by Native American Women* (1984) and even Paula Gunn Allen's *Spider Woman's Granddaughters* (1989) omit reference to the intersectional concerns of queer Native people. Gould overtly addresses such silences in Cree lesbian poet Connie Fife's 1993 anthology *The Colour of Resistance: A Contemporary Collection of Writing by Aboriginal Women.* In "A Maidu in the City of Gold: Some Thoughts on Censorship and American Indian Poetry," Gould contends, "Indian writers do not mince words. If we are being published now in greater numbers than ever before, still we face the actual potential of being silenced, especially if we are gay or lesbian writers."[36] As this overview demonstrates, the rise of 1980s and early 1990s anthologies often (but not always) countered such silences.

While more collections of Native women's, women of color, and queer of color writing would be published in the ensuing years, I suggest that three twenty-first-century anthologies—*This Bridge We Call Home* (2002), *Without Reservation: Indigenous Erotica* (2003), and *Sovereign Erotics: A Collection of Contemporary Two-Spirit Literature* (2011)—mark the field's coming of age in their claims for Indigenous difference, erotic wholeness, and Two-Spirit diversity. The long-awaited sequel to *This Bridge Called My Back,* Anzaldúa and AnaLouise Keating's *This Bridge We Call Home,* like the first anthology, includes selections by Chrystos and Max Wolf Valerio. Valerio's autobiographical essay "'Now That You're White Man': Changing Sex in a Postmodern World—Being, Becoming, and Borders" expands the parameters of queer Native studies by addressing transsexuality. At the same time, *This Bridge We Call Home* also includes the most direct discussion to date about how Native women's concerns diverge from those of non-Native women of color when Deborah A. Miranda queries, "What do I ask of you, sisters of color? I ask, remember the differences between indigenous and diasporic; between indigenous and exile; between still-colonized native and freed slave; between *choosing* education as a way to speak, and having literacy shoved down your throat in a boarding school far from home, beaten into you."[37] Thus more than twenty years later, *This Bridge We Call Home* calls for the promises of *This Bridge Called My Back* to be fulfilled—not through a simplistic understanding of coalition but through a rich and varied recognition of difference.

In another overtly political claim, First Nations Anishinaabe author Kateri Akiwenzie-Damm's edited collection, *Without Reservation: Indigenous Erotic,* returns the erotic to its historical place of importance in Native studies. The first anthology of Indigenous erotica, *Without Reservation* redresses what Akiwenzie-Damm identifies as "the utter lack" of "sex and sexuality" in Indigenous texts—a concern of particular import to queer Indigenous studies.[38] While Brant and Vickie Sears (Cherokee) published in Tee Corinne's 1991 collection of lesbian erotica, *Riding Desire,* those pieces are little known, an absence reflective of the dearth of productive conversations about any form of Indigenous sexuality (much less queer Indigenous sexualities).[39] In terms of texts from queer Native writers, Akiwenzie-Damm's trans-Indigenous, pansexual collection includes Brant's "So Generously," which chronicles the steamy relationship between two poets; a range of Chrystos's poems such as "Hot My Hair Smells of Your Cunt"; several poems by Samoan author Dan Taulapapa McMullin's about fa'afafine (Samoan Two-Spirit people); and powerful poetry by First Nations authors Daniel David Moses (Delaware) and Gregory Scofield (Métis).

Fittingly, I conclude this section with the first collection of queer Native literature published since the GAI's *Living the Spirit:* the 2011 anthology *Sovereign Erotics: A Collection of Contemporary Two-Spirit Literature,* edited by Driskill, Justice, Miranda, and Lisa Tatonetti.[40] The anthology's expansive array of authors, genres, styles, and topics reflects both the continuity and the change in the canon of queer Native literature. *Sovereign Erotics* begins with a nod to *Living the Spirit* in the form of Paula Gunn Allen's poem "Some like Indians Endure," the first piece in both texts. In addition, the collection includes recent work by Kenny and Gould, who were also in *Living the Spirit.* Miranda's "Coyote Takes a Trip" echoes Brant's and Daniel-Harry Steward's revisions of the classic trickster narrative from *Living the Spirit,* while pieces like Jaynie Lara's "Being Two-Spirit" mirror the first collection's explicit interest in defining Two-Spirit identities. *Sovereign Erotics* also represents the shifts in genre and content that occurred in the twenty-three-year gap between anthologies. Thus the collection contains Justice's fantasy fiction, Akwesasne Mohawk author James Thomas Stevens's lyric poems on English waterways, and short stories by Creek writers Janet McAdams and Chip Livingston that invoke the pounding beat of dance clubs. Ultimately, *Sovereign Erotics,* like the anthologies of the 1980s and 1990s, reaffirms the contemporary existence of Two-Spirit people and historical traditions of gender variance while also demonstrating that writing by queer Native people cannot be confined to such parameters.

Queer Native Drama

Kenny's queer 1970s poetry and the anthologies of the 1980s mark two different origin stories for a genealogy of *overtly* queer Native literature; however, the work of the earliest recognized gay Native author, Oklahoma Cherokee Rollie Lynn Riggs (1899–1954), predates both those literary moments. Riggs was a prolific writer who composed some thirty-three plays, two poetry collections, numerous folk tunes, short stories, and an unfinished novel. Though Riggs, like most prominent artists of his time, was not open about his sexual preference to the larger public, he was part of the queer literary community of the thirties, forties, and fifties. So, for example, he worked with Aaron Copeland, who published several of Riggs's songs in *Old American Songs* (1950) and talked to him about turning his play, *The Cherokee Night* (1936), into an opera. Riggs is best known for *Green Grow the Lilacs* (1931), which was adapted into the long-running Broadway hit *Oklahoma!* in 1943.[41] Jace Weaver (Cherokee) resurrected Riggs's understudied plays in the late 1990s, while Womack offered the first serious analysis of Riggs's implicit depictions of queerness and Indigeneity in *Red on Red* (1999), arguing that "Riggs's Indian identity and gay identity [were] the two most relevant aspects of his life and work."[42]

The story of Riggs's recovery as a queer Native author underscores the way genealogy maps relationship as much as chronology in the literary history of Native American and Aboriginal literatures. So, for example, Weaver, as a Cherokee critic, was particularly interested in Riggs as an Oklahoma Cherokee writer. It was at least in part because of this tribal relationship that Weaver resurrected Riggs's understudied plays in the late 1990s. Womack likewise maps his reading of Riggs through the lens of Native literary nationalism, arguing for the importance of tribally specific readings of Indigenous authors by Indigenous critics. Justice extends this queer nationalist work in his critical monograph, *Our Fire Survives the Storm: A Cherokee Literary History* (2006). Justice's reading of Riggs, while addressing Riggs erotic attraction, emphasizes the author's place in the Cherokee literary tradition. Thus Riggs's various recoveries accentuate the importance of Indigenous nationalism and the palimpsestic nature of affiliation within a genealogy of queer Native literature.

It would be more than thirty years after Riggs's death before another Native playwright, Cree dramatist Tomson Highway, came to prominence. Highway's *The Rez Sisters,* which debuted in 1986 at the Friendship Center in Toronto, is considered one of the most influential plays in Native theater and was the first Native production to tour Canada. Emily Dictionary, one of the seven "sisters" that populate the play (including blood sisters, sisters-in-law, and adopted daughters), has butch characteristics and laments the loss of Rose, who she "loved like no man has ever loved a woman."[43] Highway's *Dry Lips Oughta Move to Kapuskasing* (1989), which also takes place on the fictional Wasaychigan Hill Indian reserve, flips the script to center male characters. The trickster Nanabush appears in both plays but changes gender from male (in *Rez Sisters*) to female (in *Dry Lips*), functioning as a classic example of the long-standing tie between trickster figures and gender variance, a tradition invoked often in Two-Spirit literature. More recently, Highway published *Rose,* a third installation in what he has promised will be a seven-play cycle in 2000, as well as a stand-alone play, *Ernestine Shuswap Gets Her Trout* (2005), and Cree language versions of his first two plays: *Iskooniguni Iskweewuk* (*The Rez Sisters*; 2010) and *Paasteewitoon Kaapooskaysing Tageespichit* (*Dry Lips Oughta Move to Kapuskasing*; 2010).[44]

First Nations author Daniel David Moses began publishing in the same era as Highway, though his early work has no overtly queer content.[45] Moses's most overtly queer text is *The Indian Medicine Shows* (1995), which, interestingly enough, is also his first drama to center white characters. Comprised of two one-act plays—*The Moon and Dead Indians* and *Angel of the Medicine Show*—that both take place in the late nineteenth century, *The Indian Medicine Show* examines the intersections of internalized homophobia and racialization. Since 2000, Moses has published a poetry collection, *Sixteen Jesuses* (2000); several more plays, including *Pursued by a Bear: Talks, Monologues and Tales* (2005) and *Kytopolis: A Play in Two Acts* (2008); and, most recently, a new book of poetry, *A Small Essay on the Largeness of Light and Other Poems* (2012). Moses continues to be an award-winning and prolific poet, playwright, and essayist.

Another important voice in Indigenous theater is that of Muriel Miguel (Kuna/Rappahannock), a founding member of the feminist performance troupe Spiderwoman Theater. Along with including queer issues in Spiderwoman's body of work, Miguel published several one-woman shows including *Cabaret,* which was expanded into a full-scale Spiderwoman Theater production titled *Cabaret: An Evening of Disgusting Songs and Pukey Images.*[46] Initially produced in 1979, the expanded production, according to Sue-Ellen Case, "seemed to compose a utopic blend of differences among women: lesbian, straight, women of color, white women, old young, women of size, thin women, etc. However these same differences apparently caused a rift within the ensemble."[47] In the next Spiderwoman production, *The Fittin' Room,* which premiered in New York City in 1980, "both heterosexuality and lesbianism were scrutinized: 'Butch Meets Butch—Encounters in New York City Bathrooms' was a soap opera throughout."[48] A subsequent split occurred, in which several non-Native members left Spiderwoman as the troupe's "focus tightened onto Native American experiences and issues, with only a very minor interest in staging the lesbian."[49] Miguel, who played Pelajia Patchnose in the original Native Earth production of Highway's *The Rez Sisters,* later developed *Hot 'n' Soft* in 1992, a play that turns on the story of a lesbian coyote, a trickster tradition fast becoming a hallmark narrative of queer Native literature. Speaking of *Hot 'n' Soft*'s inception, Miguel explains,

> It came about because I was reading and seeing a lot of erotica and I thought, "Oh, skanky, oh yuk. This is lousy stuff." When people talk about pornography they aren't really talking about the erotic. After reading a lot of the trickster stories I realized that they were all male, but it couldn't possibly be that way in reality. When you think about it, the anthropologists that wrote these were male and so we ended up with male tricksters. One of the things that's wonderful about tricksters is that they change gender but female tricksters are rarely mentioned. So I decided to take that as my premise, that the trickster is a female, and I also decided to make the premise that Coyote is a lesbian. On top of that I added all this erotica, but erotics like the taboos that we, as lesbians, don't talk about, like hair, or two-timing, or being uncomfortable, or getting older.[50]

As her description suggests, Miguel's writing and performance consistently expands the boundaries of her own dramatic work as well as the focus of North American theater more broadly. Of her lifelong work with Spiderwoman Theater, Miguel says, "This type of theater is so interwoven, like Native people, interwoven with everything. The only thing you can say is, 'Is it theater? Is it Native theater? Is it queer theater?' But when you get down to it, it interconnects, and that's the only way we can work, by interconnecting it."[51] This emphasis on a web of relationship in which queerness, Indigeneity, and art coalesce further underscores its centrality to a genealogy of queer Native literatures.

The subsequent generation of queer Native playwrights includes Highway's nephew, Bill Merasty, and Grassy Narrows First Nations playwright/performer Waawaate Fobister (Anishinaabe). Merasty, a noted Cree actor, has written two plays: *Fireweed* (1992) and *For Godly and Divinia/Godly's Divinia (A Love Story)*, an Aboriginal adaptation of *Romeo and Juliet* staged in 2000. Fobister's first play, *Agokwe,* which depicts the initial meeting and erotic attraction between two gay Aboriginal teens from different reserves, premiered in 2008 to much acclaim. Most recently, Fobister, Miguel, and noted Cree performance artist Kent Monkman were published together in a collection edited by Jean O'Hara titled *Two-Spirit Acts: Queer Indigenous Performances*.[52] In the end, an overview of queer Native drama reveals the import of the Aboriginal literary canon to Two-Spirit studies and shows how representations of same-sex desire multiply from the few veiled allusions of Riggs's plays to the many frank and often humorous treatments of queerness found in the work of late nineteenth- and early twentieth-century Indigenous playwrights.

Queer Native Fiction

Queer Native fiction, like drama and the early women of color anthologies, emerges in the 1980s. But before turning to the Two-Spirit/lesbian, gay, bisexual, transgender, transsexual, intersex, and queer (LGBTIQ2) authored texts of the 1980s and beyond, I first look to an example of recent queer recoveries that are beginning to explode in the field. Michael Snyder's ongoing work on Riggs's classmate at the University of Oklahoma, Osage novelist John Joseph Mathews (1894–1979), merits reference in this context. Mathews, as one of a handful of Native writers published in the early twentieth century, holds an important place in the Native American canon. Though Snyder refrains from claiming Mathews—who was in a heterosexual marriage—as queer, he highlights the homoerotic themes of Mathews's 1934 novel *Sundown* and places Mathews in the context of a queer literary community, contending such recoveries underline "the historical continuity of Indigenous same-sex desire" and are therefore "a step toward 'decolonizing the mind.'"[53] Snyder's rereading extends Warrior's work on Mathews in *Tribal Secrets,* in which Warrior marks "Mathews' place in Native intellectual history."[54] I would add that understanding this web of relationships and undertaking analyses of queer Native writers, images, and echoes—what queer theorist José Esteban Muñoz terms "queer ephemera"—enables us to mine multiple levels of affiliation and further Warrior's call that critics attend to "historically silent voices from a full, diverse range of contemporary American Indian experience. . . . [T]he voices of poor and urban Natives extremely alienated from tradition, gay and lesbian Natives who face persecution and discrimination in their own communities, women with a feminist or women-centered analysis, and other doubly and triply marginated voices."[55] Like Snyder, my work builds on Warrior's by expanding our knowledge of contemporary Native intellectual traditions through an analysis of queer Indigenous voices *and* queer resonances in Indigenous literature.

Contemporary fiction varies widely in its depiction of Indigenous experiences, ranging from tribal trickster narratives to representations of urban alienation; however, as we move toward the present day, a distinct focus on issues of sovereignty emerges. As mentioned in the Introduction, the first Native novel with a queer Indigenous protagonist, Paula Gunn Allen's *The Woman Who Owned the Shadows,* was published in 1983. Allen's Ephanie Atencio shares a lesbian attraction with her childhood friend, Elena, and later recovers from abusive or ill-chosen heterosexual marriages through a same-sex relationship as an adult. Though most contemporary reviewers failed to mention the text's queer overtones, some fifteen years after its initial publication, as previously noted, Allen's novel would be the focus of many of the first essay-length critical analyses of queer Native literature.

Two years later, in 1985, Brant follows Allen's *The Woman Who Owned the Shadows* and Brant's previously mentioned anthology *A Gathering of Spirit* with a collection of short stories, poetry, and essays titled *Mohawk Trail.* The specific traditions and landscape of the Bay of Quinte Mohawk ground the collection, which begins with a story of the Longhouse in a section called "Native Origins." Brant ends the section with "Coyote Learns a New Trick," in which the trickster "stuff[s] . . . diapers into her underpants so it looked like she had a swell" in order to fool Fox, a pretty female.[56] By concluding the tribally grounded "Native Origins" section with this piece, Brant explicitly frames same-sex desire as part of—rather than apart from—long-standing Indigenous traditions. Here, Brant's writing aligns with Kenny's to claim a historical continuity for Two-Spirit erotics. But while Brant grounds much of her fiction in Haudenosaunee tribal tradition, she also vividly describes the violence and alienation that characterizes the experiences of some LBGTIQ2 Native people. These nuanced considerations of queer Indigenous realities reoccur in Brant's 1991 short story collection *Food & Spirits* and her 1994 collection of personal essays, *Writing as Witness.* Throughout her work, Brant highlights how Two-Spirit ideologies help Native people heal from the ongoing reverberations of settler colonialism, a prevalent theme in queer Native literature and theory.

Vickie Sears (1941–1999), who often appeared alongside Brant, Chrystos, and Gould in the anthologies of the 1980s and 1990s, published her only monograph, *Simple Songs,* in 1990. Many of the characters in her fourteen short stories are children in the foster care system who grapple not only with the difficult realities of that life, which Sears knew personally, but also with the experience of moving between Native and white communities. As Brant explains, "Herself a survivor of the foster-care system, Sears finds solace and empowerment through the things of Earth and the love between women. Her short stories emphasize these possibilities of self-recovery."[57] Looking across their canon, these early queer Native women writers often consider issues of mixed-blood identity, gendered violence, and the healing power of writing.

While Pomo/Miwok author Greg Sarris's novels *Grand Avenue* (1994) and *Watermelon Nights* (1998) both contain queer characters, *The Woman Who Owned the Shadows* was the only novel with a queer Indigenous protagonist until Anishinaabe fiction writer Carole laFavor's 1996 *Along the Journey River.*[58] LaFavor's Renee LaRoche, a lesbian detective on the Minnesota Red Earth Reservation, follows thieves, murderers, and Ojibwe traditions while juggling a steamy relationship with her white lover, Samantha Salisbury. *Evil Dead Center* (1997), laFavor's second book, continues the Renee LaRoche saga. These two novels merit much more notice in classrooms and scholarship than they have received to this point. LaFavor, an AIDS/HIV activist as well as a writer and woodcarver who died in 2011, pays close attention in both novels to the imbricated nature of tribal land, sovereignty, and sexuality.[59] In fact, in many ways, laFavor's work can be read as a precursor to perhaps the best-known queer Native novel, Womack's 2001 *Drowning in Fire,* which depicts Josh Henneha's coming of age as a gay Creek boy in 1970s rural Oklahoma. The contemporary sections of Womack's novel, set in 1993, layer the story of Josh's relationship with Jimmy Alexander, his former Creek schoolmate, together with a historical narrative of the Muscogee fight against U.S. government allotment policies. Four years after *Drowning in Fire,* Daniel Heath Justice published the first Native fantasy novel: *Kynship: The Way of Thorn and Thunder* (2005). Justice's trilogy—*Kynship, Wyrwood* (2006), and *Dreyd* (2007)—was initially published by Kateri Akiwenzie-Damm's Kegedonce Press and then compiled in an omnibus edition—*The Way of Thorn and Thunder: The Kynship Chronicles*—by the University of New Mexico Press in 2011. Like his critical work, Justice's creative work, too, constructs relationship through the lens of nationhood: *The Kynship Chronicles* maps a third-gender tradition onto an allegorical retelling of the Cherokee Nation's fight to retain sovereignty. Together, Brant, laFavor, Womack, and Justice index the ties between tribal sovereignty and Indigenous erotics that have been vital to queer Native literature since the 1970s publication of Kenny's "Winkte."

The Poetic Tradition in Queer Native Literature

Though fiction—especially full-length fiction—garners a lion's share of public attention, poetry functions as the cornerstone of the queer Native literary canon. Such prevalence is evidenced in the aforementioned anthologies as well as in the monographs of queer Native poetry that followed Kenny's *Only as Far as Brooklyn.* Perhaps this is because, as Audre Lorde tells us, "poetry is not only dream and vision; it is the skeleton architecture of our lives."[60] The early 1990s saw a significant rise in the publication of the "dream[s] and vision[s]" of queer Native poets: by 1992, Chrystos, Gould, and Fife had all published their first collections and Yuchi/Comanche poet Joe Dale Tate Nevaquaya's manuscript *Leaving Holes,* though not published until 2011, was the cowinner of the first Diane Decorah Memorial Award (today the Native Writer's Circle of America's First Book Award for Poetry).[61] Collectively, these poets offer what Dakota theorist Vine Deloria Jr. termed "calls for recognition of the humanity and nationality of Indian existence."[62]

The first collection to follow Kenny's was Chrystos's 1988 *Not Vanishing,* which was published the same year as *Living the Spirit.* One of the most important voices in queer Native literature, Chrystos's strong and often confrontational poems engage the intersections of poverty, oppression, erotic desire, dominant appropriation of Native images, and lesbianism. Her poetry regularly rejects conventional capitalization and punctuation to confront "300 years" of history in which "sacred beliefs have been made into pencils / names of cities gas stations."[63] At the same time, Chrystos calls the non-Native queer community to task for a legacy of racism while also crafting beautiful erotica in poems like "O Honeysuckle Woman." Chrystos highlights the imbricated nature of the political and the erotic throughout her subsequent work—*Dream On* (1991), *In Her I Am* (1993), *Fire Power* (1995), and *Fugitive Colors* (1995). Miranda cites the "multilevels of sensory information and resistance" in Chrystos's writing, marking its importance in the Indigenous literary tradition.[64] Additionally, she shares a conversation with Chrystos that speaks directly to the political necessity of articulating an Indigenous erotic: "I once asked Chrystos what she thought about the poor publication record and lack of critical analyses of American Indian women's erotics and love poetry. She thought for a moment, then replied, 'American Indian writing is invisible; American Indian women's writing is more invisible; American Indian women's poetry, still more invisible. And Native women's love poetry and erotics are so invisible, so far back in the closet, that they're practically in somebody else's apartment.'"[65] This conversation, which took place in 1998, continues to resonate today, speaking to the importance of mapping the queer Indigenous archive and to the necessity of work that centers Indigenous erotics and refutes settler colonial logics of erasure.

The connections between and among the queer Native women writers of the 1980s and 1990s can be seen, as well, in the common themes and, at times, style of their work. Like Chrystos and Brant, Gould, as I discuss at length in chapter 5, explicitly ties Indigeneity to the erotic. Additionally, Chrystos, Gould, and Fife overlap in their consistent turn toward autobiography. Consequently, Gould's poetry—*Beneath My Heart* (1990), *Earthquake Weather* (1996), and *Doubters and Dreamers* (2011)—chronicles the California history of her people, the Koyoonk'auwi Maidu, and the personal history of her sometimes-difficult relationship with her Native mother and white father (then an occasional cross-dresser and later a male-to-female [MTF] transsexual) as well as offers powerful depictions of same-sex desire. Likewise, Fife's first collection, *Beneath the Naked Sun* (1992), which preceded *The Colour of Resistance*, parallels Chrystos's poetry in form and content by largely eschewing punctuation and capitalization and directly confronting settler colonialism. In "the revolution of not vanishing," Fife says she is "ready to / follow the path" Chrystos "bulldozed."[66] Fife's later collections—*Speaking through Jagged Rock* (1999) and *Poems for a New World* (2001)—continue to map the relationships among many of the writers referenced here and acknowledge sympathies between Indigenous peoples and international communities in poems like "Peace Is Not Genocide," which condemns the 1999 NATO bombing of Yugoslavia during the Kosovo War.

Victoria Lena Manyarrows, along with publishing in Silvera's previously mentioned *Piece of My Heart* and numerous other 1990s journals and anthologies, also maps claims for transnational and trans-Indigenous affiliations in her 1995 *Songs from the Native Lands: Poetry*. The collection turns on a metaphor of survival and invokes Nicaragua, Chili, Guatemala, El Salvador, China, South Africa, and Iraq. In the process, Manyarrows, much as the editors of "Native Women" did ten years prior, contends,

"We have no borders / there are no boundaries between us."[67] Manyarrows's explanation of the impetus for her creative work further reinforces the lines of affiliation on which this chapter turns: "For me, writing and visual art has always been a vehicle for political and personal change, as well as spiritual exploration and expression. When I was in my early 20s, writing helped me to integrate my spiritual identity and sense of self with my political awakening and involvement in the feminist, American Indian and lesbian movements and communities, in particular."[68] These interwoven identifications and commitment to political change inform the vast majority of texts referenced in *The Queerness of Native American Literature.*

Also publishing his first book in the early 1990s and working from a similar feminist framework was First Nations writer Gregory Scofield, who has since become one of the preeminent contemporary writers in Canada. Scofield's 1993 *The Gathering: Stones for the Medicine Wheel* begins with a Cree language story—"kaskitêw-maskwa osisima" ("Black Bear's Language")—and is subsequently divided into sections based on the four directions. Scofield terms his chronicles of urban experience "survival poetry": "Raw, unflinching / Watching your back in some skid row bar / Down here / Each line will give you a day—or make it your last."[69] *Native Canadiana/Songs from the Urban Rez* (1996) likewise probes the relationship between Aboriginal identity and urbanity as well as more overtly engaging queer sexuality. In *Love Medicine and One Song* (1997), Scofield dramatically shifts tone, offering lyric poems, or "medicine songs," that emphasize the intersections of Cree images, Cree language, and the erotic. Scofield published paired books of poetry and memoir—*I Knew Two Métis Women* and *Thunder through My Veins: Memories of a Métis Childhood*—in 1999. These texts not only craft Scofield's history but also emphasize his continued attention to the stories of women through his sensitive and often humorous snapshots of his mother, Dorothy Scofield, and aunt, Georgina Houle Young. *Thunder through My Veins* has since become a staple in Canadian universities. Most recently, Scofield published *Singing Home the Bones* (2005), *Kipocihkân: Poems New and Selected* (2009), and *Louis: The Heretic Poems* (2011). Scofield's feminism links his work to the anthologies of the 1980s and early 1990s; his representations of Two-Spirit urbanity situate his poetry alongside that of Kenny, Chrystos, Gould, and Fife; and his attention to Cree language ties his writing to Highway's.

Among the many queer Native American and Aboriginal writers who published their first books in the 1990s is poet/theorist/essayist Deborah

A. Miranda, who, as mentioned previously, also published in anthologies like *This Bridge We Call Home* and *Sovereign Erotics*. Like Gould's collections, Miranda's *Indian Cartography* (1999) refutes the history of erasure that claims California Indians disappeared in the face of Euro-American "progress" while also investigating the contours of poverty, sexual abuse, strength, and love. Though *Indian Cartography*'s "Strawberries" and "Sometimes the Open Hand of Desire" have lesbian overtones, Miranda's earliest collection with overtly queer themes is *The Zen of La Llorona* (2005), which focuses on family history, the aftermath of her mother's death, and the possibilities of what Miranda calls the "indigenous erotic" (4). *Bad Indians: A Tribal Memoir* (2013), Miranda's most recent publication, combines history, poetry, primary documents, and personal photographs in a powerful tribal/personal memoir that pushes the boundaries of genre classification by moving fluidly from poetry, to fiction, to family recollections, to rewritings of common (and horrifying) California classroom assignments. In this way, Miranda, like Scofield, redefines traditional form to more effectively narrate—and in Miranda's case reclaim—Indigenous history.[70]

While the connections between Indigenous peoples in North America have been evident for centuries in trade networks, familial relationships, and political and literary texts, global ties between Indigenous peoples, though also historical, have not always been visible to outsiders. These complex trans-Indigenous relationships seen in the Indigenous anthologies, poetry collections, and queer Native activism discussed throughout this chapter are especially evident in the writing of lyric poet James Thomas Stevens, who published his first book, *Tokinish,* in 1994. His second collection, *Combing the Snakes from His Hair* (2002), melds free verse poetry, drawings, and autobiography with formalist conventions and Iroquoian allusions. Steven's 2006 collaboration with Samoan writer Caroline Sinavaiana, *Mohawk/Samoa: Transmigrations,* marks the sustained interest contemporary queer Native writers have in trans-Indigenous relationality by pairing their Mohawk and Samoan cultures, art, and poetry. Likewise, Steven's 2007 collection, *A Bridge Dead in Winter,* situates the Jesuit history in China alongside that of the Jesuit encroachment in Iroquoia. Stevens's other books include *dis(Orient)* (2005), *The Mutual Life* (2006), and *Bulle/Chimère* (2006).

Along with those previously mentioned, twenty-first-century queer Native poetry collections include Sharron Proulx-Turner's (Métis) *What the Auntys Say* (2002) and her two 2008 texts: *She Is Reading with a Blanket in Her Hand,* a book of dedication poems, and *She Walks for Days inside a Thousand Eyes: A Two-Spirit Story,* mixed-genre poetic fiction that weaves together the historical and contemporary stories of Two-Spirit women. Proulx-Turner's most recent book is a poetry collection titled *The Trees Are Still Bending South.* Additionally, Janet McAdams not only has published two collections of poetry, *The Island of Lost Luggage* (2000) and *Feral* (2007), and a novel, *Red Weather* (2012), but also began her work as the founding editor for the Salt Press Earthworks series on Native American poetry, which includes books by Miranda, Stevens, and Driskill. Driskill's 2005 *Walking with Ghosts,* one of Earthworks's earliest offerings, melds embodied ruminations on Cherokee history with an exposure of the ongoing violence toward queers of color and transsexuals. Valerio likewise engages transsexuality in his 2006 memoir *The Testosterone Files.* The continued expansion of the queer Native literary canon can be seen in the publication of the first overtly queer work by writers like Abenaki poet Cheryl Savageau, whose early poetry collections—*Home Country* (1992), which she expanded into *Dirt Road Home* (1995)—center family relationships without directly addressing queerness. By contrast, Savageau's 2006 *Mother/Land* contains erotic themes in wonderfully steamy poems like "Where I Want Them" and "Red." The late 2000s see a marked increase in the publication of collections by queer Native poets, with new texts by established writers—including Kenny's *Connotations* (2008), Gould's *Doubters and Dreamers,* and Scofield's *Louis: The Heretic Poems,* as well as a large body of work from a new generation authors. Chip Livingston's two gorgeous poetry collections—*Museum of False Starts* (2010) and *Crow-Blue, Crow-Black* (2012)—and the many talented poets included in the 2010 international queer Indigenous issue of the journal *Yellow Medicine River,* edited by Ahimsa Timoteo Bodhrán, exemplify the vibrant nature of queer Indigenous literature in the current era.

Queer Indigenous Critiques

Many of the prominent creative writers in the field also theorize queer Indigeneity, and in fact, queer Native studies has come into being as a distinct area of critical inquiry in the twenty-first century. But as noted in the Introduction, queer Native studies has roots in earlier scholarly interventions. An example of this rich past is Kenny's "Tinselled Bucks: An Historical Study in Indian Homosexuality," first published in the winter 1975/1976 *Gay Sunshine*. As chapter 2 discusses further, Kenny documents the prevalence of Two-Spirit (then still "berdache") traditions in historical sources, making an argument for the recovery of queer Native histories. Allen's groundbreaking 1981 essay "Beloved Women: Lesbians in American Indian Cultures" follows Kenny's work to situate same-sex and multiple gender traditions as part of a continuum in Indigenous cultures. While Allen published a significant number of books of poetry and criticism, she is best known for her first critical monograph, *The Sacred Hoop: Recovering the Feminine in American Indian Traditions,* which is also, as previously noted, the text in which she presents an early articulation of an Indigenous erotic. After its 1986 publication, *The Sacred Hoop* quickly became a staple text in women's studies classrooms, where Allen's focus on the lives and literature of American Indian women filled a curricular gap. In this wide-ranging collection of essays, Allen discusses negative shifts in attitudes toward "women and gays among American Indians" within a chapter titled "How the West Was Really Won"; charts the Indigenous origins of mainstream feminism in "Who Is Your Mother? Red Roots of White Feminism"; and establishes a historiography of lesbians in Indigenous cultures in "*Hwame, Koshkalaka,* and the Rest: Lesbians in American Indian Cultures" (a revised version of "Beloved Women").[71] In this last, often cited chapter, Allen draws attention to the scholarly silence about the existence of "affectional alliances" between Native women, arguing that this logic of elimination "fosters [a false] impression of uniform heterosexuality among Indian women."[72] While Allen's transhistorical reading of lesbianism and her broad claim that "traditional tribal lifestyles are more often gynocratic" and "are never patriarchal" can be critiqued from a twenty-first-century perspective, her suggestion that Indigenous kinship structures queer heteropatriarchal understandings of family (and women's roles in particular) prefigures Mark Rifkin's nuanced theoretical work in *When Did Indians Become Straight?*[73] Thus once again, we see that the twenty-first-century renaissance of queer Native literature and theory rests on long-standing Indigenous intellectual traditions. Perhaps, then, this body of writing and thinking can be best described as palimpsestic: the work of twenty-first-century writers and theorists layers with that of creative writers and scholars of the 1970s and 1980s, while all such work, as Allen reminds us, relies on much earlier Indigenous cosmologies.

These genealogical connections are also seen in Highway's critical work. As a native Cree speaker, Highway considers the intersections of Indigenous language, history, and cosmology as seen in *Comparing Mythologies,* which he presented as the 2002 Charles B. Bronfman Lecture in Canadian Studies, and his essay "Why Cree Is the Sexiest of All Languages." Though these reveries on Cree language—which Cree-Métis scholar Emma LaRoque terms part of the "Cree-ative process"—might at first seem to have little in common with Kenny, Allen, and Brant's recoveries of the historical existence of gender variance and same-sex desire in Indigenous communities, I suggest Highway's analyses relate directly to such work.[74] As he reminds his readers, "in Cree, and in other Native languages, speaking of sex and the natural functions of the body is not verboten."[75] Throughout his drama and essay, Highway uses language to map historical continuity among Indigenous peoples and traditions; the fluidity of gender performance is not, he tells us, anything new to Native people. Highway's twenty-first-century pieces on Cree language and cosmology resonate not only with the many other queer Native writers interested in language and language recovery—Scofield and Miranda come immediately to mind—but also with the historical, theoretical, and creative work undertaken in queer 1980s Native writing, further marking the transnational, trans-Indigenous, and decolonial affiliations between past and present queer Native writing and between Aboriginal and Native American writers.

Brant's collection of personal essays, *Writing as Witness,* which provides the epigraph to this chapter, and Gould's 1994 essay "Disobedience (in Language) in Texts by Lesbian Native Americans" also expand this body of theoretical texts, while Womack's critical and creative works—*Red on Red* and *Drowning in Fire*—function as a watershed moment in queer Native studies. Together, Kenny, Allen, Brant, Highway, Gould, and Womack mark a shift from literary criticism *about* queer Native and Aboriginal literatures to a Two-Spirit/queer Native *theory* undertaken *by and for* queer Indigenous peoples. As noted in the Introduction, these theoretical interventions are marked by a commitment to an embodied theory of the erotic. Miranda's 2002 "Dildos, Hummingbirds, and Driving Her Crazy: Searching for American Indian Women's Love Poetry and Erotics" and Driskill's 2004 "Stolen from Our Bodies: First Nations Two-Spirits/Queers and the Journey to a Sovereign Erotic" extend two such important interventions. Miranda argues that "if we want justice, we must work for the erotic," while Driskill's theory of a "Sovereign Erotic" describes "an erotic wholeness and/or healing from the historical trauma that First Nations people continue to survive."[76] Such psychic and physical healing is "rooted within the histories, traditions and resistance struggles of [Indigenous] nations."[77] Further theoretical interventions can be seen in Justice's, Highway's, and Scofield's pieces in Curve Lake First Nations writer Drew Hayden Taylor's (Ojibwe) 2008 collection, *Me Sexy: An Exploration of Native Sex and Sexuality*; in the 2010 special issue of *GLQ: A Journal of Lesbian and Gay Studies*, "Sexuality, Nationality, Indigeneity," edited by Justice, Rifkin, and Bethany Schneider; and in Driskill, Chris Finley, Brian Joseph Gilley, and Scott Lauria Morgensen's edited collection of critical essays, *Queer Indigenous Studies: Critical Interventions in Theory, Politics, and Literature* (2011), which was published as a companion to *Sovereign Erotics*. Today, the theories, literatures, and voices of queer Native American and Aboriginal peoples in North America proliferate with a breadth and depth that extends long-standing Indigenous histories while also presenting a decolonizing challenge to present-day U.S. and Canadian settler societies.

This genealogy of expansion and explosion—of continuity and connection—is at the heart of *The Queerness of Native American Literature*. Contemporary queer Indigenous literatures and theories index a Native literary archive that stretches both backward and forward in active continuity. The authors referenced in this chapter and all those queer Native writers, thinkers, weavers, teachers, and activists, named and unnamed, who came before them constitute an Indigenous intellectual tradition that testifies to Indigenous survivance, to the fact that queer Native peoples and histories "in guilt / in blood / in shame / in disappearance / . . . never quite manage[d] / to be disappeared."[78] A first but by no means complete or final map of relationship(s), this genealogical recovery highlights queer Native authors who not only speak, write, and imagine a scholarly field into being but, far more important, ensure that Indigenous peoples and knowledges never vanish under or into the weight of settler structures.

· CHAPTER 2 ·

The Native 1970s

Maurice Kenny and *Fag Rag*

why must we lie . . .
knowing,
hide facts
of these lovers
under bricks
of legends!

—Maurice Kenny, "Loves into Legends"

IN THE SUMMER OF 2009, I sat at a painfully ancient microfilm machine, whirring through rolls of film, searching for traces of twentieth-century Native literary history in what, at first glance, might appear to be unlikely collections. The microfilm room was located directly in the path of the college library tour, and the well-rehearsed patter of university tour guides signaled that incoming students and their parents were about to stand immediately behind me. Whenever this happened, I squirmed a bit. My discomfort arose not from the 1930s library-issue wooden chair but instead from the fact that, when the whirring stopped and the images rolled to a halt, my screen most often projected penciled and photographic images of naked white men in various stages of erotic engagement.

While chapter 1 offered an early (and provisional) map of queer Native literature as a genealogical recovery of the field, chapter 2 turns to this unlikely archival recovery, analyzing the texts and contexts of queer Native literature in 1970s gay newspapers and journals. Doing so allows us to recognize how this literature intervenes in our understandings of Native, gay, and queer of color literary canons, since none of these, as study of the anthologies listed in the previous chapter shows, acknowledges queer Native studies in all its complexities. A return to Ferguson's commentary about the regulatory nature of canon formation reminds us that all such imaginative groupings "outline trajectories for ethical subject formation" by defining (and, in the process, delimiting) "what it means to be a human, a citizen, and a moral being. As champions of normativity, these formations can only be consummated through the regulation of nonheteronormative difference."[1] With this admonition in mind, what sorts of knowledges might nonheteronormative subjects like Greta Garbo, gay cruising, or the queer space beneath the Brooklyn Bridge constitute? What might be learned from erotic parodies of Wordsworth, A. E. Houseman, and Byron? Or what's to be made of a reverie on a misplaced apostrophe in a homophobic slur? In terms of regulatory canonical imperatives, such topics already evade anticipated literary trajectories by failing to fulfill the ancestor-centered, buffalo-littered, landscape-focused expectations of Native writing. Yet as I scrolled through the microfilm of *Fag Rag* looking for poems from Maurice Kenny, the first known gay Native author to publish overtly queer literature in the United States, these images were exactly what I found.

Born in 1929 Watertown, New York, Kenny has been publishing since the 1950s and has, to this point, written more than twenty-five books of poetry, two collections of short fiction, two prose collections, and innumerable pieces in journals and edited collections while also working in radio and television and undertaking important editorial work with *Contact/II* and his own Strawberry Press. To name just a few of Kenny's many honors, he has garnered two Pulitzer Prize nominations—one for *Blackrobe: Isaac Jogues, b. March 11, 1604, d. October 18, 1646: Poems* (1982) and another for *Between Two Rivers: Selected Poems, 1956–1984* (1987)—and won the American Book Award for *The Mama Poems* (1984).[2] Kenny's oeuvre is not primarily focused on Two-Spirit themes and, in fact, his first five collections—*The Hopeless Kill, and Other Poems* (1956), *Dead Letters Sent, and Other Poems* (1958), *With Love to Lesbia: A Sheaf of Poems* (1958), *And Grieve, Lesbia: Poems* (1960), and *North: Poems of Home* (1977)—include no explicit reference to same-sex desire. The earliest collection of Kenny's poetry to include overtly queer work is his wonderful but difficult-to-find *Only as Far as Brooklyn: Poems* (1979).[3]

As chapter 1 noted, in 1975, four years before *Only as Far as Brooklyn* debuted, the first organization for Two-Spirit/lesbian, gay, bisexual, transgender, transsexual, intersex, and queer (LGBTIQ2) Native people in the United States, the GAI, was cofounded by Randy Burns and Barbara Cameron.[4] Kenny talks of meeting Cameron, Burns, and Sharol Graves (Crow) in the memoir, which begins his 1995 *On Second Thought:*

A Compilation, saying they were "young, beautiful people centered in their cultures, eager to give back to their cultures as they had been gifted with so much."[5] He goes on to name the mid-1970s as a time when "a world opened, and a prism of light and color pervaded this world."[6] While Kenny does not directly address the GAI in *On Second Thought,* his name is listed as a contact in some of the association's early literature and he speaks of this era as one of camaraderie and discovery: "In those days there weren't many Native writers who were published. We were friends and helped each other by suggesting publications and readings. We shared what little was out there."[7] He writes, "I was in a circle, a sacred circle of life with like kind, my own kind, native poets. I was no more the loner, the outlaw, nor even delinquent."[8]

Though they have, until now, been relatively unknown, the seventeen poems Kenny published in *Fag Rag* between 1974 and 1978 are tied to this period in his life as well as to the rise of gay publishing in the late 1960s and early 1970s. Such publications marked the beginning of what has been called the "gay cultural renaissance," a sea change that followed in the wake of the 1969 Stonewall Rebellion.[9] In the United States, as Gregory Woods explains in his survey of the gay male literary tradition,

> gay publishing . . . dates from the moment of gay liberation. . . . In 1969 the poet Paul Mariah founded *ManRoot* magazine and the ManRoot press in San Francisco. In 1970, also in San Francisco, Winston Leyland founded *Gay Sunshine* magazine. In 1971, the Boston Gay Liberation Front established *Fag Rag* magazine and then, in 1972, the Good Gay Poets publishing house. In 1973, Ian Young's pioneering gay poetry anthology, *The Male Muse* was published. In 1974, Andrew Bifrost founded *Mouth of the Dragon* ("A Poetry Journal of Male Love") in New York.[10]

While Woods's list continues, I stop here to note that, upon returning to these journals and newspapers, I found that Kenny's work appears in four of the five earliest publications that mark the post-Stonewall renaissance: Kenny published "A Night, a Bridge, a River" and "Greta Garbo" in the fall 1974 issue of Fag Rag; an essay, "Tinselled Bucks: An Historical Study in Indian Homosexuality," and a poem, "United," in the winter 1975/1976 issue of *Gay Sunshine: A Journal of Gay Liberation;* "Apache" in the June 1975 edition of *Mouth of the Dragon;* and "Winkte" and "Loves into Legends" in the 1977 spring/summer issue of *ManRoot.* His frequent publication in *Fag Rag* far outstripped the amount of work he placed in all the other journals combined during the 1970s. The regular inclusion of Kenny's work in *Fag Rag* disrupts a sense of these early journals as largely white and at the same time enlarges the parameters and concerns of a coeval literary movement Kenneth Lincoln termed the "Native American renaissance," which has been most often discussed through analyses of texts that focus on loss, cultural recovery, and a return to the physical space of the reservation.[11] In what my project marks as an important correspondence, the inaugural date of the Native American literary renaissance—1969, the year N. Scott Momaday's *House Made of Dawn* (1968) won the Pulitzer Prize for literature—parallels that of the gay cultural renaissance. In both cases, as in the literature and politics of so many nondominant groups, the resurgence of a more visible literary tradition is linked with political activism.[12] Thus the Gay Liberation Front that formed in the wake of Stonewall is key to the inception of periodicals like *Fag Rag,* just as journals such as *Akwesasne Notes, Many Smokes,* and *Wassaja* arose in the late 1960s and early 1970s as part of the ongoing assertion of American Indian rights.[13] Through the recovery and analysis of Kenny's writing from *Fag Rag* at this significant historical moment, this chapter expands our understanding of both these literary canons and the previously unmarked intersections between them, showing that the current rise of queer Native studies and Two-Spirit critiques have their roots in an earlier time and in unexpected venues.[14] But an analysis of queer Native literature from this period of widespread cultural change offers more than canon expansion, as important as that work is in the field. Kenny's writing from the periodicals of the gay cultural renaissance also highlights the ways in which Two-Spirit texts have, from their inception, offered new ways of reading, seeing, and imagining the world.

Contextualizing *Fag Rag*

Given that he's been publishing and editing poetry and fiction for sixty years now, Kenny's oeuvre is vast, but as a scholar of LGBTIQ/Two-Spirit literature, I thought I had read the bulk of it. In fact, I had traced the images of queerness through his work, writing about his poem "Winkte," which was previously believed to be the first piece of queer Native literature published, and the queer-themed poems in *Only as Far as Brooklyn* for

Penelope Myrtle Kelsey's edited collection, *Maurice Kenny: Celebrations of a Mohawk Writer* (2011).[15] But scrolling through the microfilm of *Fag Rag* changed everything I thought I knew about the inception of queer Native literature.

Fag Rag, which was billed as "a Gay Male Newspaper," published its first issue in June 1971.[16] The cover of the sixteen-page debut edition spoofed Grant Wood's classic 1930 painting *American Gothic* with a pencil drawing that includes the dark-coated, bespectacled farmer of the original, still clutching his pitchfork. In contrast, however, his partner is not a stern white woman but a bald, slightly pudgy white man wearing a buttoned-up shirt, overalls, and a kindly smile. The first *Fag Rag* contains an array of articles, including a piece titled "Fallen Superstar" on folk icon Phil Ochs's derogatory use of the term "fag" during a concert; a several-page spread on the medicalization of queerness called "Doctor, Doctor: Fags and Shrinks"; a piece on coming out titled "To Be 19 and Gay"; a section titled "Cocksucker" that explicitly addressed oral sex; and essays on Vietnam, the Cuban Revolution, and the Black Panthers. Sprinkled amid the initial eclectic mix of editorials and essays were three unattributed poems.[17]

There was rarely a set publication schedule for the newspaper during its sixteen-year run, and in fact, the fall 1971 editorial commentary in the second issue addressed the difficulty the volunteer editorial staff had in producing *Fag Rag* issue 2 at all due to disagreements over the content and scope of the publication. The unattributed editorial introduction, titled "*Fag Rag* Blues," noted that "staff meetings" were "often . . . long and bitter arguments. . . . The intensity of our meetings and the animosity which many of them produced indicate that there was more at stake than simply whether or not a given article was printed. The kinds of disagreements we had can best be understood in the context of what has been happening with Gay Liberation Fronts all over the country. The last few months have seen the collapse of many GLFs all over the place."[18]

This split in the politics and expectations that drove the editorial staff of *Fag Rag* was mirrored in the diversity of reader expectations. Each issue published letters from readers in the opening pages of the newspaper. These letters ranged from heartfelt responses to *Fag Rag*'s coverage of the political upheavals of the day—which included not only the ongoing schisms in the gay rights movement but also pieces on feminism, sexism, and the politics of the prison industrial system—to frequent calls for less didactic content of this sort in favor of more (and more explicit) erotica in

Figure 1. Front cover of June 1971 Fag Rag, *the first issue of the newspaper, which offers a queer revision of Grant Wood's classic 1930 painting* American Gothic. *Used with permission by Wilcox Collection, Kenneth Spencer Research Library, University of Kansas Libraries.*

both text and image. The latter call was answered: the inclusion of essays with erotic content and photographs and drawings of male bodies and sexual acts subsequently became regular aspects of the newspaper. As a result, in many cases *Fag Rag* is categorized as a gay male porn magazine, a designation I would debate—although the parameters of pornography are a slippery slope indeed.

By the time Kenny was first published in *Fag Rag*—issue 10, fall 1974—the size of the newspaper had doubled, with most issues averaging thirty pages. The number of poems included in each edition had increased exponentially as well, and, as opposed to the practice of the early issues, most subsequent poems were attributed, though not always titled, from *Fag Rag* issue 5 onward. In addition, the newspaper often interspersed two-page sections of poetry with the essays, letters, and art that made up each issue. In terms of content, the most frequent topics continued to be some form of coming-out narratives, pieces on the medicalization of homosexuality, and sex-positive essays/erotica like *Fag Rag* issue 3's "Cocksucking as an Act of Revolution."[19] The editors continued, as well, to attempt to include a widely defined diversity in the newspaper; while the bulk of photographs and drawings were of young white men, there were also images of people of color and interracial couples (usually black and white men), as well as editorials focused on racial, cultural, and social diversity. So, for example, there were articles offering "third world perspectives"; essays on the intersectional concerns of the Vietnam conflict, welfare policy, and the industrial prison complex; and pieces on alternative political or spiritual movements such as communism and paganism. Occasionally, articles by writers marking themselves as queers of color were also included, such as *Fag Rag* issue 4's "I Am a Black Faggot," in which the unnamed, first-person author points out the specificities of his experiences as a black gay man, noting that the cultural "norm was and is heterosexist, middle-class conscious, male supremacist whites."[20] Though the newspaper could be radical within work of this type, which called out the racialized hierarchies both in and outside queer communities, the limited inclusions of such pieces suggest an additive model characteristic of 1970s and 1980s multiculturalism—a worldview that centers on whiteness by offering the proverbial "seat at the table" to nonwhite artists, writers, and activists while still leaving white power and privilege intact. In *Feeling of Kinship* (2010), David L. Eng speaks of just this sort of occlusion when he marks the imbricated nature of white privilege and queer liberalism, pointing to the ways this often invisible intersection "constitute[s] normative gay and lesbian U.S. citizen-subjects . . . [who are] induct[ed] . . . into an abstract and universalizing liberal narrative of political enfranchisement and inclusion."[21] In the face of this seemingly progressive policy of multicultural "inclusion," racial privilege—which Eng, following critical race studies scholar Cheryl I. Harris, terms a "racialized property right"—functions unacknowledged and unmarked, veiled by the benevolent cloak of white liberalism. Sociologist Cathy J. Cohen terms this assimilationist paradigm a "civil rights framework," arguing that such strategies use a rhetoric of rights acquisition that incorporates a citizen-subject into existing hierarchies rather than changing the system itself.[22] The racialized ideologies underpinning this seat-at-the-table rhetoric would be challenged by the rise of women of color feminism and, as discussed in chapter 1, by important collections such as Cherríe Moraga and Gloria Anzaldúa's *This Bridge Called My Back* and Beth Brant's *A Gathering of Spirit*; however, this work was still ten years from publication when *Fag Rag*'s first issue rolled off the press.

Repatriating the Brooklyn Bridge

The earliest pieces Kenny published in *Fag Rag*—"A Night, a Bridge, a River: (Beneath Brooklyn Bridge)" and "Greta Garbo"—differ significantly from the poem thought for many years to be the first piece of contemporary queer Native literature: Kenny's "Winkte." Initially published in the spring/summer 1977 edition of the gay literary journal *ManRoot* and later reprinted in *Living the Spirit*, "Winkte" repeats laudatory claims such as "We were special to the Sioux!" and "To the Cheyenne we were no curiosity!"[23] The poem, which takes as its title a Lakota word that is the most widely known tribal term for a multiply gendered person, recoups the place of Two-Spirit people in Native nations by evoking the historical acceptance of diverse gender traditions among Plains nations like the Sioux, Cheyenne, Pawnee, Ponca, and Crow. By highlighting the inclusion, acceptance, and importance of Two-Spirit people, who, the speaker notes, "had power with the people" and were "good for the Nation," Kenny points to the heterocentricism and homophobia that, in some cases, had since elided or driven underground those traditions. Thus "Winkte" disrupts heteronormative representations of Indigenous masculinity while still fulfilling the expected narrative of cultural recovery in American Indian renaissance–era literature by calling for a return to historically recognized tribal traditions. "A Night, a Bridge, a River: (Beneath Brooklyn Bridge)" and "Greta Garbo," by contrast, present a literary narrative about urbanity, sex, and the overlapping nature of oppressions. As a result, these poems, together with Kenny's other work in *Fag Rag* during this period, demonstrate the intersectional concerns of 1970s Native writing, posit Indigeneity as an unacknowledged concern of the gay cultural renaissance, and challenge the heteronormative framing of the Native American literary renaissance and Red Power era.

"A Night, a Bridge, a River: (Beneath Brooklyn Bridge)" is an eight-stanza snapshot of the coming of spring in New York City, which backgrounds the speaker's walk home with his lover and their later phone conversation. The parenthetical half of the title—"(Beneath the Brooklyn Bridge)"—is important here because it situates the speaker and the initial action of the poem at a site famous for gay cruising, as many readers of *Fag Rag* would recognize. Through this parenthetical aside, Kenny probes the way the public/private divide circulates within both geographical and psychic sites of knowledge. Lauren Berlant and Michael Warner explain that the shared knowledge of such public spaces is one way queer people "have learned to find each other; to map a commonly accessible world; to construct the architecture of queer space in a homophobic environment."[24] By specifically naming Brooklyn Park, a locale regularly frequented by gay men, as the public space of "A Night, a Bridge, a River: (Beneath Brooklyn Bridge)," Kenny hails those in the know, both citing and creating community through an articulation of queer geography.

Kenny begins the body of the poem with a description of place that invokes the "spansion and wave" of the bridge and river below. The speaker recalls "poems colliding with river tugs / tankers answering in epics."[25] After setting a rose-tinged scene in which there are frosted mugs of beer, shouts of playing children, and "fairy-land lights" lining the streets, the poem shifts in the third and central stanza from atmospheric description to direct address: "Home-way you broke off an elm twig / you charged like a Sioux / striking bare legs with wet kisses of leaves" (8). This playful simile, with its suggestion of a counting coup, is not, as might be expected by scholars of queer Native studies, the fulcrum of "A Night, a Bridge, a River: (Beneath Brooklyn Bridge)." Instead, the second half of the poem takes an elegiac tone, focusing on the weight of individual rather than cultural loss. Thus the speaker wakes alone the morning after his romantic encounter to a telephone that "screamed in the sunshine / like the bite of a rabid dog"

(8). The elm branch that had rained "wet kisses of leaves" the night before now hangs on the wall, wilting and "crucified with scotch-tape," while the bright daylight and empty bed burn away the fairytale glow of the previous evening (8). The last stanza then makes a final, temporal shift that situates the night, the bridge, and the encounter in memory: "Now I remember cheap hotels . . . broken lilies, ladies, raisins" (8). The speaker's emotional loss culminates in a final image of "welfare clients of love," have-lesses in the world of romance who are offered not plenty but the meager leavings of a morning after (8). "A Night, a Bridge, a River: (Beneath Brooklyn Bridge)" thus captures the ebullient beauty of a shared erotic encounter, the jarring discord of a lonely awakening, and the wistful frame of remembrance. The politics here are neither solely queer nor solely Indigenous and may, in fact, be familiar to many Native and non-Native, LGBTIQ2, or straight-identified readers who, seduced by spring air, have loved and lost in rapid succession. Consequently, Kenny's first piece in *Fag Rag* departs from the narrative of cultural loss/recovery that characterizes "Winkte" and so many of the better-known, renaissance-era texts by Momaday, Leslie Marmon Silko (Laguna Pueblo), James Welch (Blackfeet/Gros Ventre), or Simon Ortiz (Acoma Pueblo). Instead, "A Night, a Bridge, a River: (Beneath Brooklyn Bridge)" can be read alongside an ongoing LGBTIQ literary tradition that figures the Brooklyn Bridge as a site of queer connection and, in fact, can be seen as an intervention into that body of work.

José Esteban Muñoz concludes *Cruising Utopia* (2009) by ruminating on the place the famous suspension bridge holds within the parameters, ephemera, and possibilities of queer utopia. Muñoz cites Walt Whitman's, Hart Crane's, and Samuel R. Delany's writing on the iconic structure and leaves us with a reading of the queer poet Elizabeth Bishop's "Invitation to Miss Marianne Moore." He suggests the "queer dynamic duo" of the author and her subject offer a "spectacle of queer transport" that builds an intertext on and with this earlier body of LGBTIQ literature.[26] The bridge therefore functions as what Muñoz calls "a dense connective site in the North American queer imagination."[27] Kenny's piece underlines Muñoz's claim that the Brooklyn Bridge has symbolic resonance in the queer imagination: its queer geography has been claimed, mapped, and erotically employed as a connective locale by LGBTIQ2 people for more than a century. Yet Muñoz's pairing of queerness with the urban geography of the Brooklyn Bridge both articulates and erases the intersectional nature of this particular queer landmark. Thus for Muñoz's geography of queerness to become visible, a concurrent geography of Indigeneity must be simultaneously elided. Andrea Smith describes just this pattern in "Queer Theory and Native Studies: The Heteronormativity of Settler Colonialism" when she explains, "A critical limit often not explored by queer of color critique is the limits of settler colonialism. As such, indigeneity frequently disappears within these projects."[28] The addition of Kenny's writing to the body of queer literature on the Brooklyn Bridge, then, enables us to re-Indigenize *both* the space itself *and* the idea of the queer imagination, reminding us that non-Native queer identities in the United States are examples of settler sexuality, which historically depends on Indigeneity.[29]

The Brooklyn Bridge itself sits on what was traditionally Algonquian land in King's County, New York. By the late 1600s, Dutch settlers had purchased or seized most of the land in what is now Brooklyn through settler colonial incursions into Indigenous territories. While these Native histories and presences are queerly absent in Muñoz's gay utopic visions, they were apparent not only to those who colonized this land but also, two hundred years later, to those who celebrated the completion of the bridge: in May 1883, at the bridge's opening gala, the Carlisle Indian Industrial School band played, led by Lakota author Luther Standing Bear, who was in the first class at Carlisle.[30] Standing Bear claims with pride in *My People the Sioux* (1928) that the Carlisle band was "the first *real American band* to cross the Brooklyn Bridge."[31] Alan Trachtenberg points to the many resonances contained in Standing Bear's deployment of the term "band" here, which functions as both a collection of musicians and a reference to tribal community that "evokes, by contrast and by irony, [the Lakota concept of] *Tiospaye*."[32] Trachtenberg shows, too, that Hart Crane's epic poem *The Bridge* (1930), which concludes with an account of a Brooklyn Bridge crossing in a section titled "Atlantis," rests on the invocation of Indigeneity.[33] Meanwhile, Douglas Cazaux Sackman notes that Yankton Sioux Chief White Ghost was brought to the bridge a year after its completion as a highlight of his New York City tour.[34] According to an unnamed reporter for the January 1885 *The American Missionary,* Chief White Ghost—"about fifty-six years of age" and "practically a heathen man"—to their surprise, "hardly evoked an expression of wonder" when "crossing the Brooklyn Bridge in mid-air and above the masts of large vessels."[35] *The American Missionary*'s expectation of awe situates the bridge and surroundings as settler space and the visiting White Ghost as primitivist signifier brought from "wigwam life into . . . scenes of a great city."[36] In this equation, both the bridge and New York City are clearly framed as antithetical to Indigenous understanding. Yet this belief could not be further from the truth; besides these more publicized visits, the bridge was often traversed as well by the famed Kahnawake Mohawk steelworkers and members of New York's Little Caughnawaga community.[37]

These Indigenous traces seem queerly indiscernible for many outside of Native studies and Native communities, just as Muñoz, though he references both the bridge and Crane, sees no record for the structure before Whitman's odes to the settler history of America. Moreover, in each of the aforementioned cases, the *intersections* of queerness and Indigeneity vanish, leaving the bridge as *either* a marker of an Indigenous presence *or* a marker of queer geography. Yet as "A Night, a Bridge, a River: (Beneath Brooklyn Bridge)" shows, Indigenous traces exist *within* the bridge's queer literary history, marking not only the historical importance of the bridge to Native narratives but also the contemporary presence of queer Indigenous people in the urban locale of New York City. These "postindian echoes," to borrow a term from Anishinaabe theorist Gerald Vizenor, reverberate like the beat of the Carlisle Indian Industrial School band's drums, disrupting the martial rhythm of a settler narrative of progress.[38] While Muñoz resists such linear narratives of Euro-Western progress—which he terms "straight time"—by queering the temporalities and geographies the bridge represents, he stops short of recognizing the importance of Indigenous voices to his project of queer recovery. Instead he turns to Bishop's poem about the bridge, forwarding her "invitation to desire differently, to desire more, to desire better."[39] I take up that invitation here by arguing that if we are really to "desire differently," as Muñoz suggests, we must listen for the reverberations of queer Indigeneity. This chapter's recovery of Kenny's poetry from the gay cultural renaissance offers one such possibility by revealing Indigeneity at the heart of queer utopia. At the same time, Kenny's work from these non-Native 1970s journals also shows that the first overt queer Native literature rests not on reservation land or tribal structures, like Momaday's and Silko's better-known narratives from the era, but on a bridge famously claimed as a marker for settler progress.

Disability, Sex, and Secrecy, or Cruising Greta Garbo

The second Kenny poem in the fall 1974 issue of *Fag Rag* is "Greta Garbo," which was later revised and reprinted in *Only as Far as Brooklyn.*

Significantly darker than "A Night, a Bridge, a River," the Garbo piece reinforces my observation about the range and diversity of work in post-1969 renaissance-era literature, as the poem focuses on correlations between disability, age, vulnerability, and loss. The poem's three stanzas of eight, twenty-two, and six lines compare a disabled soldier cruising in Brooklyn Park to Garbo, who is directly addressed throughout the piece and who would have been sixty-nine at the time of the poem's publication. The first stanza sets the stage:

> The Park's darkness
> Increased
> With the cripple's loneness.
> The leg, braced, ached.
> His coiled fingers shining
> Like ice or wax,
> Were as broken
> As your heart must be.[40]

From the outset, then, the poem makes complex claims through what at first seem to be entirely disparate images—juxtaposing a soldier's painful war wounds and gay cruising with Greta Garbo's heart. But as the piece develops in the second stanza, the parallels crystallize: the problematic nature of the gay male aesthetic is compared to the unrealistic expectations the viewing public and popular press have of screen idols. In each case, the viewer regulates the body, demanding able-bodiedness and youth as expected markers of perfection. So though the soldier smiles "handsomely" at the speaker when they meet in the park's darkness, he is also cognizant of such regulatory expectations and is therefore "fearful" (27). The narrator explains that the soldier "hid[es] / The brace and mangled hand / As [Garbo] hide[s] [her] face." Fatalistically, the narrator comments that "God meant his youth / To be broken, / Your beauty aged: / War and time take what they want!" (27). Noted communications studies scholar David Serlin, who works on the intersections between queerness and disability, offers a reading of physical disability, masculinity, and queerness that can expand our understanding of Kenny's rhetoric. Serlin charts the development of military techniques of surveillance, which by the time of the U.S. Civil War drew a "cultural distinction between the 'tragically' disabled and the congenitally 'deformed.'"[41] "This delineation,"

Serlin explains, "relied in part on the difference between disability induced by modern technology or warfare and disability induced by heredity or illness, a premodern model of judging disabled bodies by invoking the medieval 'monstrous birth.' The former kind of disability confirms one's service to the modern state, to industrial capitalism, to warfare: it helps the veteran's body preserve patriotic values and masculinity."[42] The distinction Serlin invokes would seem to circulate in Kenny's "Greta Garbo," as well, given the speaker's emphasis on the brace and wounded hand as war wounds. Thus though disability and aging are coded as loss throughout, the poem is striking in its tender description of the disabled soldier, who is seen by the speaker as both "tragically" impaired and physically attractive. This depiction is especially notable given its context in *Fag Rag,* which, as referenced in this chapter's opening vignette, regularly featured photographic and artistic renditions of lithe, able-bodied young white men. As Scott Herring comments in his analysis of the shifting images in queer publications of the 1970s, news magazines like *The Advocate* "imagined . . . gay readers as 'heavily capitalized' consumers and interpellated them into a normalized racial and class identity via an aesthetics of chic and fashionability."[43] By focusing on a central figure who stands outside what Herring calls "gay male metro print norms," Kenny highlights these regulatory expectations for gay male appearance and, in doing so, subtly critiques the prevalence of limited and limiting depictions of masculinity, beauty, and the erotic.[44]

At the same time, however, "Greta Garbo" is not outside the aesthetic binaries it critiques. In fact, one could argue that Kenny's narrator, too, equates youth and able-bodiedness with male beauty and social acceptance. The latter equation is underlined in the second half of stanza two: "The soldier's memory / Of straight leg and fingers / Does nothing to erase his pain / And give him the love / He seeks nightly in a Brooklyn Park" (27). Love, sex, and able-bodiedness are linked in this description of the soldier, and all are bound to a nostalgic past, leaving the present as a realm of "pain," loss, and loneliness. Kenny presents a common understanding of disability through these images. In *Extraordinary Bodies: Figuring Disability in American Culture and Literature,* a landmark text in disability studies, Rosemarie Garland Thomson argues that "the meanings attributed to [such] extraordinary bodies reside not in inherent physical flaws, but in social relationships in which one group is legitimated by possessing valued physical characteristics and maintains its ascendancy and its self-identity by systematically imposing the role of cultural or corporeal inferiority on others. Representation thus simultaneously buttresses an embodied version of normative identity and shapes a narrative of corporeal differences that excludes those whose bodies or behaviors don't conform."[45] Speaking of the ways these social relationships between bodies and power have been constituted historically, David Johnstone explains that there have been numerous models of disability in contemporary U.S. culture. So "prior to the development of the modern welfare state, disability was conceived as a product of individual personal tragedy."[46] In such understandings, "disability was regarded as *impairment*—it impeded the capacity of disabled individuals to live or act as 'able-bodied' individuals, and so impeded their enjoyment of rights and liberties. Their disability rendered them 'invisible.'"[47] The subsequent rise of social democracy and the welfare state moved disability into the realm of state concern. In the decades after World War II, the state "initiated the realization of rights through legislation and policy, and was the enabler of rights by providing services."[48] This state-defined disability model had, instead of erasure or loss, a "care and support orientation" that "incorporated" disabled people "rather than encouraging change within society to reflect their politics or identity."[49] In each construction, however, disabled people are either erased or acted for or upon rather than with. Such discussions of disability can be closely tied in both form and content to discourses about Indigenous people in North America. In both the United States and Canada, Indigenous people have been demonized, pathologized, and patronized in representation and legislation and, like disabled people, have often been marked for death in the politics of biopower. The legacy of these policies and histories includes pressing health such as the prevalence of diabetes or the spread of HIV/AIDS in Native communities; these ongoing health crises make discussions of disability an important consideration in contemporary Native nations and communities.[50] One of the earliest pieces of overtly queer Native lit, then, raises complicated intersectional concerns that will not begin to be adequately addressed in the academy until the rise of disability studies in the 1990s.

Recovering Kenny's work from this period enables us to see how a renaissance-era writer offers the possibility of coalition in the space marked for difference. To return to Eng, rather than working within queer liberalism's politics of erasure, in which the property of whiteness—and, as "Greta Garbo" reminds us, of able-bodiedness—is effaced by a rhetoric of neoliberal multiculturalist inclusion, Kenny's coalitional politics stem from what Cohen terms "not [a] shared history or identity but . . . [a] shared marginal relationship to dominant power that normalizes, legitimizes, and privileges."[51] Indeed, Kenny's overt attention to physical disability indexes a pervasive concern in Indigenous literatures. The list of physically disabled characters in Native literature can go on ad infinitum. Old Grandma in *Ceremony,* Yellow Calf in *Winter in the Blood,* Yellow Kidney in *Fools Crow,* and Mercury Thunder in *The Grass Dancer* are just a few examples. What this early piece of queer Native literature brings to the fore, then, is a physical reality that ties Kenny's work to American Indian literatures and also serves a bridge to a non-Native writing on "extraordinary bodies," enabling us to trace lines of affiliation through and between these texts and peoples.

In addition to Kenny's focus on disability, the rumors of the screen icon's bisexuality further advance the argument that the sorts of intersections apparent in "Greta Garbo" have the potential to "advance strategically oriented political identities arising from a more nuanced understanding of power."[52] In this case, though, the allusions to the open secret of queer sexuality are somewhat more expected given the well-known ties between queerness and secrecy. Queer studies scholar Elisa Glick explains that

> modern gay identity is pervaded by the trope of the secret. Building on the work of Michel Foucault and D. A. Miller, the literary and cultural critic Eve Sedgwick has argued that gay identity is fundamentally shaped by the dualism of secrecy and disclosure, but since "telling" is both prohibited and required, queer identity is always an internal contradiction between opacity and transparency, at once hidden and revealed. It is this double bind between secrecy and disclosure that Sedgwick refers to when, arguing for the enduring centrality of the epistemology of the closet for gay people and culture, she points to the way that homosexual identity has been "distinctly constituted *as* secrecy" from its inception.[53]

This trope of secrecy is clearly at play in "Greta Garbo," where the speaker describes, on one hand, the soldier's late-night cruising at the park, his queer desire, and his attempt to conceal his injuries, while on another, Garbo's famed seclusion, her aging, and, to those in the know, her rumored bisexuality. In a brilliant bit of doubling, Kenny probes the way the public/private divide circulates within both geographical and psychic sites of knowledge. So, for example, the soldier's cruising is half hidden as he "slouch[es] into the resolution of the night," yet the act of cruising necessarily occurs in public space (27). As with "A Night, a Bridge, a River: (Beneath Brooklyn Bridge)," here, too, we see how the shared knowledge of public space functions as a "map [to] a commonly accessible world," thereby fashioning "the architecture of queer space in a homophobic environment."[54] This slippage between public and private and the relay between them also permeates Kenny's deployment of Greta Garbo as both an actual public figure and a metonym for queer knowledge. Like Kenny's allusion to queer geography, his allusion to Garbo relies on an implicitly shared understanding. The poem's multivalence rests not simply on the function of fame, which places private figures in the public eye, thereby conveying an illusory sense of intimate knowledge, but also on the legendary image of the "divine Garbo" more specifically. Film studies scholar Melinda Szaloky calls this long-discussed impact "the Garbo affect," which Szaloky describes "*both* as a vestige of an irreparable human lack and as the promise that there is something left behind as *unattainable.*"[55] Garbo's screen image promises and withholds simultaneously, as does Kenny's reference to the public/private slippage of her sexuality. Like the queer resonance the (secret) space "(Beneath the Brooklyn Bridge)" would hold for many readers of *Fag Rag,* Kenny's use of Garbo, too, turns on what, for this reading audience, would be the public knowledge of queer rumor.[56]

The final stanza of "Greta Garbo" in *Fag Rag,* which is omitted from the version Kenny later published in *Only as Far as Brooklyn,* focuses on questions of age and temporality. The narrator exclaims, "Both the lily / and the weed / Have a single season: / Strange! / One spring / Seems sufficiently enough!" (27). The lily/weed comparison underscores the inadequacy of class or fame to halt the progress of age—despite their seemingly disparate status, both the unnamed soldier and Garbo have the same "spring" or "season" of youth. Additionally, the narrator's claim invokes the point often made in disability studies about the shifting nature of able-bodiedness, which, like youth, is always already both contextual and temporary. In each case, Kenny's intersectional juxtapositions trace heretofore unaddressed nodes of connection and disjunction in 1970s Native literature, thereby changing the way we perceive the concerns of the American Indian renaissance: by centering on the open secrets of physical disability and queer desire, Kenny intertwines identities and oppressions that relate but are not confined to Indigeneity. Making this sort of relationality visible moves us toward a coalitional politics that Cohen deems transformative—the space where "one's relation to power, and not some homogenized identity, is privileged in determining one's political comrades."[57]

Erotic Parody as Queer Possibility

As this chapter shows, just as Kenny's work disrupts any singular narrative for 1970s Native literature, so, too, does his poetry from the gay cultural renaissance disrupt any search for narrative cohesion within his own body of writing. Thus his debut pieces in *Fag Rag*—"A Night, a Bridge, a River: (Beneath Brooklyn Bridge)" and "Greta Garbo"—are followed a year later by "Two Parodies: With Apologies to Wordsworth" in the November/ December 1975 issue of *Fag Rag*. These pieces, which are burlesque revisions of "My Heart Leaped Up When I Beheld" and "She Dwelt among the Untrodden Ways," offer tongue-in-cheek rewritings of two classic Wordsworth poems. Though Kenny's title poses an "apology" to Wordsworth, he could, like Wordsworth himself in his preface to *Lyrical Ballads*, simply claim, similarly, to be "a man speaking to men."[58] The first parody, "My Prick Leaps Up," takes Wordsworth's meditation on the beauty of nature and grounds it firmly in the erotic:

> My prick leaps up when I behold
>   naked beauty on the sand;
> so was it when my cruise began;
> so is it now that I am damned;
> so be it when I shall grow old,
>   oh! let me toy!
> the Queen is mother to the Boy;
> and I could wish my nights to be
> bound thigh to thigh in sexuality.[59]

Thus Wordsworth's ode to the sublime nature of "a rainbow in the sky" and subsequent desire for "days . . . / Bound each to each by natural piety" takes a queer turn. The overt eroticism of Kenny's parody poems contrasts with the secrecy and innuendo of "Greta Garbo." While both reference gay cruising, "My Prick Leaps Up" does so in irreverent, joyous celebration of queer desire. Unlike "Greta Garbo," which cites the "single season" of youth and beauty, thereby tying age to loss, Kenny's "Two Parodies" writes desire as both constant and circular. The arousal felt "now" at the sight of a naked man upon the sand will still be felt when the narrator "grow[s] old" (12). Thus at least in the case of erotic desire, age is not an inevitable signifier of abjection. In addition, the circularity suggested by the line "the Queen is mother to the Boy" implies, in a Butlerian wink to performance, that queer culture is taught and mimetically replicated: the "Boy" does not mature alone and is not essentially queer but rather is mothered/educated by a queer parent in the form of the "Queen" (12).

Kenny's second parody in this pair, "He Cruised among the Trodden Ways," employs the same meter as Wordsworth's "She Dwelt among the Untrodden Ways" but humorously reverses the poem's message. Whereas Wordsworth's Lucy was unknown and unpraised by all save the poem's narrator, Kenny's young unnamed hustler was "a fag who's cock was highly praised / by every queen and bum" (12). That Lucy and Kenny's hustler both fade into obscurity—Lucy through death and Kenny's character through a lack of popularity due to overexposure—suggests that even if virgins were "to make much of time," as Robert Herrick famously suggested, they may, in Kenny's world, still end up "welfare clients of love."[60] While such playful prose might be easily dismissed in a period in which American Indian literature was rife with more somber calls for tribal autonomy and cultural recovery, it's important to recognize that the overt eroticism of "My Prick Leaps Up" is common not only to post-Stonewall-era gay journals but also to Indigenous oral traditions, which often include trickster stories that either humorously or matter-of-factly reference sex, the erotic, desire, and/or genitalia. While Kenny's parodies in no way overtly invoke these histories, neither are they beyond the pale of Indigenous oral and written literary traditions. They, in fact, could be argued to play an important role in rupturing monolithic ideas about the Native literary canon, which function, as Ferguson reminded us, as singular "trajectories for ethical subject formation" that "specify what it means to be a human, a citizen, and a moral being" and "regulat[e] . . . nonheteronormative difference."[61] In contrast to such limited understandings of canon, queerness, and Indigeneity, Daniel Heath Justice contends, "a place of legitimized queerness *matters* to Native cultures . . . to both tribal politics of sovereignty and a sovereignty of aesthetic (and erotic) expression."[62] With these cautions and possibilities in mind, I suggest we embrace Kenny's erotic parodies *alongside* classic 1970s texts like James

Welch's *Riding the Earthboy 40* (1971) or Simon Ortiz's *Going for the Rain* (1976) to more effectively recognize the rich diversity and breadth of the Native 1970s.

Kenny's delight in this form of erotic imitation is evident as he publishes "Three Parodies: With Apologies to A. E. Housman" a year later in the fall/winter *Fag Rag* issue 18.[63] Like "Two Parodies: With Apologies to Wordsworth," the poem takes the structure and meter of a classic verse and gives it a queer turn. In this case, Kenny parodies Housman's "Into My Heart," "When I Came Last to Ludlow," and "With Rue My Heart Is Laden," which were all published in Housman's 1896 *A Shropshire Lad,* a collection that catalogues a loss and loneliness tied to Housman's unrequited love for his Oxford schoolmate and later roommate, Moses Jackson. While the title cues the reader as to which famous poet the piece pays homage, Kenny relies on his audience to be familiar with the poems themselves. Kenny's parodies are numbered—"1," "11," and "111"—rather than named, and each begins with a four-line comic stanza that offers memories of cruising followed by a second and final stanza that laments those practices as, for the speaker at least, a thing of the past.[64] Were it not for the 1976 publication dates, the three pieces would read as the late 1980s and early 1990s post-AIDS pandemic lament that can be seen in the work of writers like Essex Hemphill, Mark Doty, and Paul Monette.[65]

Like Housman's works, Kenny's poems pose an idyllic scene in stanza one and then turn to loss and death in stanza two. In "1," which parodies "Into My Heart," the speaker recalls the "thighs" and "kisses" of "Dan's and Bill's." The space of cruising, the park, is now one with "no outlet," its "endless greens" bringing not satisfaction but thoughts of "husky boys that I could get, / And cannot love again."[66] Here this inability to love is lost due to an unexplained choice by the speaker rather than age. In "II," Kenny follows Housman's lead in "When I Came Last to Ludlow"; however, where Housman romanticizes "two friends," "honest" and "hale," who walked beside him in the Ludlow moonlight, Kenny's speaker recalls "two lovers" who "slept beside" him in "Whitman's Park" (9). This warm memory dims in light of present-day reality: "Tonight Jack sleeps in a prison / and Vic loves a needle" (9). In a progressive litany of loss, the parodies move from loss by choice to loss due to drug use and imprisonment to loss due to death. Thus in "111," which imitates "With Rue My Heart Is Laden," the poet first delightedly recalls the joys of the erotic, invoking his "lust" for "many well-hung hustlings" and "forty sweet-lipped lads," but then laments the fact that "handsome boys are [now] laid" in the parks they once cruised, leaving "cold-thighed lovers . . . weeping" (9). As a result, Kenny's later set of parody poems, while still playful, align with "A Night, a Bridge, a River"; both poems document experiences commonly referenced in post-Stonewall literature—the aftermaths of same-sex relationships. However, such explicit attention to erotics was *not* common to publications of 1970s American Indian literature, where, as noted in the Introduction and chapter 1, references to sex were markedly heteronormative until Allen's 1983 novel *The Woman Who Owned the Shadows,* which was not analyzed by critics as a queer text until the 1990s.

Like Kenny's prior work in *Fag Rag,* the queer performances of his parodies have a marked geographic locale that separates these pieces from the better-known canon of Native American literature that arises simultaneously. So, for example, Momaday's protagonist Abel finds Los Angeles a site of alienation and empty pan-Indian rituals in *House Made of Dawn.* Likewise, Silko's *Ceremony* depicts the urban space of Gallup as one of loss and victimization, a dangerous site populated by displaced Navajo and Pueblo peoples whose alcoholism and violence results from their experiences of settler colonial oppression and their psychic disconnection from their nations. While the painful realities of urban relocation for Indigenous peoples are well documented, Kenny reminds us that urban spaces are not solely the site of trauma. These considerations tie to Mark Rifkin's questions about "an *ethics of sovereignty,* a set of normative principles that can inform discussions about what can and should count as a claim to Indigeneity."[67] Rifkin suggests, "The narration and realization of [tribal] sovereignty depends on a vision of exclusionary enclosure, it casts difference from available standards of Indianness as a threatening incursion and engages space as a quantum of territory over which tribal control can be extended as jurisdiction."[68] In *Red Land, Red Power: Grounding Knowledge in the American Indian Novel,* Cherokee Nation scholar Sean Kicummah Teuton describes this trend as "a tribal realist approach to identity, experience, and politics in their novels: the protagonists cannot recover their lands, their pasts, and their lives until they reconnect with the elders, healers, and other members of their communities."[69] Kenny's poetry, whether playful or serious, forces readers to engage just such questions of space and identification: while a common understanding of the renaissance-era Native canon (such as that which Teuton details) situates redemption solely in the return to reservation relationships and geographies, Kenny's early work in *Fag Rag* depicts urban spaces as potential sites of connections. This connection hinges on a return to an explicitly constituted erotic, which is another way these poems expand the parameters of 1970s literature.

In her recuperation of Native women's erotic poetry, Deborah A. Miranda notes that "there is a significant difference between the creation of poetry and the embrace of the erotic, and it may be that a crucial level of physical safety must be reached before erotica can be publicly shared by an oppressed population. Created by people of color or sexual minorities, poetry can be dangerous."[70] While Miranda suggests work like Kenny's is important and risky, it could be argued that the "danger" of Kenny's erotica is to some degree contained by *Fag Rag*'s paean to whiteness. For example, his earlier "Two Parodies: With Apologies to Wordsworth"—in which he pairs his first parody, "My Prick Leaps Up," with "He Cruised among the Troddened Ways"—is surrounded by drawings of well-muscled, shaggy-haired white men receiving fellatio (drawn by "Razzel Dazzel.75"). The frame on the page, then, is undoubtedly an image of settler sexuality, which could limit Kenny's disruptive potential in the early literature of the post-Stonewall publishing renaissance if we think in terms of the journal's 1970s audience. For much of Kenny's audience, the absence of any Indigenous markers undoubtedly meant the poems were coded as non-Native. While those in the know, like members or allies of the GAI, might read it differently, such readings would require a deliberate intervention into *Fag Rag*'s framing narrative.

"Tinselled Bucks" as Narrative Intervention

Kenny provides some of that contextual framing with "Tinselled Bucks: An Historical Study in Indian Homosexuality" and his poem "United," both published in the winter 1975/1976 issue of *Gay Sunshine*.[71] "Tinselled Bucks" and "United" were later republished with "Winkte" in *Living the Spirit*. In terms of their original publication context, *Gay Sunshine*, a San Francisco paper edited by Winston Leyland, was, like *Fag Rag*, an eclectic blend of poetry, interviews, art, and political pieces on contemporary gay politics.[72] Kenny's essay was placed in a special "Latin American" issue that, according to the editorial note, was primarily "devoted to material from (or about) Mexico, Argentina, and Guatemala."[73] "Tinselled Bucks" appears toward the end of the issue and is described by the editors as a "historical article on homosexuality among North American Indians

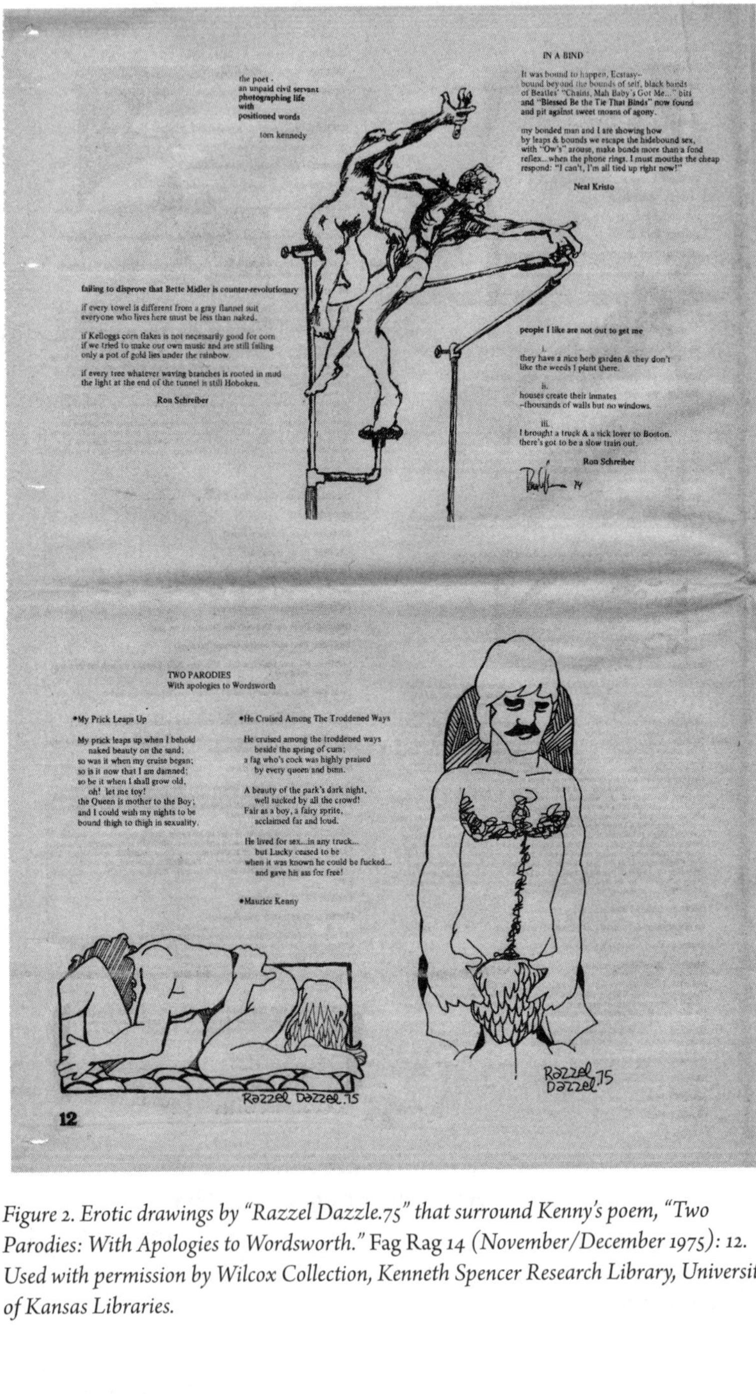

the poet -
an unpaid civil servant
photographing life
with
positioned words

tom kennedy

IN A BIND

It was bound to happen, Ecstasy–
bound beyond the bounds of self, black bands
of Beatles' "Chains, Mah Baby's Got Me..." bits
and **"Blessed Be the Tie That Binds"** now found
and pit against sweet moans of agony.

my bonded man and I are showing how
by leaps & bounds we escape the hidebound sex,
with "Ow's" arouse, make bonds more than a fond
reflex...when the phone rings. I must mouthe the cheap
respond: "I can't, I'm all tied up right now!"

Neal Kristo

failing to disprove that Bette Midler is counter-revolutionary

if every towel is different from a gray flannel suit
everyone who lives here must be less than naked.

if Kelloggs corn flakes is not necessarily good for corn
if we tried to make our own music and are still failing
only a pot of gold lies under the rainbow.

if every tree whatever waving branches is rooted in mud
the light at the end of the tunnel is still Hoboken.

Ron Schreiber

people I like are not out to get me

i.
they have a nice herb garden & they don't
like the weeds I plant there.

ii.
houses create their inmates
–thousands of walls but no windows.

iii.
I brought a truck & a sick lover to Boston.
there's got to be a slow train out.

Ron Schreiber

TWO PARODIES
With apologies to Wordsworth

•My Prick Leaps Up

My prick leaps up when I behold
naked beauty on the sand;
so was it when my cruise began;
so is it now that I am damned;
so be it when I shall grow old,
oh! let me toy!
the Queen is mother to the Boy;
and I could wish my nights to be
bound thigh to thigh in sexuality.

•He Cruised Among The Troddened Ways

He cruised among the troddened ways
beside the spring of cum;
a fag who's cock was highly praised
by every queen and bum.

A beauty of the park's dark night,
well sucked by all the crowd!
Fair as a boy, a fairy sprite,
acclaimed far and loud.

He lived for sex...in any truck...
but Lucky ceased to be
when it was known he could be fucked...
and gave his ass for free!

•Maurice Kenny

12

Figure 2. Erotic drawings by "Razzel Dazzle.75" that surround Kenny's poem, "Two Parodies: With Apologies to Wordsworth." Fag Rag 14 *(November/December 1975): 12. Used with permission by Wilcox Collection, Kenneth Spencer Research Library, University of Kansas Libraries.*

during the 18th and 19th centuries [that] concludes [the] special Third World section."[74] While this chapter focuses on *Fag Rag*, it's important to note the pedagogical work Kenny undertakes in "Tinselled Bucks," as it disrupts the quiet absorption of Kenny's poetry into the white male aesthetic that characterizes the post-Stonewall gay publishing renaissance.

In "Tinselled Bucks," Kenny presents a history of Two-Spirit peoples, who, since he writes nearly fifteen years before the coining of the term, he calls either "homosexual" or "berdache."[75] He begins by noting the gaps in the extant genealogies of Indigenous histories, claiming "new world writings mostly ignore any manifestation of male love in the natives of the new land."[76] Kenny posits instead a gay imaginary in which the West is inhabited not only by multiply gendered Indigenous peoples but also by queer cowboys, miners, and trappers, who "habitually cohabitated with each other, or [with] Indian males."[77] The lengthy piece, which takes up two full three-column newspaper pages and a portion of a third, reviews a broad selection of the extant literature in settler histories, referencing a combination of anthropological accounts from scholars like George Bird Grinnell, Ruth Benedict, Paul Radin, and Margaret Mead; eighteenth- and nineteenth-century journal entries and travelogues from trappers, military men, and missionaries; and "as told to" accounts like *Black Elk Speaks, Wooden Leg: A Warrior Who Fought Custer,* and *Lame Deer Seeker of Visions.* Though the piece at times makes sweeping generalizations about the performance and function of gender and sexuality in Native communities, it also represents a researched and documented record of Indigenous erotics, mapping a range of Two-Spirit references that were almost undoubtedly unfamiliar to the vast majority of *Gay Sunshine*'s and *Fag Rag*'s readers, given that Kenny's essay preceded the crossover popularity of work like Walter William's *The Spirit and the Flesh* (1986), Will Roscoe's *The Zuni Man-Woman* (1991) and *Third and Fourth Genders in Native North America* (1998), and Sue Ellen Jacobs, Wesley Thomas, and Sabine Lang's collection *Two-Spirit People* (1997) by many years.[78]

There was, of course, a fair amount of (often problematic) anthropological research on the figure of the "berdache" by the 1970s. In fact, as Qwo-Li Driskill, Chris Finley, Brian Joseph Gilley, and Scott Lauria Morgensen point out in their introduction to *Queer Indigenous Studies,* "Anthropology foregrounded Native American gender and sexual diversity as an ethnographic cornerstone for the cross-cultural study of gender and sexuality."[79] At the time of the 1976 publication of "Tinselled Bucks," one of the best collections of references in circulation would still have been Sue-Ellen Jacobs's 1968 "Berdache: A Brief Review of Literature." The shift from the early approaches Jacobs details to the late 1980s and 1990s research that followed Kenny's piece is significant. Speaking of this shift, Driskill, Finley, Gilley, and Morgensen suggest "the advent of the term *Two-Spirit* began a new era in the study of past and present Native American gender and sexual diversity. As a critique of anthropological writing based in colonial and western notions of gender and sexuality, the category Two-Spirit creates a distinct link between histories of diversity and Indigenous GLBTQ2 people today."[80] The editors of *Queer Indigenous Studies* map an anthropological narrative that begins with early pieces "that studied the practices of gender 'deviants'" and then moves to 1980s studies that were "concerned with discovering the reasons why American Indians had 'tolerated' same-sex sexuality and gender variance while Euro-Americans remained hostile, misogynist, and heterosexist."[81] They mark Roscoe's *The Zuni Man-Woman,* in particular, as "a new direction[,] . . . the first scholarly account to question correlations between contemporary GLBTQ identities and historic gender diversity and to foreground Indigenous cultural perspectives."[82] "Tinselled Bucks" plays a potentially important role in this narrative, given both its original 1976 publication in *Gay Sunshine* and its subsequent republication in the GAI's 1988 collection, *Living the Spirit.* In light of the historical narrative Driskill, Finley, Gilley, and Morgensen sketch, Kenny's review of these anthropological references can be read as part of the critical intervention Indigenous people made in and through the academic discourses that had functioned for so long as disciplinary mechanisms. Thus Kenny's writing in the journals and newspapers that constituted the gay publishing renaissance not only expanded multiple canons from the era but also functioned as a critical imperative to his contemporary readers, demanding his 1970s audience attend to an embodied history of Indigenous sexuality that predates Stonewall by hundreds of years.[83] Moreover, Kenny's visibility in popular gay print culture of the 1970s provides a creative and a scholarly cornerstone for contemporary Indigenous and queer of color theories. As such, this piece functions together with the work in the early women/queer of color anthologies cited in chapter 1 as part of the activist claim for a differently defined queer subject—a subject who, in this case, fractures both the heteronormative imperative of Native nationalist movements like the American Indian Movement (AIM) and the white homonormativity of dominant queer culture.

Settler Frames and Indigenous Static

In 1976, the fraught landmark of the U.S. bicentennial and one year after the formation of the Gay American Indians, Kenny published a number of poems in *Fag Rag* that paralleled the appearance of "Tinselled Bucks" in *Gay Sunshine.* The first, in the February/March issue 15, titled "No Name," would be printed in a slightly revised version in *Only as Far as Brooklyn.* The next five all appeared in the same fall/winter issue, *Fag Rag 18*: "'Kill Fag's': Graffiti on the 7th Ave. Subway, N.Y.C., June-1976," "Yemen Boy," "Three Parodies: With Apologies to A. E. Houseman," "Papago," and "Recuerdo." Like "No Name," "Yemen Boy" and "Papago"—retitled "Papago II"—would later be published in Kenny's *Only as Far as Brooklyn.*

While most issues of *Fag Rag* scattered five to eight poems throughout, issue 18 included thirty-three, with groups of poems clustered under subtitles. "'Kill Fag's': Graffiti on the 7th Ave. Subway, N.Y.C., June-1976" is situated within a section labeled "Tough" directly above a piece by Jerry Chadwick titled "Poem after Le Roi's TOILET, after My Best Friend Got Beaten Up, after Richard Heakin Got Killed *to All the Fags Who Did Nothing.*" As the titles suggest, the poems in this section consider violence, whether in words or action, against gay men. The Chadwick piece meets hate crimes and the failure to stop such violence with a powerful anger, as seen in the final two lines: "may your grief screech brakeless as this hate / I try to chant but scream."[84] "'Kill Fag's'" focuses on the weight of a misplaced apostrophe in angry graffiti scrawled at a New York subway stop, taking a humorous approach to such violent sentiments. The speaker notes in the first stanza, "Strange trips ride the minds / of strap hangers these nights. / It used to be: 'fuck faggots' . . ."[85] His speaker continues, humorously, "[N]ow it's: 'kill fag's.' / It is not the criminal law / or the sexual abuse // that bothers me, offends my sense / of death or usage. It's the apostrophe / which severs the 'g' from the 's' // making the kill a personal possessive / vendetta" (8). Kenny uses the shift in meaning afforded by the punctuation error to consider the power of internalized homophobia, ultimately asking if the author of the graffiti intended "to thrust the knife or point the gun // at his own existence . . . threatened / by the fear, dread of revelation / or the joy of male embrace!" (8). The poem's recognition of the violence that stems from social stigma points to both inward and outward manifestations of surveillance. The graffiti writer is envisioned as a victim of panopticonic forces, which, in the narrative of Kenny's piece, incites him to discourse.[86]

In such a construction, the imagined young man becomes a sympathetic symbol of the dangers of repression instead of a perpetrator of a hate crime. Through this reversal, Kenny mediates the impact of the scrawled homophobic epithet when his poem's speaker reacts with empathy rather than anger by recognizing the imbricated nature of power and fear, anger and desire.

The next page of the fall/winter 1976 *Fag Rag* includes "Yemen Boy" within nine poems grouped above the heading "Boy Poems." The pieces contains references that range from gay youth coming of age to tongue-in-cheek critiques of gay male obsessions with youth to images of young men hustling—all pieces surround a large black and white photograph by Michael Thompson of an attractive young man smoking a cigarette. Kenny's poem, which falls directly below the photograph, is bolded and printed as a vertical line of text:

Yemen Boy
sitting
on a
stool
of the
corner
candy-
store
exuding
honey
flies
buzzing
on his
throat.[87]

The double entendre of the boy sitting in a candy store while flies buzz is filled with sexual innuendo given its placement amid explicit poems that reference "cocksuckers," "fucking," and "erotic games." And while the piece could be seen to traffic in ethnic exoticism, it also holds the distinction of being the only poem on the page to even obliquely reference ethnicity or nationality. Yemen, a region of the Middle East historically renowned for its production of high-quality honey, a staple of the Middle East diet for centuries, thus serves here as the indicator of a recognized ethnic difference. The combination of the title and the scent of honey the boy "exud[es]" marks him as a diasporic subject. Stephanie Oliver notes that through references to smell, "diasporic subjects are often constructed as carrying the traces of past homelands on their bodies."[88] This diasporic trace is further emphasized by the fact that the rest of the poems in the section focus either on a fetishized understanding of youth as the sole space of desirability or on some aspect of gay cruising, such as Kenny's own darkly comic Houseman parodies, which appear slightly above "Yemen Boy" on the right side of the two-page poetry spread. Finally, besides including "Yemen Boy," the only "Boy Poem" that engages national diversity, *Fag Rag* issue 18, like most issues of the newspaper, underscores Herring's observations about "gay male metro print norms" in its photographic images and drawings. The cover is a Kent Clark photo of two naked men pressed together from thigh to abdomen while the photos and drawings throughout depict what appear to be young white men, reinforcing my previous observations about the limited nature of the newspaper's rhetoric of multicultural inclusion.

A number of odd editorial decisions further validate this reading of *Fag Rag* issue 18's narrative frame. One is the seemingly random reproduction of a buffalo hunt scene on the inside cover of the first page. The unattributed picture, inset sideways on the bottom right of the page of the "Letters" section that begins the issue, shows three men in front of a herd of running buffalo. The man at far left, in Plains dress with a full headdress, sits astride a dark horse rearing over the form of a fallen buffalo. To the right of the Plains hunter is a white man in fringed buckskin chaps and jacket, and in front of that figure is a third in a black suit coat and bowler hat.[89] All three have rifles and are depicted in a pose of wild abandon as they shoot buffalo from a stampeding herd. The faint background reveals two more figures, one in recognizably Plains garb and one in suspenders and shirt. Nothing in the letters section or the information on the facing page addresses the picture, so the original intention behind the insertion of the picture as a companion to the letters is unclear; however, the irony of situating this picture on the first page of an issue with so much of Kenny's work is unavoidable.

The inclusion on later pages of the newspaper of "Indigenous" filler art—such as circles surrounding recognizably Southwestern geometric designs, a stylized bird, and the front and back of a human figure with body paint reminiscent of Zuni ceremonials—functions similarly. Like

Figure 3. Kent Clark photo of two men standing, naked bodies pressed together, within a bed of ferns. Fag Rag 18 *(fall/winter 1976): cover page. Used with permission by Wilcox Collection, Kenneth Spencer Research Library, University of Kansas Libraries.*

© Copyright 1976, Fag Rag, Inc.

FILTH FOLLIES

LETTERS

Dear Fag Rag:

Wow!! Double wow and damn!! Smile . . .

I just had one of the greatest experiences and most complete highs of my-life (at least that part of it behind bars such as my last four years have been), a causal gay acquaintance who with the sharing of your fine paper — paper that is such a blah prosaic term for the collection of fantastic articles thoughts moods poems and artwork I have just experienced . . . .

Really fantastic I know I'll read and read again I see that you allow those of us inside to on the bum for a copy or subscription hope you'll consider putting me on the list and when I get out I promise to subscribe . . .

The issue I have just seen is the June/July 1976 — again don't let this go to any of your heads but you all definitely have your shit together!!

In gay pride and unity . . . .

Truly yours,

"Cuddles" AKA/L. Hickman

Sylvia Sidney — I love you agree with you are if we met alot of you and you alot of me farout style, sense of timing and choice of words — uncomparable — better stop this or you'll think how gauche a love letter from a sister in sin and sarcasm . . . You are truly terrific!!!!!

Dear Fag Rag:

You latest issue (16/17) is one of your best, at least since #7&8. I must complain, however, about the latest installment of Arthur Evans' series "Of Witchcraft: The Gay Counterculture." The author's arrogance and smugness has finally brought out reservations I have felt about his writing for a long, long time.

Much has already been written here about the fallacy of the "Golden Age" of matriarchy that allegedly existed before the begin-ning of recorded history. The point needs to be repeated. I'm all prepared to admit that "civilization" is a grievous mistake and that we are all its alienated victims, but I'm not sure such regret and nostalgia can do us much good at this late date.

This latest installment contains much evidence of intellectual sloppiness with Evans' sweeping, superficial overview of America's history of conquest and genocide. His romanticized version of pre-history leaves us with the implication that matriarchy was universal, and gays everywhere venerated. He seems oblivious that homophobia and the subjugation of women may also have prehistorical roots.

The author seems to dwell on his idealized past as if it could save us, if only we could "Go Back." He has moved from the city and onto the land—more power to him— but he is in a very privileged position, indeed. Besides, I like living in the city, however alienating that choice may be. My native state of Vermont is too remote for my tastes and needs. And New Hampshire, where I spent the most miserable years of my childhood, is so infused with a police state mentality that Boston—with all of its crime, racial strife, pollution and high taxes—is much preferable.

Evans presents us with a real enough dilemma, but one for which he offers no alternatives—except, perhaps, individual "solutions" which are no solutions at all. It is nothing new to suggest that contemporary "civilization" is doomed, but he could have done better in his article had he predicted the ultimate nuclear holocaust as the Final Solution to our agony and alienation. In the end, what he leaves us with is as self-deluded and dangerous as is the common belief that mere legal reform is the essence of gay liberation.

Love & struggle,

John Kyper

Greetings from the North, en route to S.F.!

Luv,

JK

MIRROR, MIRROR ON THE WALL in FAG RAG #16/17 WAS WRITTEN BY THOMAS DOTTON. The printer dropped the name by accident.

Dear Fag Rag:

I sympathize almost entirely with the second 5-year plan but find it hard to do much for it here. Minnesota has few radicals and fewer radical faggots. And the majority of faggots here that are politically involved get siphoned off into the DFL, home of Hubert Humphrey. Other good minds get sucked into religion of some kind. Sickening. I know only three other radical faggots, one of them the friend from Minnesota whose letter on fantasies appears in 16/17, and the other two are anarchists involved with the coop food movement here, which is the largest radical activity around. I'm not involved in anything right now, although I've dabbled in area gay politicking (my kind, I've found, isn't wanted) and was heavily into the coops for a year, during which we had to weather a full-scale attack from an avowedly Stalinist faction known as the Coop Organization. Since these people exhibited all the worst tendencies of authoritarian Marxism, I've often wondered how one of their core, a severely ambivalent faggot when I knew him, can live with the contradictions. From one closet into another, I guess.

These days I'm fairly despondent about sex and love for myself. I find I've stepped from the closet into a cage. Now I can see the rest of the world, but there are bars (yes, I mean the pun) delimiting my movement in it. My alternatives?—gay churches and coffeehouses sponsored by churches, both of which I regard as worse than the bars.

It's no wonder, then, that my circle of friends is largely straight radicals. I'll give them credit for being by and large conscious of their sexism and open to gay revolution as a viable concept if not something they can fight for. The majority of them are women, of course, a tiny part of them lesbian (lesbians are far more politically conscious than the faggots here) or genuinely bisexual. It all means practically no sex for me. It needn't, I know, but if I have to endure another night being turned off by every word that comes out of his mouth while struggling to maintain the initial fascination with his body—well, I just won't do it. (Oh, hell, I probably will.) Actually, I like most women better than most men, gay or straight. And actually, I have a handful of very dear gay friends whose apoliticism doesn't bother me so much that I'd think of cutting them off; right now, they're my lifeline.

What am I trying to say? Perhaps that I'm fantasizing better times in Boston or San Francisco or Toronto. Mostly that circumstances here haven't even allowed me anything to retreat from into Respectability, Normalization and Good Taste. That makes me pretty sad.

For nonviolent gay revolution,

Ray Olsen

Dear Fag Rag:

Your article on "*Competing Religions*" was great and so honest. I am a former Catholic clergyman who was caught up in the evilness of the gay church. The Church almost destroyed me in body, mind and soul. The vulgar prejudice, hatefulness, the evil gossip, spitefulness, dishonesty and the hypocrites who are contaminating everyone and everything inside and outside the churches are a real fact of life here in New York City. So you think you hvae it bad in Boston? *No way baby.* The garbage pail of theatrical religion is right here. The sinners are not the people who attend these false churches, but the drag queen clergymen who are leading them down the paths of destruction. Thanks for being honest enough to tell it like it is in your paper. You've hit the nail on the head. Believe me, I know, I've been there.

Rev. James Stuart, Jr.

Dear Fag Rag:

In his article on overpopulation, Mitzel makes a lot of good points, but the overall attitude bothers me. First, the use of the term "breeding," usually reserved for animals. Is Mitzel comparing straights to animals as a form of put-down? He should re-read Charley Shively's excellent piece on animals and sexuality (Fag Rag No. ?). The tone of the article, and especially the subtitle "Sterilize the Straights" imply an overbearing rejection of straight people, the parenting experience, and children themselves. What about those of us in the gay community who already are parents or are thinking of becoming parents? I agree that childbirth and the institution of the family have been shrouded in myth and romance; much of it very yukky, but I suspect there may be a reasonable and unselfish joy in childbirth and child-rearing that Mitzel does not wish to recognize. The issue isn't childbirth itself; it's the social use of childbirth to put down homosexuals and single people that should be challenged.

Yours,

Allen Young

2

Figure 4. Unattributed picture of a buffalo hunt, inset sideways on the bottom right of the page of the "Letters" section, showing three men in front of a herd of running buffalo. Fag Rag 18 *(fall/winter 1976): inside cover of the first page. Used with permission by Wilcox Collection, Kenneth Spencer Research Library, University of Kansas Libraries.*

the reproduction of the western painting, these graphics are unattributed, uncontextualized, and scattered among poems that invoke Apollo, Aphrodite, Joan of Arc, a Russian peasant woman, and the wonders of New York City living. Given the lack of any further information, it would seem that these stylized tribal graphics and the western picture in *Fag Rag* issue 18 are simply accoutrements, decorative accompaniments for the queer-themed, deracinated texts among which they are scattered. The Native-themed art is likely intended to emphasize the liberal multiculturalism of the newspaper, signaling an interest in and openness to nondominant cultures. In this reading, they function as part of an uninterrogated multiculturalist imperative that replicates the settler logic it seeks to challenge.

There are a number of issues at stake in a comparative frame of this sort. As Siobhan B. Somerville notes in *Queering the Color Line: Race and the Invention of Homosexuality in American Culture,* "all too often, it is assumed that being a person of color is 'like' being gay and that sexual orientation is 'like' racial identity," an "analogy [that] obscures those who inhabit both identifications . . . [and] implicitly posit[s] whiteness and heterosexuality as the norm."[90] While Somerville focuses here on a black/white racial dyad, Morgensen specifically analyzes the intersections of Indigeneity and settler sexuality in the United States. He argues, "Modern sexuality produces non-Natives in relation to Native people in the multiracial space of a white settler society."[91] In such a narrative, "when white settlers in the United States proclaim civilization's advancement," as, for example, in the case of the LGBTIQ rights movement that undergirds *Fag Rag*'s publication, "they also confirm their (il)legitimacy by resituating the Native peoples they (seem to) supplant as part of their own histories and inner lives."[92] These "Indigenous" graphics, which can be seen in other issues of *Fag Rag* as well, reinforce Morgensen's claims, as do articles over the course of the newspaper's production that cite the berdache as a precedent for nondominant forms of sex/gender identifications. So, for example, in "Witchcraft: The Gay Counterculture," which was initially published as a lengthy, nine-part article series in *Fag Rag* (1975–1976) and then as a book in 1978, Arthur Evans repeatedly invokes the figure of the berdache to ground his narrative of gay history. Much like in the newspaper's deployment of "tribal" art, in Evans's work Indigenous history is writ large as "gay" history, and white settlers naturalize their rights at citizen subjects by first comparing themselves with and then appropriating the histories of those they dispossessed. As a result, "white settler gay men" claim "the ancestors

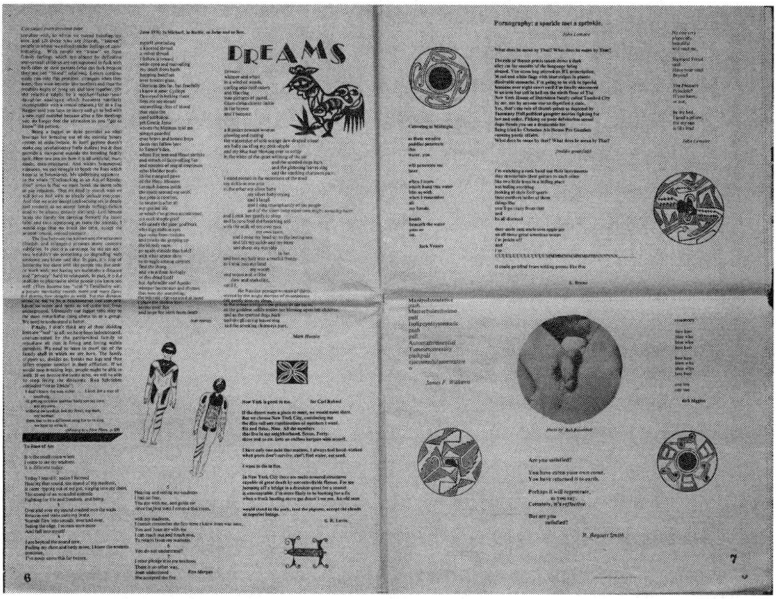

Figure 5. Unattributed line drawings reminiscent of southwestern Indigenous art scattered among poems that invoke Apollo, Aphrodite, Joan of Arc, a Russian peasant woman, and the wonders of New York City. Fag Rag *18 (fall/winter 1976): 6–7. Used with permission by Wilcox Collection, Kenneth Spencer Research Library, University of Kansas Libraries.*

of racial and national others as their own subjectivities to justify or inspire revolutionary anticolonialism and sexual liberation."[93] This discourse surrounds Kenny's work in *Fag Rag,* creating what James H. Cox terms a "white noise" that "enact[s], enhances[s], and justify[es]" colonialism.[94]

The one poem Kenny publishes in *Fag Rag* issue 18 that mutes this white noise is "Papago," which appears ten pages after the "Boy Poems."[95] I argue the poem functions as a kind of static in the issue when considered in relation to the settler frame previously discussed. Rather than being surrounded by such tribal iconography, this poem is superimposed over a full-page line drawing by Philip Gornstein of two men having sex. A naked, dark-haired, bearded man lies on his back with bent knees spread, while another, short-haired man holds himself up on muscular arms above him in the act of penetration. "Papago" is situated at the top right of the page over the shoulder of the man looking down. Kenny's piece is a tender, five-stanza poem about emotional recovery and healing. Every stanza begins with a three-word sentence that functions as chant-like refrain. In each case, the same two words—"With these"—are followed by a third word that changes for the first three stanzas and remains the same for the last two. In the first three stanzas, the poem invokes the body: "hands," "mouth," and "flesh" connect and, in the latter two cases, serve as the catalyst for productive change.[96] The speaker's mouth, for example, "open[s]" the lover's "lips / to rain" (19). In the last two stanzas, power moves from body to language and, in a claim reminiscent of Leslie Marmon Silko's *Ceremony,* which would be published a year later, the poem itself becomes a vehicle of healing: "With these words / I bind the wound / and close the scar/ across the Arizona deserts / of your tribal home . . . // With these words / I seal an hour / and sew the rent" (19). Though there is eroticism in the piece, the explicit play of Kenny's parody poems is absent. Instead, "Papago" employs a somber tone and, also in contrast to Kenny's parodies, includes allusions to "ancient earth," "painted / and sacred mountains," and "Arizona deserts" that would mark the piece as functioning in a recognizably Indigenous aesthetic (19). Importantly, the poem contrasts rather than augments *Fag Rag*'s indiscriminate and uncontextualized use of Indigeneity. Though the citation is brief, Kenny's title together with his reference to Arizona deserts presents a tribally specific referent: the object of the speaker's affection is from a particular nation, the Papago, or more appropriately, the Tohono O'odham, a nation that inhabits a specific tribal geography in southwestern and central Arizona and Northern Mexico.[97] While my argument does not hinge on intention, such a case can be made when one considers that the companion "Papago" poem, published in the 1976 summer/fall issue of *Gay Sunshine,* is accompanied by this parenthetical explanation: "Arizona is the homeland of the Papago Indian Nation."[98] A return to Morgensen emphasizes the disruption "Papago" represents to "settler colonial logic [that] . . . disappears indigeneity so it can be recalled by modern *non*-Natives as a relationship to Native culture and land that might reconcile them to inheriting conquest."[99] Through the inclusion of the opening picture—with its cowboys and Indians hunting buffalo—and the decontextualized and appropriative deployment of "tribal" art, the editors of *Fag Rag* employ Indigeneity as object, as referent. Whether an empty signifier for progressive politics or simply a figure of artistic embellishment, the dominant narrative is one in which non-Natives use vaguely Indigenous symbols for, at times, an entirely deracinated or, at best, a generically (read vapidly) multicultural, literary aesthetic. With its reference to a specific tribal nation and the existence of contemporary American Indian people, "Papago" quietly breaks through this white noise to challenge the politics of the gay literary renaissance.[100]

Reading Backward: Kenny and/in the 1970s Canon

As Kenny heads toward the late 1970s, his major publications include *North: Poems of Home,* a chapbook published in 1977 by Blue Cloud Quarterly, and *I Am the Sun,* which appeared first in *Akwesasne Notes* in 1973 before it was reprinted as a chapbook with Dodeca Press in 1976 and again with White Pine in 1979. James Ruppert marks this piece as a landmark in Kenny's canon, explaining that it was in "1976, with the publication of *I Am the Sun,* that his work found a wide audience. The poem, based on a Sioux ghost dance song, reveals a shifting emphasis in his work—toward the oral tradition, toward performed poetry, toward persona, and toward cultural stances with political implication."[101] In 1979, Kenny published two more texts: a second collection from White Pine, *Dancing Back Strong the Nation,* and *Only as Far as Brooklyn* from Good Gay Poets, a press that, like *Fag Rag,* was started by the Boston Gay Liberation Front. Among these many publications, *Only as Far as Brooklyn,* as noted in the chapter introduction, is the only collection to explicitly address queer themes. Despite my early claims about the intersectional concerns of Kenny's work in *Fag Rag,* in this case, we can observe a clear division of content between and among the topics represented in these differing venues. This fissure speaks to the heteronormative expectations of 1970s Native literary journals, further emphasizing the necessity of including Kenny's lesser-known work from the journals of the gay cultural renaissance in analyses of his oeuvre and, importantly, in our discussions of the literary history we construct as we look back on the American Indian renaissance/Red Power era. Ultimately, this chapter's work on Kenny demonstrates that our 1970s imaginary is in radical need of expansion.

Three of the four presses in which Kenny published during this period—Blue Cloud Quarterly, *Akwesasne Notes,* and White Pine—are known for their promotion of Native writers. Blue Cloud was a publication out of the Blue Cloud Abbey in Marvin, South Dakota, that published significant Native writers for nearly two decades, while the Mohawk nation's *Akwesasne Notes,* which began in 1968, was the first national Indigenous newspaper. White Pine, an independent press that, like *Akwesasne Notes,* is a still extant, also has a history of publishing work by noted Native writers. The frequent inclusion of Kenny's writing in these venues speaks to his importance in expanding our conceptualizations of American Indian literature from this period. In fact, Abenaki author Joe Bruchac comments in a 1985 review essay, "New Leaves on the Trees of Our Nations: Five Native American Chapbooks," on "the prodigious energy of one Native American small press poet and publisher, Maurice Kenny. If any person has been a central figure in the contemporary growth of modern American Indian poetry, it is Kenny. His large output of poetry has been matched, amazingly, by an equal output of editorial energy."[102] This "prodigious" output is markedly bifurcated, however. Take, for example, Kenny's work in the 1976 special issue of *The Indian Historian,* "Dreams and Drumbeats." Kenny's two pieces in this collection—"Oka Tanna" and "Standing Strong"—both differ radically from his work in *Fag Rag.*[103] "Oka Tanna," which comprises four full pages of the forty-page issue, begins with a quotation from *Black Elk Speaks* and goes on to tell the story of the 1890 Wounded Knee massacre. Wounded Knee has long been deployed by Indigenous writers as a marker of resistance and, as such, was referenced frequently in the creative work of 1970s Indigenous writers, especially that from the period following Wounded Knee II, the seventy-one-day standoff between members of AIM and the FBI that occurred in 1973. Kenny's piece in "Dreams and Drumbeats" recounts the history immediately preceding the 1890 Wounded Knee conflict and, while the poem catalogues the loss of Lakota lives at the hands of U.S. troops, it ends with an image of the subsequent spring when "the first shoots of grass" appeared and survivors "came out to walk the graveyard."[104] Rather than reiterating the (in)famous "the nation's hoop [was] broken" litany of loss, which are the most famous words Nicholas Black Elk (n)ever spoke,[105] Kenny concludes his poem with images of life, rebirth, and the words "My people shall live!"[106] The poem, which deploys Wounded Knee as a metaphor for Indigenous coalition and survivance, echoes work Kenny published in other Indigenous journals of the period.[107]

Despite the prominence of Kenny and other queer Native writers like Allen and Brant, as well as the inception of the GAI, the narrative of the Native 1970s continues to rely on a story that parallels a heteronormative political history of the Red Power movement with a limited literary history of the American Indian renaissance. In such narratives, Kenny, if referenced at all, is known primarily for writing that, to return to Ruppert, emphasizes "the oral tradition" and "cultural stances with political implication."[108] Take, for example, the most recent book-length literary criticism to return to Indigenous politics and literature of the 1970s: Teuton's *Red Land, Red Power.* Teuton's introductory gloss of "the decade-long flurry of events" that "define the time of Red Power" includes "the 1972 march on Washington for the Trail of Broken Treaties; the 1973 takeover of Wounded Knee; the 1975 intervention of the American Indian Movement on the Pine Ridge reservation; [and] the 1978 Longest Walk on Washington."[109] Teuton parallels these highlights of Red Power political history with a return to the now-classic novels of the period—Momaday's *House Made of Dawn,* Silko's *Ceremony,* and Welch's *Winter in the Blood.* This canon is, first, based solely on novels and, even given that criteria, limits the 1970s to a certain type of Native novel; thus Dallas Chief Eagle's historical novel, *Winter Count* (1967), which chronicles the period leading up to the 1890 Wounded Knee massacre, and Gerald Vizenor's surreal debut novel, *Darkness in Saint Louis Bearheart* (1978), are not included. Teuton's lists of 1970s American Indian politics and literature represent a common understanding of the period in which neither the central political events nor the literary canon include queer events or texts. His final chapter, which looks across a number of more recent novels, locates queerness as part of a productive shift in contemporary Native texts, which have "since around the 1980s . . . increasingly represented . . . an honest engagement with the diversity of class, gender, and sexuality."[110] Teuton concludes his examination of such texts with a reading of Womack's *Drowning in Fire,* noting that "few works in Native literature take the Native gay male experience seriously enough to devote literary space for its exploration in sexual, emotional, and romantic life, in history, religion, and social organizations, and in artistic pursuits."[111] While Teuton's inclusion of Womack's important novel is laudable, *Red Land, Red Power* still presents a classic representation of American Indian history in which 1970s activism and literature is firmly bound by heteronormative limits. Thus in Teuton's narrative, Womack's work represents not an extension of the queer writing and activism occurring in the very period he examines throughout most of his text but instead a more recent point in a teleological narrative of progress. If, as Smith argues, "indigeneity frequently disappears within [queer of color] projects," we can likewise claim that queerness often disappears in Indigenous critiques, even for those like Teuton, who hail its circulation in twenty-first-century literature.[112] Strikingly, Teuton's conclusion that recent texts offer "the promise of 'other worlds'" resonates with Muñoz's "invitation to desire differently, to desire more, to desire better."[113] Early in this chapter, I expanded Muñoz's invitation by suggesting that, despite its absence from his gay imaginary, Indigeneity is at the heart of every queer utopia; I likewise suggest here that, despite its absence from the story of the Native American literary renaissance, queerness is at the heart of the Indigenous 1970s.

Coda: Utopias, Dystopias, and the Queer Resonance of the Native 1970s

If we recognize the deeply imbricated nature of Indigeneity in the gay cultural renaissance and of queerness in the Native American renaissance, we see the importance of reaching outside identitarian boundaries. These boundaries mark post-Stonewall texts like *Fag Rag, Gay Sunshine,* and *ManRoot* as non-Native and American Indian renaissance–era texts like *Akwesasne Notes* and *Many Smokes* as solely heteronormative. My recovery of Kenny's work from *Fag Rag* demonstrates how these bifurcated archives can be brought together—the queer canon Indigenized and the Native canon queered—through the inclusion of the entire range of Kenny's 1970s poetry. Kenny's intervention into the dominant narrative of *Fag Rag* from this period concludes with a collection of pieces from 1978: he published four poems in the 21/22 February/March issue ("Heading East," "Growing Pains: Five Poems," "Long Distance Telephone Call," and "Tulsa by Greyhound") and three in the 23/24 issue ("Love in Brooklyn Heights," "Poem . . . Too Late," and "Two Humors: One—With Apology to Byron; Two—Masturbatory Haiku").[114] These 1978 pieces continue to highlight the ways in which Kenny's writings in the gay press enlarge our understanding of American Indian literary history. Such work, to return to Smith's exploration of the intersections between queer and Indigenous studies, does more than "simply articulate a politics of indigenous inclusion"; it "challenge[s] the normalizing logics of academia" itself.[115] And nowhere are these normalizing logics more evident than in the exchange that serves as the coda for this chapter: a letter and published editorial response between the editors of *Akwesasne Notes* and the editors of *RFD,* a U.S.-based journal aimed at rural gay men.

In a letter dated August 16, 1977, the editors of *Akwesasne Notes* sent *RFD* what was apparently a second letter to request that *RFD* remove *Akwesasne Notes* from their mailing list. *RFD* subsequently published the *Akwesasne*

Notes removal request in full alongside their response to that letter in a one-page piece titled, in all large, bolded, block letters, "AKWESASNE WE ARE NOT THE ENEMY." Additionally, according to the *RFD* editors, *RFD* also sent copies of the letter and their editorial response to "33 people/organizations/media friends" in a printed list that includes both Native American and queer publications, organizations, and individuals.[116] Notably, Maurice Kenny is among those named as a recipient of *RFD*'s published response. The *Akwesasne Notes* letter, which is dated, signed, and on the journal letterhead, is short and to the point, offering a single paragraph explanation for their removal request: "The reason we do not want to receive your publication is because they encourage a kind of human behavior which our elders consider not normal and a detriment to our way of life. There are so many things that have come from European western society whether it be alcohol, Christianity and its church, educational system and the list goes on, that have had a destructive effect on Indian Culture. And now that list includes the type of behavior your magazine advocates."[117] The *Akwesasne Notes* editors invoke tradition as a weapon, wielding the reference to "elders" as a disciplinary mechanism, a club disguised as a shield.[118] Thus if Kenny's work, when considered as a whole, reconstitutes the Native archive in all its queerness, the exchange between *Akwesasne Notes* and *RFD* reminds us of the reasons such erotic continuity was, in some contexts, submerged, operating as a disavowed but still extant reality in Native communities. This damaging rhetoric continues today, as seen perhaps most famously in the 2004 Cherokee nation and 2005 Navajo nation decisions to enact statutes that parallel the U.S. Defense of Marriage Act by limiting marriage to a union between a man and a woman.[119] The claims that background both the *Akwesasne Notes* letter and, nearly thirty years later, the tribal statutes banning same-sex marriage frame Indigeneity as always already heteronormative and cast queer desire as a settler colonial form of deviance. Thus while gender variance may have a widespread and well-documented history in Native nations, 1970s realities, as the *Akwesasne Notes* letter makes clear, were at times much less inclusive. Kenny comments on this difficult truth in a 1980 interview with the *Gay Community News* when asked by his interviewers, Charles Shivley and Clover Chango, if he "want[ed] to say something about gay people on reservations": "'You will go to reservations and you will rarely see an overtly gay person there. If there is a limpwristed person, he/she will leave and go off to a center just the way white gays leave Iowa and go off to Chicago. . . . Reservations are usually small towns. Gays there are the unhappiest around.'"[120] Kenny's blunt assessment of homophobia aligns with that of the *Akwesasne Notes* editor; the two agree on attitudes toward queer Native folks even if they differ in their assessments of gender variance in Indigenous histories. The bleak divisions painted by these claims highlight Kenny's importance to the burgeoning academic conversations of the present day.

The exchange between these two editorial staffs speaks volumes about the need for queer and Native studies and queer Native studies scholars to revisit the discourses circulating in these coeval literary renaissances. These literary movements and historical moments are often romanticized for the proliferation of rights narratives and the new visibility of gay, Native, and Two-Spirit peoples, organizations, and literatures. A return to the 1970s and a subsequent expansion of the 1970s literary archive to include gay *and* Native literary journals enables us to see these moments differently by recognizing what chapter 1 discussed as a genealogy based on relationship. That relationality includes acknowledging the imbricated nature of two separately conceived publishing histories while still remaining cognizant of their radical differences. I've suggested throughout this chapter that such revisioning functions as "an invitation to desire differently, to desire more, to desire better."[121] I strongly believe in such productive possibilities but conclude with the *Akwesasne Notes* letter and the *RFD* reply to suggest that the expansion of these archives may also expose the gap between our reading desires and 1970s realities. The frequent reprinting of Kenny's "Winkte" has crafted a safer and more comfortable imaginary of the 1970s inception of queer Native literature than the explicit and often racially unmarked erotics of Kenny's poems in *Fag Rag*. Likewise, the queer urbanity of Kenny's work in *Fag Rag* challenges previous articulations of queer geography as settler space as well as conceptions of the Native American renaissance as a body of literature bounded by a heteronormative narrative of cultural recovery and return. Such expansions are neither comfortable nor easy. In fact, as the letter from *Akwesasne Notes* and the anecdote from the introduction suggest, certain audiences might be downright hostile to these possibilities. What this coda reminds us, then, is that Kenny's work forces us to look in multiple directions, allowing a recovery of a heroic past in which Indigeneity and queerness coalesce in poems like "Papago" and politically forward essays like "Tinselled Bucks" but also bringing us face-to-face with a heterosexist and heteronormative Native 1970s, where queer desire and Indigeneity are depicted as strange bedfellows.

Queer Relationships and Two-Spirit Characters in Louise Erdrich's Novels

Rabbit was say, . . . "What's the future for Indian gay and lesbian readers wanting to read something honest about theyselves? With no help and no stories, maybe they will become haunted like Lynn Riggs. Mebeso if writers don't write about things, they is partly responsible for turning kids into ghosts. If Indian writers write only about straight Indians and not all kinda Indians, what sets them apart from white writers making up Indian romances?"

Big Man was say, "Mebeso it's not traditional to talk about sex."

Stijaati was say, "Good god, man, did you ever listen to the oral tradition?"

—Craig Womack, *Red on Red*

THE FIRST TWO CHAPTERS expanded the canon of Native literature and Two-Spirit studies by undertaking, respectively, a broad and a specific recovery of queer Native literature and history. The queer Indigenous genealogy of chapter 1 argues for narrative of affiliation by reading across the body of queer Indigenous literature in the United States and Canada. Chapter 2 narrows that focus through an archival recovery that functions as a re-membering of the 1970s. Chapter 3 continues the process of recovery, recognition, and reconnection by turning to the work of one of the most renowned authors in American Indian literature, Louise Erdrich. Thus this chapter reads Erdrich's significant body of full length fiction to further the claim that queerness was always already at the heart of Indigenous literature. It argues for a reevaluation of our extant literary genealogies by analyzing how, over the course of more than twenty years of queer characters and images, Louise Erdrich maps relationship.

Erdrich was the first among the best-known post-1960s authors—N. Scott Momaday, Simon Ortiz, Leslie Marmon Silko, and James Welch—to engage issues of queer sexuality, and her depictions are by far the most nuanced, productive, and frequent. While Silko and Welch offer problematic depictions of queers as murderers and monsters in novels that disavow productive intersections for queerness and Indigeneity—*Almanac of the Dead* (1991) and *The Heartsong of Charging Elk* (2000)—Erdrich represents lesbian, gay, bisexual, transgender, transsexual, intersex, queer, and Two-Spirit (LGBTIQ2) identities as part of the everyday fabric of Native communities and, by the same token, represents the historical existence of gender variance as commonly accepted. In the process, Erdrich recognizes and privileges a narrative of relationality. Her texts index the fluidity of gender, the constructed nature of heterosexuality, and the importance of specifically Indigenous understandings of the range and variety of genders and sexualities. Chapter 3 thus charts Erdrich's multiple, ever-shifting, and, in many cases, still unrecognized articulations of queer affiliation through the lens of erotic, familial, and community relationship.

Breaking New Ground: *The Beet Queen* Queers the Canon

While all of Erdrich's texts explore the parameters of relationship, her earliest foray into explicit representations of queer characters and relationships comes in just her second novel, *The Beet Queen* (1986). Notably, all the text's central characters—Mary and Karl Adare, a brother and sister abandoned by their mother; Celestine James, an orphan who becomes Mary's lifelong best friend; Wallace Pfef, Karl's lover and surrogate father to Celestine's daughter; and Dot (Wallacette) James, the child of Karl and Celestine—queer conventional gender norms in some way. Julie Barak argues that Mary, Celestine, and Dot can be read as "manly-hearted women," a term anthropologists historically coined for American Indian women who inhabited third-gender roles by taking on the behaviors and occupations of men.[1] J. James Iovannone contends that such characters should more accurately be read through a "transgendered framework," as such a term "represent[s] gender identities that exist beyond the binary categories of male and female, masculine and feminine, heterosexual and homosexual."[2] Tara Prince-Hughes, on the other hand, challenges work that relies heavily on Western understandings of gender and sexuality, maintaining, "Despite recent theoretical fascination with gender instability, Erdrich demonstrates that for her characters, alternative genders are expressed by relatively stable identities marked by inclinations toward mediation, healing, community responsibility, and the work, dress, and behavior of the other sex."[3] While they differ over terminology and interpretation, these critics and others who have written on *The Beet Queen* agree that Erdrich regularly pushes the boundaries of gender and sexuality in her fiction, exceeding limited, normative definitions of each. Such recognition is reinforced when one realizes that, in terms of Native-authored novels, Erdrich's inclusion of queer characters as central figures in her fiction is preceded only by Allen's *The Woman Who Owned the Shadows*. Thus, as we'll see in this chapter, the heteronormative imaginary Kenny queers in the 1970s is also challenged in the mid-1980s and beyond by one of the most prominent Native writers in the field—though, as with Allen's work, that challenge will be neither identified nor analyzed by critics until the late 1990s.

Karl Adare and Wallace Pfef, who share an on-again/off-again relationship, are two characters that function as the center of overt queer representations in *The Beet Queen*. Both men are non-Native as, with the exclusion of Celestine James, her brother Russell Kashpaw, and brief references to their family, Erdrich's novel focuses primarily on the German American community in Argus, North Dakota. In the novel's 1932 opening, Karl is depicted as a character who straddles gender lines. He is "a tall fourteen" with a "sweetly curved" mouth and "fine and girlish" skin.[4] The novel begins as he and his sister arrive in Argus heading for the shelter of their Aunt Fritzie's house after their mother's desertion. The two run in different directions when a neighbor unleashes a dog upon Karl: Mary heads east, toward town and her aunt's butcher shop, while Karl runs back to the boxcar that takes him away from Argus and his family—and the relationships and responsibilities they represent—for many years.

Karl's meeting with Giles Saint Ambrose on the boxcar he hops out of in Argus provides the first window into Erdrich's depiction of queer subjectivity and relationality—or, perhaps more accurately here, queer desire. Giles, who mistakes Karl for a girl, offers the boy food and comfort. Giles's initial impression of Karl's femininity—"You're a girl, aren't you?"—is underlined when his teasing causes Karl to burst into tears, to which Giles responds, "Quiet down. . . . You're going to have to practice. Boys don't do this" (23, 24). This attempt to regulate Karl's gender performance highlights, in a few short sentences, both the malleability of gender and the social demands for the iteration of certain preferred gender performances. As Giles points out, expected gender behaviors—in this case, the old adage that "men don't cry"—rather than being innate or biological expressions of gender, take "practice." Gender, Erdrich teaches her readers, is a set of learned behaviors. The theory of gender performance is interrogated most famously four years *after* the publication of *The Beet Queen* in Judith Butler's 1990 book *Gender Trouble,* where Butler argues that there is no "natural" tie between sex and gender. Butler explains, "There is no gender identity behind the expressions of gender . . . identity is performatively constituted by the very 'expressions' that are said to be its results."[5] In this case, the attempt to regulate Karl's gender performance is a resounding failure as, in the face of Giles's admonition, Karl cries himself to sleep.

Later that same day, Karl initiates sexual contact with Giles, but more telling than their sexual encounter is Karl's romantic daydream, which speaks volumes about the limits of Karl's perception of queer subjectivity. When he wakes from the exhausted sleep that follows his bout of tears, Karl "planned how he and Giles would travel on the boxcar, occasionally jumping off . . . , stealing food, maybe finding an abandoned house to live in. He pictured them together, in danger from dogs or police, outrunning farmers and store clerks. He saw them roasting chickens and sleeping together curled tight in a jolting boxcar, like they were now" (24–25). While Mary heads toward the relative safety and stability of family, Karl dreams differently in the liminal space of the boxcar. Notably, though, Karl's imaginings involve scenes not of relationship but instead of transgression and isolation. The homosocial bonding he envisions takes place outside of accepted societal boundaries, outside of a larger community, and, in fact, requires he and Giles to become outlaws who run from "police," "farmers," and "store clerks," figures who represent institutional authority, dominant agrarian ideals, and U.S. capitalism.[6] Karl's daydream suggests that to be together, he and Giles must exist outside all that is valued in dominant U.S. society. Additionally, it's significant that the enclosed boxcar itself mirrors the architecture of the closet, a spatial metaphor that has been interrogated by, among others, queer theorist Eve Kosofsky Sedgwick in *Epistemology of the Closet* (1990), a book often paired with *Gender Trouble* as a marker for the rise of contemporary queer theory.[7] Sedgwick argues, "The relations of the closet—the relations of the known and the unknown, the explicit and the inexplicit around homo/heterosexual definition—have the potential for being particularly revealing."[8] As a metaphor for such relations, the boxcar, an unrooted space destined for continual motion, is always outside the bounds of whatever city or home it might pass, always outside the realm of community. Thus like his queer imaginary, the physical space in which Karl envisions his idealized relationship with Giles also serves as a symbol of disconnection and fragmentation.

Though their sexual encounter is ultimately short lived, Karl sees his sexual interaction with Giles as a landmark break with childhood: "He'd touched other boys before but just in fun, down the alleys behind the boardinghouse. This was different, and he was not sure he'd dare, but then his body filled with the rushing noise" (25). He reacts by twice telling Giles, "I love you," a statement Giles dismisses with a brusque "Oh, Jesus, it wasn't anything. . . . It happens. Don't get all worked up over it, OK?" (25). For Karl, this rejection of his emotions tangles with memories of his mother's abandonment. Even while he parrots Giles's words to himself—"It happens . . . It happens"—he feels "swallowed" by "the depth of his loss," which causes him to violently reject emotional attachment (26). Upon deciding never to "cry on the lap of anyone again," Karl jumps from the moving train, leaving his short-lived dreams of a romance and intimacy behind (26). Despite the fact that Karl later has multiple physical encounters with both men and women, he's depicted as nearly incapable of a fully developed relationship. Fittingly, he becomes a traveling salesman, who passes through towns and lovers indiscriminately. The queer possibilities for affiliation Karl experiences in the boxcar are abandoned when he lands on stable ground.

Karl's association with Wallace Pfef, a queer relationship that eventually leads to Karl's return to Argus, begins with another life-threatening jump. The two men meet at the Minneapolis Crop and Livestock Convention in 1952, twenty years after Karl abandons the boxcar. At the time of the convention, Karl's history includes "rendevou[s] with thin hard hoboes" but no lasting relationships as he "never let anything go far enough to cause [him] trouble" (55, 104). Karl and Wallace strike up a conversation and have dinner in Karl's hotel room, a place that mirrors the boxcar's enclosed and transient nature. They have sex quickly and, for Wallace, unexpectedly. Karl explains, "I held his shoulders, drew him to me. Then we lay back on the startling spread. By the time the bellhop knocked on the door we were back where we'd started, dressed" (105). Wallace's subsequent admission that he's "never done this before" causes Karl to scoff about the "little woman" he imagines Wallace keeps at home (105). Neither man, however, is romantically attached; in fact, though Karl claims numerous past liaisons with women, he overtly rejects "love and marriage" even as he silently recognizes "the truth" that he'd "always found [a woman's] touch unbearable, a source of nameless panic" (106). Like Karl's headlong jump from Giles and the train, his encounter with Wallace, too, comes to an abrupt end through self-inflicted physical pain when Karl injures himself attempting to complete a somersault on the hotel bed. If in the first case, he fled a perceived rejection by leaping from the moving boxcar, in the second, he attempts to distract himself from the possibilities of a queer connection that extends beyond the physical by jumping, high and wild, on the hotel bed. Karl explains, "When he looked at me with his clear sad eyes, I suddenly had the feeling that had always frightened me, the blackness, the ground I'd stood on giving way, the falling no place. Maybe it was true about him, the awkwardness, no experience, the awful possibility that he wanted to get to know me. . . . [J]ust to do something, just to stop the feeling. . . . [I] leapt onto the bed. I had to stop myself from falling, so I jumped" (106). In both cases, Karl's leap demonstrates his need to subvert an emotional bond through physical action and injury. Thus while *The Beet Queen* expands the parameters of its characters' sexualities, the novel initially seems to represent queer desires and relationships not only as impossible dreams but also as psychological and bodily threats.

As if offering readers the flip side of a coin, Erdrich shows a very different response to queer liaisons through her depiction of Wallace's perspective of his night with Karl. For Wallace, sex with Karl brings him not to "blackness" but instead to light and clarity through his definitive recognition of his own desires and subjectivity. As he thinks back on their encounter, he realizes, "I never knew it, had probably hidden it deep away, but I found the attraction as easy as breathing. . . . [T]here I was, member of the Kiwanis, eating prime rib and accepting choice bits of game hen from the fork of another man. Sheer madness. Yet I felt amazed, as if the clouds had blown away, as if the bare bones were finally visible. I was queer" (161). Karl's dark cloud, his "awful possibility," is for Wallace a revelation. Wallace's certainty about his queer identity is reinforced by an unexpected two-week visit from Karl. For that brief period, Wallace experiences his own version of domestic bliss: "It was enough for him to be there, wearing my clothes and towels, fixing toast for himself, at last making sense of my bed. I never knew what to ask from life, but now I did" (164). Through her depiction of these two characters' mercurial relationship, Erdrich represents a spectrum of possible responses to queer desire—from romantic dreaming to violent denial to the everyday possibility of unexpected love.

Erdrich is known for her plot twists, and one of these occurs when Karl's abrupt departure from Wallace's home where, he later explains, Wallace "drove [him] out of [his] mind with attention"—brings Karl, like a speeding comet, into the irresistible pull of Celestine James's orbit (319). It is through this second relationship or, more specifically, through the depiction of Celestine's female masculinity that *The Beet Queen* radically exceeds heteronormative gender regimes. To read Erdrich's representations of masculinity necessitates a return to Judith Halberstam's landmark 1998 text on the subject, *Female Masculinity,* in which Halberstam contends her work is "part of a cultural onslaught on the privileged reservation of masculinity for men."[9] This claim resonates, albeit somewhat ironically, in Native studies, where theories about cultural challenges to mainstream power structures abound and reservations, be they in the form of misgivings or mapped geographical locales, take center stage. Speaking of dominant understandings of heteromasculinity, Halberstam notes the liminal nature of both the term and identity, pointing out, "Although we seem to have a difficult time defining masculinity, as a society we have little trouble recognizing it, and indeed we spend massive amounts of time and money ratifying and supporting the versions of masculinity that we enjoy and trust; many of these 'heroic masculinities' depend absolutely on the subordination of alternative masculinities."[10] Halberstam subsequently investigates how masculinity can be made legible when it is desutured from the male body. Most relevant to this chapter is her argument that nonwhite female masculinities—what she terms "minority masculinities"—not only "can undo the hierarchized relations between dominant and minority sexualities" but also "have the power to reorganize masculinity itself."[11] Erdrich undertakes just such relational reorganization in *The Beet Queen.*

In Indigenous literature, this reorganization of masculinity necessitates a recognition of what Halberstam's theory, as useful as it is, omits—that female masculinities signify differently in Aboriginal and American Indian cultures, where, to name just a few examples, historical evidence of warrior women in Plains nations and gender complementarity among the Haudenosaunee challenge heteropatriarchal gender binaries. While such historical differences are by no means always directly referenced in Indigenous literatures, our knowledge of these precedents necessarily redefines contemporary performances of female masculinity in Indigenous contexts. With such histories in mind, female masculinity in Native literature can be read as the embodied trace of Two-Spirit histories in the way that, post-1962, a can of Campbell's tomato soup will always carry the trace of pop art. Thus representations of female masculinities in the work of writers like Erdrich, Chrystos, Janice Gould, Carrie House, M. Carmen Lane, or Cheryl Savageau most often evade what Judith Butler in "Melancholy Gender—Refused Identification" discusses as a fear of queer desire. Butler explains that such "gender anxiety" may "in a woman . . . induce a panic that she is losing her femininity; that she is not a woman, that she is no longer a proper woman; that, if she is not quite a man, she is like one and hence monstrous in some way."[12] Rather than presenting female masculinity as such melancholic bodily horror, Erdrich instead presents female masculinity as a type of relational affective power.

As stated previously in this chapter, Erdrich consistently crafts desire as excessive, as multiple and messy. This multiplicity is nowhere more apparent than in her representations of female masculinity, which underline Halberstam's contention that "very often the unholy union of femaleness and masculinity can produce wildly unpredictable results."[13] In *The Beet Queen,* Erdrich's depiction of Celestine James's masculinity revises the text's representations of *both* queerness and heterosexuality, showing the transformative power of gender variance. This transformation is specifically enmeshed in the power of affect. In their introduction to *The Affect Theory Reader,* Gregory J. Seigworth and Melissa Gregg build their definition of the term "affect" on Baruch Spinoza's famous pronouncement that "no one has yet determined what the body can do."[14] To understand the function of affect, they claim, we must recognize that "the capacity of the body is never defined by a body alone but is always aided and abetted by, and dovetails with, the field and context of its force-relations."[15] Affect is thus more than mere emotion; it is, in fact, a *bodily* experience that is necessarily *relational.* Unlike biological drives, which, Sedgwick reminds us, "are more immediately tied to survival,"[16] affect is instead about a lived, bodily experience often articulated through that which is felt rather than spoken; thus Sedgwick explains that "touching and affect," like "touching and feeling," "seem to belong together."[17] Such is the generative, relational power of female masculinity in *The Beet Queen,* which is illustrated most prominently in Celestine and Karl's relationship.

When Karl's abrupt departure from his lover Wallace brings him into Celestine's life and bed, their subsequent liaisons are *based* on a series of queer gender performances. Karl, as we've seen, straddles gender lines. While the narrator's early descriptions offer a cisgendered picture in which Karl's male femininity aligns with his desire for men in a seemingly neat depiction of Western homosexuality, Karl's affective response to Celestine's female masculinity alters this homonormative binary. Such is the function of affect; as Seigworth and Gregg explain, "cast forward by its open-ended in-between-ness, affect is integral to a body's perpetual *becoming* (always becoming otherwise, however subtly, than what it already is), pulled beyond its seeming surface-boundedness by way of its relation to, indeed its composition through, the forces of encounter."[18] In *The Beet Queen,* female masculinity drives or is perhaps driven by this relational, affective process of becoming.

Karl and Celestine's first encounter occurs when Karl stops at the family butcher shop his sister Mary owns and Mary and Celestine now run. After Karl enters the shop in search of his sister, he and Celestine meet and almost immediately succumb to an awkward passion based on a parody of romance novels. Celestine's female masculinity (and Karl and Celestine's own affective responses to the circulation of masculine performance) frames their erotic encounter, which strays far from the Harlequin-inspired "tales of burning love" Celestine reads. She explains, "I lunge from his grip but he comes right with me. I lose my balance. He is fighting me for the upper hand, straining down with all his might, but I am more than equal to his weight-lifting arms and thrashing legs. I could throw him to the side, I know, but I grow curious" (128). Here, Celestine describes foreplay as a contest of strength, where physical agility and brute force meet in some negotiated, erotic center of gravity. Her description of their lovemaking shows how female masculinity subverts classic ideological markers that, in Western culture, "wed masculinity to maleness and [subsequently wed that male-bodied masculinity] to power and domination."[19] While masculinity still carries the weight of power in this scene, as underscored by Celestine's use of terms like "the upper hand," those masculine attributes are tied to Celestine's female body. Speaking of this encounter, Louise Flavin argues that "the comic deflation of the traditional lovers' scene affirms the absence of romanticized love."[20] In such a reading, Karl and Celestine's performance of desire falls short of the heteronormative ideal invoked by the term "romantic love." This "failure" *pivots* on interpreting Celestine's female masculinity as lack. In such a line of thought, the sex between Karl and Celestine is not "romantic" because Celestine exceeds gendered expectations of female bodily power. However, Karl's affective response to Celestine's masculine power requires us to rethink such easy binaries.

Here again, Halberstam offers a way to revise these restricted and restricting equations. In her 2011 book, *The Queer Art of Failure,* failure is equated with "queer struggle," "the refusal of legibility, and an art of unbecoming. . . . The queer art of failure turns on the impossible, the improbable, the unlikely, and the unremarkable. It quietly loses, and in losing it imagines other goals for life, for love, for art, and for being."[21] Halberstam suggests we can find meaning and value in lack, in absence, in difference, in the also-rans. Celestine's female masculinity and her awkward love scenes with Karl situate them in this liminal space, showing, as Halberstam notes, that "failure loves company."[22] Thus while Celestine and Karl's romantic relationship may not fit a dominant narrative of heteronormative love, they share an intense erotic attraction *engendered* by the affective power of Celestine's female masculinity. Karl is drawn to Celestine like a magnet despite the fact that he "cannot figure the sum of [her]. As if [she is] too much for him to compass" (132). He is consistently surprised by the strength of his embodied response to her, and to regain equilibrium, he attempts to define Celestine's masculinity in terms he recognizes; however, his verbal pronouncements cannot contain the sum of her, and therefore they fail to adequately describe the force of her affective power. Their first meeting offers a perfect example of this struggle as Karl stumbles through the courtship ritual of flirting, saying, "'Pretty's not everything . . . You're built . . .' He stops, trying to hide his confusion. . . . 'If you curled the ends at least,' he says, attempting to recover, 'if you cut your hair. Or maybe it's the apron'" (127). Karl and Celestine's subsequent relationship is built upon such unconventional "failures." In fact, after Karl moves in with her, Celestine explains, "It is uncomfortable. In the love magazines, when passion holds sway, men don't fall down and roll on the floor and lay there like dead. But Karl does that" (134). Yet the two are drawn together by a desire seemingly out of their control, a desire contingent on Celestine's often acknowledged masculinity, which produces an odd, less-than-romantic partnership that remains queerly generative in all its failures.

Moreover, Celestine's female masculinity is augmented rather than challenged by her relationship with Karl, as their first interaction suggests, which underlines the relational, active nature of the affective experience.

For example, Celestine compares Karl's "polished fingernails" to her own hands, those "of a woman who has handled too many knives, deep-nicked and marked with lines, toughened from spice and brine, gouged, even missing a tip and nail" (133). And much as in the first scenes analyzed, the text repeatedly makes such comparisons in their sexual encounters, as well. Thus in *The Beet Queen,* female masculinity becomes legible *through* relationship. But Celestine is not merely more masculine by comparison to Karl; she is, in fact, depicted as masculine from childhood. Here she embodies Halberstam's tomboy, a figure who has "an extended childhood period of female masculinity."[23] Looking back to their adolescence, Mary describes Celestine as "strong. Her arms were thick from wrestling with her brother Russell, and she . . . was bigger than the eighth-grade boys" (37). But where the gender deviance of the tomboy is most often contained postpuberty, when "the full force of gender conformity descends on a girl," Celestine cultivates her female masculinity.[24] For example, in her late teens, when Celestine quits school to work, Mary explains that she "looked good, big and lean"; she wore "tailored suits instead of dresses and . . . a leather shoulderbag. . . . [S]he was handsome like a man. Her voice was low and penetrating and she smoked Viceroys" (67). Though Celestine clearly fails to meet dominant expectations for female gender performance, in Mary's description that failure is not perceived as lack. Here Erdrich's productive representations of female masculinity subvert the common depiction of female masculinity as abject, which Butler describes as the fear "that, if she is not quite a man, she is like one and hence monstrous in some way."[25] Instead, through Mary's eyes, Celestine's female masculinity circulates as sultry promise, smoke, and penetration. Yet interestingly, in what could be read as queer failure piled upon queer failure, we find that Celestine does not identify as lesbian. Celestine and Karl's relationship therefore subverts what Halberstam calls the "rigid insistence" of dominant cultural narratives that contend "some form or another of female masculinity indicates prelesbianism."[26] In contradiction to such insistence, Celestine's failure to enact conventionally feminine gender behavior is at the very heart of Karl's erotic attraction to her. For Celestine, such gender "failure," which she experiences and, in fact, cultivates from childhood, is the path to affective power. Erdrich thus writes female masculinity as the improbable and the impossible, as bodily excess, and as the antithesis to heteronormative "tales of burning love." Ultimately, through Karl and Celestine's relationship, *The Beet Queen* demonstrates how an eroticized female masculinity can inhabit the space of the vanished heterosexual ideal through the queer art of failure.

While the focus here is on *The Beet Queen,* this reading rests on three ideas of broader import to queer Native studies. First, the relational, reorganizational power of female masculinity in Indigenous texts has the potential to challenge dominant stereotypes about Indigenous masculinities. So, for example, the circulation of female masculinity in the work of writers like Chrystos, Gould, Daniel Heath Justice, Tomson Highway, Deborah A. Miranda, and Gregory Scofield challenges the hypermasculine representations of Indigenous masculinities so prevalent from the late 1960s through the early 1980s. Second, the articulation of female masculinity is necessarily affective, as it relies on relationship, the body, and, most often, on that which is felt but not named. This affective turn, which is so evident in *The Beet Queen,* can also be seen in films like *Johnny Greyeyes,* where Johnny's female masculinity is both a site of survivance and an affective power that can be read as an ethic of care. Third, and perhaps most importantly, such affective, transformative power holds the trace of Two-Spirit histories, of gender traditions that exist before and beyond the halls of academe. This final contention follows in the footsteps of scholars such as Craig Womack and Andrea Smith, who stake claims not for Native Studies as an addition to queer studies but, instead, for Indigeneity as the point of departure.[27] Collectively, these arguments demonstrate that the study of female masculinity in Indigenous literatures functions not as another settler colonial imposition on Native texts and lives but instead as a space of generative understanding that makes legible the embodied, relational ties between present-day Indigenous literatures and ongoing and still extant traditions of gender variance. Thus Erdrich's earliest representations of queer relationships enable a study of female masculinity that, to return to Halberstam's words, challenges "the privileged reservation of masculinity for men" from the psychic and physical locale of the reservation.[28] By reading *The Beet Queen*'s relationships through a queer theoretical lens, we not only meet but also exceed Halberstam's call for new masculinities by using affective methodologies that stem from Indigenous understandings of sexualities, genders, and the world.

In case her representations of female masculinity are not enough, in a final queer subversion, Erdrich offers an unexpectedly romantic conclusion to *The Beet Queen* through Karl's last transformation. In his youth and transient adulthood, Karl perceives queer affiliation as disconnection and fragmentation, as we've seen. At the close of the text, however, that affiliation is part of what returns him to community. The climax of the novel occurs when Wallace fixes a contest so that Dot, his namesake and Celestine and Karl's child, will win the Beet Queen competition. Karl sees "a newspaper photograph of the Beet Queen candidates . . . Behind them, with a big square grin on his face and new wire-rimmed glasses, stood Wallace Pfef" (317). A subsequent reverie about his daughter, sister, and past lover evokes this epiphany: "I give nothing, take nothing, mean nothing, hold nothing. . . . And in that darkened, bleak, smothering moment, something came back to me. One thing. Not an object, not a plan, not even the nagging words to a song, but a sweetness" (318). That "sweetness" involves memories of Dot, Mary, and Wallace. Karl explains, "[Wallace] thought I was some sort of God he worshipped. . . . He drove me out of my mind with attention, and even though I did feel sorry for him there was no question, ever, of staying. And yet I was coming back" (318–19). Karl arrives at the fair to find Wallace on the seat in the dunking booth, joking and laughing with townspeople. His earlier dismissal crumbles when a furious Dot, who has discovered Wallace's duplicity about the Beet Queen contest, dunks Wallace with no mercy. Karl sprints to the rescue: "He was out cold, I had to get there. I was running for my life" (323). Pulling Wallace from the water, Karl "drag[s] him close" and finally utters "the right words"—"Screw the management"—thereby recalling and humorously acknowledging the import of their first night together twenty years earlier (323). Karl seems to have made a radical transformation in both thought and action by acknowledging his feelings for Wallace and thereby claiming queer relationship, a connection he previously perceived as both fragmenting and dangerous. As a result, Erdrich's depictions of queerness shift radically from *The Beet Queen*'s 1932 opening to its 1972 close.

Chronologically, this shift makes sense as public attitudes toward the intersections of gender performances and sexualities changed during these time periods. While Erdrich may not be intentionally mapping Karl's transformation against the historical movement in public understanding, such histories inevitably background the text. At the turn of the century, as George Chauncey points out in *Gay New York: Gender, Urban Culture and the Making of the Gay Male World 1890–1940*, there was a vibrant assemblage of "loosely constituted clubs" and "gay social networks" that "fostered and sustained a distinctive gay culture."[29] While Chauncey focuses on New York's Bowery district, he argues that "the prominence of the Bowery fairies . . . meant their image influenced the manner in which all homosexually active men understood their behavior."[30] Thus though queerness, as Chauncey shows, was relegated to spectacle by the mainstream press and heteronormative ideals of the middle and upper classes, that spectacle was a well-known if often vilified part of the fabric of late nineteenth-century U.S. life. However, the 1930s, the point at which *The Beet Queen* begins, was a period of change. A Depression/Prohibition-era crackdown on queer practices and establishments meant "social interactions that had been tolerated in the 1920s" were "more stigmatized in the 1930s."[31] This "anti-gay reaction," Chauncey explains, "gained force in the early to mid-thirties as it became a part of a more general reaction to the cultural experimentation of the Prohibition years and to the disruption of gender arrangements by the Depression."[32] Erdrich's text follows this pattern of 1930s-era repression as evidenced by Karl's limited queer imaginary and his subsequent back-alley sexual liaisons. Likewise, Karl and Wallace's romantic reunion in the post-Stonewall 1970s, which, as noted in chapter 2, have been characterized as an era of mainstream gay liberation and sexual freedom, aligns with these historical changes in queer visibility.[33]

Whether examined episodically or historically, *The Beet Queen* offers readers diverse and multifaceted images of queerness that hinge on a reconfiguration of affiliation and affection. The text begins with classic images of queerness as deviance and loss, which have long been a trope in the literary canon; it concludes with an image of queerness as a conduit for familial return, community relationship, and in Karl's case, potential redemption. In the process, Erdrich engages theoretical concepts that will be key to the rise of queer theory in the early 1990s. Moreover, through her complex relationships, Erdrich repeatedly highlights the fluid nature of genders, desires, and sexualities, creating characters that exceed the boundaries of the conventional narratives about each as demonstrated in Celestine's female masculinity. By doing so, Erdrich's work destabilizes the foundation of the normative hetero/homosexual binary. A return to Butler demonstrates the importance of such an intervention: "The heterosexualization of desire requires and institutes the production of discrete and asymmetrical oppositions between 'feminine' and 'masculine,' where these are understood as expressive attributes of 'male' and 'female.' The cultural matrix through which gender identity has become intelligible requires that certain kinds of 'identities' cannot 'exist'—that is, those in which gender does not follow from sex and those in which the practices of desire do not follow from either sex or gender."[34] By focusing on just such disruptive gender representations—queer subjectivities that should not exist according to dominant cultural beliefs—Erdrich challenges the very basis of such regulatory constructions and, in doing so, joins gay and lesbian-identified writers like Allen, Kenny, Chrystos, and Gould to deconstruct 1980s logics of heteronormativity. Consequently, Erdrich's early work underscores the fact that my call for us to recognize the inherent queerness of Native literature is by no means a claim for an essentialist politics of identification: in this case, one of the most prominent writers in Native literature provides us with "invitations to desire differently, to desire more, to desire better" as she queers the canon of Native literature.[35]

Queer Visibility in *Tales of Burning Love*

While neither of Erdrich's two subsequent novels, *Tracks* (1988) or *The Bingo Palace* (1994), explicitly centers around same-sex relationships like *The Beet Queen*, all offer radical variations in gender identities through unconventional characters like Fleur Pillager, Pauline Puyat, Lipsha Morrissey, and Lulu Lamartine. These reconfigurations of gender norms have been the subject of a significant body of literary criticism.[36] But overt queer relationships do not reappear until *Tales of Burning Love* (1996), which takes its name from the romance novels parodied in *The Beet Queen* and 108-year-old Sister Leopolda's (formerly Pauline Puyat) comment: "My prayer is a tale of burning love, child, but you aren't ready to hear it."[37]

Tales of Burning Love revolves around the five ex-wives of Jack Mauser: June Morrissey, Eleanor Schlick, Candice Pantamounty, Marlis Cook, and the Beet Queen herself, a now-adult Dot Adare. The novel moves back and forth in time from its opening scene in 1981 to its 1995 close. Part 1, "Jack of Sunflowers," begins with Jack's story of June Morrissey's death, which Erdrich readers will recognize from her first novel, *Love Medicine*. The section subsequently explores the present day lives of Jack and Dot, who have just married after a brief courtship, and Eleanor, who flees a scandal by moving to Argus to research Sister Leopolda. The section concludes when Jack, who is drunk, broke, and single again, accidentally burns his house down. Part 2, "Blackjack Night," picks up at Jack's January 1995 funeral, where four of his ex-wives decide to find the fifth to settle a dispute over his remains. The end of the novel's second section finds all five women trapped in a van during a raging blizzard. To remain awake and alive,

Eleanor suggests, "Let's tell all. . . . Pretend this car is a confessional" (205). Dot agrees, adding, "Rule one, . . . No shutting up until dawn. Rule two. Tell a true story. Rule three. The story has to be about you. Something that you've never told another soul, a story that would scorch paper, heat up the air!" (206). Among the "scorching" stories told in part 3, "Tales of Burning Love," is that of Candice and Marlis's romantic relationship, which begins with a tug-of-war over Marlis and Jack's unborn baby. Erdrich's depiction of the two women's love functions as a queer affiliation and both defies and makes legible heteronormative imperatives.

Ultimately, *Tales of Burning Love* employs third-person perspectives to reveal the covert ways heteronormativity reproduces itself. In *The Beet Queen,* the details of Karl and Wallace's relationship and Karl's other queer trysts remain hidden from public view in the shadowed spaces of train cars, back alleys, and hotel rooms, playing, like Kenny's "Greta Garbo," on the classic trope of secrecy. By contrast, in *Tales of Burning Love,* as Lauren Berlant and Michael Warner might argue, "intimacy is itself publicly mediated";[38] the private is actually a public spectacle, as the frequent outside perceptions of Candice and Marlis's love affair demonstrate. After deciding to flee his debts when he finds he's been declared dead, Jack stops to visit his and Marlis's infant son. Once he opens the bedroom door, "he knew it instantly, saw it, understood it . . . his two former wives slept together as lovers" (261). The realization stops Jack in his tracks; he "stood in the doorway and could not set foot inside" (261). The power of this queer revelation, which brings that deemed "private" into "public" view, pacts a visceral punch. Thus from the first instance, queerness made visible disrupts the status quo.

The story Candice and Marlis tell in the freezing van also indexes the regulatory nature of the heteronormative imperative alongside the unruly possibilities of queer relationship. Marlis is pregnant and broke when Candice, who is unable to have children, invites her on a trip to the Minnesota north woods in the hopes of persuading Marlis to relinquish the baby. Though they don't begin a physical relationship on the trip, a woman in an adjacent hotel room perceives Candice and Marlis as lovers: "'You two whatevers, I get it now,' she said. 'I've heard about these things. . . . You inseminated her. I've read about this stuff,' she paused, looked darkly into the new drink she'd fixed. 'You've got to be from down in the Cities. That's where this stuff's happening. Up here we don't have the right equipment. Now you get out of here'" (346). Jack's response to his ex-wives' lesbian relationship keeps him out of the women's bedroom; similarly, this observer's response to such a possibility is to demand that Candice and Marlis leave her room. Both reactions demand separation and distance, situating queerness as abject. The second scene additionally locates the possibility of nonheteronormative sex, reproduction, and family as inherently other. Berlant and Warner's discussion of how certain understandings of social relations construct heteronormativity is useful here. They point out that "the very category of heterosexuality . . . consolidates as a *sexuality* widely differing practices, norms, and institutions."[39] At the same time, "a complex cluster of sexual practices gets confused, in heterosexual culture, with the love plot of intimacy and familialism that signifies belonging to society in a deep and normal way. Community is imagined through scenes of intimacy, coupling, and kinship."[40] As a result, very different types of "social relations [become] intelligible as heterosexuality, and this privatized sexual culture bestows on its sexual practices a tacit sense of rightness and normalcy. This sense of rightness—embedded in things and not just sex—is what we call heteronormativity."[41] By offering these outside perspectives of queer relationship in *Tales of Burning Love,* Erdrich makes the problematic and insistent construction of heteronormativity visible.

The chronology of the novel furthers this argument. The account of Candice and Marlis's lesbian relationship follows the narratives of Jack's heterosexual marriages. As the stories of Jack's relationships are narrated one after another, each is more twisted than the next. In the last, he is duct-taped to a bed, his hair removed with hot wax, his ears pierced with a silver brooch, and his feet glued into red spiked heels (332–35). Yet this dysfunctional relationship is sanctioned not just by the romance novels—or "tales of burning love"—that define romantic heterocouplehood as the be all, end all of life but also by the weight of national laws and institutions. Heterosexual marriage, like heterosexuality itself, is considered "right" and "normal," whereas, at the time of the novel's publication, "queer culture, by contrast, has almost no institutional matrix for its counterintimacies" in the United States.[42] By ending the stories of Jack's relationships with this ludicrous image and then subsequently showing that outsiders view not Jack's marriages but *Candice and Marlis's* relationship as aberrant, Erdrich exposes the fractures in the supposedly stable foundation of heterosexuality.

Such a reading is further reinforced by Erdrich's poignant descriptions of the two women's erotic desires, which construct queerness not as alterity but as productivity. In fact, theirs seems to be the only nondestructive "tale of burning love" in the book. The tender quality of Candice and Marlis's interactions is striking in comparison to the damaging examples of heterocoupling. Thus though Candice initially finds the idea of a lesbian relationship "laughable," "upsetting," and "faintly painful," she comes to the gradual realization that she finds Marlis "quietly and definitively *lovely*" (350, 353). The fabric of their desire is woven delicately over the course of Marlis's pregnancy through threads of laughter, shared meals, and intimate conversations. Erdrich's lush prose fills these seemingly platonic interactions with sensuality: "The two women are sitting at the secondhand table in Marlis's apartment, eating bread. They have a new-baked loaf between them. They tear apart the rye with dreamy fingers, wiping the soft interior, the magic crust, each scrap across a thick roll of whitish, warm, unsalted sweet butter. The oil spreads up their fingers, cuffed wrists, the corners of their mouths" (355). Their first sexual encounter is cast in the same dreamy sensuality. Candice has moved in after Marlis gives birth and, believing she's found an exhausted Marlis sleepwalking, Candice leads her back to her room, where Marlis unbuttons her pajama top. At that point, "neither dares to speak—Candice to ask if Marlis is awake, Marlis to ask if this is wrong. . . . Candice . . . feels weightless, uncanny, as though she is now reading the end of a mystery. . . . [I]t is completely right for her to lean forward and hold Marlis's face" (359). The narrator explains, "From the first touch it seemed to them that they had crossed and were held within that electrical field . . . that exists between the bodies of women" (359). In the arc of the novel, as these descriptions underscore, Erdrich undoubtedly situates lesbianism as one of the few spaces of fruitful intimate connection. While *The Beet Queen* points to the performative nature of gender and the multiplicities of desire, *Tales of Burning Love* questions the primacy and supposed normalcy of heteroromance, offering in its stead a narrative in which lesbianism constitutes the most productive social formation. As a result, *Tales of Burning Love* unmoors the "sense of rightness" that undergirds the continued circulation of heteronormative ideologies.

Erdrich's depiction of Candice and Marlis's interactions reinforces my argument that throughout the body of her work, Erdrich recognizes and, in fact, privileges a heretofore unrecognized narrative of queer relationality. Candice and Marlis's love affair, for example, speaks to the possibilities of queer parenting, which include a potential focus on kinship rather than heterocouplehood and the biologically defined nuclear family. Erdrich's texts are filled with relationships that rely on kinship networks rather than nuclear family households. To name only a brief few, Fleur is rescued by Nanapush after her family dies, and her daughter Lulu is raised by Nanapush and Margaret Rushes Bear (Kashpaw). Pauline Puyat is taken in by Bernadette Morrissey, while Pauline's daughter, Marie Kashpaw (nee Lazarre), adopts June Morrissey, who is later raised by Eli Kashpaw. Marie subsequently raises Lipsha Morrisey, who is June's son and Lulu's grandson. This brief and labyrinthine catalog of familial relationships represents just a smattering of the many nonheteronormative family units that appear in Erdrich's collective works. Such kinship networks, which rely on extended rather than nuclear family relationships, are, in fact, part of Anishinaabeg traditions and are common among Indigenous peoples generally. By contrast, the insistence on the nuclear family is part of a dominant U.S. sociopolitical structure that Mark Rifkin, in *When Did Indians Become Straight?,* ties to narratives of national identity. Rifkin exposes the way conjugal coupling and the nuclear family function as lynchpins for a racialized national imaginary in the United States by demonstrating how U.S. Indian policy juxtaposes an institutionalized model of heterocouplehood against Indigenous understandings of kinship that center around collectivities. These historical juxtapositions mark Indigenous forms of familial and geopolitical affiliation like kinship as failed or "perversely aberrant."[43] At stake, Rifkin argues, is "the consolidation of a familial norm that elides native kinship structures which challenged the jurisdictional imaginary of the incipient settler state."[44] But Indigenous understandings of kinship, while they can't be overlooked because of their prevalence in Erdrich's novels, don't map perfectly onto Candice and Marlis's relationship since the two women, like Karl and Wallace in *The Beet Queen,* are non-Native.

One way to locate the family formation created by Candice and Marlis's romantic ties, then, is through alternate readings of kinship such as those offered in queer studies. In the past years, numerous critics have used the trope of kinship to theorize queer relationships, one of the best known being Kath Weston. Weston begins *Families We Choose: Lesbians, Gays, Kinship* (1991) by discussing the proliferation of alternate understandings of family, pointing out that despite the myriad types of queer families, "The stereotyped tragedy of 'gay life' revolves around [a] presumed isolation, the absence of kin and stable relationships."[45] Such stereotypes rest on an imagined binary in which reproduction is bound to heterosexuality and opposed to queer identities, which are figured as physical and ideological threats to both reproduction itself and the heteronuclear family more generally. In such limited imaginaries, "coming out" as LGBTIQ2 always already equals alienation from a biological family and a concomitant rejection of procreation and parenting. Weston's research situates gay kinship structures outside such binaries. She argues, "By substituting images of creation and selection for the logic of reproduction and succession, discourse on gay families can—and does—remind people of their power to alter the circumstances into which they were born."[46] As a result, "Gay families not only dispute exclusively procreative interpretations of kinship, but introduce a new basis for rendering heterosexuality and lesbian or gay identity commensurable. Put simply, two things that are capable of being compared. In the context of the symbolic contrast between straight and gay families, kinship effectively bridges the opposition of straight versus gay by providing a third term capable of relating each to the other."[47] Importantly, she distinguishes such "commensurability" from "the notion of likeness that informs identity politics."[48] Kinship, Weston shows, is not sameness. Moreover, queer kinship centers on a rhetoric of choice and affiliation as opposed to a rhetoric of inevitability and biology.

In *Tales of Burning Love,* Candice and Marlis's first sexual encounter can perhaps be best understood through such theories. As the two women begin to make love, Erdrich implicitly questions the boundaries and limits of identity markers, so "it did not occur to Marlis . . . that they were doing anything that fit a category, anything that had a name. Her body seemed so powerful it was like a physical shock to her. It was for both of them as though they were inventing each gesture and act, out of nothing and as they went along" (360). Through the consciousness of her characters, Erdrich defies those who might read lesbian sex as a mirror image of the heterosexual encounters that precede it in the text. While the scene can be compared to other representations of intimacy and erotic desire in the novel, the experience of the two women exceeds limitations of "just like" or "same as," claims that in this era of queer liberalism and Defense of Marriage Act (DOMA) reforms are so often used to argue for LGBTIQ2 rights. Sedgwick refers to such discourses as "universalizing" in *Epistemology of the Closet* when she maps the common binaries employed in representations of queerness. This universalizing/minoritizing binary brings us to theoretical and conceptual "deadlock," which limits more nuanced understandings of gender and sexuality.[49] Instead, Erdrich gives her readers "more than" by suggesting Marlis and Candice come together through their experience of erotic desire to form something new. The rest of the scene furthers this claim by extracting the notion of family from the confines of heterosexuality. The narrator explains,

> As they went into it, and they did not stop to eat or sleep or do the dishes or answer the phone or go to work, as they . . . occasionally bathed or dressed each other, took care of the baby, settled into bed only to begin touching once more, they sometimes talked dreamily of what all this might mean. Implications drifted over Candice and disappeared—she remembered vaguely that she had once regarded what seemed entirely normal, now, as absurd, foreign, freakish. The baby lay between the two of them—he was a lovely little baby, with fine long fingers and dark coppery hair. (360)

The unit formed by Candice, Marlis, and the baby extends the limited understanding of conjugal couplehood. Rather than depicting lesbian identity as divorced from reproduction, the two women's love affair exceeds narrow definitions of both kin and family. To invoke Weston, this scene "question[s] not so much the 'naturalness' of a biological tie, but rather the assumption that shared biogenetic substance in itself confers kinship."[50] The familial relationship depicted here, while it does include biology, extends outward to situate affiliation in affective connection. Thus in *Tales of Burning Love,* queerness can, to use Julianne Piduck's words, "make strange the grammar of kinship, potentially rearticulating the meanings and membership of family."[51]

"Appalling, God-Given Milk": Affect, Motherhood, and Naming in *The Antelope Wife*

Though no major characters are overtly homosexual in Erdrich's next book, *The Antelope Wife* (1998), the text begins with another significantly queer relationship when a cavalry soldier, Private Scranton Teodorus Roy, first takes part in a vicious cavalry attack on an unsuspecting Ojibwe village and then follows and saves a baby girl's life by literally nursing her. At first the nursing serves to give the baby comfort, forging an affective bond between the two that, for Scranton, represents the tenacity and purity of faith. Eventually, though, that embodied faith engenders actual nourishment as Scranton begins to lactate "his own watery, appalling, God-given milk."[52] As a result, Scranton feeds the Ojibwe girl he himself stranded from her family when he participated in the physical and psychological violence of settler colonial practices. This representation of queer motherhood reminds us of Seigworth and Gregg's claim that "the capacity of the body is never defined by a body alone but is always aided and abetted by, and dovetails with, the field and context of its force-relations."[53] Scranton's lactation operates within and because of such force relations when the baby's faith and his transgressive body temporarily intervene in a settler colonial system in a manner that disrupts most readers' expectations of what is often the most privileged and naturalized relationship of all: motherhood. Erdrich's representation of Scranton is not unprecedented—there are previous literary and anthropological representations of male lactation as well as scientific studies that argue for the physical possibility.[54] However, rather than resting on Scranton's physiology, the scene foregrounds how a biological imperative—the baby's will to live—queers our preconceptions about gender and motherhood. The baby "seized [Scranton]. Inhaled him" (6). Additionally, though she is without spoken language, the baby manipulates Scranton through her instinctual responses to his actions. She is "surprisingly contented" unless he removes her from his nipple; Scranton, who reads this physical demand as not biological drive but as "loyalty," an affective attachment, reacts by leaving the baby latched to his body at almost all times. His feelings for the baby radically contrast his emotions and actions in the cavalry raid where he focused on "the feral quiet of the children," experiencing a "sudden contempt" and "frigid hate" for them (4). Moreover, rather than being horrified in the midst of battle in a way that might cause him to be a sympathetic character, Scranton found "pleasure in raising, aiming" at, and shooting down fleeing children (4). There is a dark irony at play, then, when Scranton becomes a surrogate mother to one of the Ojibwe children he previously hunted, his body the source of both affection and sustenance.

Even before Scranton finds the baby—whom, in classic colonial fashion, he names after his mother, Matilda—his relationship to motherhood disrupts the brutal dehumanization of the Ojibwe. After he bayonets an old woman and unintentionally meets her eyes, "his gaze was drawn to hers and he sank with it into the dark unaccompanied moment before his birth.... A groan of heat and blood. He saw his mother, yanked the bayonet out with a huge cry, and began to run" (4). In a visceral moment of connection engendered by the interplay of blood and amniotic memory, Scranton experiences embodied relationship. Blood runs, eyes meet, and in the interstices of the physical present and the embodied memory of the past, the monstrous nature of Scranton's brutality becomes visible. The subsequent affective bond disrupts the psychological violence of settler colonialism, though, importantly, the ensuing bond cannot and does not dispel the physical violence that has already occurred. Such is the function and inherently relational nature of affect, which "*accumulates* across both relatedness and interruptions in relatedness, becoming a palimpsest of force-encounters traversing the ebbs and swells of intensities that pass between 'bodies' (bodies defined not by an outer skin-envelope or other surface boundary but by their potential to reciprocate or co-participate in the passages of affect)."[55] In Scranton's case, that affective encounter jars him from his calculated hatred and causes him to flee the scene, which enables him to rescue the baby girl whose cradleboard has been strapped on the back of her family's dog. In a complicated relational web, Scranton is complicit in the brutal attack on the baby's family and therefore responsible for her subsequent peril, even as he later provides her with the nourishment she needs to live; he stabs and saves, kills and comforts. Within this thorny history, Erdrich's representations of motherhood not only thwart gender expectations but also affectively intervene in settler colonial narratives by turning enemies into relations. It could be said, then, that through Scranton Roy's affective engagement to motherhood, *The Antelope Wife,* like *Tales of Burning Love,* queers heteronormative kinship relations and the settler colonial narratives they so often uphold.

The Antelope Wife also offers a scene that briefly introduces a multiply gendered figure to Erdrich's fiction, a community-centered role that will be explored further in her next novel. Here, too, Erdrich explores the reverberations of settler colonial violence on the mother–child relationship. When baby Matilda's biological mother, Ozhawashkwamashkodeykway, or Blue Prairie Woman, cannot stop grieving for her lost child, the elders recognize they must give Blue Prairie Woman a new name if she is to spiritually and psychologically return to the tribe:

> They asked the strongest of namers, the one who dreamed original names. This namer was nameless and was neither a man nor a woman, and so took power from the in-between. This namer had long, thick braids and a sweet shy smile, charming ways but

> arms tough with roped muscle. The namer walked like a woman, spoke in a man's deep voice. Hid coy behind a fan and yet agreed to dream a name to fit the new thing inside Blue Prairie Woman. (13–14)

Erdrich's description of this figure of cultural liaison explicitly recalls the history of Two-Spirit people, who inhabited third- or fourth-gender roles. Will Roscoe explains, "Those alternative gender roles that have been documented . . . occur in every region of the continent, in every kind of society, and among speakers of every major language group."[56] In this scene, Erdrich situates the namer as a respected figure, endowed with a significant role and accepted by the tribe. Importantly in terms of my larger argument in this chapter, this role *hinges upon* relationship—the Two-Spirit namer has a responsibility enmeshed in the nexus of community. Gerald Vizenor's description of such roles reinforces this contention. In *The People Named the Chippewa,* he explains, "The bestowing of a name was not . . . the principal function of a namer. . . . The principal function was the transmission" of a "benefit" or "power."[57] The name giver has a dream that gives that person "a spirit power or protection which he could transmit to others."[58] While Vizenor speaks of namers more generally, Erdrich draws this same picture from tribal histories and anthropological accounts that situate those who inhabited alternate gender roles in some Native nations as shamans, spiritual leaders, and, as seen here, namers. Walter Williams discusses the Lakota tradition in which a winkte would "prepare himself for a naming ceremony by fasting and undertaking a vision quest, to gain some insight into [a] child's future."[59] The "namer" who saves Blue Prairie Woman, likewise, works with and for hir Anishinaabe people in the service of not just individual but communal survival.[60] If we turn from the role of this character in *The Antelope Wife* to consider the character's function in Erdrich's larger body of work, we find a number of important correspondences. First, with the inclusion of this powerful Two-Spirit figure, queerness is no longer solely the purview of white characters in Erdrich's novels, and, second, Erdrich's representation of the historical existence of gender diversity, though only fleetingly invoked, introduces a framework of Indigenous sociality heretofore absent in her depictions of queer relationships. This intervention becomes more fully apparent in relation to her next novel, *The Last Report on the Miracles at Little No Horse* (2001).

Gender B(l)ending and Two-Spirit Histories in the *Last Report on the Miracles at Little No Horse*

While *The Antelope Wife* touches on queer relationality through Scranton Roy's motherhood and the text's brief invocation of Two-Spirit histories, Erdrich's seventh novel, *The Last Report on the Miracles at Little No Horse,* revolves around entwined understandings of gender, sexuality, and relationship. In one of Erdrich's most entertaining plot twists, *Last Report* reveals that Father Damien Modeste, a minor character in *Tracks,* was born Agnes De Witt, a white, Chopin-playing ex-nun, who takes the robes and identity of the original Father Damien after he dies on his way to the fictionalized Ojibwe reservation in the text. Agnes lives as a man and serves as the reservation priest from her 1912 arrival until her 1996 death. Along the way, she learns to perform masculinity, schooling herself as Giles schooled Karl. She makes an often cited list of "masculine" behaviors:

Some Rules to Assist in My Transformation

1. Make requests in the form of orders.
2. Give compliments in the form of concessions.
3. Ask questions in the form of statements.
4. Exercise to enhance the muscles of the neck.
5. Admire women's handiwork with copious amazement.
6. Stride, swing arms, stop abruptly, stroke chin.
7. Sharpen razor daily.
8. Advance no explanations.
9. Accept no explanations.
10. Hum an occasional resolute march.[61]

The novel's subsequent exploration of such gender b(l)ending has been the subject of much literary analysis. Maria Orban and Alan Velie read Agnes/Father Damien as trickster, "a shape-shifter of indeterminate sex and interchangeable gender who has the ability to create and re-create identity very much along the lines of Judith Butler's 'performative theory.'"[62] Pamela J. Rader argues, "Erdrich's treatment of gender in *Last Report* reinstates a syncretic tradition wherein Ojibwe and Catholic beliefs fuse, marking Agnes's multilayered assimilation process."[63] Annette Van Dyke maintains, by "challenging the gender dichotomies of Euro-American culture, Erdrich also begins the reader's education as to what it is to be human."[64] Iovannone extends his transgender framework to *Last Report,* contending that, "while Agnes assumes the masculine role and position of a priest, she does not become a man in the Western binary sense of the word. She is positioned within the novel in a liminal space that transcends both masculine and feminine identity markers."[65] This sampling of the many fine analyses of *Last Report* mark the novel's importance in terms of Erdrich's ongoing investigations of the fluidity and transformative possibilities of gender performance.

As the number of articles on gender in *Last Report* suggest, Erdrich's portrayal of Agnes/Father Damien—with its mixing of gendered pronouns and interrogation of the boundaries and possibilities of shifting gender roles—extends the *depth* of the work she's already begun in terms of her depictions of gender performance and queer relationships; in this way, *Last Report* expands the examinations Erdrich began fifteen years earlier in *The Beet Queen.* One aspect of *Last Report,* however, also extends the *breadth* of Erdrich's queer representations: her extended acknowledgement of the Two-Spirit traditions first referenced in *The Antelope Wife.* Thus to situate her Anishinaabeg characters' responses to Agnes/Father Damien's queer gender performance, Erdrich also includes a historical scene with "an ikwe-inini, a woman-man called a *winkte* by the Bwaang," or Lakota (153). While critics like Barak and Prince-Hughes have read Erdrich's early novels, including *Love Medicine, The Beet Queen, Tracks,* and *The Bingo Palace,* through the lens of Two-Spirit traditions, such work does not account for the fact that, in those texts, Erdrich's queer characters are white. Given the history of white appropriations of a romanticized Two-Spirit identity, reading non-Native characters as Two-Spirit is questionable.[66] By contrast, in *Last Report,* both Agnes/Father Damien's adoption by the Anishinaabeg and Erdrich's inclusion of an explicitly Two-Spirit character open the possibility of Two-Spirit critiques.

Erdrich's flashback to an earlier moment in Anishinaabe history with the "ikwe-inini" is preceded by two scenes that show multiple gender traditions are still known and accepted among the older Anishinaabeg in the text. When Agnes first arrives as Father Damien, she is brought to the mission by Kashpaw, who "sensed something unusual about the priest. . . . Perhaps, he thought, here was a man like the famous Wishkob, the Sweet, who had seduced many other men and finally joined the family of a great war chief as a wife, where he had lived until old, well loved, as one of the women. Kashpaw himself had addressed Wishkob as grandmother" (64).

In a nuanced essay that parses the historical differences between transgender and Two-Spirit approaches, Deirdra Keenan maintains, "In the context of mainstream attitudes about transgender identities and Native American gender systems," *Last Report* "provides a theory and practice of gender identity formation."[67] That theory, in the case of Kashpaw and Nanapush, who represent the old-school Anishinaabeg, centers Indigenous knowledges in which multiple genders and sexualities are culturally appropriate rather than radically transgressive. Moreover, to define Wishkob's place in the tribe, Kashpaw invokes kinship, both in Wishkob's familial relationships and in Kashpaw's own relationship to Wishkob; in doing so, Kashpaw constructs Two-Spirit traditions as delineated and sanctioned by community relationship. Nanapush, too, confirms Wishkob's well-known place within the Anishinaabeg community of Little No Horse when he tries to beat Father Damien at chess by asking, "What are you? . . . A man priest or a woman priest? . . . Are you a female Wishkob?" (230–31). After throwing Agnes/Father Damien off balance, Nanapush presses his advantage: "So you're not a woman-acting man, you're a man-acting woman. We don't get so many of those lately. Between us, Margaret and me, we couldn't think of more than a couple" (232). Recognizing Nanapush's questions as chess strategy, Agnes "realized that this moment, so shattering to her, wasn't of like importance to Nanapush" (232). Each scene suggests Anishinaabeg attitudes toward sex and gender are wide ranging and complex and that positions exist for those whose gender performances exceed the Western gender binaries that came to North America as part of settler colonialism. Though the encroachment of Christianity clearly shifts historical configurations of kinship and family—as perhaps best seen in the disastrous fates of Kashpaw's wives in his move from polygamy to monogamy—the historical memory and cultural acceptance of gender diversity still exists in the Anishinaabe world of Erdrich's texts. In addition, much as in *The Antelope Wife,* such Two-Spirit figures are defined by and through the web of relational responsibilities.[68]

Erdrich's depiction of the Lakota winkte, which employs a historical flashback to return to the era in which Kashpaw's and Nanapush's memories of gender diversity were present-day realities, serves as her most extended engagement with Two-Spirit traditions to date and as yet another commentary on the potential (or, in this case, potential failure) of queer relationship and responsibility. The winkte's story unfolds within a document Father Damien writes about Pauline's ancestors: "History of the

Puyats." This "history," one of the many literary documents Erdrich layers into the narrative of *Last Report,* returns to a prereservation-era past when the "Bwaanag," or Lakota, and the Ojibwe and Michif hunted buffalo during spring and summer months. While this is not a precontact narrative—the Ojibwe hunting party uses guns and includes the presence of "Good Father LaCombe, whose job it was to bless the hunt"—it is a scene in which the subsistence patterns of the Ojibwe and Lakota remain intact (150). In Father Damien's story, the band of Ojibwe and French-Indian Michifs meet the Lakota when both groups are laden with meat and hides from successful hunts. The historic enmity between the groups erupts into an exchange of bullets and insults that culminates when the women of each group taunt the other by showing their genitals and shouting challenges. The first Pauline's father suggests a compromise: "Since it is our hotheaded women who are looking to shed blood, and as we are French and Ojibwe men who always satisfy our women, let two of the women race to the death. The winner of the race, we all agree, shall have the other's life. After this is accomplished, we will go our separate directions and meet to fight, as men and warriors, another day" (151). Pauline's mother and one of the Lakota women run a race, which instead of the loser's death, leads to another contest, this time between Pauline's father and the ikwe-inini or Lakota Two-Spirit.

In contrast to her previous depictions of Blue Prairie Woman's namer and Wishkob the Sweet as enmeshed in the web of Indigenous relationship, *Last Report* ultimately presents a Two-Spirit character who chooses self-preservation over communal responsibility. The ikwe-inini is described as "a woman-man called a *winkte* by the Bwaang, a graceful sly boy who sighed, poised with grave nuance, combed his hair, and peered into the tortoiseshell hand mirror that hung around his neck by a rawhide thong" (153). Walter Williams explains that persons inhabiting such Two-Spirit positions "mix together much of the behavior, dress, and social roles of women and men. . . . They are not seen as men, yet they are not seen as women either. They occupy an alternative gender role that is a mixture of diverse elements."[69] Native people interviewed in Williams's study described Two-Spirit people as "almost universally known to be hard workers, doing good beadwork, pottery, weaving, saddlemaking, and tanning, and being good providers for their family."[70] Like the Anishinaabe Two-Spirit figure in *The Antelope Wife,* among the Lakota, winkte such as the one Erdrich depicts here would have played a spiritual role within their nation and were "described as *wakan*" or "sacred."[71] In her classic essay, "Changing

Native American Roles in an Urban Context and Changing Native American Sex Roles in an Urban Context," Beatrice Medicine explains, "Among the Lakota (Teton Sioux) there is evidence that other facets of action were bounded within the *winkte* gloss—ritualist, artist, specialist in women's craft production, herbalist, seer, namer of children, rejector of the rigorous warrior role, 'mama's boy' . . . and the designation [of male homosexual] commonly stated in anthropology books."[72] Medicine's careful use of the phrase "facets of action" is key, since third-gender roles were often defined around occupation rather than sexual identity or sexual object choice, as is often assumed by contemporary readers. Among the Lakota, taking up such a position traditionally involved a vision quest and a sacred dream that either initiated or confirmed the dreamer's identity as a winkte.[73] Thus at the time period of the Ojibwe and French-Indian Michifs's encounter with the Lakota, the winkte, though a "graceful sly boy," would have most likely already received a great deal of spiritual guidance from tribal elders and undoubtedly would have been socially integrated into hir Lakota community. With these commonly known historical details in mind, Erdrich's preening winkte, with hir combed hair, mirror, and "eyes rimmed with smoky black," leans more toward a caricature of a modern-day queen than a valued spiritual figure (154). In this respect, Erdrich's depiction of the Lakota Two-Spirit includes a contemporary tongue-in-cheek campiness even while it invokes actual historical traditions.

Such humor in no way shuts down the possibilities of Erdrich's gender play. In fact, in the scene in which the winkte is introduced as a possible competitor in the men's footrace, Erdrich underscores the malleability of gender much as she did in *The Beet Queen,* showing it to be contextual, a socially constructed subject translated differently by different people. Thus when the Lakota put the winkte forward as one of the two possible representatives of their community, observers are "lost in debate. Was the *winkte* a man or a woman for the purposes of this race?" (153). The narrator explains, "Some of the Ojibwe, who judged his catlike stance too threatening, rejected him as a male runner on account of his female spirit. Others were wary of the scowling hunter [the second possible candidate for the race] and argued that as the winkte would run with legs that grew down along either side of a penis as unmistakable as his opponent's, he was enough of a male to suit the terms" (153–54). Again, this admittedly amusing scene allows for multiple interpretations. Given the historical existence of multiple gender traditions in both Ojibwe and Lakota communities, the community's retreat to gender binaries for the purpose of intertribal rivalry seems unlikely. As Brian Joseph Gilley explains in *Becoming Two-Spirit: Gay Identity and Social Acceptance in Indian Country,* "Historical Native ideas about gender did not employ the gender-binary, bodily-sex-equals-gender view commonly found in European society."[74] Thus the equation made here—the winkte can race as a man because he has a penis—rests on heteropatriarchal rather than Indigenous logics. Orbin and Velie, in their analysis of this scene, argue, "The way Erdrich characterizes the *winkte* in *Last Report* is entirely a matter of gesture and performance, of social construction based on the perception of negative female stereotypes from a male perspective."[75] They claim, too, that Erdrich's use of the phrase "'enough of a male' indicates a scale with varying degrees of maleness, not an either/or binary opposition."[76] It's questionable whether this scene refutes such a binary, and, instead, the debate seems to hinge on gender dichotomy, as does the narrator's later description of the race.

Such descriptive dichotomies surface when the winkte and hir Ojibwe rival strategize as they begin to run. Racing for the Ojibwe and French-Indian Michifs, Pauline's father, "the clever Montrealer," plans "to confuse his opponent" (154). The narrator explains, "This would have worked more easily had not his opponent, whose job it was as a woman to study men and whose immediacy of manhood gave him uncanny understanding, read the mind of the Frenchman" (154). Like the Ojibwe who debated hir eligibility in the race, the narrator describes the winkte as part female and part male: as a woman, the winkte studies men; as a man, the winkte has some undefined type of special "understanding." The idea of the winkte belonging to an entirely different gender category is not explored in the race scene, leaving the gender binary itself unchallenged. Additionally, none of the critics who analyze this scene discuss the repercussions of the flight when "the *winkte,* losing by a toe, swiped his dress neatly from the grass and simply kept running, across the broad plains, into the hills" (154). Since the loser of the race has promised to forfeit his or hir life as a representative of his or hir tribe, the dishonorable escape amounts to a betrayal of key Lakota values. While the winkte's disappearance might make for a neat conclusion to the comedic scene, in this desertion of community and honor, we again see Erdrich veer away from known histories of Two-Spirit people. To return to Gilley, "Because third-gender people were neither men nor women but their own gender, they were not bound by the same expectations and responsibilities. In most societies, women-men did not participate in the prestige system of hunting and war honors required of men. Women-men did not have to earn the respect of their people through acts of bravery, because they gained their prestige through the obligation to the people that was built into their role."[77] After losing the race, the winkte eschews this kinship obligation for self-preservation by running off into the sunset and ultimately rejecting communal responsibility. Yet even while claims for the transgressive nature of Erdrich's descriptive details in this particular scene are questionable, both *The Antelope Wife* and *Last Report* push mainstream audiences to recognize how Ojibwe and Lakota gender systems exceed those of their western counterparts. Catherine Rainwater contends Erdrich's texts contain "anomalous moments . . . when the reader must pause 'between worlds' to consider perceptual frameworks as important structural principles in both textual and nontextual realms."[78] While Rainwater concentrates on the function of Erdrich's figures of speech, her argument resonates, as well, with Erdrich's descriptions of queer relationship. Erdrich's relationships expand perceptual frameworks of gender and sexuality throughout her canon, whether by exposing the performative nature of gender in *The Beet Queen* and *Last Report,* destabilizing the structure of heteronormativity in *Tales of Burning Love,* enlarging the physical and affective parameters of motherhood in *The Antelope Wife,* or considering the importance of third-gender traditions to Anishinaabe community as seen in *The Antelope Wife* and *Last Report.*[79]

In many ways, the extended recognition of a community-sanctioned Two-Spirit history, rather than Agnes/Father Damien's gender performance itself, is why *Last Report* occupies a particularly important place in Erdrich's many depictions of queer relationship and nonnormative genders and sexualities. In her landmark book *Conquest: Sexual Violence and American Indian Genocide,* Andrea Smith argues we must recognize the context of settler colonialism to understand the importance of sexuality within both Indigenous histories and Indigenous peoples' present-day realities. Colonization took place "through sexual violence and . . . the imposition of European gender relationships on Native communities."[80] Justice points to a well-known historical example of this pattern, explaining,

> Native and queer subjectivities have a long and quite vexed history of interconnectedness within the early modern context of colonialism and imperialism. In 1513 Vasco Nuñez de Balboa . . . led his soldiers against the village of Quarequa. . . . [When] Balboa turned his attention to the "house of this kynge," which was "infested with

> most abominable and unnaturall lechery" . . . [H]e found "the kynges brother and many other younge men in womens apparell, smoth & effeminately decked, which by the report of such as dwelte abowte hym, he abused with preposterous venus." Balboa ordered that the men, who numbered around forty, be fed alive to his hunger-maddened war-dogs.[81]

Such violence occurs on the level of both action and ideology; thus Balboa's well-documented savagery is sanctioned and driven by particular belief systems. Qwo-Li Driskill maintains this settler colonial ideology "enforce[s] the idea that sexuality and non-dichotomous genders are a sin, recreating sexuality as illicit, shocking, shameful, and removed from any positive spiritual context."[82] Karl's comparison of queers with outlaws in *The Beet Queen* and outsiders' shocked responses to Candice and Marlis's relationship in *Tales of Burning Love* stem from such beliefs. Scott Lauria Morgensen furthers this analysis of settler colonial violence by tracing what he calls "settler homonationalism," a theory he builds on the work of transnational queer theorist Jasbir Puar. Morgensen illustrates that "modern sexuality is not a *product* of settler colonialism, as if it came into being in the United States after settlement transpired. Modern sexuality arose in the United States as a method to *produce* settler colonialism, and settler subjects, by facilitating ongoing conquest and naturalizing its effects."[83] With this troubled history of erotic colonization in mind, one can see that Erdrich offers a radically different concept of sex/gender performances in *The Antelope Wife* and *Last Report*. Her representation of Anishinaabe acceptance of Two-Spirit identities invokes Indigenous understandings of sex and gender that both exceed and predate—by hundreds of years—those offered by theorists like Butler, Sedgwick, Berlant, Warner, and Weston. Thus while such theories are useful, *The Antelope Wife* and *Last Report on the Miracles at Little No Horse* necessarily redirect current theoretical conversations about her work away from mainstream queer theory and toward the historicized critiques of settler colonialism occurring in contemporary queer Native studies.

Catachrestic Love and Queer Desire in *The Master Butchers Singing Club*

While the inclusion of Two-Spirit histories in Erdrich's fiction is of particular interest, her engagement with LGBTIQ2 characters and relationships does not by any means end in 2001 with *Last Report.* In the ten years since its debut, Erdrich published five more novels, each with at least passing mentions of queer characters and themes. In fact, Erdrich's next novel, *The Master Butchers Singing Club* (2003), is the first of her texts in which a queer Native character occupies a central role. *The Master Butchers Singing Club* initially seems to follow the path of *The Beet Queen* by focusing on the white inhabitants of Argus, North Dakota, rather than on the lives of the Anishinaabeg people living in or near Argus, which is most likely why the text has received significantly less critical attention than her other novels.[84] Fidelis Waldvogel, a white World War I veteran and German butcher, serves as one of the text's core characters. Readers come to discover as the book unfolds that Fidelis—loosely based on Erdrich's immigrant grandfather, Ludwig Erdrich—exists in a world more culturally diverse than initial appearances suggest. Thus Fidelis's story intertwines with those of several characters who have, or eventually believe they have, some claim to Native ancestry. This list includes Cyprian Lazarre, who, like Karl in *The Beet Queen,* keeps multiple secrets—which in this case means hiding both his Anishinaabe ancestry and his queer desire from public view. Through the character of Cyprian and his relationship to Delphine Watzka, who is Cyprian's partner in a physical and emotional balancing act, *The Master Butchers Singing Club* interrogates the boundaries and limits of queer kinship as well as the links between the suppression of Indigenous histories and the repression of nonheteronormative sexualities.

Readers of *The Master Butchers Singing Club* meet Cyprian and Delphine immediately after Fidelis. In one of Erdrich's classic shell games, she introduces the two as they teeter on the verge of the very thing that will eventually prove the demise of their relationship—heterosexual sex. It is 1934, and the narrator describes the scene: "In a small town on the headwaters of the Mississippi River and in a room rented solely for the purpose of making love, a man and a woman, unclothed and in bed, paused in apprehension. For several months before this hour, they had been comfortably well acquainted, even friends. . . . Inevitably, they both became curious whether there was more and they set off together."[85] Despite their nakedness and close proximity, the two do not consummate their relationship at this moment, though they do begin an intense and often romantic partnership that will be central to both of their lives for years to come. Through the twists and turns of their deep love for one another, Erdrich examines a relationship structured outside the language of hetero- or homonormative family units or erotic affiliations, thereby creating an affective bond I term "catachrestic love."

Though the first scene in *The Master Butchers Singing Club* suggests that Cyprian and Delphine are poised on the edge of a love affair, the culmination (or lack thereof) of the events in the rented bedroom more aptly reflects the shape of their relationship to come. Just as Karl leaps on the bed to distract himself from his potential emotional ties with Wallace, so does Cyprian leap from the bed at pivotal moment, as well, though for slightly different reasons. When Cyprian sees Delphine's nakedness, he reaches to touch her, "sweep[ing] her torso lightly with his knuckles, then the tips of his fingers," feeling not passion but possibility (14). He sees function in the beauty of Delphine's abdominal muscles, and the acrobatic potential of their combined strength leads him to leap onto a chair and into a headstand, where his perfectly formed nude body presents "an ideal picture of manliness" to those outside the window (15). Performance and perception, then, are immediately established as central to Cyprian and Delphine's life together, while heterosexual sex is left by the wayside.

Cyprian performs heterosexuality and heteromasculinity both in the balancing act he and Delphine put on as they travel through Minnesota and North Dakota and in his intimate relationship with her. That performance begins outside the hotel room in their first scene in the novel; when Cyprian shocks onlookers with his naked handstand, Delphine rushes to the street to distract viewers, who comment, as one woman gasps, on his "state of *male indiscretion!*" (16). What the reader knows that the viewers do not is that Cyprian's clearly displayed physical arousal comes from the possibilities he sees in he and Delphine's acrobatic act rather than from a sexual encounter between them. Delphine is fully complicit in their charade of heteronormativity: she defuses the potential outrage of those on the street by pretending to be Cyprian's wife—though notably her married name is her own, "Mrs. Watzka" rather than "Mrs. Lazarre"—and, in a show of quick thinking, uses the potential erotic lure of their imagined sexual encounters to incite viewers to attend their show. Compulsory heterosexuality works to their advantage here as dominant viewers see and desire what they believe to be true—Cyprian epitomizes a hypermasculine physical ideal, and he and Delphine's erotic encounters become the stuff of dreams for some. However, from the first, desire and relationship hinge on display, perception, and sleight of hand in *The Master Butchers Singing Club.*

Delphine and Cyprian's "marriage" is an example of one such illusion. Since heterosexuality and heterocouplehood are legitimated by law and rewarded by societal sanction, the pair could choose to legally partake of the benefits of heterosexual marriage. Significantly, though, they choose to *pass* as married rather than to actually marry. Thus they buy fake wedding rings to perpetuate their charade and use conjugal couplehood both as a prop in their act—Cyprian gives Delphine "falsely passionate" kisses for the benefit of the crowd—and as the necessary veneer of respectability they need to return to Delphine's hometown of Argus (21). Iovannone, who analyzes *The Master Butchers Singing Club* as part of his reading of Erdrich's transgender images, maintains, "The performative nature of Delphine and Cyprian's relationship enables them to survive in a world where compulsory heterosexuality is the norm. As a pair, Delphine and Cyprian are able to navigate various normative societal constructs with more ease than they would be able to if they were not members of such a partnership."[86] Such is undoubtedly the case. In addition, their choice to perform marriage rather than to legally wed suggests they recognize not only the compulsory nature of heterosexuality but also the confining nature of heteronormativity. Delphine's knowledge of this regulation is evident when she implicitly recognizes that marriage is not without its own dangers. Therefore, while she sees her cheap wedding ring as "a little piece of armor against the Lutheran ladies," she notices, too, that "the band seemed tight already, and although it was smooth she'd heard of machines and car doors catching on rings and yanking off or breaking fingers" (46, 45). Their performance offers the safety found in complying with compulsory heterosexuality and holds the threat of physical and psychic mutilation, suggesting that despite her heterosexual desire, Delphine perceives the institutionalized expectations of marriage and couplehood as potentially painful restraints. In *The Master Butchers Singing Club,* heteronormativity causes Cyprian to suppress the open expression of his queer desire, while dominant society's insistence on heterocouplehood pressures Delphine into a conformity she resists throughout the text.[87]

While the queer possibilities of *The Master Butchers Singing Club* seem myriad, Delphine and Cyprian's attempts to find a balance between their love and their differing sexual desires is far more queer for today's readers than Cyprian's lifelong desire for men. Their deep love for each other questions *both* the primacy of heteronormative kinship constructs that rest on the nuclear family *and* the homonormative focus on romantic couplehood and marriage by asking how we name, define, and value significant long-term relationships that are neither erotic nor biological. From the outset, Cyprian and Delphine's bond challenges that requirement: "They both knew the grand passion between them was an affectionate joke. They were something else. They were not-quite-but-more-than family" (50).

Despite what they become, initially Delphine joins Cyprian on the road "because she hoped she'd become infatuated with" him (18). Though not physically attracted to Delphine, Cyprian attempts to meet the demands of heterocouplehood as best he can: the two have sex several times and, in fact, experience "a mysterious bonding" in one of the only two mutually fulfilling sexual encounters they share—an anomaly that hearkens back to the intense relationship between the otherwise queer-identified Karl and Celestine in *The Beet Queen* (25). "It was," the narrator explains, "a strange experience, one they didn't talk about afterward, or, unfortunately, manage to repeat" (25). For her part, Delphine finds Cyprian's striking good looks attractive and, in their first months together, hopes they will be lovers even after she discovers Cyprian in a sexual encounter with a strange man. However, Cyprian's sexual object choice is always clear. When Delphine asks him if it was the war that brought about his desire for men, he briefly considers seizing this explanation as a way out of their awkward conversation but realizes "he'd always known. It was perfectly apparent to him that he had the feelings for men that men usually expressed for girls, then women. What could be more obvious?" (78). If we situate sexuality in erotic desire, then despite his sex with Delphine, Cyprian reads as gay (rather than bi- or asexual). Though he loves Delphine and has sex with her several times at her instigation, he does not, like Karl, find himself surprised by sudden erotic passion for a woman. Of his sexual affinity for men, Cyprian explains, "nothing he'd heard about his desire matched the feelings that he had when he was experiencing this form of love. Then, at those times, it was simply the most basic joy he'd ever felt" (77). And even while she sometimes resists it, Delphine knows this truth, as well: "[S]he had seen him, and what he did was—she couldn't name it exactly, she couldn't put it into words except clumsily—what she saw was *him*. Truly Cyprian. If someone had an essence, his was in that quick stirring between the two men, their energy and pleasure, his happiness" (175). That said, as a gay, Native man in the 1930s, Cyprian could be excused for choosing Delphine as a heterosexual cover for his queer desires. Yet their relationship exceeds such a clichéd convention, which is why their love, while it lasts, can be read as perhaps the queerest in the book.

Cyprian and Delphine's relationship, which is based on a kinship affiliation outside of both blood and sex, has no name in the English language. Their love can be seen as a catachresis, which David L. Eng points out is a "naming" that is simultaneously a "misnaming."[88] A catachresis—perhaps most appropriately in this case—names that which has no name in the English language. In "Epistemology of Metaphor," Paul de Man calls such linguistic instability inherently troubling: "Something monstrous lurks in the most innocent of catachresis: when one speaks of the legs of the table or the face of the mountain, catachresis is already turning into prosopopeia [*sic*], and one begins to perceive a world of potential ghosts and monsters."[89] "Significant others," be they hetero, homo, lesbian, gay, bisexual, transgender, transsexual, intersex, or queer, are defined in terms of sex partners, but in their catachrestic relationship Cyprian and Delphine are, to revise *Hamlet,* something more than kind and less than kin. While Cyprian has long acknowledged his erotic desire for men, the "way he felt about Delphine Watzka was an utter surprise to him, something he'd never expected in his life" (77). Before Delphine, Cyprian "had come back lonely from [World War I] and stayed that way, concentrating on his balance. His brothers had all moved far north into Cree country. His parents were drinkers. His grandparents had wandered off in disgust, headed for someplace where they could die in peace. . . . He was really alone or had been until now. Things had gone past romance [with Delphine]" (49). Though they begin as merely partners in a balancing act, in short order Cyprian and Delphine become more intimate; they live together, sleep together, and share in the physical and financial burden of their household and of caring for Roy, Delphine's lovable but destructively alcoholic father. While men are his sexual object choice, at this point in his life Cyprian chooses his relationship with Delphine as his primary affiliation, telling her in a moment of desperation, "You're all I want out of life" (76). One could argue their relationship is simply Cyprian's concession to the strictures of compulsory heterosexuality, but the narrative repeatedly suggests both he and Delphine feel something more, some nameless but equally valid affective bond with the strength and power most often reserved for family ties. Through Cyprian and Delphine's catachrestic love for each other, Erdrich explores yet another alternate configuration of family and kinship, one based not on genealogy or sex but on a largely platonic but no less significant understanding of love and intimate relationship.

While Cyprian and Delphine's union represents a distinctly important configuration of affective relationship, Cyprian's sexuality also extends Erdrich's previous depictions of queer relationship. Cyprian suppresses his desire for men through a subterfuge reminiscent of *The Beet Queen.* Like Karl, whose story takes place in and around the same geographical area (Minnesota, North Dakota, and Argus in particular) in an overlapping timeframe (the 1930s to the 1970s in Karl's case, the 1930s to the 1940s in Cyprian's), Cyprian's sexual encounters take place in alleys, bars, and park benches, though he does reference having "fallen devoutly in love with another man, whose death he still grieved" during his service in World War I (78).[90] And just as Karl, when young, can only imagine him and his lover as outlaws, so too does Cyprian see "no future in living with a man. In setting up house. He'd never heard of that except in the cities, and he imagined they were different than he was. They didn't get along with regular men" (149–50). Iovannone points out, "In order to act out his queer desires . . . Cyprian must literally go to a space that does not exist—in that such a space does not signify within dominant narratives of gender and sexuality—in order to claim some sort of existence that is representative of his actual desires."[91] Thus a queer relationship initially seems beyond the pale to Cyprian, requiring him to become urban and effeminate, someone who contrasts a "regular man." In *Long Slow Burn,* Weston discusses this common ideology, which depicts the city as *the* idealized gay imaginary. Such "urban/rural contrasts are bound up with the creation of an imagined community peopled by gay subjects."[92] Since "the search for a gay imaginary involves the pursuit of like persons gathered together in space," many who made the move from rural to urban spaces encountered disappointment—what Weston terms "anti-identification"—when they found, in the words of one of her subjects, that "gay people weren't like [them] much at all."[93] Likewise, while Cyprian can imagine gay men and gay community in the city, he cannot imagine himself there or, correspondingly, see himself reflected in those he imagines. Instead, he disidentifies with urban queerness, or what David Bell terms the demand for "metrosexuality."[94] The text suggests Cyprian's experience of Indigeneity underlies some of this psychic dissonance.

Significantly, Cyprian discloses his Native heritage to Delphine in the midst of a stilted conversation about his sexuality. After Delphine stumbles upon Cyprian in a liaison with another man, they don't address her discovery or the ensuing shift in their relationship until a disturbing event with her father finally pushes Delphine to question Cyprian directly. Their discussion is halting and pained. She raises the subject with a cryptic comment—"That man by the river. You know what I'm saying"—and then asks, "'Why do you do it?'" (76, 77). Though his mind races, Cyprian lacks the language to express his feelings and answers briefly, "I don't know" (77). Despite his reticence, Delphine is "determined to obtain the whole truth and nothing less" (77). In pursuit of that truth, she asks her next, seemingly unrelated question: "You're not a Pole with a name like Lazarre" (77). When Cyprian admits to being French, Delphine pushes him further, "Plus what else?" (77). Delphine's overlapping questions about Cyprian's sexuality and ethnicity point to the linkage between heteronormativity and white normativity. Her queries mark both facets of Cyprian's identity as alterities requiring disclosure and explanation. In response, Cyprian's imbricated revelations situate him not only as outside of the fabric of dominant narratives but, in terms of his national difference, as proud of that alterity; this response signals an initial move toward the queer diasporic space in which we leave him at the conclusion of the novel. And while Cyprian remains reticent about his sexual desire, Delphine's question about his ethnicity elicits an impassioned response:

> I'm Chippewa. Ojibwe. The word my grandpa used was Anishinaabeg—the humans. Same thing. . . . My dad was half French and my mom was part French, too. Have you heard of michifs or métis? . . . I guess not, but if you had, you'd have heard of my famous ancestor, Louis Riel, who died a martyr to the great vision of a mixed-blood nation—not a loose band or batch of hunters. A place with boundaries and an actual government taking up a big chunk of Manitoba. There's lots of us who still dream about it! (77–78)

Cyprian's Indigenous nationalism is not visible in his public life, which, as he talks to Delphine, is circumscribed by the interlocking strictures of racism and homophobia. In fact, Cyprian's ties to Indigeneity had heretofore been only briefly mentioned and, in those citations, figured as a site of loss. For example, when he returned injured from World War I, "he came home before it even occurred to him that, as an Ojibwe, he was not yet a

U.S. citizen. During his slow recuperation, he couldn't vote" (15). Yet in the face of multiple possible exclusions from settler society, Cyprian cites an alternate history of land and nation. Moreover, he refutes the iteration of "band" as a synonym for "nation," acknowledging the ways the terms circulate in dominant narratives of land and sovereignty, which often meld "tribe" and "band" with notions of the primitive to justify manifest destiny and the nationhood of settler colonies. In Cyprian's narrative, nation is bound not to the settler state but to *Indigenous* sovereignty—Native land with "boundaries" and "government." Additionally, Cyprian's nationalistic feelings and his pride at his relationship to the charismatic Louis Riel, a hero to many and the political and spiritual leader of the Métis people, proposes Indigeneity, not queerness, as a site of productive possibility and futurity. The conversation between Cyprian and Delphine therefore suggests that though he passes for white just as he passes for heterosexual because of normative assumptions about both identities, Cyprian experiences these two facets of his identity differently: here, Cyprian's Indigenous nationalism counters discomfort about his sexual desires.[95] While Indigeneity holds potential for a future tense, queerness, when imagined solely as located in urban geography, stands emphatically outside the boundaries of Cyprian's queer Indigenous imaginary.

Cyprian embraces both his Indigenous homelands and same-sex desire by the time he disappears from Argus into the queer diaspora of his future; however, the two facets of his identity remain irreconcilable within the Argus community, where such imbricated relationships are refused and where, in contrast to Delphine, Cyprian remains an outsider. Innumerable moments mark Cyprian's separation from Argus society. For example, he, Delphine, and Roy reside in Roy's house, which Delphine calls the "house at the end of the world"—a space literally and figuratively on the outskirts of Argus (302). Though the three form their own powerful bonds within the pieced-together sanctuary of the house, both their living space and their relationships evade the strictures of convention and white heteronormative community. Moreover, Cyprian's occupations as vaudevillian performer and bootlegger—he conducts secretive trips north during which Delphine suspects he has liaisons with men—further mark him as both culturally perverse and legally suspect. Outside the boundaries, identities, and relationships sanctioned by settler state logics, Cyprian operates in the sort of queer diaspora space investigated by queer of color scholars like Gayatri Gopinath, Walcott, and Eng, as underlined by his departure and brief reappearance in Argus.[96] The conclusion of Cyprian's relationship with Delphine, who functions as his connection to the largely white town of Argus and to his performance of heteronormativity, precipitates his embrace of the possibilities of queer diaspora. After recognizing Delphine's attachment to Fidelis and his children, Cyprian buys her a ring and asks her to legally marry him. Following Delphine's weary rejection of his proposal, he disappears from Argus, leaving her free to marry Fidelis. When Cyprian returns for a brief visit several months after Delphine and Fidelis marry, his reappearance underscores both his distance from Argus community and his recognition that the queer space beyond social stricture represents something more than disenfranchisement and loss. In fact, Cyprian's departure from Argus brings him not into exile but into a newly defined understanding of self, nation, and desire. These possibilities are briefly articulated when Cyprian and his new partner, Vilhus Gast (the "Snake Man"), put on a carnivalesque vaudevillian act that includes a series of comic, acrobatic gags; a python; and a spider named Mighty Tom.[97]

Here, again, we see the relational nature of Erdrich's meditations on queerness: Cyprian escapes Argus's constraints by reconciling same-sex desire with his previously articulated sense of Indigenous nationalism. This reconciliation arises directly from Cyprian's diasporic relationship with Vilhus, a Lithuanian refugee. Cyprian's first conversation with Roy after his return reveals that Vilhus is more than simply his partner in performance. The bedridden older man jokes, "My pole hasn't been painted for the last twenty-six years. What about yours?" To this, Cyprian replies, "The paint's fresh on mine" (315). This off-color exchange would mean little if not followed by Cyprian's seemingly casual comment to Delphine, "My partner's name is Vilhus Gast" (317). Delphine immediately recognizes the statement for what it is—an acknowledgement that Vilhus is both Cyprian's performance partner and his lover. Importantly, Cyprian threads this erotic relationship with Indigenous community when he tells the story of bringing Vilhus home:

> "Well, he's a lot like me . . . A performer, you know. He made it over here from Lithuania and he's a Jew. I was a real curiosity to him at first. I took him home with me." Cyprian laughed. "Boy was he surprised."
>
> "How come?"

> "There's no Jews on the reservation, I mean to speak of. I never knew one when I was growing up, any more than he'd know an Indian. Except he did know about us and said he believed we were one of the lost tribes of Israel doomed to wander, too, like his people. Always to be on the edge of things. Hounded and hunted, he said. 'Well, okay,' I said. 'So let's roam around together.' So we got this act up and since then we've been playing it steady." (317)

Given the ongoing links between performance, compulsory heterosexuality, and heteronormativity in *The Master Butchers Singing Club,* Cyprian's comment that Vilhus is a "performer" who is "like" him suggests Vilhus, too, has most likely been passing as straight. Moreover, queerness and Indigeneity reconnect in this scene *through* queer diasporic affiliation. While sexual desire circulates as the unstated impetus for Cyprian and Vilhus's initial interaction, their outsider status and common experiences of historical trauma, of being "hounded and hunted," provide the entry point to their relationship. For Cyprian, then, erotic relationship and a return to the reservation arise from that diasporic connection; thus the space of exile, outside the limit of every dominant norm, engenders alliance and reconnection. To find this space of return, Cyprian must refute the logics of a settler colonial society that cast him as an outsider in his own country, while Vilhus would have fled a nationalist invasion in which "more that 90% of Litthuania's 240,000 Jews were killed" in the Nazi occupation.[98] As Cyprian describes it, such trauma becomes the point of convergence that enables the men to move forward together, thereby enabling him to experience home as something more than that of alienation and loss.[99] This convergence is reminiscent of Gopinath's contention that queer diasporic desire makes settler colonialism visible. Speaking of *My Beautiful Launderette* (1985), she argues, "The barely submerged histories of colonialism and racism erupt into the present at the very moment when queer sexuality is being articulated."[100] Similarly, Erdrich depicts same-sex desire as the mechanism that makes diasporic trauma and queer diaspora legible.

In terms of the larger narrative of *The Master Butchers Singing Club,* however, the queer diasporic possibilities so potentially transformative for Cyprian remain fast within the walls of Roy's house, leaving the settler politics of Argus in stasis. Vilhus himself is introduced to neither Roy nor Delphine. Furthermore, outside the confines of the Watzka household,

Cyprian and Vilhaus are known solely by their outrageous performance, which makes them legend in the small town of Argus. The narrator explains,

> For weeks after Cyprian and the Snake Man had vanished . . . people stopped Delphine in the street. They treated her with shy admiration. She received the deference of one who knows, or has access to, a great artist. They addressed her with respect. They wanted details, secrets.
>
> "The python, has it eaten anyone?"
>
> "Has the spider underneath Cyprian's nose ever caused him to sneeze? If he did, what would happen?"
>
> "Where did he learn to juggle? To ride a unicycle?" (320)

While Cyprian and Vilhus are admired, they are simultaneously exoticized and set apart. Looking at performance history, José Esteban Muñoz, in *Disidentifications,* discusses what he calls the "'burden of liveness' that inflects the experience of the postcolonial, queer, and other minoritarian subjects. The story of 'otherness' is one tainted by a mandate to 'perform' for the amusement of the dominant power bloc. If there is any acceptable place for 'queers' in the homophobic national imaginary, it certainly is onstage—being 'funny' for a straight audience."[101] In the same manner, despite years in Argus, Cyprian remains the consummate outsider defined by fetishized difference who conveniently vanishes into the night after providing hours of entertainment for the locals. This temporality is part of the "burden of liveness," in which "the minoritarian subject can only exist in the moment" without "the privilege or pleasure of being a historical subject," a settler colonial erasure that is especially marked in light of Cyprian's history; though he creates diasporic connections through his relationship with Vilhaus, he remains spectacle, curiosity, in settler space.[102] Marked by disconnection, silence, a lack of community relationship, and eventual disappearance, Erdrich's depiction of Cyprian reminds us that, to use Muñoz words, "minoritarian subjects don't always dance because they're happy; sometimes their feet are being shot at."[103]

Queer Pathology and Historical Absence in *The Plague of Doves*

Erdrich's 2004 novel, *Four Souls,* picks up at the end of *Tracks,* letting her readers know at long last where Fleur went after she walked away with the bones of her ancestors when her trees toppled dangerously around loggers on the shores of Matchimanito. In many ways, every relationship in *Four Souls* could be read as queer: from Fleur's revenge-driven marriage to John James Mauser, the developer who took Fleur's land; to the surprising reversal of the affections of Miss Polly Elizabeth Gheen, Mauser's ex-sister-in-law who comes to call Fleur kin; to the joyful insanity of Nanapush and Margaret's constant battle of wits, no love falls within what would seem to be the boundaries of the everyday. The novel has less to say than *The Master Butchers Singing Club,* however, about the workings of LGBTIQ2 desire. Within those more limited parameters, one of the only potentially queer characters is John James Mauser's first wife, Placide Mauser (née Placide Armstrong Gheen), who occupies only a tertiary role in the text.

When Fleur arrives at the Mauser house in search of employment as the first step in her plan for revenge, she is hired by Placide's sister, Polly, who runs the household while Placide paints. Placide's lack of sexual desire for her husband is among the few details readers discover about her. Placide "stiffened harder than the iron banisters when she was touched," and, the narrator explains, "trying to make love to her was for young Mr. Mauser like touching the frozen body of a window mannequin."[104] Placide's real passion, which she calls a "vibrational urge," stems from her painting teacher's twice-weekly lessons where "the two seclude themselves for hours, engrossed in an intense exploration of form and color" (17). During these hours, Placide and her teacher, like Placide and her husband, practice the subtle art of Karezza, which arose as an alternative sexual practice in the late nineteenth century. In her 1896 book *Karezza: Ethics of Marriage,* feminist physician Alice Stockham, who was also involved in the free love movement, calls Karezza a "sexual science." "Karezza," she explains, "consummates marriage in such a manner that through the power of will, and loving thoughts, the final crisis is not reached, but a complete control by both husband and wife is maintained throughout the entire relation.... [I]n the course of an hour the physical tension subsides, the spiritual exaltation increases, and not uncommonly visions of a transcendent life are seen and consciousness of new powers experienced."[105] At the highest plane of success, a trance is achieved.[106] Placide's insistence she and her husband engage in Karezza is deemed a queer enough practice that, with the support of his medical doctor and the church, Mauser is able to annul their marriage and marry Fleur.[107] Through her brief but comical depiction of Placide and the exercise of Karezza, Erdrich again queers heterosexual sex and, as Peter Beidler notes, gently mocks her white characters' sexual relationships and practices.[108]

The Painted Drum, Erdrich's 2005 novel, returns to the present day to tell the story of Faye Travers's discovery of a sacred drum tuned by the hidden bones of Fleur Pillager's half-sister, a young Anishinaabe girl killed by wolves as their mother left her husband to be with her lover. Faye's journey to return the drum briefly brings her, as one of the last Pillager descendants, back to the reservation. Her journey and the repatriation of the drum spark Bernard Shaawano's retelling of Fleur's family history and the drum's origin. The narrative turns on the story of heterosexual love gone awry, of a windigo love so consuming it damages everyone it contacts. Though such love could undoubtedly be read as queer, Erdrich's most recent representations of explicitly same-sex desire can be seen in Evelina Harp's lesbian relationship, which occurs in Erdrich's 2008 novel, *The Plague of Doves.*

Evelina's first love is Corwin Peace, whose name she traces on her body "a million times" before she turns her fervent affections to their sixth-grade teacher, Sister Mary Anita Buckendorf. Through both this platonic attachment and Evelina's later lesbian affair, *The Plague of Doves* investigates how the absence of relationship impedes queer desire. Evelina's first passionate same-sex attachment arises from a powerful affective encounter—a combined experience of shame and empathy—after Sister Mary Anita discovers Evelina drawing her caricature, a jagged-toothed dinosaur in a nun's robes. The nun, whose habit emphasizes extraordinary facial features—what the narrator calls a "great raw-boned jackal's muzzle"—asks Evelina to look her in the eye, explaining such mockery has the power to emotionally wound.[109] Evelina describes her response: "My eyes spilled over again. I knew that the strange feelings that had come upon me and transfixed me were the same feelings that Mary Anita felt. I had never felt another person's feelings, never in my life" (46). This intense empathetic encounter leads Evelina to realize, "Oh God, I am *in love*" (47). Like the affective connection between Scranton Roy and the baby he nurses in *The Antelope Wife,* this queer connection balances on the difficult edge of settler history, which in *The Plague of Doves* plays out the tangled relationships among the white and Anishinaabeg families (and the convergence of the two) who live on the reservation and in the neighboring towns of Pluto and Hoopdance, North Dakota.

Evelina's continued iteration of Sister Mary Anita's name eventually leads Seraph Milk, who Evelina calls Mooshum (grandfather in Anishinaabemowin), to tell the story around which the text repeatedly circles—the vigilante hanging of three Anishinaabeg men for their supposed murder of a white farm family, a crime they did not commit. Thus while Evelina's first experience of queer relationship stems from empathetic connection, the story that drives the text emerges from its polar opposite—a racially charged violence that necessitates the radical denial of relationship. This injustice was perpetrated by, among others, Sister Mary Anita's great grandfather, Emil Buckendorf, who was instrumental in hanging Paul Holy Track; Paul's guardian, Asiginak; and Mooshum's good friend, Cuthbert Peace. The knowledge of this atrocity haunts Evelina, who finds herself related to those who hanged on the tree (her Mooshum, who was cut down before he died) and those who did the hanging (Eugene Wildstrand, Evelina's great grandfather and the father of Mooshum's wife, Junesse). Upon discovering their shared history, a logic of separation supplants Evelina's regard for Sister Mary Anita: Evelina "be[comes] obsessed with lineage" and with "trac[ing] the blood history of the murders" (86). In this case, then, biology severs rather than builds relationship: genealogy entwines with the history of settler violence to supersede the early stirrings of queer affection.[110] Thus through her depiction of Evelina's discovery and subsequent rejection of her feelings for Sister Mary Anita, Erdrich asks, What does it mean to be in relationship? What are the intersections and boundaries of queer desire and kinship?

Through Evelina's ruminations on relationship, *The Plague of Doves* interrogates the effects of violence on affective connection as seen in the troubled dynamics of Evelina's short-lived lesbian relationship. As an adult, Evelina follows a brief stint in college with a position at a mental institution that results in an affair with Nonette, a patient who battles manic depression. The fact that the space of the institution backgrounds the women's relationship brings to light the troubling history in which racialized/queer bodies and desires have been controlled and pathologized. In terms of situating their liaison historically, their 1972 encounter comes only a year before the board of directors of the American Psychiatric Association removed "homosexuality" from their *Diagnostic and Statistical Manual of Mental Disorders* (DSM). This hotly contested elision was followed by a 1974 vote by the association's membership, where the decision was upheld.[111] In the 1972 Midwest mental institution they inhabit, homosexuality is undoubtedly still considered a pathology, and Nonette's understanding of her gender performance and sexual desire circulates within this paradigm: Nonette ultimately cultivates queer gender performance and desire as a symptom of illness. Nonette has an imperious and often overly affected style; along with pretending to be French and occasionally barking orders, she flamboyantly claims a transgender identity, which she attempts to enact by, for example, wearing "a man's shirt . . . necktie and men's chino pants" with "feminine kitten heels" and "black eyeliner" (231). She looks, Evelina explains, "depressed but, it could not be denied, also chic" (231). Though Nonette is the patient and Evelina the psychiatric aide, Nonette controls their interactions, kissing Evelina as they talk on the institute's sun porch, approaching her again when they pass in underground steam tunnels, and later telling the matron Evelina had requested a patient visit during off-duty hours, a lie that culminates in their sex at Evelina's staff dorm room. However, Nonette's pursuit of Evelina stems as much from her purposeful, self-conscious performance of "illness" as from erotic desire.

Nonette's description of her illness depicts the pathologized understandings of sex and gender that were the norm in the years after the histories depicted in *The Antelope Wife* and *Last Report on the Miracles at Little No Horse.* For example, in one of her first extended conversations with Evelina, Nonette states, "I want to talk about how really, truly, sick I am" (232). She continues, "If I could just be born over, . . . I'd be born neutral. Women or man, that's not what I mean. I wouldn't have a sex drive. I wouldn't care about it, need it or anything. It's just a problem, things that you do, which you hate yourself for afterward" (232). She goes on to tell of her repeated sexual abuse at the hands of a male relative when she was nine years old, situating that assault as the moment when she begins to "smell" like sex, "feel different," and search out other sexual encounters (232). In this scene, Nonette describes patterns common to "adults and adolescents molested as children [who] are prone to episodes of frequent, short-term sexual activity, often with a number of different sexual partners."[112] She situates her gender and sexuality within this place of physical and psychic damage: "I'm messed up. I'm in a state hospital. I think I want a sex-change operation. I want to be a man so I won't have to put up with this shit" (232). Nonette's experience of transgender embodiment stands in direct contrast to the gender variance of Erdrich's Two-Spirit characters. Rather than functioning as a community-centered healer or sacred figure, Nonette deploys nonnormative gender performance as a highly individual practice, one she employs to counter the trauma of child abuse and, whether consciously or unconsciously, to distance herself from relationship. Thus for this white 1970s survivor of sexual abuse, gender nonconformity circulates as pathology.

Initially, Nonette locates sexual desire as the key to bodily and psychic boundaries. Desire, in her experience as a victim and survivor of abuse, becomes the site of trauma. As a result, for Nonette, the reverberations of assault shape her subsequent erotic interactions and gender identification. In their research on the long-term impact of childhood sexual abuse, John N. Briere and Diane M. Elliott explain that one outcome of "abuse-related fear among adult survivors" can be "an association between sexual stimuli" and various manifestations of pain, fear, and anxiety, which explains the negative connotations Nonette attributes to sexual desire.[113] If, in Nonette's estimation, desire is the root of her problems, gender variance functions as the key to mental and physical safety; rather than being a link to community, an alternate gender performance functions as physical and psychic separation. Nonette claims she "want[s] to be a man" to escape the "shit" of her life. Moreover, she subsequently challenges Evelina by claiming phallic power: "Oh, look at you, trying to be tough. You're not tough. You're like, a little college girl, right? Who the hell cares. I'm from the university, too. I have a Ph.D. Pretty Hot Dick. I am a man, posing as a woman. You want proof?" (233). Ironically, despite her claims to a transgressive gender identity, Nonette's threats hinge on heteropatriarchal logics: she attempts to cow Evelina by infantilizing her, using the gendered appellation "little girl" to negate the small amount of institutional power Evelina holds as a mental health aide; Nonette meets the perceived intellectual challenge of Evelina's college experience with the threat of hypermasculinity. With every response—from her "too big and comically masculine" attire to her unprovoked verbal attacks—Nonette wields gender like a defensive weapon, used to shield herself and wound others in a practice that differs radically from Erdrich's previous depictions of gender variance (234). In this context, we can see that Nonette's transgender identity serves as a distinctly individual self-preservation and psychological protection that contrasts Erdrich's previous narratives of queer relationship.

The disciplinary nature of the institution and its history of queer pathology further compound this distance. While from all accounts Nonette's abuser remains unpunished, her own "transgressive" behavior leads to her incarceration and an institutional attempt to "cure" her. In fact, Nonette gains her release by transforming into a Stepford version of herself with "scary cheerleader eyes" and "ultra-normal Midwest catalogue clothes"

(238, 239). Through the specter of the institution, Erdrich reminds us of painful settler histories in which bodies and desires marked as other were restrained, physically altered, and/or erased. Much as *Tales of Burning Love,* then, Erdrich counters pathological narratives of normalization, questioning the parameters and price of inclusion into the heteronorm.

While Nonette's experience of transgression privileges individuality, alienation, and conformity, through her depiction of Evelina, Erdrich highlights the necessity of familial relationship and historical continuity. Evelina's experience of their short affair counters Nonette's in nearly every way. Rather than an act of transgression or rebellion, their first kiss is, for Evelina, "no different than other times I'd kissed someone for the first time. There was the same tentative heat, the same curiosity" (234). However, Evelina recognizes the shifting nature of performance and perception when she continues, "Only she was supposed to be crazy, I was supposed to be not crazy, and we were women. Or maybe Nonette was just troubled, I was less troubled, and she claimed to be a man. She pretended she was a man. Or she pretended that she was pretending" (234). The multiple possible readings of their transgressive gender performances are of much less consequence to Evelina than her erotic response to Nonette and the fact that she "couldn't stop thinking of her" (235). In contrast to Nonette, who relates desire to fear or power, submission or domination, Evelina finds an unexpected level of comfort and ease in same-sex desire. Even though she "didn't know at the time women could kiss women in that way anywhere but in Paris," she finds their physical encounter "entirely familiar, much more so than if I were touching a boy I'd never touched before . . . because our bodies are the same" (235, 236). As a result, Evelina describes Nonette as "the one I'd always needed," constructing a romantic narrative around their queer encounters that would rival any "tale of burning love" contained in Celestine's novels.

Ultimately, though, Evelina's queer relationship results in a troubling reversal: when Nonette checks out of the mental institution, Evelina checks in. And while Two-Spirit histories are not invoked in *The Plague of Doves* as they are in *The Antelope Wife* and *Last Report,* their absence can be read as central to Evelina's breakdown. Evelina's trauma is rooted in her feelings of isolation and her lack of extant Indigenous models of queer desire. To Evelina, queers are non-Native, Indians are straight, and she herself is adrift somewhere in the middle. Before Evelina takes the position at the state mental hospital, she spends a semester at college where the white girls play Joni Mitchell and grow their hair long, while the "Dakota, Chippewa, and mixed-blood [girls] like" her either fade to the background or "swagger around furious in ribbon shirts with AIM-looking boyfriends" (222). A "middle-class BIA Indian" who "wanted to go to Paris," Evelina feels like an outsider on every front. Hiding out in the poetry section of the library, Evelina discovers Anaïs Nin: "She became my muse, my model, my everything" (223). With no other guiding models, Evelina follows this decidedly white representation of lesbian identity when she enters into a relationship with Nonette: "There was nothing in the many stories of reversal and romance among my aunts and uncles to guide me here. A kiss from another girl set me outside the narrative. . . . I was in Anaïs's story now" (235). Queer desire starkly contrasts family and Indigeneity in this estimation, leaving Evelina to find alternate forms of self-definition. But eventually, Evelina recognizes that Nin's cosmopolitan edginess has failed her.

The disastrous aftermath of Evelina's brief lesbian affair, of her attempt to inhabit "Anaïs's story" in *The Plague of Doves,* points to the importance of Two-Spirit histories for queer or questioning Native youth. Seeing no models for her own desire in the heteronormative relationships of her family, however happy they might be, Evelina looks elsewhere. She finds her place, for a brief time, in the countercultural narratives of writers like Nin and Sylvia Plath who were legendary feminist icons.[114] But in the end, she explains, they "provid[ed] the treacherous paradigm of a life I was always too backwards, or provincial, or Catholic, or reservation- or family-bound to absorb and pull off" (241). Evelina's depiction of the alienating paradigm Nin represents speaks to the cognitive dissonance she feels between her familial background and her desire; much like Cyprian in *The Master Butchers Singing Club,* this dissonance sets Evelina "outside the narrative" of her home community as she understands it. At the same time, Nin's eroticism, which rests on a romanticized outsider status grounded in individualism rather than family or nation, also fails her. She recognizes that while Nonette sees of her as part of "her illness, a symptom of which she thinks she has been cured. She, on the other hand, is what I was looking for" (240). The conjunction between Evelina's embrace of queer desire as an individually constructed, culturally discontinuous practice and her attendant feelings of communal and familial disconnection spark a deep depression that results in her being placed in Nonette's bed in the state mental hospital. Importantly, Evelina gradually emerges from her depression as a direct result of the visits and love of her family and friends. Her recovery thus hinges on relationship, emphasizing the healing capacity of familial bonds while further reinforcing the need for queer Indigenous role models.

Reading across Erdrich's canon, one could argue that the presence of Two-Spirit people and histories in *The Antelope Wife* and *Last Report* highlights the impact of their historical elision as represented by Evelina's experience in *The Plague of Doves.* In *The Antelope Wife,* Anishinaabeg gender logics play a central role in Blue Prairie Woman's psychological and spiritual healing. That renaming and mental restoration also function as a community healing since Blue Prairie Woman's pain and loss are reverberations from a larger network of settler colonial violence. In *Last Report,* the historical memory of those restorative Anishinaabeg gender logics enables Agnes's/Father Damien's nonnormative gender performance to be recognized and accepted by members of the Little No Horse community, who, in turn, accept, nurture, and, some would argue, eventually save the priest, body and soul. Evelina is a member of these same communities, but her narrative suggests that several generations after "Wishkob, the Sweet, seduced many men and finally joined the family of a great war chief as a wife," knowledge of such traditions has waned.[115] Thus she perceives herself, to return to her words, as having no "guide" and views queer desire as that which "set[s] [her] outside the narrative" of her family (235). In many ways, Evelina's experience returns us to key moments in 1980s queer of color critiques such as Gloria Anzaldúa's "To(o) Queer the Writer" and *Borderlands/La Frontera,* Cherríe Moraga's *Loving in the War Years,* Lorde's *Sister Outsider,* and, as discussed in chapter 1, the work of the many lesbians/queers of color in *This Bridge Called My Back* and subsequent women of color/queer of color anthologies. In each case, these theorists point to the importance of being able to claim erotic sensibility within their own cultural contexts. When discussing the critical imperative that brought her to theorize queerness outside dominant constructions of sexuality, Anzaldúa explains, "I think of lesbians as predominately white and middle-classed women. . . . 'Lesbian' doesn't name anything in my homeland."[116] Anzaldúa's words resonate with Erdrich's depiction of Evelina, pointing to the necessity of an Indigenous erotic that situates temporal and spatial understandings of queerness within one's own community.

To turn from the specific to the large scale, this chapter concludes with a number of claims about what such a study of Erdrich's queer relationships can show us. Perhaps most obviously, analyzing the depictions of queer images and Two-Spirit characters in Erdrich's novels recovers the author's significant intervention in the project of queering Native literatures, which is, of course, the endeavor at the center of this book. The range of desires and gender expressions represented in *The Beet Queen* is unprecedented in Native fiction at that historical moment. Thus in the mid-1980s, though it was not discussed at the time, Erdrich was not only breaking ground in Indigenous literary studies with her wide-ranging and complex depictions of erotic attachments but also consistently providing depictions of queer relationships that forwarded theoretical challenges to the heteronorm. To reiterate just a few such challenges, *Tales of Burning Love* subsequently extends the interrogation of heterosexuality that began in Erdrich's depiction of Karl and Celestine's affair. The juxtaposition of Jack's dysfunctional marriages with Candice and Marlis's relationship calls into question the primacy and normalcy afforded the latter. *The Antelope Wife* and *Last Report,* while extending Erdrich's previous investigations of gender performance, also shift the focus to Indigenous understandings of genders and sexualities by introducing the historical existence of Two-Spirit people within the Anishinaabeg community in Erdrich's ongoing historical saga. In terms of Erdrich's canon and queer Indigenous studies, her depiction of Evelina in *The Plague of Doves* emphasizes the importance of both the extant knowledge of Two-Spirit traditions and everyday representations of queer Native people. Craig Womack's Creek trickster, Rabbit, suggests that with no stories about their lives, gay and lesbian Native readers "will become haunted."[117] He further conjectures, "Mebeso if writers don't write about things, they is partly responsible for turning kids into ghosts. If Indian writers write only about straight Indians and not all kinda Indians, what sets them apart from white writers making up Indian romances?"[118] *The Plague of Doves* shows the impact of one such haunting, while Erdrich's canon as a whole meets Womack's call for the regular inclusion of queer literary representations. Strikingly, though, Erdrich's radical erotic politics have, even today, received too little critical attention. The movement from Wallace to Wishkob, then, speaks both to Erdrich's multifaceted contributions to the field of Native literature and to the productivity of recognizing and analyzing the Two-Spirit texts and images that have long circulated within the field.

· CHAPTER 4 ·

Forced to Choose

Queer Indigeneity in Film

> *I write because I am aware that whoever controls the image controls the population; that those who define us determine not only our lives, but our concept of our selves, and that colonization begins and ends with the definer, the contextualizer, and the propagandist.*
>
> —Paula Gunn Allen, "Going Home, December 1992"

IN THIS CHAPTER'S EPIGRAPH, Paula Gunn Allen suggests that definitions—or, more specifically, the circulation of particular forms of imagistic discourse—matter to Indigenous people and, I would add, to Indigenous studies. This chapter begins, then, with a question that follows her contention—if prominent writers like Allen, Maurice Kenny, and Louise Erdrich have crafted images of Two-Spirit/lesbian, gay, bisexual, transgender, transsexual, intersex, and queer (LGBTIQ2) Native people for academic and reading publics, what images have been used to depict queer Native people in the media most accessible to the general public—contemporary narrative film? I turn from literature to such visual media because of the unquestionable reality that films, whether made by Native or non-Native filmmakers, function just as Allen suggests—as interventions into modes of understanding about queer Indigeneities. In *Reservation Reelism,* Michelle H. Raheja contends "films serve as pedagogy and knowledge production for spectators."[1] While Corinn Columpar, in *Unsettling Sights: The Fourth World on Film,* likewise notes "cinema plays" a "specific role" in identity formations "by way of the multiple intersubjective interactions it fosters: those that condition film production . . . [and] those that occur when heterogeneous audiences watch films that represent Aboriginal peoples and cultures (or, for that matter, that rely on them as a signifying absence). . . . The result is an identification of the conventions by which Aboriginality is represented and, in turn, an exploration of their legibility and resonance outside as well as inside the specific national contexts in which they are employed."[2] As both Raheja and Columpar underscore in their scholarship, the importance of film has long been noted in Indigenous studies. In fact, in the past few years alone, media representations by/about Indigenous people have been analyzed, to name just a few recent texts, in monographs by Columpar, Johanna Feier, Joanna Hearne, Raheja, and Lee Schweninger and edited collections such as Denise Cummings's *Visualities,* Sigurjón Baldur Hafsteinsson and Marian Bredin's *Indigenous Screen Cultures in Canada,* and M. Elise Marubbio and Eric L. Buffalohead's *Native Americans on Film.*[3] There has not yet, however, been a book devoted entirely to queer Native film, though such work is undoubtedly on the horizon from scholars like Gabriel S. Estrada (Rarámuri, Caxcan Nahua, Chiricahua Apache, and Mestizo/a) or Sophie Mayer.

Queer Indigenous Characters and Two-Spirit Films

Perhaps the best-known iteration of a queer Native person in narrative film is the character Little Horse (played by Robert Little Star) in Arthur Penn's classic 1970 revisionist Western, *Little Big Man.* A parody of a Cheyenne heemanhe, Little Horse attempts to woo his childhood friend, Jack Crabb (Dustin Hoffman). Both Thomas Berger's 1964 novel—the book on which the film is based—and Penn's film participate in the counterculture critiques of the period.[4] They align with the multiculturalist imperatives of *Fag Rag,* which, like Penn's film, employed an inclusive but still settler-focused framework to question dominant social and political norms. Thus Penn offers a massacre scene that intentionally invokes U.S. atrocities in Vietnam and both director and novelist, despite presenting Little Horse as a swishing caricature of a queen, also craft sympathetic renderings of Indigenous characters.[5] At the same time, however, much as in chapter 2's discussion of *Fag Rag,* a white gaze—in this case Crabb's—frames and directs narrative perception. Recognizing this perspective, Maurice Kenny notes in "Tinselled Bucks" that Little Horse is "placed in the novel for comic relief," even while Berger also "gave Little Horse a husband and a certain amount of joy in the union."[6] In both Berger's novel and Penn's film adaptation, the queer Indigenous figure signifies a humorous "primitive" difference *and* a sympathetic point of identification for settler sexuality.[7]

At present, the majority of films by and/or about queer Indigenous people are not narrative films but documentaries and shorts with a number of the latter arising from Canada's vibrant Aboriginal film scene.[8] Early documentaries include Smith's previously mentioned *Honored by the Moon* and her 1988 educational film that highlights the life of novelist/activist Carol laFavor, *Her Giveaway: A Spiritual Journey with AIDS*, as well as Michel Beauchemin, Lori Levy, and Gretchen Vogel's *Two-Spirit People* (1991).[9] Among the many twenty-first-century documentaries that center around queer Native people are Rope Wolf's (White Mountain Apache) *Two-Spirits: Belonging* (2005), which focuses on urban Indian experience; Ruth Fertig's *Two Spirits* (2007), a portrait of Two-Spirit Jicarilla Apache activist Joey Criddle; Sharon A. Desjariais's (Cree/Métis/Ojibwe) *Two-Spirited* (2007), which recounts Two-Spirit dancer Rodney "Geeyo" Poucette's (Chiniki) initially difficult involvement in the traditionally female jingle dress competition; Ruth Villasenor's (Chiricahua Apache/Mexican) *Traditional Indigenous Values* (2009), which considers marriage equality and settler colonialist incursions on Indigenous knowledges; Lydia Nibley's widely viewed *Two Spirits* (2010), a full-length documentary that chronicles queer Diné teenager F. C. Martinez's life and 1991 murder;[10] and *Native American LGBT Two Spirit* (2012), a segment of the "Our Families" series, produced by Basic Rights Oregon. Crafting similar genealogical arguments as those discussed in chapter 1, each of these documentaries invokes the history of Indigenous gender diversity alongside sympathetic portraits of contemporary queer Native people.

In addition to documentaries, a remarkable range of shorts by and about queer Indigenous people—though lesser known than feature-length narrative films examined in the body of this chapter—serve as a valuable resource for queer Indigenous studies. These shorts include (but are by no means limited to) the often wickedly funny, experimental films by Thirza Cuthand (Cree) such as *Lessons in Baby Dyke Theory* (1995), *Through the Looking Glass* (1999), *Anhedonia* (2001), and *You Are a Lesbian Vampire* (2008);[11] Cree visual artist/performer/filmmaker Kent Monkman's many installation pieces, which range from the narrative dance performance of *A Nation Is Coming* (1996) to the postapocalyptic *Future Nation* (2005) to his series of comic reversals in which Monkman's fabulous alter ego, Miss Chief Eagle Testickle, challenges Western art history and non-Native artists like George Catlin—*Group of Seven Inches* (2005), *Shooting Geronimo* (2007), *Robin's Hood* (2007), and *Dance to the Berdashe* (2008); James Diamond's (Cree/Métis) explorations of transidentity—*The Man from Venus* (1999) and *Mars-Womb-Man* (2006)—and his critique of rape apologists,

I Am the Art Scene Starring Woman Polanski (2010); Kevin Lee Burton's (Swampy Cree) experimental Cree-language films *Meskanahk* (2005) and *Nikamowin (Song)* (2008); Cree/Métis filmmaker Adam Garnet Jones's animated *Thunderstorm* (2005) and autobiographical *Cloudmaker* (2006), as well as his *Demonstrations of Indianness #31* (2006), which he constructs from his grandfather's 1950s home movies, and his nearly irresistible declaration of Indigenous pride, *Wave a Red Flag* (2009); Shawn Imitates Dog's (Oglala Lakota) *Two Spirits, One Journey* (2007), an eighteen-minute drama that follows the romance of two young Pine Ridge men; Carrie House's (Diné) animated *Two-Embrace* (2009); and Jeremy Hirsch's darkly comic *Natives* (2013), a twenty-minute narrative film that explores the fascination a non-Native lesbian has with her partner's Indigenous background.[12] As to be expected, there is no single through line in the work of these writers and directors, though most privilege explorations of self, community, gender, sexuality, and Indigeneity.

Full-length experimental films that depict queer Indigenous people include Mohawk visual artist Shelly Niro's 1998 *Honey Moccasin,* Métis filmmaker Clint Alberta's *Deep Inside Clint Star* (2000), and Duane Ghastant'Aucoin's (Tlingit) *"Kichx Anagaat Yatx'I": Children of the Rainbow* (2003). In Niro's parody, the protagonist, Honey (Tantoo Cardinal, Métis), transforms into a Sherlock Holmes–style detective, complete with cloak and magnifying glass, to track down missing powwow regalia stolen by Zachary John (played by actor/playwright Bill Merasty), the queer Native owner of the Inukshuk café, who proceeds to wear the purloined regalia in a sort of private drag performance before Honey apprehends him.[13] Alberta's film walks the line between documentary and ironic, sometimes brilliant commentary on the genre itself. Composed of a series of interwoven interviews, Alberta, as Star, both questions and participates in an interrogation of sexuality, Métis identity, and queer community.[14] Meanwhile, Ghastant'Aucoin's ninety-minute multimedia production combines dance and history with spoofs of *Queer as Folk* ("Queer as Chief"), *Sex in the City* ("Sex & the Rez"), and *Buffy the Vampire Slayer* ("Bobbi the Social Worker Slayer").[15] While this brief overview offers only a sampling of the many contemporary documentaries, shorts, and experimental films by and about queer Indigenous people, this chapter focuses on three contemporary full-length narrative films (*Big Eden, Johnny Greyeyes,* and *The Business of Fancydancing*) to consider what their representations of queer Indigenous peoples and desires say about

Indigeneity, sexuality, and nationhood—the triad of imbricated concerns the introduction marked as essential in the articulation of an Indigenous erotic.

In the 2000 film *Big Eden,* Henry Hart, a white New York artist played by Ayre Gross, returns to his fictional hometown of Big Eden, Montana, after his grandfather suffers a stroke. In the idyllic setting of Big Eden, where all the men are sensitive and all the queers accepted, Henry finds love with Pike Dexter, a tribally unidentified Native man played by Inuit/German actor Eric Schweig (who starred opposite Graham Green as Rudy Yellowshirt in Chris Eyre's *Skins* [2002]). The first film written and directed by Thomas Bezucha, *Big Eden* played at gay and lesbian film festivals across the country, where it won numerous audience and grand jury awards. Much has been made by critics and viewers of the film's depiction of a queer utopia—a Montana town in which there are no homophobes—but, significantly, nothing has been noted about the film's erasure of Pike's tribal identity. In light of this absence, despite its productive depictions of dominant queer identities, *Big Eden* situates Pike, the recognizably Indigenous proprietor of the town store, in a disconnected and detribalized space. By doing so, the film subsumes *Indigenous* subjectivity within its anglicized version of a queer small-town utopia.

If *Big Eden* depicts one end of the representational spectrum, an end in which queerness leaves no room for acknowledgments of race and culture, then what happens when we turn to films that have *both* sexuality *and* Indigenous peoples as their subjects? Two of the few feature-length narrative films that meet such criteria are *Johnny Greyeyes,* a 2000 Canadian motion picture that focuses on the relationship between two Aboriginal lesbians in prison, and *The Business of Fancydancing,* a 2002 U.S. film that follows a queer Spokane poet home to a reservation funeral after his longtime absence. Like *Big Eden,* both movies interrogate Western assumptions of normative sexuality; by contrast, however, both films also recognize the centrality of tribal cosmologies to queer Native people. But despite each story's focus on a queer Native protagonist, by their conclusions, these narratives also fracture Two-Spirit identities. Whereas *Big Eden* elides Indigenous identity, *Johnny Greyeyes* and *The Business of Fancydancing* segregate Indigeneity from queer sexuality by relegating queerness entirely to off-reservation spaces. As this analysis demonstrates, when the films' protagonists cross reservation lines, they literally leave behind their queer lovers and figuratively abandon all those lovers represent as the films' storylines turn nearly exclusively to familial and cultural ties. Consequently, both films suggest that the boundaries of nation in Indigenous contexts are constructed and maintained by the heteronormative gaze and that queer Native people are therefore forced to choose between sexual and national affiliations. In the end, then, this theme of division, in which Indigenous affiliations with tribe and nation are split from expressions of queer sexuality, demonstrates how contemporary representations of queer Native people in narrative film continue to mirror the ongoing legacy of settler colonialism. In the case of *Big Eden,* Indigenous people, and thus any potential for queer Indigenous erotics, vanish under the weight of colonial desires; in the case of *Johnny Greyeyes,* though the aftermath of settler violence is both highlighted and healed by the invocation of an Indigenous erotic, articulations of queer desire are bounded by the walls of the prison; and, finally, in the case of *The Business of Fancydancing,* regulating settler logics, which long degraded and denied Two-Spirit cosmologies, are replicated and, in fact, reinvigorated by the deployment of a gay imaginary that privileges queer urbanity.

Whose Paradise Is This? Eating the Other in *Big Eden*

To briefly make the case about *Big Eden,* we can examine the film's creation of a raced sexual order in which Anglo queerness becomes the de facto norm. When the protagonist, Henry Hart, returns to his old stomping grounds in Montana, his romantic possibilities are triangulated by his unrequited love for his high school best friend, Dean Stewart, and his slow awakening to his attraction to the silent Pike, who has clearly been harboring his own unrequited desire for Henry since high school. The movie focuses primarily on Henry's angst over Dean and Dean's own anguished split over his strong emotional but seemingly asexual feelings for Henry. During this segment, Pike functions largely as comic relief when he secretly substitutes his gourmet meals for Widow Thayer's salt-laden casseroles in his attempts to care for Henry and Henry's recovering grandfather. As Pike combs through cookbooks and orders online delicacies, he is watched by a Greek chorus of backwoods locals, all white men, who seem, at some point in the distant past, to have taken up permanent residence in Pike's country store/coffee house/lending library. While Pike hones his domestic skills under the supportive but watchful eye of the local sheriff and company, Henry longs for his own domestic bliss with Dean and his two young boys. Strikingly, as the plot unfolds, the movie sets up a community for each man, marking sexuality as a place of communal coalition.

Henry's community is both the larger populous of Big Eden, who collectively plot to find him a suitable partner, and his grandfather, Sam, who quietly supports Henry's search for love as he waits in vain for his grandson to come out to him. Dean is also surrounded by both the Big Eden community and his blood relatives; in fact, Dean's tender relationship to his two boys and his role as successful father takes center stage in many scenes. The film's message is clear in each of these cases: queer sexuality does not threaten non-Native kinship ties. Such is not the case for Pike, the only Indigenous member of the Big Eden community, which is ironic given the traditional emphasis on kinship structures in Indigenous cosmologies.[16] While, like Henry and Dean, Pike is fully supported by the Big Eden community, which, in his case, is largely cast as the group of bumbling white men who inhabit his shop, *unlike* either Henry or Dean, neither Pike's family nor his tribal affiliation are ever referenced directly in *Big Eden*. In fact, besides the flute music that plays in the background of his scenes, the closest viewers come to any hint of Pike's Native heritage is when he solemnly tells Henry a story of the Pleiades, explaining,

> There's a myth in Onondagan tradition. . . . There was a nation, a great nation. And they had set up camp in the shadow of a mountain, near a lake. You see, the children of this nation, they had a favorite spot—this clearing in the trees. And there they danced a secret dance that they invented. One day, a strange man appeared. . . . He had long, grey hair flowing down his back and this long robe with white feathers, white as snow. He asked them not to dance in this way or they would draw a terrible occurrence upon themselves. But, they didn't listen. . . . And still they danced, and danced. Then, mysteriously, they began to rise. . . . They rose high enough that their parents could see them and they were terrified. . . . But it was too late: the children already belonged to the sky. . . . Yet every now and then, one of them will remember his hunger and the love of his parents who he can see beneath them. And his yearning grows

> so strong that he falls from the sky into his parents' arms and returns home to his village.[17]

This story, the single moment in the film in which Pike's Native identity is explicitly invoked, works to reify Native identity by situating Indigenous narratives in a romantic but unattainable past—Pike retells a "myth" but never references family, nation, or contemporary Native people in any way. In fact, it's not even clear if viewers are to think Pike is Onondagan or simply that he knows an Onondagan story. Perhaps most telling in the Pleiades creation story he shares, however, is the past tense itself: "There *was* a nation," which invokes the vanishing Indian myth by situating the single reference to a Native nation as a distant recollection. The suggestion that *Big Eden* erases tribal identity through the portrayal of Pike's character is underlined by the fact that the retelling of this "myth" is his single substantive piece of dialogue in the movie. In the end, Pike's character as the tall, dark, monosyllabic other who adores the white man is constructed solely to fit the needs and desires of the dominant community. This representation of Native identity fits a long-standing pattern of representation that Robert F. Berkhofer famously termed "the white man's Indian."[18] In this pattern, whites create and circulate inaccurate representations of Indigenous people in the service of systemic racism. Such misrepresentations historically undergird settler colonialism in the United States: they were deployed to contain and control Native people and lands. And as demonstrated in *Big Eden,* Berkhofer's thesis that such simplistic and subsequently damaging narratives reflect more about the whites who create them than they do about Indigenous people still holds true in the twenty-first century.

In Bezucha's film, then, Pike's "difference," as coded in his racial identity, is invoked solely in the service of settler sexuality. In this way, Pike functions as bell hooks's classic other to be eroticized and consumed by members of the dominant culture. As she points out, in such a scenario, "ethnicity becomes spice, seasoning that can liven up the dull dish that is mainstream white culture."[19] And though overt references to the vanishing Indian myth may be absent, Pike's isolation from family and nation implicitly engages this time-honored colonialist rhetoric. In the end, Pike's Indigenous identity and tribal ties, while briefly hinted at, are sacrificed by the filmmakers to *Big Eden*'s narrative focus on Anglo queerness, which the filmmakers posit as the only form of queerness. While Henry is allowed to both return to his home community *and* find love, Pike is left without that choice; his love is inherently bound to whiteness. In this way, *Big Eden* is representative of the early years of queer studies in which the monolith of white privilege lurked just beneath the surface of claims for queer coalition and emancipation when, as Nikki Sullivan points out, "in focusing almost solely on sexuality, lesbian and gay theorists and activists, and queer theorists . . . not only overlooked race, but . . . 'white-washed' the figure of the homosexual. . . . At the same time, these race-blind theorists and activists . . . fantasized a gay community that, in short, is homogenous."[20] Thus while racial and ethnic difference is invoked by Pike's body and by the film's brief allusion to an Indigenous cosmology, the complexity of actual queer Indigenous histories and people is completely elided by the governing logics of the film's white racial framing.[21] As a result, despite its at times productive focus on dominant constructions of nonnormative sexualities, *Big Eden* mirrors the founding project of settler colonialism, which is premised on the erasure of Indigeneity. This premise has chilling ramifications, since within such an ideology, as Andrea Smith notes, "Native people are a permanent 'present absence' in the U.S. colonial imagination, an 'absence' that reinforces at every turn the conviction that Native peoples are indeed vanishing and that the conquest of Native lands is justified."[22] These concerns leave us to ask just whose paradise *Big Eden* imagines.

Indigenous Erotics in *Johnny Greyeyes*

In contrast to *Big Eden*'s reductive image of Indigeneity, *Johnny Greyeyes,* the first feature film to focus on Native lesbians, presents a clear picture of the interlocking possibilities and oppressions that undergird race, gender, and sexuality, as it traces the life of Johnny, the title character, played by Métis actress Gail Maurice. This sort of intersectionality, María Lugones explains, "reveals what is not seen when categories such as gender and race are conceptualized as separate from each other."[23] The central narrative of the film follows the months before Johnny completes her seven-year sentence at the former Prison for Women in Kingston, while flashbacks and montages return viewers to scenes of Johnny's childhood and adolescence. According to Manzano, "The story was inspired by a series of interviews conducted with American Indian inmates in prisons across Canada [where] a disproportionate number of American Indians are [incarcerated] . . . 'I think it's a social problem . . . It's like the reservation system—the killing of culture, taking people's identities away, their language.'"[24] Manzano's movie, which often played alongside *Big Eden* at 2001 film festivals, alternates between the prison and Johnny's reserve. Although filmed in part on the Wikwemikong Reserve on Manitoulin Island, Johnny's homeland remains unnamed; despite this absence, Johnny's ties to family and use of Anishinaabemowin couple with the panoramas of specific reserve geographies to culturally ground the film in ways Pike's solitary recitation of decontextualized tribal lore cannot. At the heart of *Johnny Greyeyes* is Johnny's painful journey back to that reserve, which requires her to face the damaging legacies of settler colonialism and, in doing so, to forgive both her own action—her shooting of her father to stop her brother's beating—and her mother's inaction in the face of the abuse that Johnny and her brother endured throughout their childhood. Johnny's relationship with fellow inmate Lana, played by Coast Salish actress Columpa Bobb (Lee Maracle's daughter), is key to Johnny's spiritual and psychological healing. In fact, Johnny is able to begin healing from the historical trauma of settler colonialism specifically through her experience of Two-Spirit desire. By the film's conclusion, however, the narrative ultimately seems to limit such cohesive possibilities by segregating queer desire not only *to* the physical space of the prison but also *from* the physical and psychological space of the tribal nation. Thus, even while the erotic represents an avenue for psychic reconciliation in *Johnny Greyeyes*, Johnny's lesbian desire is bounded by both the walls of the prison and the geography of the nation.[25]

A temporary shift in Johnny's view of the confines of her surroundings shows that Manzano initially locates Johnny's relationship with Lana as the site of significant transformative potential. One example of the shift in Johnny's perception occurs in a conversation between Johnny and her therapist, Georgina. When Georgina asks, "Well, aren't you up for parole pretty soon?" Johnny answers jubilantly, "I don't fucking care about that anymore. I'm in love." In this scene, Johnny suggests her love for Lana has the power to dissolve the psychological restrictions of what Michele Foucault famously termed the "panopticon." Under the unceasing threat of observation, which the film underscores by repeated close-ups of security cameras panning right to left, the incarcerated subject succumbs to normalization. The panopticonic goal of such a space, then, is ultimately to persuade inmates to participate in their own surveillance; they become fully complicit participants whose compliance and self-regulation uphold and reinforce the system. As Jodie Michelle Lawston points out, "Prisons are heterotopic spaces characterized by their hyper-rationality. Every single minute and every single aspect of the prisoners' lives is measured, regulated, and controlled."[26] Johnny and Lana's differing responses to this constant surveillance are highlighted when they exchange words over the correct way to respond to the threat embodied by the guards:

> LANA: What are you worried about? Not playing basketball for a week? Is that it? Well, you can take that shit from them, but I won't.
>
> JOHNNY: They don't respect us and never will. They do what they want. We have no fucking rights. Get used to it.

Johnny's words show how deeply she has internalized the feeling of powerlessness engendered by the prison industrial complex—whether the "us" with whom she groups herself are prisoners, lesbians, Aboriginal people, Indigenous women, or any combination of these, she is recognizing and conceding to the logics of a settler ideology that situates her as abject. Unsurprisingly, given the physical dangers Indigenous women in prison must confront daily, Johnny not only concedes to this systematic dehumanization ("We have no fucking rights") but also, when angered by Lana's resistance, demands her compliance to the ideology, as well ("Get used to it").[27] And, in fact, at a key moment when Lana is clearly in danger of being abused by two prison guards, Johnny allows herself to be ushered out of the bathroom after a female guard chides, "Come on, Johnny, you know the rules." Johnny's submissive performance as she is led away without protest ties to her knowledge of her impending release—she undoubtedly regulates her behavior in order to meet the prescriptive norms of successful rehabilitation. Johnny's attraction to Lana, however, leads her to disrupt this pattern of self-surveillance a number of times.

Perhaps Johnny's most productive moments of resistance are the quiet victories of her burgeoning erotic relationship with Lana. Importantly, these occur when the two women are pictured together in scenes that highlight their growing physical and emotional intimacy. Speaking of the prohibitions against such interaction, Foucault discusses the need to divide prison populations, describing cells "like so many cages, so many small theaters, in which each actor is alone, perfectly individualized."[28] The prisoner "is seen, but . . . does not see; . . . is the object of information, but never a subject of communication," an arrangement that "impl[ies] a lateral invisibility."[29] David Spurr extends Foucault's theory of surveillance by situating it within the specific dynamics of the colonial imaginary, arguing that "when we speak of the role of the eye in establishing knowledge of the world and authority over space, we are referring to a fundamental characteristic of Western thinking. . . . [T]he gaze [or] the commanding view makes possible an understanding of the non-Western world as an object of study, an area for development, a field of action."[30] Johnny and Lana's growing intimacy rejects both the invisibility and the objectification that the constant panning of the prison cameras represents. When read through Audre Lorde's argument that "within living structures defined by profit, by linear power, by institutional dehumanization, our feelings were not meant to survive," their erotic relationship embodies unruly potential.[31] The film emphasizes the transgressive nature of the erotic, and in fact, the word *contact* is a repeated refrain in the scenes set within the prison walls, where the term is tied both to the need for emotional connection and human interaction (or that which the panopticon denies) and to the systematic regulation of the body (or that which the panopticon demands).[32] In each case, physical contact is cast as a danger to the state, and therefore unregulated erotic contact is a clear breach of prison policy.

The regulation of the body has a number of resonances here, given the history of Aboriginal and Native American people's interactions with the Canadian and U.S. governments in, to name just a few key instances, the trauma of boarding/residential schools experiences; the forced sterilization of Native women;[33] and the attack on Native peoples' bodies, genders, and sexualities by early explorers, settlers, and missionaries who ridiculed, regulated, and diagnosed Indigenous bodies and desires as a means of social control.[34] In terms of Aboriginal women's experiences specifically, a 2004 Amnesty International report states that "a shocking 1996 Canadian government statistic reveals that Indigenous women between the ages of 25 and 44, with status under the Indian Act, were five times more likely than all other women of the same age to die as a result of violence."[35] In fact, they estimate that in the twenty years prior to the report, "more than 500 Indigenous women may have been murdered or gone missing in circumstances suggesting violence."[36] This ongoing violence against Indigenous women is a direct and enduring legacy of settler colonialism; cycles of physical and psychological abuse, whether perpetrated by whites directly or by Native people as a result of their ongoing relationship to the process of colonization, can be traced to ideologies of conquest that subjugate, degrade, and kill Indigenous people. Additionally, as Luana Ross notes in *Inventing the Savage: The Social Construction of Native American Criminality,* in settler colonialism, these ideologies of conquest are bound to understandings of law and politics in concrete ways; thus "the destruction of Indigenous cultures includes the eradication of their judicial systems. Law has been repeatedly used in this country to coerce racial/ethnic group deference to Euro-American power."[37] As juridical subjects who, in most cases, have no recourse to traditional tribal justice systems, Aboriginal and American Indian women are incarcerated at rates much higher than their percentage of the general population and are most often situated far from their families and tribal nations.[38] In light of these colonial histories, it is markedly significant that Johnny and Lana find refuge from this systematic regulation through the erotic relationship they forge inside the prison walls.

Importantly, the refuge Johnny and Lana create is bound to a Two-Spirit cosmology: their relationship is defined not just in terms of same-sex desire but also by the Indigenous erotic. Thus as the women's relationship progresses, Johnny shares stories with Lana about spending "summers in the bush" with her grandparents, while Lana presses a small dream catcher into Johnny's hand when Johnny struggles with homesickness. The tie Johnny feels between her feelings for Lana and her home community is underlined when Johnny speaks of Lana (whom she calls her "friend") to her mother, saying, "She reminds me of you sometimes." Further reinforcing the argument that Johnny's relationship to Lana intersects with her ties to her mother and her reserve is the fact that Johnny's claim of familial recognition—"She reminds me of you"—occurs immediately after she tearfully explains her to her mother, "When I see you. I want to come home." These connections—a chain of signifiers that connects Lana to Johnny's mother and Johnny's mother to home—highlight the fact that, in the end, eroticism and Indigeneity are linked.

Beyond merely highlighting the existence of this Two-Spirit cosmology in *Johnny Greyeyes,* through such ties between erotic and tribal affiliations, Manzano's film challenges the logic of erasure that undergirds representations of settler colonialism such as that seen in *Big Eden.* Speaking of how the erotic visibility of Native women affects the very foundation of colonialist ideology, Deborah A. Miranda explains, "For Indian women to express the erotic is almost as frightening to America as if the skeletal witnesses in anthropology departments and national museums had suddenly risen from their boxes and begun to testify. The mythology of a nation built on 'discovery,' 'democracy,' and 'manifest destiny' begins to fall apart, and the old foundation, bereft of bones, cannot hold it up."[39]

Qwo-Li Driskill furthers such an idea, arguing, "I do not see the erotic as a realm of personal consequence only. Our relationships with the erotic impact our larger communities, just as our communities impact our senses of the erotic. A Sovereign Erotic relates our bodies to our nations, traditions, and histories."[40] Driskill also contends that "healing our sexualities as First Nations people is braided with the legacy of historical trauma and the ongoing process of decolonization. Two-Spirits are integral to this struggle."[41] To recall Robert Warrior's words, "The erotic . . . is a key to affirming the worth and the wholeness of the self. Its expression is an act of resistance and colors all other such acts."[42] *Johnny Greyeyes* depicts the beginning of just such decolonial healing in its representation of Johnny and Lana's relationship. Thus state prohibitions against contact are defied by the sensual touch of the two women's bodies as they lean against each other in a prison hallway or lay atop one another other in a prison bed. These erotic exchanges create an affective oasis of relationship, of humanity, in the midst of the pain and violence of their past and present lives. Through these interactions, then, Johnny is no longer bound by the specter of discipline—Johnny's love for Lana, which rests on an Indigenous erotic, affords her a personal and psychological sovereignty that her incarceration formerly prohibited.

While *Johnny Greyeyes* initially imbues queer sexuality with transformative power in compelling ways, the film undercuts such potential when Johnny reaches what her spiritual guide calls "a fork in the road." A painful series of events lead Johnny to this fork. First, Lana is thrown into solitary confinement after being viciously beaten by two prison guards in the scene in which Johnny is ushered from the bathroom. Then during her time away from the larger prison population, Lana, "a lifer," discovers Johnny is coming up for parole. In an apparent response to this combination of events, Lana hangs herself in her cell and dies several days later in the prison hospital. Johnny's response to Lana's death is to cut her own wrists, a suicide attempt she survives. In her subsequent solitary confinement, Johnny has a vision in which she is met and counseled in both English and Anishinaabemowen by a male-bodied spirit who tells her, "We come to meet in memory of your sister . . . who has departed from your world." As the two talk, the dialogue and flashbacks imply that to make the right choice—returning intact to her family on the reserve—Johnny must overcome the cycle of violence in which she's been entrapped since her childhood abuse and, importantly, must also release her ties to Lana after her suicide attempt. Johnny explains, "It's been with a lot of pain that I've been able to come to this place. Where I can finally let her go. If I can even do that. I still hold her at night sometimes. You told me everything comes full circle. Even when I sit here grieving for her, I grieve for other things. For the things that brought me here. For my friends, for my family. I love you, Lana." In this pivotal vision scene, Johnny struggles to deal with Lana's suicide and with her own past and present pain by smudging, praying, and gaining spiritual counsel. Within this recognizably Indigenous context, Johnny's declaration of love seems cathartic and, as with earlier scenes in the film, suggests that acknowledging the erotic is a productive move toward a sovereign erotic, the healing of the psychological scars of settler colonialism through recognizing and (re)connecting to Indigenous sexuality. But in *Johnny Greyeyes,* such productivity has its place and, despite Lana's importance to Johnny's life, that place is definitively outside the boundaries of reserve geography.

Manzano's film makes queer Indigenous desire both visible and valuable within certain parameters and, by doing so, challenges the dynamics of a settler colonial paradigm that historically situated such desire as deviant. In addition, as Manzano intended, *Johnny Greyeyes* brings to light the atrocities that Aboriginal and American Indian women continue to face in the prison system, which is a weighty and necessary goal in the ongoing fight for social justice. But to conclude this chapter's analysis there would tell only part of the story. We began with a look at *Big Eden,* critiquing how the film subsumes Indigeneity within a white version of queerness in ways that mirror the dynamics of settler colonialism. We turned to *Johnny Greyeyes* to examine how a film that focuses on Aboriginal lesbians might trouble such divisions by offering more nuanced representations of Indigenous erotics. However, despite its strengths, *Johnny Greyeyes* replicates *Big Eden*'s divisions by the end of the film—the difference being that the final scenes of *Johnny Greyeyes* privilege Indigeneity rather than queerness.

This reading of *Johnny Greyeyes* hinges on the movie's conclusion: while the film's ending provides space for complicated understandings of Native families and relationships, thereby recognizing the kinship relationships that *Big Eden* vacated, Manzano's film leaves conversations about Johnny's queer desire behind Kingston's barbed wire fences. Perhaps the clearest evidence for such a reading is that Johnny's repeated declarations of love for Lana occur only inside prison walls; thus, in relation to the constant visuals of the unbounded and beautiful landscape of the reserve, these walls become not only a literal border but a symbolic space of enclosure mirroring the architecture of the closet. Overt knowledge of Johnny's relationship and, really, of queerness itself is ultimately contained by that seemingly impermeable boundary. Lana's suicide is central to such a theory. Though Lana's death highlights the brutality of the prison system and speaks to the disturbingly high suicide rate among Aboriginal and Native American people, it follows the convenient literary trope of the tragic queer in which, like the vanishing Indian who falls away in the face of manifest destiny, the queer is fated to either a literal or symbolic death. As Gregory Woods points out, "The mythology which represents the invert as an inherently tragic figure materialized in Western culture towards the end of the nineteenth century, and took hold of the imagination of individual writers . . . in the early decades of the twentieth. . . . By mid-century, the idea of the tragic queer was firmly established in literature, both straight and gay."[43] This long-standing pattern served, at least in part, as a way for authors to acknowledge sex/gender diversity without having to fully address how the continued existence of queerness fundamentally challenges the heteropatriarchal logic undergirding dominant institutional and familial norms. Lana's suicide can be read as following such a pattern; her death, though tragic, leaves Johnny free to return to her reserve unencumbered by all but the trace of her queer lover.

And such *is* the nature of Johnny's return after her parole, as is made evident in a letter to her mother, which demonstrates that when Johnny returns to the reserve and to the fold of her reconstituted family, she relegates queerness to a space of silence. As the camera follows Johnny onto the bus home, breathtaking scenes of Manitoulin Island are accompanied by a voiceover in which Johnny reads a letter to her mother:

> I couldn't have survived the past seven years without you. Knowing I had you and a place to go back to has given me courage and strength. Something to dream about and look forward to. I picture our house. My brother. You and me. The three of us sitting together, sharing stories. I will miss certain things. I need you to

> understand this when you see me. So that you won't get hurt if I grow quiet or if I cry. It is a hard thing to leave a family for a second time. I just wanted to let you know, mom, how much I love you.

There is little doubt that the "certain things" that will cause Johnny to "grow quiet" are her memories of her love for Lana and her friendship with other Aboriginal lesbians in the prison, who, together with her Native therapist, Rebecca, constitute the "family" she leaves behind Kingston's walls. Given such a reading, Johnny's "quietness" exemplifies her response to what Janice Gould has called "the patriarchal injunction that demands . . . silence and invisibility [from Native lesbians]. If we would only stay politely and passively in the closet and not flaunt our sexuality, we could be as gay and abnormal as we like."[44] Brian Joseph Gilley discusses how the same sort of cultural regulations function for Two-Spirit men, explaining how they can

> transform themselves into "straight-acting" Indians. . . . They . . . completely ceased any discussion of men, sex, or gay culture. Except for the very resistant, most Two-Spirit men participated in some sort of "passing" behavior, whether it was changing their mannerisms, not using "gay talk," or changing their style of dress when around non-gay Indians. Passing is an important skill to master because it allows Two-Spirit men to participate in cultural and social practices without drawing potentially negative attention.[45]

Though Manzano's film focuses on lesbian identity, the outcome is much the same, since all overt reference to the erotic ends when Johnny leaves the prison. As she returns home, the cinematography emphasizes tribal geography, solitude, and, in the last few minutes of the film, familial kinship when the camera comes to rest on Johnny, her brother Clay, and their mother as they reunite for the first time in many years. The final scene in *Johnny Greyeyes,* in which the three embrace at Johnny's father's grave after her mother says the Lord's Prayer, underlines such a reading: the family unit, which had been fractured by ongoing echoes of settler colonialism via alcoholism, violence, and the prison industrial complex, is reconstituted by Indigenous people on Indigenous ground. In addition, given the heteropatriarchal resonance of the Indian Act in Aboriginal histories, it's notable that kinship ties and the reconstituted family rest not only on a return to the reserve but also specifically on a return to the mother in this scene. Yet as the strains of "Amazing Grace" underscore, this fragmented and fragile family structure is still by no means utopic; while some aspects of "what once was lost" may be found, others are sacrificed for that redemption. Thus *Johnny Greyeyes* privileges Indigenous nationhood and the healing of Aboriginal families while isolating queer sexuality from nation and family. If, to return to Joane Nagel's words from the introduction, "national and sexual boundaries are mutually reinforcing" and "implicit in the meaning of national boundaries ('who are we?') are certain prescriptions and proscriptions for sexual crossings," then this separation has weighty consequences: the conclusion to *Johnny Greyeyes* suggests that once a queer Native person crosses into the reserve, the answer to questions of national identity, or "who we are," precludes considerations of sexuality.[46]

"Not Your Tribe": Homonormative Geographies in *The Business of Fancydancing*

This analysis of *Johnny Greyeyes,* which contends that Manzano presents viewers with a reserve in which cultural and familial ties take precedence over considerations of sexual diversity, maps a division replicated by Sherman Alexie's *The Business of Fancydancing.* Alexie's directorial debut follows award-winning poet Seymour Polatkin, played by Coast Salish actor Evan Adams of *Smoke Signals* fame, as he returns to his reservation for a childhood friend's funeral. For Alexie, Seymour's queerness takes center stage. Alexie explains this choice, saying, "I've spent more time in urban situations and in the art world. I've made more friends who are gay. So it's a huge part of my life. . . . Part of me writing about gay people in this movie was a larger social effort. I knew a lot of Indians will see this movie, and there's *a lot* of homophobes in the Indian world, so I wanted to slap them in the face a bit."[47] But as with *Johnny Greyeyes,* Alexie's "slap in the face" is perhaps not as radical as it might first appear. Like Johnny, Seymour too is ultimately depicted as fragmented, but while Manzano's dichotomy of sexual and tribal affiliations come late in the film, Alexie poses Seymour's fragmentation, his "choice," as his film's lynchpin.

I focus here on two facets of Seymour's life, the first of which is his relationship with his ex-girlfriend, Agnes Ross, played by Michelle St. John (Cree). When Agnes, the daughter of a Jewish mother and a Spokane father, first meets Seymour, he is president of the Native American Student Alliance at St. Jerome the Second University, where they both attend college. Upon recognizing her, Seymour tries to recruit Agnes into the organization, saying, "You're on my list. . . . This is a list of every student who checked the American Indian, Alaskan Native, Pacific Islander, miscellaneous Indigenous box on their application for enrollment."[48] In response, Agnes insists she did not check the box. She explains, "My mother was Jewish so that makes me Jewish." In fact, according to her "biography" on Alexie's website, Agnes "was born in Seattle, and never once set foot on the Spokane Indian Reservation even though it was only a short five-hour drive away."[49] Rather than being tragically alienated by this classic urban-reservation divide, however, Agnes is depicted as fully incorporated within the Spokane community into which she moves after graduating from St. Jerome's. In fact, Agnes is intimately connected with Seymour's childhood friends, who, at the time of his return, he has not seen for more than nine years. Agnes's integration into the Spokane community Seymour left behind is demonstrated in the scenes in which she teases and chides the friends present at the house, prepares Mouse's body for his funeral, and sings a haunting song in the Spokane language ("Osinilshatin," cowritten with Jennifer Kreisberg of Ulali). As Agnes's experiences show, despite her nontraditional upbringing, a return to the reservation—and to the Spokane culture it represents—is undoubtedly possible in the world of Alexie's fiction.

Why, then, is such a return seemingly *impossible* for Seymour? According to the film's narrative arc, Seymour ultimately believes he must choose between erotic desire and his Spokane heritage. Thus, as with *Johnny Greyeyes,* while the reservation may be metonymic of Indigeneity, the same cannot be said for queer sexuality. In fact, in Alexie's narrative, Seymour's sexuality seems predicated on a depiction of queerness reminiscent of *Big Eden*—to be queer, according to *The Business of Fancydancing,* means to privilege a dominant version of sexuality that precludes Indigenous understandings of the erotic (which, as the Introduction showed, turn on interrelated concepts of land, Indigeneity, and desire). In doing so, *The Business of Fancydancing* examines settler colonialist logics similar to those in *Big Eden.* While the film does not elide Indigenous relationships as does *Big Eden,* it does depict queer Indigeneity as inherently damaging to such relationships. Speaking of the intersections between queerness and dominant conceptions of Indigeneity, Craig Womack argues that "a queer Indian presence *fundamentally* challenges the American mythos about Indians in a manner the public will not accept. . . . [I]dentifying an Indian as lesbian or gay makes the Native radically resistant to the popular tendency to make Indians artifacts from the past, since no one associates such terms with the warrior days when men were men and buffalo were scared."[50]

Given Alexie's comments about the film and his frequent discussion of same-sex desire in his public appearances, there is little doubt that he recognizes queer Indigeneity as having this same sort of radical signification. However, though Alexie offers a gay Native character with the deliberate intention of queering heterosexist understandings of Indigeneity and the reservation, the film's protagonist ultimately finds such erotic integration unmanageable. This reading is underscored early in the story after Seymour's white lover, Steven, answers a late-night call about Mouse's suicide. When Seymour makes it clear that Steven can't accompany him to the reservation for the funeral, Steven argues: "They're not your tribe anymore, I'm your tribe." With this quote, Steven divides Seymour's loyalties between Indigeneity and sexuality, posing the two as oppositional choices.[51]

Steven's rhetoric of "tribe," which argues for a kinship relationship rather than simply a sexual or romantic bond between he and Seymour, is reminiscent of Christopher Nealon's theory of "foundlings." Nealon refers to an understanding of queerness "defined by a particular relationship to the idea of history," which "allegorizes a movement between solitary exile and collective experience."[52] This "relationship . . . entails . . . imagining, on one hand, an exile from sanctioned experience, most often rendered as the experience of participation in family life and the life of communities, and on the other hand, a reunion with some 'people' or sodality who redeem this exile and surpass the painful limitations of the original 'home.'"[53] According to Nealon's theory, then, Seymour's "original 'home,'" as represented by the reservation, is supplanted by his attachment to an urban, gay identity. As discussed in chapter 3, Kath Weston examines the gay migration from rural to urban spaces, arguing that "the gay subject is most commonly represented as a subject bereft of community," a depiction that impedes the construction of a "gay imaginary," a shared understanding of identity Weston bases on Benedict Anderson's concept of imagined community.[54] The desire to find community is key, Weston argues, for many LGBTIQ2 people who move to urban spaces. As Steven's claim to "tribe" suggests, the notion of exile and chosen community are also at work in *The Business of Fancydancing*; however, in Alexie's film the structure of Native nationhood complicates any easy realignment of loyalties and kinship affiliations. The film makes clear through vignettes of storytelling about

Seymour's childhood that, at least into his high school years, Seymour had a close group of family and friends on the reservation. Seymour's nine-year absence thus represents a symbolic "choice" of community exile—a choice his childhood friends equate to betrayal, as their harsh comments to and about Seymour demonstrate throughout the funeral. But interestingly, they comment on his abandonment of the reservation rather than his sexuality. It is Seymour himself who maintains the reservation as a heterosexual space by situating absence as his only option.

This choice between queerness and Indigeneity is further reified by Agnes's continued romantic attachment to Seymour. If Agnes is read as a voice of tradition in *The Business of Fancydancing,* then her longing for Seymour's heterosexuality takes on marked significance in the film. In the end, Agnes's overt acceptance of Seymour's queerness is undermined by her ever-present desire for him and for a heteronormative life with him. But Agnes is not alone in mourning Seymour's "loss." Seymour's own desire at times mirrors the same ideological and geographic divisions. These conflicting desires are perhaps best demonstrated in a scene in which Seymour and Agnes share an intimate conversation and a kiss in the closet-like space of the attic. In what is clearly a well-loved habit from their time together as a couple, the two complete one another's poetic quotes and dream of what life might have been had Seymour been straight:

> SEYMOUR: Do you ever think what life might have been like with me?
> AGNES: Once or twice a day.
> SEYMOUR: I don't know why we let sex get in the way. I mean, I can't slip you the tongue a hot twenty minutes of every day, but I can give you the best things you ever had for the other 23:40.
> AGNES: . . . What, do you think you can just stop being gay? I mean, do you really think you can just turn it off?
> SEYMOUR: No, there's nothing I can do about that. I think about the straight life sometimes. Sometimes, I want to be the Indian guy that brought you home to the rez. And sometimes I want to be the Indian who stayed behind. And sometimes, I wish there was a cute little boy or girl who looked like me and you.
> AGNES: [tearful] There could have been.
> SEYMOUR: I know.
> AGNES: You know, you can always come back here. You don't have to come back just for me.

SEYMOUR: The only reason I'd come back is for you.
AGNES: Why are we spending all this time talking about the impossible?
SEYMOUR: Because the rest is silence.

Given Agnes's symbolic value in the film, this scene underscores the film's rhetorical message: one cannot be queer *and* Native on the reservation. While Seymour's lack of sexual response to Agnes's kiss defuses any stereotypical suggestion that his sexual object choice might be in question, the scene itself makes some weighty claims about the consequences of queer desire on Indigeneity. For Seymour, a heteronormative life with Agnes is the only promise life on the reservation holds for him, and we see in this scene and elsewhere that such a promise is tempting. But in Seymour's view, his sexual object choice precludes that possibility and thus precludes him from living on the reservation. In this case, Seymour can only imagine himself as straight, or at least as living a heteronormative life when he envisions himself on the reservation (which may, in part, explain his portrayal of the reservation as "a prison"). His echo of Hamlet's final words—"the rest is silence"—in answer to Agnes's question therefore casts him as the tragic, divided hero while reinforcing the idea that all that falls outside an imagined vision of heterosexual intimacy cannot be voiced.

To return to Weston's theory of how an urban/rural dichotomy figures in the construction of a gay imaginary, central here is not the actual regulation of sexuality on the reservation—though that potential exists—but instead that Seymour predicates his sexuality on exactly the sort of "whitewashed" representations of queerness endemic to early gay and lesbian studies.[55] Weston references what she calls "the classic tale of the escape from surveillance into freedom, in which the anonymity of city life becomes a precondition for coming out and 'being gay' or at least expressing 'gay feelings.' . . . In most stories of the Great Gay Migration," she explains, "the rural is not only the space of dead-end lives, oppression, and surveillance. It is also a landscape emptied of gay people."[56] Though Weston proves that queer migration and the urban/rural split are far more complicated than these "classic" narratives, this dead-end, heterosexual rural geography *is* the landscape of Seymour's imagined reservation. Moreover, Seymour maintains this limited vision of Indigeneity in spite of his knowledge of queer Indigenous histories. Unlike Evelina in *The Plague of Doves*, who saw queerness as "outside the narrative" of her family, Seymour calls himself "Two-Spirit" and, in fact, tells a story of coming out to his traditional grandmother, who accepts him fully.[57] Notably, however, he does so as part of a performance of Indigeneity for a largely white audience at a poetry reading. While *Johnny Greyeyes* presents a rift between the Indigenous erotic and reserve life, *The Business of Fancydancing* suggests Two-Spirit cosmologies are inherently fiction.

The choice that precludes queer Indigenous realities by leaving queerness on one side of the reservation border and Indigeneity on another is further accentuated by a consideration of Seymour's childhood friend and college lover, Aristotle. While Seymour's pleasure at being with Agnes is evident, the pain and anger he and Aristotle feel at seeing each other is just as apparent. And to make matters more complicated, Seymour's two ex-lovers and friends—Aristotle and Agnes—are now in a romantic relationship themselves, presenting the classic specter of Eve Kosofsky Sedgwick's triangle.[58] Though the film opens to Seymour and Aristotle with their arms around each other's shoulders at graduation, it's by no means initially obvious they share more than homosocial bonds. Thus when Aristotle delivers lines like, "We were brothers, man. We were *more* than brothers," the queer implication is not immediately evident. In fact, despite the fact that Seymour asks Agnes wistfully if Aristotle is "still thunder between the sheets," and we actually see Aristotle and Seymour share a kiss on the lips while in bed together in a flashback, few of my undergraduates read Aristotle as queer when they initially view the film. While their readings are undoubtedly a telling example of the power of compulsory heterosexuality on audience interpretations, they also speak to the film's depiction of Aristotle's choices. On the reservation, Aristotle's known alliances are with women. Though he may, like the Two-Spirit men in Gilley's study, be "participat[ing] in some sort of 'passing' behavior" in order to be socially accepted, he is still following the established social order of the rest of the film, keeping his queerness, or all "the rest," in "silence." Thus rather than identifying as Two-Spirit, queer, or bisexual, Aristotle fulfills heteronormative expectations for Indigenous masculinity in ways that suggest, for nonheterosexual men, the reservation can be as much of a panopticon as Johnny's prison. While they may choose opposite paths, *both* Seymour *and* Aristotle's actions bear out the same idea: whether one stays or leaves, heteronormativity defines reservation life.

This claim is underlined by the penultimate scene in the movie in which, when Seymour drives away from the reservation, he is doubled—or, as is more likely by such a narrative, halved—as he pulls out of the driveway. This moment begs a number of questions. But one thing that is not left to interpretation is the outcome of Seymour's visit: his departure from the reservation equals a psychic split. When Seymour leaves the funeral, he literally is pictured in two places—one Seymour watches himself drive away, while another leaves, looking through the windshield to see himself standing in the driveway as he backs out. This scene is spliced with Agnes singing "Osinilshatin" at the funeral, Aristotle dancing in Seymour's review mirror, and Seymour taking off his fancydancing regalia and throwing it to the floor piece by piece before he begins sobbing. Each of these scenes makes a powerful statement about loss and division, about the psychological damage of being forced to choose. In Seymour's vision of himself as eternally split or, to return to Nolan, as "an exile from sanctioned experience," we see the classic urban/rural (urban/reservation) divide as inevitably isolating him from home, tradition, and cultural connection. In Agnes's final scene, she sings in Spokane of the consequences of precisely such divisions, saying, "Who are you when you turn your back? / Where do you go when you leave here? / You can't hide from the truth / Can't run from where you belong / Some things you can't choose / Sometimes you can't have it all / I know your dreams remind you / Where you belong / Memories hold you tight / When there's no comfort in white arms / Loneliness will bring you back / Where you belong."[59] Meanwhile, Seymour's heartbroken rejection of his fancydance regalia suggests he sees no such inevitable return home.[60] And in fact, in the final scene, the film concludes as Seymour crawls into bed with his white lover once back in Seattle. In the screenplay, Steven asks, "Where have you been?," to which Seymour replies, "I was gone. But now I'm back,'" while in the film, Seymour simply holds tightly to Steven from behind, kissing him repeatedly as Agnes's haunting commentary rings on.[61] In each case, whether read as mirror or critique of the divisions contemporary Native and non-Native cultures can demand of queer Indigenous people, *The Business of Fancydancing* leaves no room for a healthy Two-Spirit existence.

The Transformative Possibilities of Indigenous Studies

The body of this chapter focuses on how films like *Big Eden, Johnny Greyeyes,* and *The Business of Fancydancing* replicate the legacies of settler colonialism in their depictions of LGBTIQ2 Native people, leaving queer Indigenous people with an untenable choice in which they are, as this chapter's title suggests, "forced to choose." They must either, like Johnny, embrace family and nation in the silence of desire or, like Seymour, embrace sexuality at the expense of tribal and familial alliances. On one hand, as Raheja notes of Indigenous media more generally, such representations of queer Indigenous people "capture the imagination by signifying at least some sort of *presence,* however vexed, in a representational field defined primarily by *absence.*"[62] On the other hand, the films discussed here parallel the disciplinary divisions laid out by the Introduction, suggesting that contemporary narrative film, which undoubtedly offers the most widely viewed representations of queer Native people, often reenacts (or at least reflects) fragmenting visions of the erotic. Thus *Big Eden* and *The Business of Fancydancing* posit queer desire as white, the reserve/reservation as straight, and Two-Spirit identity as tenuous and unsustainable. Despite its limiting conclusion, *Johnny Greyeyes* offers the single exception to this pattern, suggesting a queer erotic can intervene in the cycles of colonial violence that continue to circulate in Indigenous communities. In the end, the film's complex representations of erotic sovereignty call attention to the productive possibilities of queer Indigenous studies, which, Estrada argues, "draws more awareness to specific nationalist, traditionalist and [often] community-oriented perspectives of Two-Spirit peoples."[63] As my readings throughout *The Queerness of Native American Literature* have demonstrated, recovering the intersections of queerness and Indigeneity through the recognition that Indigenous knowledges are always already queer allows us to better understand—and thus perhaps eventually circumvent—the damaging fragmentations that occur when the erotic is envisioned as a geographic barrier to Indigenous community. Instead of forcing a choice, queer Indigenous studies offer nuanced imaginings of Indigeneity in which queerness is not apart from but a part of Native literature and lives.

· CHAPTER 5 ·

Indigenous Assemblage and Queer Diasporas in the Work of Janice Gould

I've always felt that my memory of California, my imaginative landscape, is not entirely my own but is embedded in the memory of many tribal people, my own tribe, the Koyangk'auwi Maidu, and in the other small nations of Indian people who inhabited California before it was ever named and was still Turtle Island.

—Janice Gould, *The Geography of Home: California's Poetry of Place*

TOGETHER, the Introduction and the first four chapters of *The Queerness of Native American Literature* undertake multiple forms of recovery—the genealogical, the archival, and the thematic—and forward an expansive map of relationship(s). Chapter 5 furthers this story of recovery and relationship by looking across the work of Janice Gould, an important but understudied writer. At the same time, the final chapter extends the scope of this study by considering how queer Native literature speaks to Leslie McCall's contention that "different methodologies produce different kinds of substantive knowledge."[1] This chapter reads across Gould's three poetry collections—*Beneath My Heart, Earthquake Weather,* and *Doubters and Dreamers*—to consider how Gould's writing moves us toward a queer Indigenous methodology.

Assembling Indigenous History / Indigenizing Assemblage

Janice Gould explains in the introduction to her 1996 collection, *Earthquake Weather,* that her mother, Vivian Beatty, was born in Belden, California, to Harry and Helen (Nellie) Beatty, who were both mixed-blood Koyoonk'auwi people still living in what historically would have been Konkow territory.[2] When Vivian's mother Nellie died of cancer, Vivian was subsequently adopted by three white sisters—Beatrice, Henrietta, and Clara Lane—living in the San Francisco Bay area. Though Gould is unsure "if there was ever a legal adoption," this geographical and psychological relocation can, to some degree, situate Vivian as a member of the "stolen generation" or "lost birds"—American Indian and Aboriginal children removed from their extended families and cultural heritages by adoption policies that functioned as cultural genocide.[3] These damaging practices remained in place in the United States at least until the 1978 National Indian Child Welfare Act and in Canada until the passage of the 1984 Child and Family Services Act, at which point they were curtailed (though not by any means eradicated, as seen in the recent U.S. Supreme Court decision *Adoptive Couple v. Baby Girl*).[4] The personal histories of members of the stolen generation are often painful and complicated and can involve losses of cultural ties and familial connection. These experiences are certainly elements of Gould's representations of family history, yet in her poetry, the emerging story is not solely one in which identity and tradition are sutured to an unrecoverable past upon her mother's adoption, a fraught pairing Gerald Vizenor terms "tragic victimry."[5]

Both Eva Marie Garroutte (Cherokee Nation) and Scott Richard Lyons (Ojibwe/Dakota) interrogate the definitional boundaries of contemporary Indigenous identities and the ongoing demarcating, defending, and sometimes policing that enforce them. Garroutte begins *Real Indians: Identity and the Survival of Native America,* which analyzes the changing processes of Native identification in Indian Country, by recognizing, "The question of 'real Indianness' has more force today than ever before."[6] Lyons examines similar questions in *X-Marks: Native Signatures of Assent* as he surveys the differing criteria for Indigenous identification and tribal citizenship. He contends, "Perhaps the first thing we should do is stop asking the perennial question, what is an Indian? . . . I would suggest that for analytic purposes we turn our attention instead to the social processes that create intersubjective Indian identities."[7] Garroutte and Lyons refuse the indelible suturing of *change* to *loss* in their examinations of the legal, national, and cultural definitions of contemporary Native people and nations in the United States. In doing so, these scholars reject, to use Jabir Puar's words, the "question of temporality that doggedly binds all cultural forms navigating the yesterday of tradition with the futurity of the modern."[8] David L. Eng borrows from Martin Heidegger to discuss this racialized and nationalistic understanding of time as a form of "worlding," in which "the perpetually anachronistic non-West is forced to play catch-up with an exalted European present and presence invariably constituted as the here and now."[9] Gould's reconstruction of her familial history and tribal connections similarly questions the idea of irreparable cultural disintegration and victimization. Rather than a teleological narrative of loss in which movement away from the tribal past (or "the yesterday of tradition") inevitably places her mother, Vivian, and then, by default, Gould herself in a deracinated "here and now," Gould instead presents a palimpsest of pasts and presents that fluidly intersect, overlap, and rearrange through the *felt* experience of history and memory. The product and the process of such reconstruction can be seen as an example of what I term "Indigenous assemblage."

In one of the most influential recent articulations of assemblage, Puar builds on the foundational ideas of Gilles Deleuze and Félix Guattari to contend that we must "rethink race, sexuality, and gender as concatenations, unstable assemblages of revolving and devolving energies, rather than intersectional coordinates."[10] In this configuration, assemblages are both intensely relational and "spatially and temporarily contingent."[11] This process-oriented understanding of identity is particularly useful for reading Gould, whose depictions of her personal history, in terms of both her California Indian ancestry and her articulation of queerness and the erotic, function as just such dynamic assemblages in which experiences of self, family, sexuality, and culture ebb and flow in what Deleuze and Guattari might term a territorializing/deterritorializing spiral, their differing iterations contingent on geographic and temporal locales. In Gould's work, assemblage describes the flexible and often transitory nature of what the films in chapter 4 imagined as more discrete intersectional coordinates.[12] Rather than applying Puar's or Deleuze and Guattari's articulations of assemblage *to* Gould, I argue that Gould's assemblages provide an example of *queer Indigenous writing as critical methodology.*

Gould's mother's integration into the Lane family can be read as one of the many such assemblages that mark Gould's texts. In this case, the physical relocation geographically removed Vivian and, subsequently, her daughter from Konkow land.[13] But rather than the stark schism so often employed in portrayals of Indigenous urbanity, Gould represents Vivian's resilient relationships to land, family, and culture as a particular kind of assemblage that Ho-Chunk scholar Renya K. Ramirez calls an urban "hub." This temporal and geographical concept "emphasizes the importance of Indians' relationship to *both* homeland and diaspora" and, significantly, allows for the two spatial and ideological constructs to be imagined simultaneously.[14] Ramirez's concept of the hub is necessary because urban Indians are so often depicted as estranged from the stuff of Indigenous identity, as if "Indian" and "urban" are always already dichotomous. These tragic configurations ignore both that urban Indian communities are vibrant examples of Indigenous survivance and that the history of Indigenous cities in North America predates European contact by hundreds of years, proof of which is written on the land in the form of earthworks, ancient roads, and ancestral pueblos.[15] Despite the best attempts of U.S. government assimilation policies, "urban Indian" is not an oxymoron.

Gould portrays her mother, Vivian, as operating within an urban hub after her adoption and move to Berkeley. So while acknowledging that her Konkow grandmother Nellie's passing "caused a huge disruption in [her] family," Gould also explains that Vivian "returned frequently after her mother's death" to Belden, the Feather River, and her relatives who remained there.[16] Additionally, though Vivian's "siblings dispersed," Gould highlights the fact that several go back to live or regularly visit the Konkow land of their birth.[17] If assemblage functions "as a series of dispersed but mutually implicated and messy networks," then it can be seen to work in this case as the loosely organized, changeable networks of affiliation through and around which Vivian, and later Gould, organize their Koyoonk'auwi ties after removal.[18] Mishuana R. Goeman (Seneca) points out that such dominant assimilation and relocation practices were "not only about a movement of bodies off reservation, but also about respatializing a consciousness and relationship to land or mapping space as settler places."[19] Favoring a stagnant and limited vision of Indigeneity that was to be erased and replaced by assimilation into dominant identities in urban locales, the ideologies behind relocation practices denied the possibility of dynamic, evolving assemblages. However, as Gould shows, Vivian's adoption/relocation, though difficult, still allows for the process of Indigenous assemblage rather than inevitably creating an indentitarian dead end. As opposed to the static Indigenous identities and nations of settler colonial logics, Gould's depictions of family demonstrate that Indigenous ties are not fixed, linear maps strictly bounded by and confined to mission, reserve, or reservation geographies but are instead breathing, *active* entities capable of transformation and continuance.[20] These flexible assemblages are deterritorializing Indigenous traces in both Gould's family history and her writing.

Queer Diasporas in *Beneath My Heart*

As a way to more effectively discuss the affective and spatial nature of these active processes, we can think of Indigenous assemblage together with David L. Eng's articulation of queer diasporas, which was discussed briefly in chapter 3's analysis of Cyprian. Building from the work of theorists like Gayatri Gopinath and Martin F. Manalansan IV, Eng argues,

> As a methodological tool, queer diasporas directs our attention to . . . the epistemological coordinates of how we are thought—in order to focus on the politics and problems of racial knowledge. As a structure of feeling, queer diasporas also indexes lost or forgotten desires, those stubborn remainders of affect that individuate through their ardent refusal of the orthodoxy of conventions, the great expectations of social agreement. Lastly, in the binding force of the what-can-be-known, queer diasporas suggests how we might think the unknowable . . . "a might-have-been which is more than truth." Queer diasporas thus opens upon a landscape of other histories and knowledges, preserving in the process a space for social and political reinvestment.[21]

In this conceptualization, queer diasporas have "subjects in waiting," Eng's example being queer Asian migrants, who disrupt the mandates of queer liberalism by inhabiting geographies outside understandings of the nation-state. As discussed in chapter 2, queer liberalism focuses on incorporation of queer subjects *into* the logics of the settler nation—inclusion into what Lisa Dugan has called homonormative modes of thinking, acting, and being and Puar has theorized as the rise of a troubling homonationalism.[22] Subjects in waiting deterritorialize such reiterative understandings of queerness by assembling self in the often unseen spaces independent of (or at least unacknowledged by) nation-state ideologies. Thus spatially and epistemologically, such assemblages emerge and exist in the shifting locales of queer diasporas.

This idea of a dynamic subject in waiting who is always already outside queer liberalism is key to Gould's three texts: *Beneath My Heart, Earthquake Weather,* and *Doubters and Dreamers.* If we read "Autobiography," a poem from Gould's first collection, *Beneath My Heart,* through the paired lenses of assemblage (the fluid process/product of self-construction) and queer diaspora (the affective/spatial/ideological dimensions of that process), we can see Gould's speaker engages questions of "how we are thought," disrupts the "orthodoxy of convention," and also evidences the trace of affective desires.[23] I offer the poem in its entirety to more concretely demonstrate this point:

I was born of a half-breed mother
and a transvestite father
on All Fool's Day
in the year of forty-nine.

I was born on a park bench
outside a museum
one morning of warm rain.
Huge ferns protected my mother and me.

I was born clutching blue light.
The weight of secrets
lolled on my infant tongue.
A stone was planted in my heart
the day of my birth.

At an early age I wanted
to run off with the gypsies
for the tambourine
and the gold hoop in my ear.
Later I wanted to join the circus
till I realized a dread of clowns
and trapeze artists.

Often I stayed away from school.

After a while I manifested
a tendency to howl,
cry inconsolably,
and choose the wrong women.
The appendix may be consulted
for a list of lovers, pets,
travels, etc.

Three things help me get by:
a sense of navigation
unending loneliness
and black coffee.[24]

In "Autobiography," the speaker is figured from birth as outside the structures of power that undergird the settler nation: she is a mixed-race child of queer parents born beside a museum.[25] With these few images, settler colonial legacies of land loss, homelessness, racism, homophobia, and anthropological violence are all invoked. Thus "Autobiography" underlines Beth Brant's claim in *Writing as Witness* that "writing is an act that can take place in physical isolation, but the memory of history, of culture, of land, of Nation, is always present—like another being. This is how we create. Writing with all our senses, and with the ones that have not been named or colonized, we create."[26] Gould's poetry assembles such named and unnamable energies and, like Eng's queer Asian migrants, her speaker, a subject in waiting, exists outside U.S. national identities and dominant versions of queer identities and subsequently outside queer liberalism's mandate of citizen sameness. Yet at the same time, as Brant and Eng suggest, rather than being a space of exile, such physical and psychic locales carry within them alternate possibilities for the creation of Indigenous knowledge. The creative reconstructions that take place in such spaces, then, are acts of assemblage.

These alternate possibilities and knowledges, the trace of what Brant terms "another being," can be seen in "Autobiography" within Gould's description of the speaker's embodied history. When Gould commented on her deployment of history during a 2011 American Studies Association panel, she stated, "It's all autobiography."[27] Thus if we read the speaker as some version of the author herself, we can see that Gould suggests these creative possibilities exist beyond the tragic boundaries of her mother's "stolen generation." As one such possibility, the poet herself is an assemblage, carrying a history that is present from birth; thus, in Gould's poem, the baby holds "light," mouths/tongues "secrets," and houses "stone" in her *physical* body (19). In this extended metaphor, blood and bones serve as the repository of knowledge, and thus the speaker creates, and finally becomes, an embodied assemblage.

A similar movement occurs in the opening poem of the collection. Like "Autobiography," the poem and section titled "Coyotismo" begins with the transformative movement of birth. The ubiquitous Coyote, a gender-shifting trickster who makes frequent guest appearances in queer Indigenous poetry and fiction, explains, "My mother lay on her side to birth me. / This was millennia ago / when the earth was still fresh / with the energy of being."[28] In ways reminiscent of the urban Indian, the trickster's identity undergoes a perceptual shift in the city where the sometimes-sacred figure is perceived instead as profane. After birth, Coyote travels the roads of suburbia unrecognized, poor, and disrespected; she scavenges, begs, and ingests garbage.[29] Throughout these urban migrations, Coyote's body, which circulates as a metaphor for the queer, female Native body, is sexualized and perceived as abject: "People laughed at me. . . . // They joked about my sex, / said nasty things about my genitalia" (11). Gould suggests, then, that internal and external perceptions of Indigenous bodies are radically different. Whereas the figure of the baby in "Autobiography" holds embodied knowledge—an internal perception of a tribal trace as power—Coyote's confrontations with damaging external stimuli craft the queer, female Indigenous body as painful contact zone. However, in "Coyotismo," rather than accepting the indentitarian act of being named and contained by the colonizer, Coyote rearranges knowledge, creating queer assemblage outside the boundaries of the settler state.

Deborah A. Miranda points out that "like minority women everywhere, Native women carry varying levels of marginalization within our identities: woman, Native, poor, lesbian, disabled, reservation/urban, and so on. However, for Indian women there is the added effect of internalized colonization and of what I call 'Intergenerational Post-Traumatic Stress Syndrome.'"[30] "Coyotismo" brings this experience to the fore. As an Indigenous signifier, Coyote bears the weight of trauma, her body and psyche serving as sites of a settler colonial violence that attempts to both maim and contain her. Coyote first internalizes this psychological violence—"I was always angry. // . . . / I became vengeful." Then she externalizes it—"I scooped hot coals / and threw them in [the moon's] fat face. / Sure, it burned my hands—/ but she is marked with permanent surprise" (11). Likewise, after Coyote is hypersexualized when "night began a rumor / that I'd hump anything that moved," she pulls night's tongue with a ferocity that creates the Milky Way, "a trail of stars no one can clean up" (12). Coyote, like the baby of Gould's "Autobiography," is a subject in waiting born outside the confines of the settler colonial nation and heteronormative logics. A Two-Spirit trickster, she embraces that queer diasporic space, creating a dynamic assemblage with the affective power of an anger that shapes the universe.

"Coyotismo" concludes with the same sort of affirmation we saw in "Autobiography," a claim for a self understood through the process of assemblage—that is, in this case, constructed through a changeable, active, and, importantly, *embodied* erotic knowledge: "No poetry exists which wasn't first on my lips. / I was a live seed planted by a women / in another woman's womb. / All things insatiable belong to me" (12). In ways reminiscent of Paula Gunn Allen's theory of the Indigenous erotic in which a creator figure "made the first food from her own body-seed," Coyote's knowledge is not only held within the body but also sent out into the world when the act of creation and the practice of creativity meld.[31] Dian Million examines how such transformations take place within Indigenous texts. Speaking of First Nations writers' testimonies against colonial violence, she contends, "Native women's personal narrative explore[s] the racialized, gendered, and sexual nature of their colonization. In doing so, they [transform] the debilitating force of an old social control, *shame,* into a social change agent."[32] Gould's coyote story functions similarly, transforming the abject narrative written on her objectified body into a generative, world-defining fury. Million argues Native women's experiences and writings are often delegitimized by academic gatekeepers who equate felt experience, testimonial anger, and "social distress" with "individual pathology."[33] On a national level, "Canada and the United States resisted the truth in the emotional content of this felt knowledge: colonialism as it is *felt* by those who experience it."[34] Gould's poetry attacks such resistance by insisting that the queer space of the subject in waiting is not only productive but also *re*productive. Moreover, as in the origin stories Allen references, here reproduction itself is reconfigured when Coyote claims to be a "seed planted by a woman / in another woman's womb" (12). While noted queer studies scholar Lee Edelman focuses on queerness as death drive, maintaining queers should recognize and embrace their status outside the "reproductive futurism" that undergirds U.S. heteronormativity, Gould gives us queerness as an *affectively generative act.*[35] Coyote's queer birth shows how the flexibility of the Indigenous erotic exceeds, as it has for centuries, Euro-American configurations of Indigeneity, sexuality, and desire. To embrace, as Edelman suggests, the concept of queers having "no future" in ideological configurations of reproduction and the nation-state is a position fundamentally incongruent with an Indigenous concept of the erotic. The queer diasporas of Gould's work thus present a more relevant theoretical framework for queer Native literatures: the regenerative and transformative assemblages that exist in the inherently queer space of the sacred.

"Thinking the Unknowable": Embodied Movement in *Earthquake Weather*

These affective narratives of embodied difference translate into the movements through space, time, and cultural knowledge that recur across Gould's texts.[36] If we again consider "how we might think the unknowable . . . 'a might-have-been which is more than truth,'" we can locate this understanding in the way embodied movement (that which is affectively felt) and bodily movement (the physical experience of migration/relocation) circulate in Gould's work.[37] Such movements are vital aspects of Gould's assemblage. To consider how these embodied movements work to reconstruct (or assemble) the "unknowable" or the "might-have-been," we turn to Gould's second collection, *Earthquake Weather.*

Gould's preface begins with the story of her family's move from San Diego to Berkeley when she was nine. This relocation to the house of her mother's adoptive mother has many resonances, but key among them, to use Gould's words, is how "Berkeley's proximity to the Sierra Nevada and the small town of Belden, on the Feather River, where [her] mother Vivian Beatty was born in 1914" was a catalyst that caused Gould to become "firmly attached and sensitive to [her] California Indian, or Konkow heritage."[38] Here we begin to see the way physical movement enables an exploration of queer diasporic space. Part of Gould's project in *Earthquake Weather* and in her visits to her family's ancestral land as they're documented in the text is to reassemble "the unknowable," to reconstruct the "might-have-been." In other words, Gould's return to Koyoonk'auwi territory functions as an embodied, affective homecoming in which the felt experience of a specific geographical locale produces what in Western terms would be epistemologically inaccessible: the unrecorded histories of her family and nation.

The connections, memories, and affiliations Gould crafts through these spatial and psychic homecomings are ephemeral, changeable, and affectively encountered assemblages. They rest within the body and are particularly tied to her physical and emotional returns to the land of her mother's birth. Because of the traumatic reverberations of settler colonial interventions in California, Gould does not and, in fact, *cannot* provide an American Indian renaissance–era story of a quantifiable Koyoonk'auwi identity, recovered by a physical return to bounded geographical locale and a subsequent cultural reconnection to the specific tribal practices of her family. Such cultural knowledge, she tells us, has been violently disrupted by colonization. Gould offers instead an affectively embodied assemblage or "colonialism as it is *felt* by those who experience it."[39] Part of such affective experience is cultural loss—a territorializing reality of California history—but another just as valid reality involves the deterritorializing act of reconstruction and reconnection, which Gould consciously undertakes throughout her texts.

In *Earthquake Weather,* this affective knowledge manifests in Gould's journeys to Belden and the Feather River. These locales, sites of a deep, embodied pleasure, engage the senses through the smells of cedar and rich soil, the taste of strawberries, and the coolness of river water on sun-warmed skin. Her trips also offer affective encounters with familial history, such as when Gould describes standing in a nineteenth-century cemetery, reading "the fading names of my mother's family."[40] This land, which cradles the bodies of her ancestors, is, to use her words, both "a source of deep pleasure" and "a source of sadness and loss" (x). These sights, smells, and feelings, which are "intense" bodily experiences of affective connection to land/ancestry, exist *alongside* the assertion that "there was a limit to how much I could know from a familial or 'tribal' source. So many of my relatives had died" (x). An affectively experienced Indigenous presence and a settler-induced absence therefore exist simultaneously. Gould chronicles *both* this narrative of ongoing relationality *and* familial and tribal loss: "The displacement and dissolution of my Indian family represents one aspect of the colonization that took place in northern California. This colonization amounted . . . to a social and political upheaval that occurred at the level of community and, perhaps more crucially, within families."[41] That California Indian people have lost lives, land, and in many cases, tribal connections due to colonial practices of theft, relocation, missionization, and genocide is well documented. Gould recognizes the specificities of these histories in poems such as "History Lesson," "Easter Sunday," "Blood Sisters," "We Could Not Forget," and "Tribal History." But despite how these painful histories reverberate in her and her mother's geographical relocations, Gould reconstructs tribal and familial networks through the process of Indigenous assemblage. Thus, while recognizing the violence of such historical trauma and cultural loss, Gould notes as well, "I've always felt that my memory of California, my imaginative landscape, is not entirely my own but is embedded in the memory of many tribal people, my own tribe, the Koyangk'auwi Maidu, and in the other small nations of Indian people who inhabited California before it was ever named and was still Turtle Island."[42] Here, she describes an embodied land/memory matrix, a felt connection to Koyoonk'auwi territory and relatives, established through the active interplay of individual recollection, collective memory, and lived experience. Speaking of just this possibility, Chickasaw scholar Jodi A. Byrd contends, "For American Indians who have lived for tens of thousands of years on the lands that became the United States two hundred and thirty years ago, the land both remembers life and its loss and serves itself as a mnemonic device that triggers the ethics of relationality with the sacred geographies that constitute Indigenous peoples' histories."[43] By reading Gould's affective response to her homeland and her reconstructions of personal history as embodied and dynamic assemblages, we can recognize how the geographical relocations of settler colonial histories do not have to "respatializ[e] a consciousness and relationship to land or [necessarily map] space as settler places."[44] The active nature of assemblage therefore highlights the decolonizing possibilities of alternate responses. Perhaps Brant puts it best when she contends, "Our writing is, and always has been, an attempt to beat back colonization and the stereotyping of our Nations. But the writing is *not* a reaction to colonialism, it is an active and new way to tell stories we have always told."[45]

Queer Re/Deterritorializations

The trope of movement circulates across Gould's three collections as she experiences, imagines, and, in the process, assembles personal and tribal history. I've looked briefly at the effects of bodily movements (physical relocations and cultural removals) and embodied movements (the affective encounters Gould presents as the felt experience of a land/memory matrix). The embodied movements of *queer* transformations are woven throughout Gould's work as well as in her depictions of the queer spaces she and her father inhabit. *Beneath My Heart,* as we've seen, begins with a queerly born coyote assembling the world. In this way, Gould alludes to both Indigenous oral traditions and, as chapter 1 showed, literary antecedents such as Brant, Tomson Highway, Muriel Miguel, and Daniel-Harry Steward.[46] In each of these texts, the trickster's proclivity for gender blending is emphasized, much as in Gould's "Coyotismo." By centering such queer assemblage, the opening poem of Gould's first collection sets the stage for the subsequent examinations of sexuality and the erotic that appear in all three of her books.

In *Beneath My Heart,* the deterritorializing nature of queer desire is implicitly referenced in poems like "The Beaver Woman" and "Black Bear," which anthropomorphize animal narrators who have female companions, and explicitly referenced in poems like the previously mentioned "Coyotismo" and "Autobiography," as well as in "Waiting for a Miracle," "Foster Family," "My Crush on the Yakima Woman," "A Married Woman," "When We Return to Aztlán," and, finally, the wonderful erotica of texts like "The Woman I Love Most" and "To Speak Your Name." All these pieces present the erotic as a central facet of the narrator's movement from youth to adulthood. Just as in Gould's representations of her family's movements to and from Koyoonk'auwi territory, the affective experience of a queer diasporic subject who exists outside the logics of the settler nation—in this case because of queer desire—continues to frame her acts of assemblage.

Gould's articulations of queer desire illustrate a key aspect of assemblage, the movement between territorialization and deterritorialization. In reference to such movements, Deleuze and Guattari contend that assemblage includes "*territorial sides,* or reterritorialized sides, which stabilize it, and *cutting edges of deterritorialization,* which carry it away."[47] This section considers how deterritorializing formulations of queer desire circulate. In contrast to the discrete threads of identification in *Big Eden, Johnny Greyeyes,* and *The Business of Fancydancing,* which depict clearly defined boundaries around/for sexual identities, assemblages move through and outside indentitarian layers; in fact, in many cases, Gould actively constructs alternate knowledge to deterritorialize—or "carry . . . away"—damaging understandings of self. Speaking of the utility of such work, Nikos Papastergiadis, in *The Turbulence of Migration: Globalization, Deterritorialization, and Hybridity,* contends, "The concept of deterritorialization has been a useful mode of understanding the fissures within language and cultural identity. It suggests more than just a kind of intellectual mobility but refers to a critical sensibility of innovation and improvisation. Through the process of extending forms as they are translated into different contexts or transforming concepts through elaboration with new materials, the deterritorialized subject both develops a more dynamic relationship between past and present, and offers new interpretations of the flows in the world."[48] Gould's depictions of queer desire illustrate the innovative, improvisational, and dynamic translation of deterritorialization. Thus in *Beneath My Heart,* assemblage both stabilizes (re/territorializes) existing ideological paradigms about sexuality, desire, or Indigeneity and destabilizes (deterritorializes) those same paradigms through the articulation of decolonial concepts of the erotic.

Two pieces in particular in *Beneath My Heart*—"Waiting for a Miracle" and "Foster Family"—engage the speaker's coming of age as a queer subject whose configuration of self, like Coyote's, rubs against that projected through territorializing heteropatriarchal logics. In "Waiting for a Miracle," Gould presents the reader with two women whose definitions of the miraculous leave an ideological gap between them.[49] The speaker begins, "Mama and I are both the same. / Each of us wait for a miracle."[50] While the opening frame suggests a spiritual and psychological uniformity, the narrative then moves in this stanza and the next from comparison to contrast, developing two distinctly different vantage points:

> For years Mama prayed I'd change
> into a normal girl. She thought
> I needed an operation.
> Take something out
> or put something in
> to make me right. (21)

The speaker counters the mother's reading of queerness as either bodily lack or bodily excess with her own vision of the divine: "I keep saying, Mama, / it's enough of a miracle / for a person to accept herself / the way she is" (21). Thus the territorializing understanding of queerness as deficiency is countered by a common aphorism about self-acceptance, which, rather than a banal pronouncement of individual worth, serves in this context as the "*cutting edges of deterritorialization,* which carr[ies] . . . away" the mother's troubling disciplinary demand for physical and psychic heteronormativity.[51]

The movement from the mother's perspective to the speaker's in "Waiting for a Miracle" initially seems to offer a clear transition between territorialization and deterritorialization. Reading between the two points of view, the audience sees the speaker encounter normalizing (territorialized) logics in stanza one and then sees her own (deterritorializing) claim for the "miracle" of self-acceptance in stanza two. When these differing definitions of "miracle" are contrasted, the daughter's redefinition can be interpreted as a recognizable narrative of queer resistance to the demands of heteronormativity. But in the turn to the third and final stanzas, yet another movement occurs, reminding us "one can never posit a dualism or a dichotomy, even in the rudimentary form of the good and the bad. You may make a rupture, draw a line of flight, yet there is still a danger that you will reencounter organizations that restratify everything, formations that restore power to a signifier, attributions that reconstitute a subject."[52] Gould's "line of flight," her speaker's claim for emancipatory understanding, is reterritorialized: "Nevertheless, I wait. / I pray to change. / . . . / But no miracle occurs" (21). With these prayers, perception shifts again. If into the first pairing of "miracles" we can read resistance to dominant iterations of homophobia and heteronormativity, the last presents a reversal when the speaker "pray[s] not to feel anymore," prays to "stop / loving women," thereby internalizing the mother's heteronormative definition of "miracle" (21). In "Waiting for a Miracle," meaning lies in the spaces among these narrative reversals, where the audience, though not, in the end, the speaker, can recognize the manifestations of internalized homophobia and, subsequently, see how Gould makes visible the production and repetition of psychological trauma.

The psychic movements in "Waiting for a Miracle," in which configurations of queerness circulate in a re/de/territorializing spiral, are echoed in "Foster Family," which also takes as its subject queer coming-of-age and, subsequently, the queer as subject in waiting. In "Foster Family," queer affiliations are shown to draw lines of kinship and alliance outside biological or state-mandated family structures. The poem, which is set in an Oregon October, begins when two girls—the speaker, who seems to be the foster child of the title, and her companion, the biological daughter of the foster family—ride out to an apple orchard. Within the trees, with their classic connotations of desire and forbidden fruit, the speaker explains, "We each rode silent, / in separate hungers."[53] The two girls gallop back to the house, arriving "in the kitchen, mud-spattered, / breathless" (40). Like the mother in "Waiting for a Miracle," in this family, too, the mother wields the disciplinary mechanism of shame and social control. The speaker comments, "Your mother's hand slapped / flat on the table. / She tore into you like a badger, / snarled the words *love* / and *lesbians* / . . . / I saw that night we had things in common / besides the way your face fought humiliation" (40). In Foucauldian proliferation, the girls' unspoken desires are articulated in/through the very act of prohibition. The mother in this vignette uses, perhaps, the girls' proximity, their flushed faces, their giddiness after a long gallop, as evidence for her "charges" against them, citing as fact what they themselves had heretofore only imagined. José Esteban Muñoz examines the parameters of such queer evidence in *Cruising Utopia,* explaining, "Historically, evidence of queerness has been used to penalize and discipline queer desires, connections, and acts."[54] As a result, he argues, the way to "prove queerness and read queerness, is by suturing it to the concept of ephemera . . . [the] trace, the remains, the things that are left, hanging in the air like rumor."[55] In this scene, the mother leaves "hanging in the air" the possibility of queer desire, even as she attempts to territorialize or foreclose it. Yet the trace of queer erotics remains, held tight to the speaker's chest when she "escape[s] to the narrow bed / [her foster] family provided" (40). The re/de/territorializing spiral we saw in "Waiting for a Miracle" therefore reveals itself again in "Foster Family." The queer ephemera left hanging after the mother's denouncements become, in the distorted space between the original utterance and the speaker's perception, a lingering trace of queer possibility, a line of flight. Perhaps the psychic movements of Gould's characters open a window on what Muñoz might call a "future in the present," when the young narrator sees "an anticipatory illumination of a queer world, a sign of an actually existing queer reality, a kernel of political possibility within a stultifying heterosexual present."[56]

The intersection of "love" and "lesbians," spit like a curse from the mother's lips in "Foster Family," becomes the site of erotic play in Gould's wonderfully steamy poems like *Beneath My Heart*'s "The Woman I Love Most," "To Speak Your Name," and "Our Bodies in the Half-Light." The subject in waiting, placed outside the bounds of family and nation in the previous pieces, finds existence not in acceptance by and incorporation into the strictures of the nation-state but through the affective experience and deterritorializing articulation of queer desire. Brant calls such erotic writing both "gift" and "give-away," pointing out, "Land. Spirit. History, present, future. These are expressed in sensual language."[57] She explains, as well, "It is now possible for lesbian Natives to give voice to *all* of who we are. Keeping ourselves secret, separating parts of ourselves in order to get heard and/or published has been detrimental to our communities and to our younger sisters and brothers who long for gay and lesbian role models."[58]

As noted in the Introduction, the importance of the erotic has been the subject of much discussion in queer Indigenous studies, where Native writers and critics like Brant, Gould, Chrystos, Qwo-Li Driskill, Chris Finley, Daniel Heath Justice, Miranda, Robert Warrior, and Craig Womack, among others, have argued for its centrality to Indigenous literatures and lives. Gould herself explores the intersections of writing and Indigenous erotics in her essay "Disobedience (in Language) in Texts by Lesbian Native Americans," where she explains, "I have imagined the art of writing as the art of risk-taking, the art of leaping into the forbidden territory of the heart and soul, of tasting the fruit of holistic and psychic knowing that is fed, as Lorde eloquently noted, by the erotic."[59] Likewise, in the introduction to her collection *The Zen of La Llorona,* Miranda writes,

> Love and the erotic are powerfully creative forces in human lives, in what Joy Harjo calls "The epic search for grace". . . . Grace isn't about a culminating moment of perfection or the achievement of a sublime mystical state. Grace, or what I call an indigenous erotic, has a particular context for this particular continent: the perpetual act of balancing. . . . But both love and the erotic are at odds with the violence and domination that structures any colonizing or patriarchal culture. Thus, in colonization and patriarchy love is turned into grief, and the erotic is distorted.[60]

What Miranda terms the "Indigenous erotic" and Driskill terms "sovereign erotics" has the power to disassemble colonizing rhetorics about Indigenous sexualities and deterritorialize desires, as a return to Gould's work demonstrates.

In "The Woman I Love Most," "To Speak Your Name," and "Our Bodies in the Half-Light," Gould revisits the affective, embodied imagery of "Autobiography." Here, the affective turn is mapped through the Indigenous erotic: a topography of desire that includes a felt relationship between bodies and landscape. Thus the speaker explains, "The woman I love most / opens beneath her skin. / I feel the blood of her womb / waiting for me. / When she flowers, / red petals will cover parched land."[61] The pulse of body and blood are regenerative in this scene; the erotic heals "parched" land from drought. This decolonizing articulation of desire carries away/ deterritorializes the heteronormative logics the speaker encounters in "Waiting for a Miracle" and "Foster Family." These lines of flight occur, too, in "To Speak Your Name," where the classic tie between queerness and secrecy is exchanged for speech: "To speak your name / between your warm thighs / above the curve of your belly / in the cave of your mouth / close to your closing eyes, / this is what I want."[62] Gould depicts speech as erotic act when the articulation of a lover's name becomes, itself, a bodily caress. Moreover, the act of naming a queer lover serves as an example of erotic sovereignty. According to Miranda, in this sort of "erotic acknowledgement," a lover "makes herself visible and patriarchal culture suddenly invisible. In that instant, as she creates herself, each lover grasps what Lorde calls the power of the erotic, and what I suggest to be more specifically the power to create, to become visible, and become the creator of her own visibility—to assert presence in a physical, historical, and political sense."[63] This creativity is seen not just in "The Woman I Love Most" and "To Speak Your Name" but throughout Gould's poetry and essays, where the erotic serves as a creative force that deterritorializes settler colonial understandings of sexuality to engender Indigenous visibility and voice.

Lines of Flight/Lines of Inheritance: Fear of the Queer

Another location from which to view the territorializing/deterritorializing spiral of embodied movements and queer transformation in Gould's work is in her depictions of the queer spaces her father inhabits. Just as *Beneath My Heart, Earthquake Weather,* and *Doubters and Dreamers* explore the "autobiographical" account of Gould's own desires, so too do these texts explore the parameters of her father's queer desire as constructed through the lens of his daughter's poetic personae. Looking back, we see that "Autobiography" frames this conversation with the speaker's opening claim: "I was born of a half-breed mother / and a transvestite father."[64] That single-line reference is the extent of Gould's allusions to her father in *Beneath My Heart,* but *Earthquake Weather*'s "Thursdays" and "My Father" consider the psychological reverberations of this queer transformation.

"Thursdays" and "My Father" alternate between situating queerness in occupation/attitude and in the body within two poems that craft queer affiliation as a father/daughter inheritance. The prose poem "Thursdays" begins with a childhood prohibition: "They say one should never wear green on Thursday, for fear of being labeled a queer. This we heard when we were young, but it was difficult to determine what a queer was."[65] The narrator then posits a series of questions about what constitutes queerness. Is a recluse queer? Is an intellectual queer? A "lunatic" who stands in the road and "sh[akes] his fist at amused motorists" queer (31)? Is the male-to-female (MTF) cross-dresser queer? What if that cross-dressing occurs when "taking women's roles in comic operas" (31)? In the subsequent paragraph the musings continue, moving from objective question to specific claim: "Could a girl be queer? Could a woman? What would such a lady look like, and what would she do? I suspected I was queer" (31). The speaker embarks on a reverie of the risks of wearing green on Thursday, which leads to a lament about the heteronormalizing logics of "Home Ec": "Every girl was obliged to take this class, to learn how to be a good homemaker for her future husband and family" (32). The poem pokes fun at the equation of sewing a skirt with the successful performance of femininity and then concludes by employing sewing as a metaphor for queerness. The slippery nature of identitarian logics are questioned throughout, since queerness can be signified by anything from colors to occupation to seemingly arbitrary and unrelated actions. An amorphous permutation—an assemblage of the most random configurations—in "Thursdays," queerness is a line of flight that multiplies at will. Such a multiplicity, Deleuze and Guattari contend, "has neither subject nor object, only determinations, magnitudes, and dimensions that cannot increase in number without the multiplicity changing in nature. . . . An assemblage is precisely this increase in the dimensions of a multiplicity that necessarily changes in nature as it expands its connections."[66] Gould presents queerness as just this sort of unruly, multiplying de/re/territorializing configuration, an assemblage that is "both/and" (or perhaps "neither than") rather than "either/or."

Muñoz's examination of queer evidence resonates in this multiplicity, much as it did in Gould's earlier work, since each vignette Gould offers in "Thursdays" is one in which "evidence of queerness [is] used to penalize and discipline queer desires, connections, and acts."[67] But just as the narrator's definitional attempts fail, so do her attempts to conform to the arbitrary markers of heteronormativity. Through the queer permutations of memory, she is often forgetful, "sometimes [wearing] a dark green skirt to school on Thursdays" (31).[68] At the same time, a softball injury, the bane of butch lesbians everywhere, prevents the speaker from completing her sewing project. This failure has social and cultural ramifications. She explains, "The success of my skirt would demonstrate that I was a real girl with an interest in being female and eventually a wife and mother [and] would prove a love for my body, a vanity in my looks, a desire to be desired by boys" (32). The boundaries of identity thus remain unsecured in the narrator's life, and the slippery nature of this public slide into queerness is matched, at the poem's conclusion, by private "evidence" of her father's queerness, a "trace . . . hanging in the air like rumor."[69]

"Thursdays" concludes with the narration of the father's prowess at sewing "the hardest thing of all, the buttonhole and button" (32). As a "symphony" played on the radio, Gould's father "would put his knees primly together, . . . his face register[ing] satisfaction" while he sewed (33). But like the speaker's failure, the father's success at this marker of hetero-femininity carries with it the territorializing trace of alterity: "'Don't ever tell your friends your father knows how to sew,' Mom would say. 'People will laugh. They won't understand. They'll say he must be a queer!'" (33). The speaker's "suspicioning," to again use Womack's term, situates her questions as "action, full of desire for concrete resolution, a certainty it never achieves."[70] Gould suspicions what constitutes queerness, suspicions her own queerness, and finally presents her father's sewing as the queer trace that, if publicly articulated, might cause others to suspicion, as well. Ever adaptable and multiplicative, queerness, when suspicioned, "increase[s] in number . . . [by] changing in nature."[71] Functioning like the mother's territorializing denouncements in "Foster Family," the very act of suspicioning enables the shifting assemblage of queerness to proliferate, to "[change] in nature as it expands its connections."[72] Here, as Puar might say, "there is no entity, no identity, no queer subject or subject to queer, rather queerness coming forth at us from all directions, screaming its defiance."[73] Affiliated here with color, there with intellectualism, then with insanity, and now with a well-sewn buttonhole, in "Thursdays," Gould shows not only that evidence of queerness always already "hang[s] in the air like rumor" but also that such deterritorializing rumors run in the family.[74]

In "My Father," Gould directly returns to the "transvestite father" of "Autobiography" at a time when the suspicioned queerness seen in "Thursdays" has come to fruition.[75] The playful tone of "Thursdays" is replaced here with a more somber, though no less slippery, rumination on queerness. The poem begins,

> I have tried to understand
> what makes me afraid, wondering
> what my sisters and I will do
> with the body of my father
> when he dies.
> While in his seventies
> he changed his sex,

becoming a woman
like us.[76]

This struggle to come to terms first with the embodied movement of her father's cross-dressing and, a few years after her mother's death, with her father's decision to surgically transition from male to female is addressed here and in Gould's 2010 essay, "My Father, Cynthia Conroy." Gould's poem and essay draw lines of affiliation and demarcation, claiming at once fear and love, relationship and distance. In both pieces, Gould frames her father's transsexuality, his transition from father to mother, as an unsettling line of queer inheritance.[77]

As the first stanza of the poem demonstrates, in "My Father," Gould considers what it means for queerness to be written on the body in legible form. Unlike the act of sewing, her father's cross-dressing and eventual surgical MTF transition are lines of flight that can't be contained, or territorialized, by the walls of their family home. In Gould's poem and essay, transsexuality is figured as excess and the transsexual body, with its inherent liminality, figured both as the space of a deterritorializing, liberatory desire in the brief vignettes of Gould's father and as the site of a painful transphobia for the speaker herself. This discomfort returns us to Eng's contention that "the concept of queer diasporas" can function "as a rejoinder to the political and psychic dilemmas of queer liberalism."[78] As previously noted, Eng sets up a contrast between the homonormativity of "queer liberals today, who appear before the law demanding rights and legal protection for their intimacies," and subjects in waiting, who are always already outside such discourses.[79] We can consider the figure of Gould's father as one such displacement, a subject whose present, as depicted by Gould, is structured by the temporal and spatial logics of waiting.

The early narratives of Gould's father's cross-dressing are described in just these terms. He waits, as Gould notes in *Doubters and Dreamers*, to "[do] what dads do without a family near—/ funny things, perverse, all a little queer."[80] Gould's father, who was born in England in 1916, came of age at a time when doing "perverse" or "funny things" in public had serious consequences; thus he had to wait until some sixty years later to pursue his desire to transition—hence the story behind another movement addressed in Gould's work: her family's relocation from San Diego to Berkeley, which was a result of Gould's father leaving his job in sonar development at a company that contracted with the U.S. Navy. As they packed, Gould's mother explained that this move was tied to his arrest for cross-dressing, which she described to the young Janice as a one-time event, the result of a college dare. Gould's mother explains in 1957, "[That arrest record] means that your father is vulnerable. The government does not want to have anyone in its employ who could divulge state secrets."[81] Such queer evidence and the "oddly fraught" explanation that followed are refuted by Gould's father years later. There was "no dare involved," he explained. "It was simply something I did."[82] As Gould describes it, her father's cross-dressing must have been infrequent because he was so rarely alone, though she, one of her sisters, and her mother inadvertently met Cynthia at one point or another. Her father's waiting for the "right" temporal and spatial locations to cross-dress similarly aligns with his MTF transition, which he does not begin until after her mother's death, when he is in his seventies. "About that time," Gould explains, "Dad started the process of becoming Cynthia," who was "the oldest patient they had treated at [his Trinidad, Colorado,] clinic."[83]

The queer space that Cynthia inhabited for years before she emerged to become the public articulation of the "private" family secret can be read as the temporal and spatial articulation of queer diaspora. A subject in waiting, Cynthia challenges the binary logics of gender and sexuality, the mandates of heterocouplehood, and the supposedly stable logics of Western kinship structures, as well as the demands of homonormativity. Gayatri Gopinath speaks of such interventions, contending, "When queer subjects register their refusal to abide by the demands placed on bodies to conform to sexual (as well as gendered and racial) norms, they contest the logic and dominance of these regimes."[84] Berlant and Warner, likewise, address nation-state policing of queer identities, identifying a "national heterosexuality," which "is the mechanism by which a core national culture can be imagined as a sanitized space of sentimental feeling and immaculate behavior, a space of pure citizenship. A familial model of society displaces the recognition of structural racism and other systematic inequities."[85] Gould's father's cross-dressing ruptures the familial model. Even the trace of this practice in the form of his prior arrest record necessitates his departure from his position at the U.S. Navy laboratory. He is outside not only structures of the nation-state, which criminalize his actions and desires, but also the space of the nuclear family, where his cross-dressing and trans desires are perceived, at least by Gould, as irreconcilable with normative structures of parenthood and with homonormative models of gay subjectivity.[86] Speaking of the ways transgender people shift the language of kinship, Jack Halberstam argues that "with the rise of a visible transgender community in the last two decades and the boom in queer families, U.S. publics have had to contend with the real and abiding shifts in their understandings of kinship, belonging, normativity, and gender stability."[87] The trans body, then, disrupts territorialized lines of familial, sexual, and gendered divisions. This disruption functions as a line of flight recognized in Gould's honest portrayal of her discomfort with Cynthia.

As we have seen, the first stanza of the poem "My Father" depicts the speaker's fear of the transwoman her father has become, locating the cause for that fear in a seemingly unruly body that, even in death, is unmanageable. The poem's next two stanzas narrate the pretransitioned body. The second stanza considers the body before transition: "As a man, my father was not beautiful. / The skin on his face was fish white, / he was ruddy at the neck, / his muscles were stringy" (43). Her father's "stringy" appearance is paired with a description of his actions that, like the image of him "primly" sewing in "Thursdays," suggests he failed to meet the standards of heteromasculinity: "Standing, he gave no pose of strength, / nothing stern, nothing possessive. / He never wished to take up space" (43). The third stanza then considers the transitioned body. However, a clear before-and-after break exists between these descriptions: while the pretransitioned father is described in detail, the transitioning and the transwoman, Cynthia, remains at a distance. So though the third stanza begins with a question—"As a woman, is my father beautiful?"—for the speaker in "My Father," Cynthia remains ultimately unknowable (43). Gould describes only Cynthia's voice, which "is softer," but then immediately situates that voice as an inauthentic performance of femininity: "I know it's the voice he uses as Cynthia" (43). Posttransition, Cynthia is seen only through the mediated frame of quoted letters: "He wr[ites], 'Now that I am a woman / I like to go out dancing'" (44). Cynthia's letter goes on to explain that after being walked to her car by "Eduardo," "suddenly he was feeling me up, / his hands on my breasts. / It was a strange sensation. / I liked it very much'" (44). Just as in Gould's dismissal of the authenticity of Cynthia's voice on the telephone, the speaker's response to her here is an othering marked by visceral anger: "Those letters! / I threw them on the floor. / I wanted to stomp on them" (44). The disruption represented by transsexual bodies and desires is painfully evident in the poem where Cynthia signifies excess and physical, psychic, and familial transgression, existing in a queer diasporic space disavowed by both nation and family.

Gould's own identification as a butch lesbian who invariably crosses normative boundaries of gender and sexuality might seem to suggest the potential for affiliation, but as queerness multiplies, changing in number and kind, it demonstrates what Deleuze and Guattari call the "principle of asignifying rupture." They explain, "A rhizome may be broken, shattered at a given spot, but it will start up again on one of its old lines, or on new lines. You can never get rid of ants because they form an animal rhizome that can rebound time and again after most of it has been destroyed."[88] Though queerness may be domesticated or reterritorialized on some fronts, in, for example, homonormative practices and ideologies of sameness or in related formations of a queer liberalism that reinvigorate and extend the mandates of the nation-state, it still carries with it the possibility of excess in the spaces outside such mandates and in the subjects in waiting, like Gould's father Cynthia, who reside there. In a moving passage in "My Father, Cynthia Conroy," Gould ruminates on this possibility: "I was not comfortable with Cynthia. I wanted to be, and I tried to be, but for years I had avoided seeing her one-on-one, especially after the sex change. I don't fully know the reasons for this discomfort. My dad scared me, but I expect that this is because I could identify in a visceral way with Cynthia's discontent with being a man. That sense of identification, a kind of inward knowing about my dad's—and my own—transgressive longings, was something I could not articulate."[89]

Gould's fear as expressed in her poem "My Father" and essay "My Father, Cynthia Conroy" recognizes and, in fact, hinges on this understanding of her father's and her own queerness spiraling between territorialized and deterritorialized alterity. Affiliation functions not as the sort of affective bond we saw in Erdrich's depictions of female masculinity but as the root cause of the disruption and distance the poem and essay depict.

In the poem, Gould moves from her mediations on her father and the anger over his letters and physical transition directly into a narrative about the ways her own body has been queerly read. Her father's letters remind her of her mother's belief that Gould, as a young girl, was "not normal" (44). Her mother takes her to the doctor, claiming that "if he found anything wrong," she would kill her daughter and then herself.[90] This scenario, which Gould repeats in both poem and essay, marks the queer body as a legible text that signifies both lack and loss. In such a reading, queerness has the power to sever kinship bonds; thus, in Gould's childhood, her own queerness, if articulated, holds the possibility of severing the relationship between herself and her mother, while, as an adult, her response to her father's/transmother's queerness likewise increases the distance between them. However, at the same time, the seamless move from her father's to her own potentially transgressive body in "My Father" offers again a possible line of inheritance, a point of connection, a queer line of flight that Gould acknowledges even as, according to her overt claims, she would prefer not to: "*O, my father, / father I never knew, / father who never was / yet was my only father, / who do you imagine I am?*" (45). In these repeating scenarios, the queer body is the asignifying rupture, the rhizome that "rebound[s] time and again after most of it has been destroyed."[91] As a result of this return, Gould has no choice but to confront the overlaps in her and her father's transgressive narratives.

Gould's honest portrayals of the fears that erupt in the face of the trans body highlight both the efficacy and the tension involved in deploying queer diasporas as a theoretical lens. On the one hand, her depictions of the disruptive nature of her father as transwoman point to the power of spaces and identities that exist in the margins and shadows, in sites outside familial and national recognitions. On the other hand, however, her particular narrative also demonstrates the problems the concepts of queer assemblage and queer diasporas have for Native studies, where questions of familial identity and cultural affiliation so often take center stage. Gould addresses these difficulties head on in "My Father, Cynthia Conroy," writing, "There was another social awkwardness when we met people outside the family. How did we explain our Native American heritage? It would mean creating a fictional Native American father, if our 'mother,' Cynthia, was white."[92] In this case, the rhetoric of biology and genealogy, so central to Indigenous studies, territorializes the trans body. While Lyons, as I noted earlier in this chapter, argues we must "stop asking the perennial question, what is an Indian?" Gould's experience of her father's transition suggests it's not that easy.[93] What's striking here is the way this particular genealogical narrative hinges on heterocouplehood, attaching lineage and Native identity to a heteronormative family configuration. Mark Rifkin traces the way this pairing of heterocouplehood and Indigeneity has functioned as a state mandate within U.S. Indian policy, demonstrating how nondominant configurations of "home, family, and political collectivity are presented as endangering the state."[94] Within Gould's work, configurations of transsexuality hit just such indentitarian walls when heterocouplehood is marked as necessary to genealogical lineage. Thus in *Earthquake Weather,* the Indigenous assemblages of *Beneath My Heart* are contained (or at least constrained) in the face of the rupture embodied by the transmother and her queer line of inheritance.

Assemblage, Queer Diaspora, and the Space Between: *Doubters and Dreamers* and Political Reinvestment

This chapter began with an epigraph that speaks to how Gould's sense of an Indigenous collective memory shapes her understanding of California and self. The processes involved in these reconstructions of self, family, and Indigeneity are active, shifting practices of becoming that, in the context of Gould's writing, I term "Indigenous assemblages." Alongside the always contextual processes of assemblage, the methodology of queer diasporas helped us discuss the affective experiences and embodied spaces outside and between dominant narratives of being, keeping in mind, as Deleuze and Guattari note, that "*between* things does not designate a localizable relation going from one thing to the other and back again, but a perpendicular direction, a transversal movement that sweeps one *and* the other away, a stream without a beginning or end that undermines its banks and picks up speed in the middle."[95] The spaces between and/or outside settler colonial projections of Indigeneity and nation-state demands of hetero/homonationalisms are of particular interest to *The Queerness of Native American Literature* and are central to Gould's work. Thus after considering the ways theories of assemblage and queer diasporas frame *Beneath My Heart* and *Earthquake Weather,* this chapter concludes with a brief analysis of Gould's most recent collection, *Doubters and Dreamers,* where familial histories are both reiterated and reconstituted through Indigenous assemblage, thereby, as Eng would say, creating the "space for social and political reinvestment[s]."[96]

In *Doubters and Dreamers,* descriptions of Gould's travel from Berkeley to Belden and Berkeley to the coast are chronicled in poems like "Renegade" and "New Year's Day." The intimate enclosure of a car's interior serves a place of possibility where laughter, songs, and stories are shared "when the tank is full" and the car heads "a steady fifty / up [a] river road," whose "ancient waters," the narrator later explains, "[cover] our dead."[97] These journeys embody affective encounters, recalling and reassembling the familial, national, and sexual identities fractured by settler incursions into Koyoonk'auwi territory. Gould's poetry, then, deploys the metaphor of movement to craft Indigenous assemblage in the imaginative geographies of history, nation, family, and sexuality that exist within the body.

In "Tribal History," the first of two sections in *Doubters and Dreamers,* Gould returns to the process of Indigenous assemblage that marked *Beneath My Heart.* Thus one of the threads of *Doubters and Dreamers* is the evocation of a Koyoonk'auwi presence on the land now claimed as California. This rehistoricizing is particularly significant in terms of California history, where the intentional genocide of Indigenous people is still so often glossed over in dominant texts and classrooms. As Miranda points out in her introduction to her powerful poetry collection, *Indian Cartography,* "To this day, schoolchildren in many parts of California are required to create dioramas of Missions, complete with happy, productive Indians working in fields, at looms, and worshipping in the sanctuary of a benevolent Catholic god."[98] Gould's poems refute this erasure by insisting that California Indian history and presence be acknowledged.

The first poem in the section, "Indian Mascot, 1959," is a sestina that revolves around the tension between settler colonial erasures and Indigenous recognitions. The narrator remembers the rivalry between the University of California, Berkeley, and Stanford University, when Berkeley students—to mock their rivals, who were then called the Stanford "Indians"—would hang Native effigies. After fall parties, the speaker explains, "students [would] parade foggy streets in mock / processions, bearing on shoulders scrawny effigies of dead, / defeated Indians cut from trees, where, / in the twilight, they had earlier been hung."[99] This practice evokes a debate between the speaker's mother and father. If we read this poem as autobiography, Gould's white father claims, "'it's only in jest.' / . . . / 'They don't mock // real, live Indians,'" while her Koyoonk'auwi mother, whose personal history of adoption and relocation Gould addressed in *Earthquake Weather,* demurs (1). She notes, by contrast, that the "kids [who] perform mock / war dances, whooping, re-enacting scenes of a debacle / white folks let loose" are children of the settlers who literally killed Indigenous people in just this way three generations before (1). The overt recognition of this historical violence is followed by a comment about the emotional toll of colonialism: "How many dead / Indians do they need to feel okay? This whole thing wears / on my soul" (2). The exchange evokes the ongoing attempts at colonial disavowal of settler violence even as that violence is reenacted, reminding us again of Million's argument about the affective weight of colonial trauma. Coming after Gould's previous ruminations on her father's queerness, the exchange also can be seen to reference the weight of the settler colonial imagination in histories of U.S. queerness. Scott Lauria Morgensen argues that "the biopolitics of settler colonialism continues to attempt to eliminate Native nations as a difference that can disturb the finality of settlement."[100] This practice is seen in Gould's representation of the exchange between her father and mother. The conversation disrupts "the temporality of settler colonialism, which predicts indigeneity's erasure by positing authenticity as a past split from a progressive present."[101] In this light, the conversation functions as yet another example of how Indigenous histories can be depicted as distinct from current settler realities; according to the father, the hanging of these "scrawny effigies of the dead" holds no trace of actual historical practices and therefore should have no affective weight in the present for his Koyoonk'auwi wife and daughter. But Gould refutes such worlding in "Indian Mascot, 1959."

Besides crafting her mother as a Koyoonk'auwi woman who overtly contests the biopolitical erasures of settler practices, Gould also uses the poem's final, three-line envoi to further this point. The envoi speaks especially to settler colonial temporalities by highlighting an Indigenous present and presence in California: "living Indians at Feather Falls / leave tobacco to mark that, indeed, / we're still here, lungs full of indigenous air" (2). Though not noted specifically in the poem, the 640-foot drop of Feather Falls, which is in Middle Rock Canyon, is Koyoonk'auwi territory and, today, is near "the principal modern Konkow community."[102] With this reality in mind, Gould's conclusion marks the existence not only of Gould and her mother Vivian, whose ties to Koyoonk'auwi community had been fractured (though not severed) by Vivian's adoption, but also of those who were able to remain permanently on the land. Gould's California in 1959 is the space of survivance, of historical continuance, where Native people speak of and refute historical and present practices of settler colonial violence.

In "Renegade," Gould again acknowledges the movement of assemblage and the presence of urban hubs, writing, "Mama was no reservation squaw. Abandoned / but not disowned, she married white and went back home / only when the tank was full, smoking at a steady fifty / up the river road, taking each snake-eyed turn in stride."[103] Rather than being a litany of tragic victimry, the family's movement to and from Berkeley to Belden and the Feather River and her mother's connection to/distance from

Koyoonk'auwi culture is humorously invoked here. Thus as the family returns to the land of their Indigenous ancestors, the speaker explains that she and her siblings "chortled with songs sacred to our people, Wee-mo-way / and Kumbaya" (3). By invoking pop and Christian songs as "sacred," "Renegade" plays with expectations that metonymically link "Indian" to "tradition," situating both in a precontact past.[104] Garroutte addresses these dominant misconceptions in a chapter humorously titled "What If My Grandma Eats Big Macs?":

> [The] assumption that unbroken continuity forms the sine qua non of Indian cultural integrity is fundamental to many other cultural definitions of Indianness. This premise, as historian James Clifford writes, reflects a Western, linear story about tribal existence in which culture is assumed to have an essentially straight and unbroken trajectory toward an end point of either survival and maintenance or disintegration and assimilation. This story makes no accommodation for "sharp contradictions, mutations, or emergencies"—the eventualities of which real life is, in fact, composed. In other words, it is an unrealistic construct that reflects a great deal about the racial beliefs of those who formulated it and very little about the real world and the real people who inhabit it.[105]

Instead of foreclosing Indigenous futures based on the temporal settler logics Garroutte addresses here, in *Doubters and Dreamers* Gould again creates Indigeneity as part of a living, breathing assemblage. Thus as in her previous collections, Gould acknowledges the violence of California's colonizing history and the subsequent cultural fragmentation experienced by California's Indigenous peoples. However, as we have seen, Gould also claims a deep connection to land and Konkow ancestry as evidenced yet again in the poem's conclusion, when the children go to sleep to the sound of "the river in its restless bed, ancient waters covering our dead" (4). In the end, *Doubters and Dreamers* refutes a narrative of erasure by assembling—seeing, naming, and affectively experiencing—Koyoonk'auwi history and landscape.

Assembling Conclusions

Eng and Gopinath critique the way classic diasporic studies situate homeland as part of the "patriarchal and heteronormative underpinnings" of diaspora that focus on "genealogical notions of racial descent, filiation, and biological traceability."[106] Gopinath contends, "Queer diasporic cultural forms," by contrast, "suggest alternate forms of collectivity and communal belonging that redefine home outside a logic of blood, purity, authenticity, and patrilineal descent."[107] This chapter demonstrates that Gould both claims and disavows such genealogies, locating identity in affective affiliation to Koyoonk'auwi territory while still recognizing the inadequacies of her and her mother's relationship to Koyoonk'auwi cultural knowledges. But even while Gould readily acknowledges the losses incurred from California's settler history, none of her texts traffic in Vizenor's tragic victimry; instead Gould posits networks of affective and familial affiliation that weave back and forth from the urban hub of Berkeley to Belden and the Feather River. Like spider webs, these networks are at once flexible and delicate; they can be rended if stretched too far but also repaired by those who built them. Moreover, these ever-shifting networks are tied to geographical movements, visible only in certain light from certain locations. By imagining these relationships in the face of California's genocidal history, Gould offers not simply a depiction of but *a methodology for* how to "think the unknowable" or, if we were to read through an affective lens, how to *feel* the unknowable. In the process, the web of Gould's project, the "zigzag / of [her] path / back home / or away" in *Beneath My Heart, Earthquake Weather,* and *Doubters and Dreamers* replaces a narrative of tragic victimry with the powerful, active, and generative practice of Indigenous assemblage.[108]

Two-Spirit Futures

THIS STUDY BEGAN by looking at moments that attempt—but never quite manage—to sever queerness from Indigeneity, arguing that when we examine queer Native literature and theory more closely, we find a map of complex relationship(s). That argument moves and develops across the book and appears, in some form, in every chapter. The first relationship *The Queerness of Native American Literature* maps, then, is that between the inception of American Indian literary studies as a distinct discipline and the inception of queer Native literature and theory as a distinct body of work. Using Paula Gunn Allen's foundational writing across categories as synecdoche, the Introduction demonstrates the imbricated nature of these two areas of study, which are often imagined as disparate. As an agent of academic change, Allen facilitated early intellectual dialogue and exchange in Native literary studies; as a poet, essayist, and theorist, she simultaneously sparked vibrant, sometimes contentious scholarly conversations about queer Native people and texts. The Introduction also brought Allen's important tribal-feminist study and manifesto, *The Sacred Hoop,* into the expanding collection of embodied theoretical analyses of the Indigenous erotic. Layering Allen's, Beth Brant's, Qwo-Li Driskill's, Deborah A. Miranda's, and Robert Warrior's work, this chapter identified commonalities and differences among queer of color and Indigenous erotic imaginaries, noting the latter's deep ties to land, Indigenous nationalism, and sovereignty. Out of this return to Allen, then, comes one of the book's key refrains: Native literature was always already queer.

To further this claim, *The Queerness of Native American Literature* then looks toward multiple types of recovery: the genealogical, the archival, and the thematic. Chapter 1 demonstrates that the roots of the relationship cited in the Introduction branch in multiple directions. Thus what seems a recent blossoming of queer Indigenous poetry, fiction, essays, and theory—a twenty-first-century "renaissance," if you will—actually traces back to time immemorial. By following these roots from the mid-twentieth century to the present, this first chapter charts a genealogy, contending that the texts, trends, and affiliations in queer Native literary studies form yet another map of relationship(s) and are themselves practices of meaning making. Chronologically, this much-needed history of the field gestures back to Lynn Riggs's work in the 1930s and then reviews queer texts from the 1970s to the present. This chart of relationship and affiliation emphasizes the previously unrecognized importance of queer / women of color anthologies to a Two-Spirit literary genealogy as well as the transnational, trans-Indigenous affiliations between Indigenous writers in Canada, the United States, and beyond, a connection that predates these anthologies and continues to this day. After considering 1970s poetry and 1980s anthologies, chapter 1 then looks across the genres of drama, fiction, poetry, and theory. In the process, this chapter illustrates the richness, depth, and vibrancy of queer Native literature and theory.

Extending *The Queerness of Native American Literature*'s recovery work, chapter 2 focuses on one particular archive—Maurice Kenny's writing from the 1970s gay cultural renaissance—in order to argue for an expansion of our 1970s imaginaries. Concentrating primarily on the poems Kenny published in *Fag Rag* between 1974 and 1978, chapter 2 uses this work to make a number of arguments about how such a recovery might help us better recognize and forward relationship. One such unearthed correlation involves the gay cultural renaissance and the Native American literary renaissance. Both of these watershed moments share common temporal markers—the 1969 Stonewall Rebellion, on one hand, and N. Scott Momaday's 1969 Pulitzer Prize, on another—similar expansions of political protests, and parallel increases in literary production; however, little has been said about the potential interconnections between the two historical periods. The recovery of Kenny's work from the journals of the gay cultural renaissance thus disrupts a common sense of these literary venues as solely white. Moreover, Kenny's poems about the Brooklyn Bridge allow us to expand and reclaim a particular psychic and literary geography. To reiterate the words of José Esteban Muñoz, Kenny's oeuvre from this period serves as "an invitation to desire differently, to desire more, to desire better," thereby enabling us to re-Indigenize *both* urban space *and* the idea of the queer imagination.[1] Finally, chapter 2's recovery concomitantly challenges a heteronormative understanding of the Red Power era, reminding us, again, of the fact that Native politics, literatures, and histories were always already queer.

Chapter 3 further recovers and narrates relationship by turning from queer archive to queer image to read nearly twenty-five years of Louise

Erdrich's fiction. Beginning with her second novel, *The Beet Queen,* and concluding with her eleventh, *The Plague of Doves,* this examination, like those of the previous chapter, privileges a narrative of queer affiliation while also broadening the spectrum of analyses within *The Queerness of Native American Literature.* Thus chapter 3 looks at the relationships of Erdrich's overtly bisexual or homosexual characters—such as Karl Adare, Wallace Pfef, Candice Pantamounty, Marlis Cook, and Evelina Harp—while also reading queerness as "facets of action" rather than exclusively as subjectivity.[2] Along the way, the chapter considers queer relational practices: the affective power of female masculinity, the queer visibility of heteronormativity, and the affective, embodied experience of male lactation. Moreover, chapter 3 shows how Erdrich challenges certain forms of relationship by questioning the primacy of heteronormative kinship narratives and, in the catachrestic love between Cyprian and Delphine, our contemporary emphasis on romantic couplehood. The chapter concludes by arguing that, along with forwarding complicated theories of sexual desire and gender performance that predate or parallel those of queer studies, Erdrich's body of work emphasizes the necessity and restorative power of Two-Spirit histories in Indigenous communities. Similar to the Introduction and first two chapters, then, chapter 3 uses the trope of relationship to contend that *both* the archive *and* the canon of Native literature have been queer from the start.[3]

Chapter 4 turns from literature to visual media to consider what it means to queer Native studies that, as Michelle H. Raheja argues, "films serve as pedagogy and knowledge production for spectators."[4] Much as in chapter 1, chapter 4's brief overview of queer Indigenous filmmakers and films begins to map a particular queer history of author and image. Thus the chapter marks the prevalence of Indigenous documentaries and also offers a rich sampling of a number of contemporary shorts that are directed by queer Indigenous filmmakers or include queer Indigenous characters. As a result, chapter 4 furthers chapter 3's contention that analyses of queer authors and queer images represent equally important avenues of inquiry in queer Native studies. Like the previous analyses in *The Queerness of Native American Literature,* those in chapter 4 hinge on questions of relationship, asking what three twenty-first-century narrative films—*Big Eden, Johnny Greyeyes,* and *The Business of Fancydancing*—say about the affiliations between Indigeneity, sexuality, and nationhood, the triad of concerns so central to articulations of the Indigenous erotic. The chapter subsequently demonstrates that while each film interrogates normative Western assumptions about sexual desire, they at the same time quarantine queer desire from reserve or reservation geographies, thereby denying relationship and representing sexual and national affiliations as opposing "choices" for LGBTIQ2 Native people. More than a quarter of a century ago, Allen contended, "Image casting and image control constitute the central process" that Native people "must come to terms with, for on that control rests our sense of self, our claim to a past and to a future that we define and that we build. Images of Indians in media and educational materials profoundly influence how we act, how we relate to the world and to each other, and how we value ourselves."[5] This claim marks the value and consequence of literary and media analyses of queer images and ephemera and, as I argue at the conclusion of chapter 4, marks, as well, the importance of deploying queer Native studies as an intersectional critical lens.

Chapter 5 serves as both a final recovery in its analysis of the work of Janice Gould, an important but understudied writer, and an extension of chapter 4's call for deploying queer Native studies as an analytic. Chapter 5 undertakes such work by demonstrating how Gould's three poetry collections—*Beneath My Heart, Earthquake Weather,* and *Doubters and Dreamers*—present a theory of Indigenous assemblage. Building from the work of Gilles Deleuze, Félix Guattari, and Jasbir Puar, chapter 5 cites Gould's embodied reconstructions of queerness, self, and Koyoonk'auwi ancestry as generative methodology. Through a reclamation of relationship, Gould's practice of assemblage both confronts and rebuts the narratives of tragic victimry so often linked to California Indian histories. As opposed to the intersectional understandings of identity analyzed in chapter 4, in which discrete—and therefore fixed—threads of self could be suppressed when crossing tribal boundaries, Gould's relational assemblages present a more fluid sense of sexuality and Indigeneity. Both temporal and spatial, these assemblages coalesce around the shifting nature of events, experiences, and perception, around the known and unknown. The inherently transitory and flexible nature of assemblages thus offers a productive way to consider how the ties between Indigeneity and queerness might be imagined and reconstructed in the wake of attempted genocide. Consequently, Indigenous assemblage is linked to what Dian Million terms the "felt" experience of colonialism.[6] To address this affective quality of assemblage, chapter 5 employs David L. Eng's notion of queer diasporas.

As structures of feeling, queer diasporas both describe a space outside sanctioned nation-state identities and "index lost and forgotten desires" to "suggest how we might think the unknowable."[7] Eng argues such a concept "queer[s] the black Atlantic by expanding the oceanic limits of its social cartographies."[8] Holding in mind the many lines of trans-Indigenous affiliation chapter 1 mapped, I suggest a need to *simultaneously* interrogate the diasporas, migrations, and movements within and across American Indian and Aboriginal contexts to recognize the transnational contexts present *within* the coastlines of the land we now call North America. Through the paired lenses of assemblage and queer diaspora, then, chapter 5 demonstrates how Gould's work enacts just such an expansive and reparative methodology.

A brief turn to Deborah A. Miranda's brilliant tribal memoir, *Bad Indians,* helps us see the significance of such a transformative methodology. Speaking of the way contemporary California settler narratives describe histories of conquest in the formative spaces of elementary education, Miranda asserts that now is the "time for the Mission Fantasy Fairy Tale to end."[9] Constructing an intentional assemblage as a way to initiate this end, Miranda uses charts, letters, anthropological and mission records, newspaper clippings, poetry, archival documents, short stories, and cassette tapes of family conversations to create an alternate "Mission history," one that foregrounds both the genealogy of settler violence and the survivance stories of California Indian people. By weaving together these layered narratives, *Bad Indians* enacts the methodological process of Indigenous assemblage, terming the resulting products—lines of flight that see history *and* present anew—"mosaics." The dynamic activity of piecing often jagged cultural shards into a larger picture includes acknowledging rather than merely shunting aside the most painful of psychological and cultural fragmentations: "We've lost our language, our lands, our religion, our literature (stories and song). None of these things are recuperable, no matter how hard we work."[10] Miranda recognizes that nations gifted with more extant bodies of cultural knowledge might question the sum of the remaining pieces. Yet like Gould, in the face of such questions, she rolls up her sleeves and keeps moving forward, showing us how a messy, ongoing theoretical practice happens in the twenty-first century. Miranda concludes, "I'm not whole. And yet, I *am* whole. What the hell! I'm a whole mosaic. Deal with it, world. White and Indian, and not only that, but Indian and reinventing myself in this Post-Colonial Art Project I've inherited."[11] In the end, Indigenous assemblage is not only about a call to decolonize but also about the importance of ongoing recoveries and reclaimed relationship(s), which is, finally, the project of *The Queerness of Native American Literature.*

The genealogical and methodological recoveries at the center of *The Queerness of Native American Literature* will, I hope, provide a basis for further histories and new scholarship. Ultimately, queer Native literatures represent a vast and, in many ways, still unmined field of study. The queer Native authors and queer Indigenous images I reference here by no means make up a comprehensive list. My work, for example, privileges monographs when there are so many essays, pieces of short fiction, and, especially, so much poetry outside that textual form. Issues of access to and the fiscal constraints of the publishing industry, as well as the sometimes difficult day-to-day realities of Indigenous authors' lives, make the production of monographs the exception rather than the norm for queer Native writers. The more we uncover texts from the 1970s, 1980s, 1990s, and earlier, the larger the group of authors and collections appear to be: like the horizon, the "end" is always an optical illusion, ever expanding as we move forward. One conclusion this book makes apparent, then, is that a narrative of paucity, in which queer Native authors and texts are both anomalous and few, is inaccurate; in its stead, I propose a narrative of richness and abundance.

While comprehensive coverage is (thankfully) impossible, *The Queerness of Native American Literature* contributes to this generative process of expansion by mapping the first branches of a genealogy for subsequent scholars to extend and revise. For instance, the gap between Riggs and Kenny will, I hope, get smaller and smaller as future scholars delve into archives, libraries, and oral histories, looking, as I did in chapter 2, in unexpected places and using our ever-growing access to new materials to chart still undiscovered histories and texts.[12] These recoveries therefore necessitate a move away from novels and into the poetry and essays found in small Native and non-Native journals and newspapers as well as into the often widely dispersed archive of personal correspondence. Combing through letters, journals, and newspaper clippings can be painstaking, but it enables us to reconstruct at least some small portion of the daily lives and friendships of these early writers. Similarly, we have not scratched the surface of the small-scale collaborations that mark the 1970s and 1980s. So many association newsletters, special journal issues, and small-press anthologies remain to be recovered and, in an ideal world, digitized so this writing can return to circulation. Thus canon expansion will continue to be an integral part of the field's development as we move further into the twenty-first century. This expansion, as my work on Kenny demonstrates, is not simply about *more* texts; it is, instead, about *how the archive enables us to rethink and revise our assumptions about the field.*

As I look forward to the recovery of texts from Riggs to Kenny, I also want to highlight the pressing need for documentation of queer Native histories of alliance. I am especially interested in the rise of the many small queer Indigenous groups from the Red Power/Stonewall era to the present. My hope is that, as I write, Native scholars and activists together with non-Native allies are talking, teaching, thinking, and writing about organizations like the Gay American Indians, WeWah and BarCheeAmpe, and Nichiwakan Native Gay and Lesbian Society. Scott Lauria Morgensen offers us further context in the latter half of *Spaces between Us,* but extensive oral interview and archival work would be invaluable to the field. An example of the significance of such studies can be found in the case of the Greater Vancouver Native Cultural Society (GVNCS). While little published work exists on this still active and lively Indigenous organization, the GVNCS undoubtedly arose as a group whose purpose and focus was distinct from that of the GAI. Centered around drag performance and queer nightlife, the GVNCS presents a vastly different model of queer Indigenous collectivity than many other queer political groups of the 1970s and 1980s. As a result, the GVNCS undoubtedly breaks away from the civil rights framework that so often drives mainstream LGBTIQ organizing. Given the ways these settler frameworks reinscribe nation-state policies and fracture alternate kinship organizations, the GVNCS may well offer a productive community-based model of relationship. Brant argues that Two-Spirit people "are not 'just like everybody else.'"[13] Neither, I would add, are they "just like" each other. Exploring the radical differences *within* queer Native communities would help dispel the homogenizing and romanticized vision of queer Indigeneity that often circulates in conversations about Two-Spirit people and histories. In my Midwestern classrooms, for example, where I have been teaching queer Native literature courses since 2001, the initially surprising *lack* of resistance to queer Native studies from my largely non-Native and Christian students hinges on this romantic vision of an Edenic precontact past. To hearken back to

Craig Womack, it is my suspicion that contemporary Native men in drag might disrupt the comfortable distance of nostalgia in productive ways.

While *The Queerness of Native American Literature* looks to collaborations between Aboriginal and Native American writers north of Mexico, the field itself extends across multiple borders and, in fact, around the entire expanse of Turtle Island. Indigenous imaginaries are not bound by the North American continent but, rather, are built on intercontinental and transoceanic networks of attachment. The continued expansion of the field's geographical horizons, then, promises rich possibilities for queer Indigenous scholarship.[14] These cooperative artistic and scholarly practices of alliance are active examples of decolonial practice, yet at the same time, many Indigenous–Indigenous relationships are not about settler ideologies at all but instead about extending ancient Indigenous practices of relationship.[15] This connectivity rests on tribal realities both past and present: Indigenous peoples have always shared networks of affiliation, trading and adapting goods, languages, traditions, and resistance movements in the active process of transforming and expanding Indigenous knowledges. Looking back to the alliances evidenced by *A Gathering of Spirit, Living the Spirit,* the "Native Women" issue of *Fireweed,* and *The Colour of Resistance* helps us recognize that such trans-Indigenous methodologies have been at the heart of queer Native studies since its inception.

To conclude, I turn to my title and ask: What is to be gained by considering "the queerness" of Native American literature? As I have attempted to demonstrate, queering Indigenous literary history and engaging specifically queer Indigenous literary history forces us to reconsider foundational moments in Native studies. Moreover, the writers, artists, and scholars discussed in *The Queerness of Native American Literature* both build upon and extend preexisting intellectual genealogies and geographies. These genealogies and geographies represent archives of more diverse social roles, indexes of creative kinship relations, and essential meaning-making practices through which to generate and organize knowledge. A paradigm through which we can make felt experience legible, the "queerness" of Native American literature thus delineates a living, breathing, erotic mode of understanding *and* a transformative methodology that, as Beth Brant asserts in the epigraph with which I began this project, hold the power to "merg[e] the selves that colonialism splits apart."[16] Placing Indigenous erotics at the center of theoretical inquiry not only strengthens approaches to queer and Indigenous studies but also forwards restorative, decolonial practices. Ultimately, it transforms the ways we perceive and engage our world.

Acknowledgments

THIS BOOK WAS A LONG TIME COMING, so I have many thanks to extend. First, to my family, Edna Tatonetti; Nancy, Robert, and Matthew Lear; Judy, Mike, and Timmy Conner; Dan Tatonetti; Cam, Debbie, Jason, and Josh Tatonetti; and Cara, Dave, and Emma Pavek, your love sustains me even while I am far from the salty breezes of home. And to my dad, Frank Tatonetti, I still miss you.

Thanks to the Pennsylvania compound, Tara Pauliny and Rebecca Dingo, for so many years of draft reading, good wine, stolen cookies, and fierce love. And to Jennifer and Henry Phegley for continuing our Ohio State tradition of reading women in KC.

Thanks to Debra Moddelmog and Brenda Brueggemann for invaluable early mentorship. Who knew, Debra, what would happen when you introduced me to Beth Brant's "A Long Story" so many years ago?

My University of Wisconsin Oshkosh crew—Denise Clark, Aaron Dunckel, Lynn Freeman, Charlie and Anna Hill, Jordan Landry, and Jeanie Grant Moore—I miss you. Thanks for summer evening fires, Fratello's dinners, and Door County memories.

In Manhattan—first, to my super friends, Jenn Anthony, Val Padilla Carroll, and Tanya González, thanks for being my family in Kansas. To my SOS sisters, my gratitude for standing shoulder to shoulder. To Abby Knoblauch for tissues, Wisconsin cheese, and unfailingly good advice on drafts and life. To Kara Northway for surprise chocolates, sharp wit, and smart comments. To Michele Janette for friendship, intellectual companionship, and bathroom renovations. To Cameron Leader-Picone for great conversations and always having my back. To Shireen Roshanravan and Tushabe wa Tushabe for our collaborations in queering the universe. And to Dave Defries, Greg Eiselein, Bret Flanders, Brian Johnson, Anne Longmuir, Wendy Matlock, Anne Phillips, Annie Recking, Kim Smith,

Joe Sutliff Sanders, Karin Westman, and Naomi Wood. Who could ask for more wonderful colleagues and friends?

Special thanks to Chad Allen for so many years of great mentoring, fabulous trips, invaluable friendship, and reading sections of the manuscript. Sharing work and conversations with you has fundamentally shaped my thinking and enriched my life. To Jeff Berglund for encouragement and the shout-outs about my early queer Alexie piece. To Susan Bernardin for friendship, travel, wineries, and excellent beer. We have many writing retreats to come, my friend. To Jim Cox, especially for our MLA conversation in which you made me believe I could write an Introduction. To Qwo-Li Driskill, Daniel Heath Justice, and Deborah Miranda for being friends, sometimes-readers, sometimes-letter writers, inspiring writers and theorists, and wonderful collaborators on *Sovereign Erotics*. To Brian Gilley for influential scholarship and reading a short section of the Introduction. To Janice Gould for music, poetry, and permissions. To Jane Hafen for introducing me to *Johnny Greyeyes* and pushing me to publish; my early work on Alexie never would have made it to print otherwise and the Erdrich is also due to you. To Joanna Hearne for warm friendship and so generously sharing your vast knowledge of Indigenous film. To Rob Innes and Kim Anderson for comments on my female masculinities essay. To Maurice Kenny for permissions and the gifts of your books, which made me cry. To Scott Morgensen for academic inspiration, encouragement, and generously sharing resources. To Meg Noodin for friendship and for taking on the *SAIL* book review editorship. To Mark Rifkin for the *GLQ* comments and brilliant scholarship. To Mikko Tuhkanen and Ellen McCallum for invaluable feedback on the Cambridge essay that became chapter 1. And to Craig Womack for foundational work in queer Indigenous studies; my students will still be giddy about Skyping with you when this book comes to print.

Thanks to Robert Warrior for his generosity in including my book in the Indigenous Americas series, where I am published alongside my academic heroes. Thanks to Jason Weidemann and Danielle Kasprzak, to my challenging and invaluable anonymous readers (the improvements are yours, the remaining deficits mine), and to all the fine folks at the University of Minnesota Press for help bringing the book from laptop to material reality.

Thanks to Kansas State University for an invaluable sabbatical semester and for the USRG funds that allowed me to travel to the American Native Press Archives. To Daniel Littlefield at the American Native Press Archive for research help with 1970s Native periodicals. To the University of Wisconsin Oshkosh for the Race and Ethnicity Fellowship. To the University of Kansas Kenneth Spencer Research Library for help with the Wilcox collection, permissions, and material reproductions.

Sincere thanks to my SUROP and undergraduate student intern help: Maria Calhoun, for tracking down the early Kenny collections; Molly Sanders, for research on Kenny, Allen, and laFavor; and Elyse Stadlmayr and Brent Weaver for invaluable support in the final stages of manuscript formatting.

I send love, laughter, and gratitude to all my students, especially those in 710, 650, and 680. You made me think harder every time. Among these folks, shout-outs to Josh Abrams, Sandi Cox, Betty Jean Curran, Ashley Denney, Dan Hornsby, Suzie Lear, Melissa Prescott, Maureen Orth, Laura Thacker, and Jessica Reyes.

Thanks to Lorraine Reimers and Samson the wonder cat for making home feel like home.

And to our Atlanta escapees, Krista and Dagney Walton, thanks for the sabbatical home where so much of this book was drafted, for paper hats and *Grease* sing-alongs, an impressive Tybee sunburn, ghost tours in multiple countries, Scottish folk music, ATL beer fest, Flying Biscuit breakfasts, London theater, Russian orthodox churches, and, most recently, otherworldly Icelandic vistas. The best trips and conversations are yet to come, boo.

Notes

Introduction

1. In this book, I employ common usage and collectively refer to Indigenous peoples whose nations and/or communities are located within (what is now) the United States as "Native American" or "American Indian." For Indigenous peoples whose nations and/or communities are located within (what is now) Canada—First Nations, Inuit, and Métis—I use the collective term "Aboriginal." In my work, "Native" and "Indigenous" function as broader, transnational terms. Attempting to accurately address the similarities and differences between Native American and Aboriginal histories is inevitably complicated. For example, as markers of the dominant imaginary, the borders between these settler nations in some cases run directly through tribal nations. At the same time, however, as I discuss at various points in this book, Indigenous peoples in the United States and Canada, while sharing common experiences of settler colonial incursion and assault, have disparate histories with U.S. and Canadian government policies. Historically, U.S. Native studies scholarship has often elided these differences through the imposition a U.S.-centric vision of the field, a fact made clear in the early organizing discussions around the name for the Native American and Indigenous Studies Association. I attempt to avoid those erasures here but also recognize the limits of both my project and my understanding as a non-Native, U.S. scholar. Additionally, I highlight the fact that this book focuses on writing in English published in the United States and Canada. My research addresses a small number of Native language and no French Canadian publications and does not cross the border into Mexico, though those borders are just as significant, just as contentious, and just as permeable.

2. Roscoe, *Zuni Man-Woman*, 22.

3. Quoted in Roscoe, *Changing Ones*, 4.

4. Ibid.

5. Jacobs and Cromwell define gender variance as "cultural expressions of multiple genders (i.e., more than two) and the opportunity for individuals to change gender roles and identities over the course of their lifetimes." See Jacobs and Cromwell, "Visions and Revisions of Reality," 63–64.

6. Jacobs, "Is the 'North American Berdache' Merely a Phantom?," 29.

7. See Williams, *The Spirit and the Flesh*; Roscoe, *The Zuni Man-Woman* and "Native North American Literature"; Jacobs, Thomas, and Lang, *Two-Spirit People*; Gilley, *Becoming Two-Spirit.*

8. Jacobs, Thomas, and Lang, "Introduction," 2–6.

9. Driskill, Finley, Gilley, and Morgensen, "Introduction," 11.

10. While some queer Native people employ "Two-Spirit," there also has been resistance to the term. "Two-Spirit" was quickly co-opted by the non-Native community and thus some see it as having New Age connotations that romanticize Indigenous identities. As the term's creators recognized, "Two-Spirit" is pantribal and lacks a relationship to a specific nation, gender role, or tribal practice. Finally, many Native people are simply more comfortable identifying as lesbian, gay, bisexual, trans, queer, and so on. See Driskill, Finley, Gilley, and Morgensen, "Introduction"; Driskill, Justice, Miranda, and Tatonetti, "Introduction"; Gilley, *Becoming Two-Spirit;* Jacobs, Thomas, and Lang, *Two-Spirit People;* Lang, *Men as Women, Women as Men;* Roscoe, *Changing Ones;* Williams, *The Spirit and the Flesh.* See Driskill for an argument for the use of "Two-Spirit" rather than "gay" or "lesbian"; "Stolen from Our Bodies," 62n3. See Womack for a brief discussion of the efficacy of the term "queer"; *Red on Red,* 300–301. See Epple, "Coming to Terms with Navajo Nádleehí," and Stevens, "Poetry and Sexuality," for critiques of the term "Two-Spirit."

11. Brant, *Writing as Witness,* 18.

12. See Van Dyke, "A Tribute to Paula Gunn Allen (1939–2008)," for more on Allen's history.

13. Simard, "A Wilderness Unlittered by Academic Trash," 4.

14. Ibid.

15. See Tatonetti, "The Emergence and Importance of Queer American Indian Literatures."

16. Jaimes and Halsey, "American Indian Women," 333. For more on the circulation of the figure of the berdache in non-Native communities, see Morgensen, *Spaces between Us.*

17. Jaimes and Halsey, "American Indian Women," 333.

18. Mihesuah, *Indigenous American Women,* 43.

19. See Denetdale, "Carving Navajo National Boundaries" and "Securing Navajo National Boundaries"; Justice, "Notes toward a Theory of Anomaly"; Womack, *Red on Red.*

20. Denetdale, "Securing Navajo National Boundaries," 134.

21. Ibid.

22. Justice, "Notes toward a Theory of Anomaly," 208.

23. Pulitano, *Toward a Native American Critical Theory,* 28; Womack, "A Single Decade," 23. For further critiques of Allen, see Krupat, *Ethnocentricism;* Vizenor, Manifest Manners; and Pulitano's scathing (and some might say disrespectful) chapter on Allen, *Toward a Native American Critical Theory,* 19–57.

24. Ferguson, *Aberrations in Black,* 66.

25. The term "queer of color" speaks both to nonwhite populations and, more often, to a body of critical approaches to race, sexuality, and gender that arose in the period of which I write. See Ferguson, *Aberrations in Black,* and Holland, *The Erotic Life of Racism.*

26. Sandoval, *Methodology of the Oppressed,* 42.

27. Ferguson, *Aberrations in Black,* 112.

28. Moraga, "*La Güera,*" 29.

29. For a conversation about such differences, see Kim, McCall, and Singer, "Introduction."

30. Ferguson, *Aberrations in Black,* 117–18.

31. Rifkin, *The Erotics of Sovereignty,* 38.

32. Holland, *The Erotic Life of Racism,* 32. Though Holland at times works in both black studies, Native studies, and also on the confluence between the two fields, she is very specifically talking about queer black studies here; however, her configuration of the erotic resonates, as well, in Native contexts.

33. Womack, *Red on Red,* 300.

34. Medicine, "Changing Native American Sex Roles," 150. Medicine employs this phrase when parsing out the difference between "homosexual" and a person who inhabited the social role of "winkte" or "hemaneh."

35. Puar, *Terrorist Assemblages,* xv.

36. See Justice, "Notes toward a Theory of Anomaly"; Morgensen, *Spaces between Us;* Rifkin, *When Did Indians Become Straight?* and *The Erotics of Sovereignty;* Smith, "Queer Theory and Native Studies"; Womack, *Red on Red* and *Art as Performance.*

37. Lorde, *Sister Outsider,* 53, 54, 55.

38. Ibid., 59.

39. Ibid., 39.

40. Warrior, "Your Skin Is the Map," 340.

41. Ibid., 343.

42. Brant, *Writing as Witness,* 17, emphasis added.

43. Miranda, *The Zen of La Llorona,* 4.

44. Miranda, "Dildos, Hummingbirds, and Driving Her Crazy," 138.

45. Driskill, "Stolen from Our Bodies," 52.

46. Rifkin, *The Erotics of Sovereignty,* 4.

47. Allen, *The Sacred Hoop,* 24.

48. Brant, *Writing as Witness,* 17.

49. Allen, *The Sacred Hoop,* 25.

50. Ibid.

51. Rifkin, *The Erotics of Sovereignty,* 34.

52. Nagel, "Ethnicity and Sexuality," 108.

53. McCall, "The Complexity of Intersectionality," 1774.

1. A Genealogy of Queer Native Literatures

1. See Warrior, *Tribal Secrets.*

2. Womack, *Red on Red,* 280.

3. Kenny, "Apache."

4. As I'll discuss later in this chapter, Canada also had a significant rise of queer politics and literature during this period. Beginning in 1978, the Greater Vancouver Native Cultural Society, one of the first queer community groups, held social events for the Two-Spirit community.

5. Quoted in Gengle, "Reclaiming the Old New World," 40.

6. This heteronormative silence occurs even in excellent anthologies such as Cherokee-Quapaw/Chickasaw writer Geary Hobson's 1979 *The Remembered Earth.* In "Adowe: We Return Thanks," the opening piece in Hobson's edited collection, Kenny describes an Indigenous poetic tradition that, despite his reference to "the humor of the delightfully erotic 'coyote' and 'trickster' stories," is markedly—and rather ironically—heteronormative. See Kenny, "Adowe," 14. Abenaki author/editor Joe Bruchac's 1983 *Songs from This Earth on Turtle's Back* and Cherokee scholar/poet Rayna Green's important 1984 collection *That's What She Said* follow this same pattern. While these collections manifest themes of consequence to Native studies, such as oral traditions and tribal/cultural continuity, they elide, by omission, the existence of multiple gender traditions and same-sex desire. Thus, while queer Native writers like Kenny, Allen, and Brant were involved in these anthologies, neither their writing nor their contributor biographies reference same-sex desire or mark them as gay and lesbian writers in these or other 1970s and early 1980s collections often cited as landmarks of the Native American literary renaissance.

7. "Akwesasne We Are Not the Enemy," 51. Many thanks to Scott Morgensen for generously sharing this resource with me. See his insightful analysis of *RFD* in *Spaces between Us,* 67–77.

8. McCall, "The Complexity of Intersectionality," 1776.

9. Ibid.

10. See Kranich and Kranich, "A Bibliography of Periodicals by and about Women of Color," and the Women's Institute for Freedom of the Press, "Celebrating Our Diversity." There were also Native women's newsletters from this period such as *The Wisconsin Tribal Women's News Najinokwe,* founded 1974 in Madison; *Ohoyo,* founded in 1979 in Wichita Falls, Texas; and *Shenabe Quai,* founded in 1979 in Turtle Lake, Wisconsin. These newsletters focused on Native politics and women's health, condemning infractions against/assaults on treaty rights and settler policies. See Kranich and Kranich, "A Bibliography of Periodicals by and about Women of Color," 40.

11. Ferguson, *Aberrations in Black,* 129.

12. My aim in this overview of anthologies is to be illustrative rather than exhaustive. There are many collections omitted from my survey, and this research offers particularly rich possibilities for future recoveries and analysis.

13. Chrystos, "I Walk in the History of My People," 57; Cameron, "Gee, You Don't Seem Like an Indian from the Reservation," 47.

14. Valerio, "It's in My Blood, My Face," 44.

15. Writing some twenty years later, Deborah Miranda will say, "The voices in *Bridge* are not inadequate or inarticulate. Those voices helped save my life. But I craved the indigenous voices that knew the paradox, pain, and deceit of a colonized homeland beneath my feet—and beneath the feet of every American." See Miranda, "'What's Wrong with a Little Fantasy?,'" 193.

16. Allen, Mary Bennett (Seneca), Brant, Cameron, Chrystos, Gould, Elaine Hall (Creek), Terri Meyette (Yaqui), Mary Moran, Katei Sardella (Micmac), Vicki Sears (Cherokee), and Valerio.

17. Brant, "Introduction," 9.

18. Brant, *Writing as Witness,* 13.

19. See Allen, *Trans-Indigenous.*

20. Holland, *The Erotic Life of Racism,* 71.

21. Chaske, Fife, Champagne, King, and Sun, "Native Women," 6.

22. Morgensen explains that "beginning in the 1970s, Native gay, lesbian, bisexual, and transgendered people met in new networks formed in the wake of migration to cities that supported both urban Native and radical gender/sexual politics. . . . Alongside Gay American Indians in the United States, groups that arose in the 1980s included American Indian Gays and Lesbians (AIGL) in Minneapolis, WeWah and BarCheeAmpe in New York City, and Nichiwakan in Winnipeg; in the late 1970s, Vancouver already hosted the Native Cultural Society, which brought Native people together in an annual drag ball and other activities." See Morgensen, *Spaces between Us,* 78.

23. For more on this gathering and queer Native organizing in Minneapolis, see MacDonald, "Two-Spirit Organizing." For more on this period of queer Indigenous activism, see Morgensen, *Spaces between Us,* 77–87.

24. McLeod, "Empowering Two-Spirit People."

25. Roscoe, *Zuni Man-Woman,* xiv.

26. Burns, "Preface," 1.

27. Allen, Ben the Dancer (Yankton Sioux), Brant, Chrystos, Gould, Nola M. Hadley (Métis), Kenny, Richard La Fortune (Yupik), Carole La Favor (Ojibwe), Joe Lawrence Lembo (Cherokee), Daniel Little Hawk (Lakota/Southern Cheyenne/Aztec), Joe Dale Tate Nevaquaya (Comanche/Yuchi), Lawrence William O'Connor (Winnebago), Debra S. O'Gara (Tlingit), M. Owlfeather (Shoshone-Métis/Cree), Erna Pahe (Navajo), Kieran Prather (a non-Native ally), Roscoe, Tala Sanning (Sioux), Daniel-Harry Steward (Wintu), Midnight Sun

(Anishinaabe), Mary TallMountain (a straight Koyukon-Athabascan ally), Hulleah Tsinhnajinnie (Seminole/Muscogee/Diné), and Anne Waters (Seminole/Choctaw, Chickasaw, Cherokee).

28. Morgensen, *Spaces between Us,* 81.

29. Anzaldúa, "Haciendo Caras, Una Etrada," xvi.

30. Ibid., xxii.

31. Ibid., xxi.

32. The inclusion of Allen, Brant, Chrystos, and Gould highlights their significance in the field, as these four authors are the most commonly anthologized queer Native writers of the 1980s and 1990s.

33. In terms of queer Native writers, Silvera's collection includes Susan Beaver (Mohawk, Grand River Territory), Brant, Chrystos, Connie Fife (Cree), and Victoria Lena Manyarrows.

34. Silvera, "Introduction," xiii.

35. Manyarrows, "The Drum Beats," 141.

36. Gould, "A Maidu in the City of Gold," 238.

37. Miranda, "'What's Wrong with a Little Fantasy?,'" 200.

38. Akiwenzie-Damm, *Without Reservation,* xi.

39. Brant's poem "Language/Desire" describes a same-sex encounter with an explicitness heretofore absent in Native literature, while Sears's short story "Baskets and Rugs" intersperses memories of the first-person Native narrator's first sexual encounter with a white woman and her developing relationship with a Native woman.

40. Contributors are Indira Allegra, Allen, Louise Esme Cruz (Mi'kmaq), Driskill, Laura Furlan (Chiricahua Apache, Osage, and Cherokee), Gould, Carrie House (Diné), Justice, Kenny, Michael Koby (Cherokee), M. Carmen Lane (Mohawk/Tuscarora), Jaynie Lara (Yaqui), Livingston, Luna Maia (Yaqui), McAdams, McMullin, Miranda, Moses, D. M. O'Brien (Omushkego Cree), Malea Powell (Miami/Shawnee), Savageau, Sarah Tsigeyu Sharp (Cherokee/Lakota), Kim Shuck (Cherokee/Sauk and Fox), Stevens, William Raymond Taylor (Osage), Joel Waters (Oglala Lakota), and Womack.

41. Weaver, "Foreword," xii.

42. Womack, *Red on Red,* 273.

43. Highway, *The Rez Sisters,* 97.

44. Along with his plays, Highway has published children's books and a semi-autobiographical novel, *Kiss of the Fur Queen* (1998), which depicts the events and aftereffects of the Okimasis brothers' abuse at the hands of the head priest of a Residential School.

45. Like Kenny, Moses published a poetry collection, *Delicate Bodies* (1980), with blewointment, a press that arose in the wake of the Stonewall Rebellion. Moses followed with two plays, *Coyote City* (1988) and *The Dreaming Beauty*

(1988), before publishing another poetry collection, *The White Line* (1990), and a series of plays throughout the 1990s: *Big Buck City* (1991), *Almighty Voice and His Wife* (1992), *City of Shadows* (1995), *Brebeuf's Ghost* (1996), and *The Witch of Niagara* (1998).

46. Spiderwoman Theater, which originated from the lesbian feminist and women of color feminist art and activism I previously discussed, is the oldest continually running women's theater company in North America. Miguel founded it together with her two sisters, Lisa Mayo and Gloria Miguel, and their first production, *Women in Violence,* premiered in New York in 1976. Spiderwoman productions are often described as weavings that interconnect stories, movements, dance, comedy, and drama. See Canning, *Feminist Theaters in the U.S.A.,* and Case, "Introduction."

47. Case, "Introduction," 5.

48. Canning, *Feminist Theaters in the U.S.A.,* 84.

49. Ibid. Case cites Schneider, "See the Big Show," and Dolan, *The Feminist Spectator as Critic,* as evidence for this claim.

50. Quoted in Abbott, "Spiderwoman Theater and the Tapestry of Story," 176.

51. Quoted in Haugo, "Weaving a Legacy," 223.

52. *Two-Spirit Acts* includes Fobister's *Agokwe,* Miguel's *Hot 'n' Soft,* and three pieces by Monkman: *Justice of the Piece, Séance,* and *Taxonomy of the European Male.*

53. Snyder, "'He Certainly Didn't Want Anyone to Know That He Was Queer,'" 50.

54. Ibid., 25.

55. For more on queer ephemera, see Muñoz, *Cruising Utopia,* 65–81; Warrior, *Tribal Secrets,* 4–5.

56. Brant, *Mohawk Trail,* 32.

57. Brant, *Writing as Witness,* 17.

58. Better known for his fiction, Sarris turned his hand to drama in *Mission Indians,* which opened at San Francisco's Intersection Theater in 2002. While Sarris's short stories ("Joy Ride") and children's fiction ("How a Mountain Was Made") have been performed by San Francisco's Word for Word Performing Arts Company, *Mission Indians,* which includes queer characters, is his first piece written for the theater. For more on Sarris, see Rifkin's insightful analysis of *Watermelon Nights* in *The Erotics of Sovereignty,* 153–214.

59. LaFavor is also the subject of Mona Smith's documentary, *Her Giveaway: A Spiritual Journey with AIDS.*

60. Lorde, *Sister Outsider,* 38.

61. The press originally slated to publish Nevaquaya's collection went bankrupt and the typewritten manuscript was subsequently lost for years. After a long

and circuitous journey, *Leaving Holes & Selected New Writings* was published in 2011 by Mongrel Empire Press.

62. Deloria, "Foreword," ix.

63. Chrystos, *Not Vanishing*, 7.

64. Miranda, "Dildos, Hummingbirds, and Driving Her Crazy," 143. See also Rifkin's chapter on Chrystos in *The Erotics of Sovereignty*, 215–66.

65. Miranda, "Dildos, Hummingbirds, and Driving Her Crazy," 146.

66. Fife, "The Revolution of Not Vanishing," 49.

67. Manyarrows, "We Have No Borders," 79.

68. Manyarrows, "Artist Statement."

69. Scofield, "Survival Poetry," 34.

70. Another memoir that precedes Scofield's and Miranda's is Cree author Kevin White's 1993 *Where Eagles Dare to Soar.*

71. Allen, *The Sacred Hoop*, 203. "Who Is Your Mother" came out in a 1984 issue of *Sinister Wisdom*, which, as previously noted, was the same multicultural journal that first published Brant's *A Gathering of Spirit.*

72. Ibid., 246, 245. Morgensen points out that white anthropologists' "promotion of berdache naturalized specifically *masculinist* colonial discourses and generic or specific references to male embodiment and desire as focal points of the sexual nature and rights defined in sexology and homosexual emancipationism by white men." See *Spaces between Us*, 47.

73. Allen, *The Sacred Hoop*, 2.

74. LaRocque, *When the Other Is Me*, 30.

75. Highway, "Why Cree Is the Sexiest of All Languages," 39.

76. Miranda, "Dildos, Hummingbirds, and Driving Her Crazy," 14; Driskill, "Stolen from Our Bodies," 51.

77. Driskill, "Stolen from Our Bodies," 51.

78. Allen, "Some Like Indians Endure," 24.

2. The Native 1970s

1. Ferguson, *Aberrations in Black*, 66.

2. See Kelsey, "Reading the Wampum"; Wilson, "Maurice Kenny"; or Kenny, "Introduction" and "Waiting at the Edge," for more on Kenny's personal and literary biography.

3. My gratitude to Maurice Kenny for my copy of this powerful collection.

4. See Morgensen's *Spaces between Us* for more on the rise of the GAI and other queer Native social/activist groups.

5. Kenny, *On Second Thought*, 58.

6. Ibid.

7. Ibid.

8. Ibid.

9. Winston Leyland, the editor of *Gay Sunshine,* claims to have initially coined this term, which he defines as "a rediscovery of Gay Cultural heritage and its expression, especially since Stonewall, through art, music, literature, film, and in many other ways." See Leyland, *Orgasms of Light,* 9.

10. Woods, *A History of Gay Literature,* 10. Woods gives us an important starting point for the many small gay newsletters and newspapers that sprang up all over the country at this time. Winston Leyland, speaking of this same period, offers a slightly different list of the post-Stonewall publications that, he explains, "acted as vehicles for the spread of movement ideas. The first of these papers was New York's *Come Out!,* the initial issue of which appeared in November 1969. As the movement spread to other parts of the country, other gay papers were started, most of them closely allied to local gay groups: *The Gay Liberator,* the first issue of which appeared in Spring 1970, was published by Detroit's Gay Liberation Front. The short-lived papers, *Lavender Vision* and *Gay Dealer,* came out of Philadelphia and Boston respectively. And Boston's *Fag Rag* began publication in the summer of 1971 as an independent gay paper." See Leyland, *Orgasms of Light,* 7.

11. See Lincoln, *Native American Renaissance.*

12. See, for example, Ferguson's chapter "Something Else to Be" in *Aberrations in Black,* 110–37; Taylor, "The Historical Evolution of Black Feminist Theory and Praxis."

13. What I point to by deploying Lincoln's term is the rise of a particular publishing history in the 1960s. I by no means suggest American Indian literature or activism in the United States began in the 1960s. For an intellectual history of Native writers, see Warrior, *Tribal Secrets.* In addition, there's a long history of activism in Indian country from contact to present. To name just a few twentieth-century pantribal groups, the Society of American Indians, which officially formed at Ohio State University in 1911, is often marked as one of the earliest formal groups; the National Congress of American Indians was founded in 1944; the National Indian Youth Council formed in 1961; and both the United Native Americans and the American Indian Movement formed in 1968. In terms of the rise of American Indian newspapers and journals, an excellent collection of the many national and tribally specific publications in print during this period is Princeton University's American Indian Periodicals collection, which contains more than six hundred publications and is available in microfiche. I accessed this collection at the American Native Press Archives in Little Rock, Arkansas, and I am indebted to Daniel Littlefield for his help with my work there.

14. I see this recovery as similar to Warrior, Weaver, and Womack's reminder of Simon Ortiz's early contribution to Indigenous nationalism in their collaborative project on Indigenous nationalisms. The archive repeatedly shows us that

"new" literary, activist, or theoretical movements are rarely originary. See Weaver, Warrior, and Womack, *American Indian Literary Nationalism.*

15. See Tatonetti, "Two-Spirit Images in the Work of Maurice Kenny."

16. *Fag Rag* began publication in 1971 and ceased publication in 1987 with volume 44. Publication was irregular and there are a number of combined issues. Poems are published in most issues of the newspaper but are not in any particular order or section and are often scattered throughout the text. Because my initial interest in this project evolved from my interest in how queer Native literature can be read in the context of the Native American literary renaissance, my recovery work and subsequent analysis focuses on the 1970s.

17. The lack of bylines on editorials, articles, and poetry continues until *Fag Rag*, no. 5. The first issue of *Fag Rag* "was put together by: kevin mc girr, lester heumann, steve barru, charlie, steve mirman, steve lowell, bob, john mitzel, larry martin, allan troxler, donald, allan berube, john rebelle, Richard, marcus, craig smith." See *Fag Rag*, 1. This list of uncapitalized, often incomplete names is followed by a tongue-in-cheek statement: "Dr. Reuben tells us in *Everything You Wanted to Know about Sex but Were Afraid to Ask:* 'Few homosexuals use their real names; they generally choose aliases with sexual connotations, Harry, Peter, and Dick are the most favored.'"

18. "*Fag Rag* Blues," 3. The Gay Liberation Front organized after the June 27 police raid on the Stonewall Inn. The group officially split in 1972, not long after *Fag Rag*, no. 2, was published. However, a number of LGBT organizations emerged from this early queer activism, including the Lavender Menace, OutRage!, the Organization for Lesbian and Gay Action, and Stonewall.

19. "Cocksucking as an Act of Revolution."

20. "I Am a Black Faggot," 20.

21. Eng, *The Feeling of Kinship*, 47.

22. See Cohen, "Punks, Bulldaggers, and Welfare Queens."

23. The first line of the poem as it was originally printed in *ManRoot,* which I cite here, differs from the version later published in *Only as Far as Brooklyn* where the line shifts to present tense: "We *are* special to the Sioux!" See Kenny, *Only as Far as Brooklyn,* 10. The other changes between the two versions include the elision of the word "red" from the line "Into red war or the hunter's lonely woods," the elision of several commas before introductory clauses, and the addition of a stanza break between lines eight and nine. All subsequent references to "Winkte" cite the original *ManRoot* publication. See Kenny, "Winkte," 26.

24. Berlant and Warner, "Sex in Public," 551.

25. Kenny, "A Night, a Bridge, a River," 8.

26. Muñoz, *Cruising Utopia,* 188.

27. Ibid., 189.

28. Smith, "Queer Theory and Native Studies," 53.

29. See Morgensen, *Spaces between Us.*

30. Thanks to Kathleen Washburn for bringing this fact to my attention in a conversation at the Native American Literature Symposium.

31. Standing Bear, *My People the Sioux,* 171.

32. Trachtenberg, *Shades of Hiawatha,* 282.

33. Ibid., 279–81. In his foreword to Michael Castro's *Interpreting the Indian,* Kenny himself contends that Crane's "*This Bridge* . . . is certainly 'all American' as Whitman would have declaimed, but shows an immediate lack of concern for American history and no understanding or sympathy with either the earth or the First Peoples' place upon it." See Kenny, "A Change of Worlds," xi.

34. Sackman, *Wild Men,* 55–56.

35. American Missionary Association, "The Indians," 114, 115.

36. Ibid., 114.

37. Michael W. Robbins and Wendy Palitz explain that "during most of the great age of urban building in New York in the early twentieth century, a disproportionate number of the workers in high steel were indeed Indians. Working all over the United States and Canada, they were some of the best craftsmen America ever produced. Most of them were Mohawks, of the Iroquois people, and they hailed from Quebec province, upstate New York, and, eventually, Brooklyn. . . . The legend began in 1886, when the Dominion Bridge Company built a cantilevered railroad bridge over the St. Lawrence River. The bridge traversed land owned by the Kahnawake and Akwesasne Mohawks, who in partial payment were given jobs on the project. Dominion Bridge expected Mohawks to occupy themselves with the most menial, unskilled work on the site, such as unloading boxcars. Instead, the Indians were soon climbing all over the bridge." See Robbins and Palitz, *Brooklyn: A State of Mind,* 256. See, too, the documentary *To Brooklyn and Back: A Mohawk Journey,* in which Kahnawake Mohawk filmmaker Reaghan Tarbell traces her family's connections to this vibrant New York community.

38. See Vizenor, *Manifest Manners.*

39. Muñoz, *Cruising Utopia,* 189.

40. Kenny, "Greta Garbo," 27.

41. Serlin, "Crippling Masculinity," 161.

42. Ibid., 161–62.

43. Herring, "Out of the Closets, Into the Woods," 348.

44. Ibid., 359.

45. Thomson, *Extraordinary Bodies,* 7.

46. Johnstone, *An Introduction to Disability Studies,* 97.

47. Ibid.

48. Ibid., 99.

49. Ibid.

50. Morgensen's chapter "'Together We Are Stronger': Decolonizing Gender and Sexuality in Native AIDS Organizing" offers an excellent reading of

health sovereignty and Native activism. Morgensen explains that "Native AIDS organizers . . . challeng[e] colonial power over Native peoples and its internalization among them. While the biopolitics of the settler state and global health operate by requiring the participation of Native people, Native health activists engage that power more complexly than simply considering their participation in state or global health programs to be a form of co-optation. . . . Asserting Native sovereignty over the *conditions* and methods of health potentially disrupts the entire institutional apparatus of settler colonialization. But in the context of fighting AIDS and the genocidal legacies of disease for Indigenous people, calls for health sovereignty specifically challenge the biopolitics of settler colonialism that presumes Indigenous people are destined to die." See Morgensen, *Spaces between Us,* 196–97.

51. Cohen, "Punks, Bulldaggers, and Welfare Queens," 43.

52. Ibid.

53. Glick, "The Dialectics of Dandyism," 129.

54. Berlant and Warner, "Sex in Public," 551.

55. Szaloky, "'As You Desire Me,'" 199.

56. When I employ the term "queer rumor," I am thinking of Muñoz's reading of queer ephemera in *Cruising Utopia,* a concept I examine at length in chapter 5.

57. See Cohen, "Punks, Bulldaggers, and Welfare Queens," 22. In looking forward to my work on Indigenous assemblage in chapter 5, I also suggest that "Greta Garbo" articulates an early understanding of assemblage. In assemblage, individual and group identities, like power, coalesce situationally, forming and transforming through juxtaposition and heterogeneous relationship rather than through any sort of inherent consistency or sameness. Ultimately, the poem prefigures Deleuze and Guattari's sense of becoming in its focus on temporality and the instability of knowledge and secrecy, as well as in its insistence on the necessarily contingent and participatory nature of *Fag Rag*'s reading audience.

58. Wordsworth, *Lyrical Ballads and Other Poems,* 259.

59. Kenny, "Two Parodies," 12.

60. Herrick, "To the Virgins, to Make Much of Time"; Kenny, "A Night, a Bridge, a River," 8.

61. Ferguson, *Aberrations in Black,* 66.

62. Justice, "Notes toward a Theory of Anomaly," 208.

63. To clarify, just as the issues of the newspaper were often published at differing times, so too did the citation practices shift, with some issues citing publication months and others seasons.

64. I follow the original here in using multiples of the numeral one rather than Roman numerals to mark the three sections of "Three Parodies."

65. Hemphill, *Ceremonies;* Doty, *My Alexandria* and *Atlantis;* Monette, *Borrowed Time* and *Love Alone.*

66. Kenny, "Three Parodies," 9.

67. Rifkin, *The Erotics of Sovereignty,* 33.

68. Ibid., 34.

69. Teuton, *Red Land, Red Power,* 33.

70. Miranda, "Dildos, Hummingbirds, and Driving Her Crazy," 142.

71. In "Two-Spirit Images in the Work of Maurice Kenny," I analyze this essay next to "Winkte," marking both as the earliest pieces of Native literature and citing both as having appeared in "the same Winter 1975/1976 issue of *Gay Sunshine.*" See Tatonetti, "Two-Spirit Images in the Work of Maurice Kenny," 20. I based that claim on the citation from *Living the Spirit,* which was incorrect. As I note here, Kenny published "Tinselled Bucks: An Historical Study in Indian Homosexuality" together with "United" in *Gay Sunshine*'s winter 1975/1976 issue. "Winkte" is first published in *ManRoot*'s spring/summer 1977 issue. I briefly discuss the context of "Tinselled Bucks" in "Indigenous Fantasies and Sovereign Erotics."

72. Leyland explains,

> Issue No. 1 of *Gay Sunshine* was published in August 1970 by a group of people associated with Berkeley's Gay Liberation Front. The title of the paper reflects in part the fact that "sunshine" was a counter culture slang word for acid (LSD), as well as the general implications of light: a new gay dawn. The first five issues of the paper, issued monthly, were geared toward the local political needs of the Bay Area's new gay movement, although some copies were distributed in other cities throughout the country. Even in these early issues cultural articles and poetry began to appear. . . . Following the collapse of Berkeley GLF in early 1971, the original Gay Sunshine collective was dissolved and the paper underwent a crisis of identity, suspending publication. A small group of people, with [Leyland] as coordinator . . . decided to bring the paper to San Francisco and resume publication as an independent cultural/political gay journal which would strive for a national readership. With Issue No. 8 (Summer 1971) the paper took this route.

See Leyland, *Orgasms of Light,* 7.

73. "Editor's Note," 1.

74. Ibid. A portion of this paragraph was previously published in "Two-Spirit Images in the Work of Maurice Kenny."

75. From a contemporary perspective, we can recognize the inaccuracy of both terms: casting multiply gendered Native people as "homosexual" offers a transhistorical reading that erases specificity by flattening out the complexity of both desire and gender performance, while "berdache," as I note in chapter 1, has

a troubling etymology and a problematic anthropological past. However, in 1975, these were the terms at Kenny's disposal.

76. Kenny, "Tinselled Bucks," 16.

77. Ibid. While Kenny may have expanded the gay imaginary for Native and non-Native men, he has difficulty imagining productive possibilities for Indigenous women, claiming "for the most part, Indian women lived miserable lives and were sometimes known to commit suicide to rid themselves of their abject bondage to a merciless husband." See Kenny, "Tinselled Bucks," 16.

78. Kenny published the poem from which I take this chapter's epigraph, "Loves into Legends," during the same period as "Tinselled Bucks." Appearing in *ManRoot* in 1977, "Loves into Legends" engages similar concerns about non-Native historical figures: "If Billy the Kid / wasn't / Pat Garret's / chicken-lover / I'll eat . . . / If Mike Fink / didn't shoot / his young buddy, / Carpenter, / In the name / of jealousy, / I'll drop my . . . / many a cowboy / put the pistol / in his mouth, / and not because / he lost his cow . . . / why must we lie . . . / knowing, / hide facts / of these lovers / under bricks / of legends!" See Kenny, "Loves into Legends," 102.

79. Driskill, Finley, Gilley, and Morgensen, "Introduction," 10.

80. Ibid., 11.

81. Ibid.

82. Ibid., 12.

83. Speaking of *Living the Spirit,* which was published more than ten years after "Tinselled Bucks" was first published in *Gay Sunshine,* Morgensen notes, "St. Martin's Press originally advertised the book for sale to the very gay and lesbian readers prepped to consume Native culture as representing their roots." In this framework, the fact that "Tinselled Bucks" was originally published in *Gay Sunshine* could also be read as reinforcing a dominant cultural narrative that constructs mainstream queer modernity on an Indigenous past. While Morgensen makes this claim as part of his larger project, he also recognizes the agency of queer Native people like Kenny and those in the GAI, who "showed their ability to adapt non-Native desires to their own ends." See Morgensen, *Spaces between Us,* 11.

84. Chadwick, "Poem after Le Roi's TOILET," 8.

85. Kenny, "'Kill Fag's,'" 8.

86. I avoid the more commonly used term "graffiti artist" here. Graffiti is an important form of public art, but there's a significant difference between that art and hate speech.

87. Kenny, "Yemen Boy," 9.

88. Oliver, "Diffuse Connections," 86.

89. It is possible that the clean-faced white figure in the fringed buckskin is female—a sort of Calamity Jane figure.

90. Somerville, *Queering the Color Line,* 7, 8.

91. Morgensen, *Spaces between Us,* 16.

92. Ibid., 17.

93. Ibid., 74.

94. Cox, *Muting White Noise,* 11.

95. "Papago" is republished under the title "Papago II" in *Only as Far as Brooklyn.* I discuss "Papago I" and "Papago II" from that collection in "Two-Spirit Images in the Work of Maurice Kenny," 126–28.

96. Kenny, "Papago," 19.

97. The Tohono O'odham officially reclaimed their name for themselves in 1986, when a new constitution was approved.

98. Kenny, "Papago," *Gay Sunshine,* 23. The poem titled "Papago" in *Gay Sunshine* is retitled "Papago I" when republished in *Only as Far as Brooklyn.* To further clarify, though both the poem in *Gay Sunshine* issue 29/30 and that in *Fag Rag* issue 18 are each titled "Papago," they are two different pieces that will later be paired as "Papago I" and "Papago II" in *Only as Far as Brooklyn.*

99. Morgensen, *Spaces between Us,* 3.

100. Kenny's final poem in the fall/winter 1976 issue of *Fag Rag,* titled "Recuerdo," begins with an epigraph from the Edna St. Vincent Millay poem of the same name. Millay begins each of the three stanzas of her 1922 poem with the same two lines: "We were tired, we were very merry— / We had gone back and forth all night on the ferry." Her piece charts an evening in the lives of a couple, perhaps lovers, perhaps friends, who stay up all night in exhilarated play that ends only at dawn. In Kenny's response, the speaker describes a "smile" exchanged by two schoolboys from "doorways filling with rain / splashing your brown cheek / and my school books." The repeated refrain that "nothing was accomplished" but "the smile" suggests an unconsummated attraction. Thus the poem's conclusion in which the speaker explains, "We kissed and split / the echo of our moans / in the ticking clock," may describe action or imagination. See Kenny, "Recuerdo," 21.

101. Ruppert, "Maurice Kenny," 455.

102. Bruchac, "New Leaves on the Trees of Our Nations," 473. See Norma Wilson's excellent chapter on "America's Indigenous Poetry" in *The Cambridge Companion to Native American Literature* for more on the history of American Indian poetry.

103. The second piece, "Standing Strong," is not listed in the table of contents and thus is sometimes omitted from discussions of this special issue.

104. Kenny, "Oka Tanna," 19.

105. The transcripts from Nicholas Black Elk's interviews with John G. Neihardt show that the most quoted words from *Black Elk Speaks*—"The nation's hoop is broken and scattered. There is no center any longer, and the sacred tree is dead" (270)—were John G. Neihardt's editorial addition. See Tatonetti, "Disrupting a Story of Loss," for more. I further analyze representations of Wounded Knee

and the ghost dance in "Catholics, Carlisle, and Casting Stones"; "Dancing That Way, Things Began to Change"; and "Behind the Shadows of Wounded Knee."

106. Kenny, "Oka Tanna," 19.

107. See, for example, Kenny's poems in various issues of *Many Smokes,* such as "Yonnondio"; "My Nation, Behold It"; and "I Was Tired of What's Happening: (In Memory of Pedro Bissonette)." Bissonette was an AIM leader involved in Wounded Knee II, who was killed by BIA police. Kenny's work during this period responds directly not only to Bissonette's death but to Wounded Knee II specifically; the original printing of "I Am the Sun," for example, was in a special issue of *Akwesasne Notes* that focused on "The First Month at Wounded Knee." Like "Oka Tanna," "I Am the Sun," which is subtitled "(A Song of Praise, Defiance, and Determination)," also quotes Black Elk and references the 1890 Wounded Knee massacre. In this case, Kenny does employ the famed Black Elk quote penned by Neihardt as his epigraph. Though he cites Neihardt's vanishing Indian rhetoric, Kenny's poem subsequently refutes the implicit erasure of such claims when the speaker states vehemently, "We will put the center back / in your country; / We will circle stones and make the hoop / in your country; We will plant the seed of the sacred tree." See Kenny, "I Am the Sun," 48.

108. Ruppert, "Maurice Kenny," 455.

109. Teuton, *Red Land, Red Power,* 6.

110. Ibid., 198.

111. Ibid., 225.

112. Smith, "Queer Theory and Native Studies," 53.

113. Teuton, *Red Land, Red Power,* 233; Muñoz, *Cruising Utopia,* 189.

114. The 1978 23/24 issue does not designate particular months or a season, such as summer or fall, for the issue. When the strikingly illustrated pieces first rolled across the screen of the microfilm machine, I realized I had come across early poems from *Greyhounding This America.* The full-page spread has the words "Poems by . . . Maurice Kenny" inscribed over a rectangular print of an urban landscape, a series of three-story brick brownstones pictured at the top left of the page. To the right of that picture is a small pen-and-ink drawing of a 1970s-era bus with passengers disembarking. Underlying the poems themselves is a U.S. map that lists cities and the straight-line mileage between them, and at the bottom right is a photograph of a widely smiling, dark-skinned adolescent boy wearing a t-shirt and beaded necklace. The layout on the page speaks to Kenny's interest in and experience of travel, which he discusses in stark honesty in *Greyhounding This America,* a collection that is a written account of a recorded dialogue between Kenny and Larry Jackson, his publisher, as they discuss his draft. In the course of their conversation about each piece, Kenny narrates his poems, sharing inspiration, intent, and, at times, darkly personal stories from his life. The collection also includes drawings by Hopi/Miwok poet Wendy Rose, a close friend of Kenny's

and an important poet in her own right. A comparison shows that the poems in *Fag Rag* issue 21/22 provide a queer corollary to Kenny's 1988 collection *Greyhounding This America,* since, despite their close connection in theme, only one of the four poems, "Tulsa by Greyhound," is in the later collection.

115. Smith, "Queer Theory and Native Studies," 44.

116. "Akwesasne We Are Not the Enemy," 51.

117. Quoted in "Akwesasne We Are Not the Enemy," 51.

118. The *RFD*'s vehement response, which is significantly longer, begins with a hyperbolic disclaimer: "The attached letter came to us as a shock and disappointment. We were appalled that *Akwesasne Notes* would try and pass us off in such a prejudiced, sexist way. To include us in a list of 'destructive effects on Indian Culture' as imposed by 'European western society' is to deny an important aspect of Native American culture that existed ages before white man came here." In many ways, *RFD*'s claims are another example of Morgensen's argument in *Spaces between Us* that non-Native social movements articulate their sexuality in relation to what he terms "the colonial object berdache."

119. See Denetdale, "Carving Navajo National Boundaries" and "Securing Navajo National Boundaries"; Wilson, "Changed Embraces, Changes Embraced?"; Womack, *Art as Performance,* 384–86.

120. Kenny, "Maurice Kenny."

121. Muñoz, *Cruising Utopia,* 189.

3. Queer Relationships and Two-Spirit Characters in Louise Erdrich's Novels

1. Barak, "Blurs, Blends, Berdaches," 55.

2. Iovannone, "'Mix-Ups, Messes, Confinements, and Double-Dealings,'" 41.

3. Prince-Hughes, "Worlds in and out of Balance," 8.

4. Erdrich, *The Beet Queen,* 1.

5. Butler, *Gender Trouble,* 25.

6. For a trenchant analysis on the changing attitudes of tramps and hoboes and their lives in what he terms "hobohemia" from 1877 to the twenty-first century, see DePastino, *Citizen Hobo.*

7. Much has been written about the history, deployment, and problems with the ubiquitous metaphor of the closet. See, for example, Brown, *Closet Space;* Chauncey, *Gay New York;* Ross, "Beyond the Closet as Raceless Paradigm in Black Queer Studies"; Seidman, "Are We All in the Closet?" and *Beyond the Closet;* Signorile, *Queer in America.*

8. Sedgwick, *Epistemology of the Closet,* 3.

9. Halberstam, *Female Masculinity,* xii.

10. Ibid., 1.
11. Ibid., 29.
12. Butler, "Melancholy Gender—Refused Identification," 168.
13. Halberstam, *Female Masculinity,* 29.
14. Seigworth and Gregg, "An Inventory of Shimmers," 3.
15. Ibid.
16. Sedgwick, *Touching Feeling,* 20.
17. Ibid., 21.
18. Seigworth and Gregg, "An Inventory of Shimmers," 3.
19. Halberstam, *Female Masculinity,* 2.
20. Flavin, "Gender Construction," 20.
21. Halberstam, *The Queer Art of Failure,* 88.
22. Ibid., 121.
23. Halberstam, *Female Masculinity,* 5.
24. Ibid., 6.
25. Butler, "Melancholy Gender—Refused Identification," 168.
26. Halberstam, *Female Masculinity,* 52.
27. See Womack, *Red on Red;* Smith, "Queer Theory and Native Studies."
28. Halberstam, *Female Masculinity,* xii.
29. Chauncey, *Gay New York,* 42.
30. Ibid., 34.
31. Taylor, Kaminski, and Dugan, "From Bowery to the Castro," 104.
32. Chauncey, *Gay New York,* 331.
33. I want to recognize the broad strokes I employ here in my depiction of queer histories in the United States. While there are undoubted shared historical markers, like the Depression, Prohibition, the Cold War, and the Stonewall Rebellion, there are also radical differences in such histories in light of disparities in gender, class, race, and region. See, for example, Beemyn's collection *Creating a Place for Ourselves.*
34. Butler, *Gender Trouble,* 17.
35. Muñoz, *Cruising Utopia,* 189.
36. For essays on Erdrich and gender that engage these early novels, see, for example, Barak, "Blurs, Blends, Berdaches"; Baringer, "'Captive Woman?'"; Brehm, "The Metamorphoses of an Ojibwe Manido"; Castillo, "The Construction of Gender and Ethnicity" and "Women Aging into Power"; Cornell, "Woman Looking"; Hansen, "What if Your Mother Never Meant To?"; Stokes, "What about the Sweetheart?"; Tanrisal, "Mother and Child Relationships"; Van Dyke, "Of Vision Quests and Spiritual Guardians." For an annotated bibliography of Erdrich criticism through 1994, see Burdick, "Louise Erdrich's *Love Medicine, The Beet Queen,* and *Tracks.*" Laura Furlan Szanto (now Laura Furlan) builds on Burdick and offers another excellent annotated bibliography of Erdrich criticism

through June 2000; see "Louise Erdrich's *Love Medicine, The Beet Queen,* and *Tracks.*" Beidler and Barton's revised and expanded edition of *A Reader's Guide to the Novels of Louise Erdrich* offers a bibliography of key resources on Erdrich through the early 2000s.

37. Erdrich, *Tales of Burning Love,* 53.

38. Berlant and Warner, "Sex in Public," 553.

39. Ibid., 552.

40. Ibid., 554.

41. Ibid.

42. Ibid., 562.

43. Rifkin, *When Did Indians Become Straight?,* 15.

44. Ibid., 48.

45. Weston, *Families We Choose,* 2.

46. Ibid., 202.

47. Ibid., 202–3.

48. Ibid., 203.

49. Sedgwick, *Epistemology of the Closet,* 91.

50. Weston, *Families We Choose,* 211.

51. Pidduck, "Queer Kinship and Ambivalence," 442.

52. Erdrich, *The Antelope Wife,* 8.

53. Seigworth and Gregg, "An Inventory of Shimmers," 3.

54. For a review of both the literary and scientific precedents for male lactation, see Swaminathan, "Strange but True."

55. Seigworth and Gregg, "An Inventory of Shimmers," 2.

56. Roscoe, *Changing Ones,* 7.

57. Vizenor, *The People Named the Chippewa,* 14.

58. Ibid.

59. Williams, *The Spirit and the Flesh,* 37.

60. I employ the third-gender pronoun "hir" here and elsewhere in the text to indicate the alternate gender position of the Two-Spirit figures in Erdrich's texts.

61. Erdrich, *The Last Report on the Miracles at Little No Horse,* 74.

62. Orbin and Velie, "Religion and Gender in *The Last Report,*" 28.

63. Rader, "Disrobing the Priest," 221.

64. Van Dyke, "A Hope for Miracles," 67.

65. Iovannone, "'Mix-Ups, Messes, Confinements, and Double-Dealings,'" 61.

66. For more on non-Native appropriations of the concept/term "Two-Spirit," see Womack, "Politicizing HIV in Indian Country"; Gilley, *Becoming Two-Spirit,* 121–32.

67. Keenan, "Unrestricted Territory," 2.

68. Iovannone's discussion of this scene, though it invokes Indigenous traditions, does so by employing the term "transgender." As my earlier readings of

Erdrich suggest, I agree with Iovannone's contention that "any sustained exploration of Erdrich's theorization of gender must be attuned to her use of both Native and non-Native sources" (42). However, Iovannone's reading of "Two-Spirit," which he defines as "a blending of traditional masculine and feminine attributes," focuses primarily on the semantics of the word "two" in "Two-Spirit" (42–43). As a result, even as he cites the rationale for the term's coining, Iovannone unintentionally dismisses the historical foundation behind that activist decision when he claims "Two-Spirit" does not reject "the primacy of binary designations of gender" (43). In fact, "Two-Spirit" does not rest on a system that keeps intact Western gender binaries; instead, the term is specifically intended to cite the distinct histories of Indigenous genders and sexualities. Those histories already include the sort of nuanced understandings of gender and sexuality that Iovannone attributes to a transgender theoretical framework. Thus, while transgender theory can offer insight into Erdrich's texts, it cannot—or at least should not—supersede the specifically Indigenous framework of a Two-Spirit critique in all readings of her work. Moreover, it is simply inaccurate when applied to multiply gendered Anishinaabeg characters in historical scenes such as that under discussion. Replacing the problematic anthropological term "berdache" with "transgender" rather than "Two-Spirit" creates another historical elision. See Iovannone, "'Mix-Ups, Messes, Confinements, and Double-Dealings.'" For further discussion of the history behind and meaning of the term "Two-Spirit," see Herdt, "The Dilemmas of Desire"; Jacobs, Thomas, and Lang, "Introduction"; Driskill, Finley, Gilley, and Morgensen, "Introduction"; Gilley, "From Gay to Indian."

69. Williams, *The Spirit and the Flesh,* 2. Will Roscoe also acknowledges cross-dressing, though he disputes its frequency: "The most visible marker of berdache gender status was some form of cross-dressing, although this occurred much less consistently than is usually assumed. In some tribes, male berdaches did not cross-dress at all or only partly." See Roscoe, *Changing Ones,* 8. For a counterargument that details the existence of this cultural practice among the Zuni, Wapato, Tolowa, and Hoopa, see Pilling, "Cross-Dressing and Shamanism among Selected Western North American Tribes." Though commonly used due to the absence of a better term, "cross-dressing" clearly reifies a gender binary.

70. Williams, *The Spirit and the Flesh,* 58.

71. Ibid., 32.

72. Medicine, "Changing Native American Roles in an Urban Context," 150.

73. See Williams, *The Spirit and the Flesh,* 28; Roscoe, *Changing Ones,* 8.

74. Gilley, *Becoming Two-Spirit,* 8.

75. Orbin and Velie, "Religion and Gender in *The Last Report,*" 31.

76. Ibid.

77. Gilley, *Becoming Two-Spirit,* 10.

78. Rainwater, "Reading between Worlds," 168.

79. For an excellent piece on Erdrich and audience, see Roemer, "They Talk, Who Listens."

80. Smith, *Conquest,* 139.

81. Justice, "Introduction," 9.

82. Driskill, "Stolen from Our Bodies," 54.

83. Morgensen, "Settler Homonationalism," 117.

84. Among these analyses, Austenfeld, Cornelia, and Lischke and McNab center on Fidelis Waldvogel and the German and German American histories his character invokes. Embry, too, examines Erdrich's deployment of German ethnicity in "Ethnic Nostalgia"; Rowe offers a postcolonial reading of *The Master Butchers Singing Club* and *Last Report* in "Buried Alive"; Georgi-Findlay compares transnational encounters in Silko's *Gardens in the Dunes,* Welch's *The Heartsong of Charging Elk,* and Erdrich's *The Master Butchers Singing Club* and *Last Report;* Iovannone's previously referenced essay is the only reading that engages Erdrich's depictions of gender and sexuality.

85. Erdrich, *The Master Butchers Singing Club,* 14.

86. Iovannone, "'Mix-Ups, Messes, Confinements, and Double-Dealings,'" 48.

87. Even when Delphine marries Fidelis, she resists the normative imperatives of heterocouplehood: she keeps her house, which is one of the conditions she imposes when she agrees to marry Fidelis, and continues to live separately from him until some unspecified time after Roy's death.

88. Eng, *The Feeling of Kinship,* 64.

89. de Man, "Epistemology of Metaphor," 21. Derrida, too, has famously examined catachresis, which he figures at various times as the "abuse of metaphor," violence, and monstrous excess. See Derrida, "White Mythology"; Kronick, *Derrida and the Future of Literature,* 187–88n4; Rajan, *Deconstruction and the Remainders of Phenomenology,* 48–51.

90. To clarify, Karl is fourteen at the 1932 start of *The Beet Queen,* while Cyprian is thirty-two when he and Delphine begin to travel together at the 1934 start of *The Master Butchers Singing Club.* Both travel in and around the same Midwest states, and both live for a time in Argus. In fact, Karl's sister, Mary, inherits and runs the butcher shop of Fidelis's rival, Pete Kozka, where Fidelis works when he first moves to Argus in 1922. However, neither Mary nor Karl are referenced in *The Master Butchers Singing Club,* nor does Cyprian encounter or hear about other Anishinaabe characters, such as Fleur Pillager, Pauline Puyat, or Russell Kashpaw, who live or have lived in Argus and worked at Kozka's at various times, as chronicled in *Tracks* and *The Beet Queen.* However, Cyprian does seem to be related to the infamous Lazarres, who appear throughout Erdrich's texts as Step-and-a-Half warns Delphine, "I know his family, the Lazarres. Bunch of no-goods. You watch yourself around that Cyprian and hang on to your money." See *The Master Butchers Singing Club,* 208. In the big reveal at the end of the book, readers discover

that Step-and-a-Half is also Anishinaabe, though that's unbeknownst to anyone in Argus except Roy.

91. Iovannone, "'Mix-Ups, Messes, Confinements, and Double-Dealings,'" 46.

92. Weston, *Long Slow Burn*, 48.

93. Ibid., 49.

94. See Bell, "Eroticizing the Rural."

95. In Sedgwick and Frank's landmark essay on affect, "Shame in the Cybernetic Fold," they analyze the work of American psychologist Silvan Tomkins, pointing out that, for Tomkins, "shame is the exemplary affect for theory" (518). Their reading of Tomkins leads them to contend, "Without positive affect, there can be no shame; only a scene that offers you enjoyment or engages your interest can make you blush. Similarly, only something you thought might delight or satisfy can disgust. . . . [S]hame, as precarious hyperreflexivity of the surface of the body, can turn one inside out—or outside in. . . . [S]hame is characterized by its failure ever to renounce its object cathexis, its relation to the desire for pleasure as well as the need to avoid pain" (520–21). Cyprian's ongoing experiences of shame resonate with this theory of affect in which his sexual desire for men acts as a point of attachment that he repeatedly fails to renounce and, as such, intersects with both pleasure and a drive to "avoid pain."

96. I discuss the intersections of Indigeneity and queer diaspora at length in chapter 5.

97. Iovannone employs Mikhail Bakhtin's performance theory to read Cyprian and Vilhus's vaudeville act: "In creating a performance space where non-normative desires can be expressed, Cyprian troubles the legitimacy and authenticity of gender and sexuality categories." See Iovannone, "'Mix-Ups, Messes, Confinements, and Double-Dealings,'" 47. Muñoz's *Disidentifications* also offers a productive though less celebratory lens for reading this scene. Muñoz considers what he calls the "'burden of liveness,'" which I discuss later in this chapter.

98. Cassedy, "We Are All Here," 78.

99. Though the reference to Vilhus is brief, the weight of this comparison could be analyzed at length. Both occupying countries maintained similar ideologies—"Manifest Destiny" in the United States and Hitler's "New World Order" in Nazi Germany—and employed similar practices of containment and eugenics, such as reservations/concentration camps and forced sterilization. Toland is frequently cited as evidence that Hitler studied U.S. Indian policy: "Hitler's concept of concentration camps as well as the practicality of genocide owed much, so he claimed, to his studies of English and United States history. He admired the camps for Boer prisoners in South Africa and for the Indians in the wild west; and often praised to his inner circle the efficiency of America's extermination—by starvation and uneven combat—of the red savages who could not be

tamed by captivity." See Toland, *Adolf Hitler*, 702. See Bachrach's "Deadly Medicine" for a discussion of Germany's eugenics programs and Gonzales, Kertész, and Tayac's "Eugenics as Indian Removal" for one example of eugenics programs in American Indian histories. The Indian Health Service practice of sterilization is well documented. Lawrence explains that the sterilization of Native women, often without their knowledge or consent, was "a common occurrence during the 1960s and 1970s. Native Americans accused the Indian Health Service of sterilizing at least 25 percent of Native women who were between the ages of fifteen and forty-four during the 1970s" (400). See also Johansen, "Reprise/Forced Sterilizations," and Smith, *Conquest*, 79–107.

100. Gopinath, *Impossible Desires*, 2.

101. Muñoz, *Disidentifications*, 185.

102. Ibid., 189.

103. Ibid.

104. Erdrich, *Four Souls*, 7.

105. Stockham, *Karezza*, quoted in Bode, "Columbia's Carnal Bed," 56–57.

106. For more on Karezza and its place in nineteenth-century feminist and free love movements, see Gordon, "Voluntary Motherhood." Karezza is also considered in Beidler, "Mauser's Illness," and is included in innumerable sex manuals from the late nineteenth century to the present.

107. It's unclear whether Placide's painting teacher is a man or a woman, so along with the practice of Karezza, it's also possible to read Placide as a lesbian, which would recast her lack of desire for her husband. However, given the offhand nature of Polly's comment about her sister practicing Karezza with the painting teacher, I believe such a reading is unwarranted.

108. See Beidler, "Mauser's Illness."

109. Erdrich, *The Plague of Doves*, 44.

110. Evelina's attachment to Sister Mary Anita is not entirely severed by her discovery. When Evelina leaves the state mental institution, her first visit outside the family is to St. Joseph's convent. Once there, she explains, "I couldn't bear to tell her the truth, so I said something else. 'I've been thinking about becoming a nun!'" (249).

111. For more on the heated debate over removing homosexuality from the list of psychiatric pathologies, the subsequent introduction of the new category "ego-dystonic homosexuality" into the 1980 edition of the DSM, and its 1986 removal, see Bayer, *Homosexuality and American Psychiatry;* Chauncey, "From Sexual Inversion to Homosexuality"; Suppe, "Classifying Sexual Disorders"; Minton, *Departing from Deviance;* and an excellent segment of the radio program *This American Life* titled "81 Words."

112. Briere and Elliott, "Immediate and Long-Term Impacts of Child Sexual Abuse," 61.

113. Ibid., 58.

114. See Badia, *Sylvia Plath and the Mythology of Women Readers,* for a fascinating analysis of how the figure of the Plath reader has become an iconographic symbol of depression and immaturity used to mark young, female readers.

115. Erdrich, *The Last Report on the Miracles at Little No Horse,* 64.

116. Anzaldúa, "To(o) Queer the Writer," 163.

117. Womack, *Red on Red,* 309.

118. Ibid.

4. Forced to Choose

Thanks to Qwo-Li Driskill and Mark Rifkin for invaluable comments on the *GLQ* article that forms the basis of this chapter.

1. Raheja, *Reservation Reelism,* x.

2. Columpar, *Unsettling Sights,* xiv.

3. See Feier, *We Never Hunted Buffalo;* Hearne, *Smoke Signals* and *Native Recognitions;* Schweninger, *Imagic Moments.*

4. See Kadsan and Tavernetti, "Native Americans in a Revisionist Western."

5. For more on *Little Big Man*'s allusions to the My Lai massacre, see Slotkin, *Gunfighter Nation.*

6. Kenny, "Tinselled Bucks," 27.

7. This second point, which further underscores Morgensen's reading of berdache in *Spaces between Us,* is especially evident given *Little Big Man*'s place on so many online lists of queer-related films, where Little Horse functions as a signifier of queerness writ large.

8. The film references that follow are a sampling of films that either include a queer Native character or are made by queer Indigenous directors/writers. Thus this list, which is by no means comprehensive, includes both Native and non-Native and queer and straight-identified filmmakers. For more on the rise of Aboriginal film, see Gittings, *Canadian National Cinema,* 215–30.

9. Smith's *Her Giveaway* is part of a body of documentaries/educational videos about Native Americans and HIV/AIDS that include *American Indians against HIV/AIDS Leadership Project,* Smith's *That Which Is Between* and *An Interruption in the Journey;* Alaskan Native Barbara Byron's *I'm Not Afraid of Me;* Sandra Osawa's (Makah) *AIDS and the Native American Family;* and Muscogee Creek/Cherokee Lisa Tiger's *Lisa Tiger's Story.* See Vernon, *Killing Us Quietly,* and Machiorlatti, "Video as Community Ally and Dakota Sense of Place."

10. Nibley's film is by far the most widely screened of these documentaries due in part to an impressively effective publicity campaign. To give a sense of the film's reach, Nibley's documentary was shown at the White House on June 15, 2012.

11. Cuthand, like so many Indigenous performance artists, works in multiple media. She's also part of the breakthrough group of Aboriginal artists who follow in the wake of the landmark exhibition curated by Lee-Ann Martin and Morgan Wood titled *Exposed: Aesthetics of Aboriginal Erotic Art.* John G. Hampton argues that, in the years since *Exposed,* "artists like Thirza Cuthand, Kent Monkman, Adrian Stimson, and Terrance Houle have brought the discourse surrounding sexuality in Aboriginal communities out of the smokehouse." See Hampton, "Unsettling Sex," 2.

12. For a discussion of Desjariais's *Two-Spirited* and Imitates Dog's *Two Spirits, One Journey,* see Estrada, "Two-Spirit Film Criticism."

13. Heather Norris Nicholson argues that Niro's queer character is an intentional call for Two-Spirit inclusion in Indigenous community: "Zachary John's presence on Grand Pine is a call for Aboriginal communities to be more open about matters of sexuality. . . . Her wish was, she explained at the initial screening, to contribute to [a] wider healing process." See Nicholson, "Visual Irony," 165. *Honey Moccasin* also includes a scene in which Honey's daughter, Mabel (Florene Belmore), screens a film based on Daniel David Moses's poem "Inukshuk."

14. Alberta, who was born Clint Morrill and also went by Clint Star and Clint Tourangeau, died in 2002. His final film was *Miss 501: Portrait of Luck* (2002). See Asals, "Memoriam for Clint"; Mayer, "This Bridge of Two Backs"; Columpar, *Unsettling Sights,* 117.

15. I omit Alberta's film from my chapter analysis because of its status as a documentary and both Niro's and Ghastant'Aucoin's film because their surrealist narratives garner different audiences than productions like *Big Eden* and *Johnny Greyeyes,* which are frequently listed as favorites for a broader viewing public. While Alexie's film, like Alberta's, Niro's, and Ghastant'Aucoin's, also parodies conventions of filmmaking with the inclusion of an interview sequence and frequent references to the filmic gaze as seen in Mouse's and Steven's filming; *The Business of Fancydancing*'s storyline, like those of *Big Eden* and *Johnny Greyeyes,* meets more mainstream narrative conventions.

16. There is a large body of work on kinship ties in Native communities going back to the early twentieth century and spanning multiple disciplines. For just a few examples, see Deloria, *Speaking of Indians;* DeMallie and Ortiz, *North American Indian Anthropology;* Purdue, "Race and Culture"; Rifkin, "Romancing Kinship."

17. *Big Eden.* All subsequent quotes from the film are from this DVD. Henry's retelling of the Pleiades narrative is based on a story from the oral traditions titled "The Seven Brothers of the Star Cluster." A version of this oral story can be found in Parker, *Seneca Myths and Folktales.* Thanks to Eric Gansworth for identifying the narrative.

18. See Berkhofer, *The White Man's Indian.*

19. hooks, *Black Looks,* 14.

20. Sullivan, *A Critical Introduction to Queer Theory,* 66–67.

21. The claim that queerness is often marked as white and that queer theory and queer literatures have at times functioned as racial and cultural erasures has been well documented. See, for example, Anzaldúa, "To(o) Queer the Writer"; Barnard, *Queer Race;* Cohen, "Punks, Bulldaggers, and Welfare Queens"; Lugones, "Heterosexualism and the Colonial/Modern Gender System"; Moraga, *Loving in the War Years;* Ng, "Race Matters"; and Sullivan, *A Critical Introduction to Queer Theory,* 57–80. *Big Eden* undoubtedly mirrors these previously discussed theoretical absences.

22. Smith, *Conquest,* 9. Smith is referencing Kate Shanley.

23. Lugones, "Heterosexualism and the Colonial/Modern Gender System," 192.

24. Silva, "*Johnny* Looks at Women Behind Bars," 6H.

25. I want to be clear, however, that the film falls far from reinforcing the myths that women become lesbians as a reaction to male violence or that lesbianism is simply a means of surviving the experience of prison. Instead, Two-Spirit identity is inherently tied to redemption and return in *Johnny Greyeyes,* creating what Driskill calls "doubleweave": a space of possibility in which queerness and Indigeneity productively intersect and no one is forced to choose. See Driskill, "Doubleweaving Two-Spirit Critiques."

26. Lawston, "Women, the Criminal Justice System, and Incarceration," 9.

27. Lawston details the horrific realities for women in contemporary prisons: "Approximately twenty-five percent of women in prison report being sexually abused while in a correctional institution. The actual number of sexual assaults is likely much higher given that, like women on the outside, many women survivors of sexual abuse and rape do not report it. Feelings of humiliation and degradation, which are common to women who are sexually assaulted, are compounded for incarcerated women by the threat of retaliation by prison staff if the women were to expose the abuse." See ibid., 4. Manzano intends, as noted earlier in the piece, to bring attention to these abuses through *Johnny Greyeyes*'s representations of and engagement with this ongoing legacy of violence.

28. Foucault, *Discipline and Punish,* 200.

29. Ibid.

30. Spurr, *The Rhetoric of Empire,* 25.

31. Lorde, *Sister Outsider,* 39.

32. There are multiple examples of how the word "contact" becomes a metonym for physical and psychological regulation. In one scene, for instance, Johnny turns to the guard before hugging her mother good-bye after a visit to ask, "Can we have contact now?" Her query emphasizes the rigid regulation of physical intimacy. In another, Johnny writes a letter to her brother, Clay, saying, "Little brother. I know about losing people. It would be six months before I leave

these walls. I stayed the strong one. Seven years. Contact. Hands only. Just when I dream do I go to the good place. This world here. This world is not my world. It has been taken from me. Choose a good path. You're young and free. Don't ever lose that, brother."

33. The Indian Health Service practice of sterilization was a eugenically motivated attack on Indigenous people. Jane Lawrence explains that the sterilization of Native women, often without their knowledge or consent, was "a common occurrence during the 1960s and 1970s. Native Americans accused the Indian Health Service of sterilizing at least 25 percent of Native women who were between the ages of fifteen and forty-four during the 1970s." See Lawrence, "The Indian Health Service and the Sterilization of Native American Women," 400. See also Johansen, "Reprise/Forced Sterilizations"; Smith, *Conquest,* 79–107.

34. The earliest reference to Two-Spirit people comes from the journals and travel narratives of priests, traders, and explorers who read the landscape and the people through the lens of their own cultural beliefs. Thus expressions of alternate gender roles and sexualities were distorted or buried under the weight of the imperial gaze. Will Roscoe details his findings on these documents, saying, "I have identified some 57 secondary sources published between 1500 and 1900 that refer to gender and sexual diversity in the Americas. . . . An analysis . . . reveals that the dissemination of contact accounts of North American gender diversity cut across several discursive domains: [Two-Spirit people] were invoked first and longest in a moral discourse, then in historical discourse and a discourse on prodigies, and finally, in the nineteenth century, in the discourses of the social sciences and medicine." See Roscoe, *Changing Ones,* 179.

35. See Amnesty International, "Stolen Sisters." In Canada, the 1868 Indian Act was put into place so the state could legally define who is Indian. When the original regulatory codes of the 1868 Act were amended in 1876, the revision instantiated a heteropatriarchal settler logic that tied "status," or federal recognition, to male lineage; this frightening act of settler imperialism stood in a direct contradiction to the belief systems of many Indigenous nations that defined their societies along matrilineal lines. In addition, the Indian Act granted status to non-Native women who married Native men with status and stripped the status from Native women who married white men. Audra Simpson argues that "juridical efforts to incorporate or expel or contain difference such as the Indian Act were a way of disciplining Indigenous *and* white bodies to a Victorian norm of white settler citizenship or Indian wardship." See Simpson, "From White into Red," 254. See also Barker, "Gender, Sovereignty, Rights."

36. Ibid.

37. Ross, *Inventing the Savage,* 12.

38. See the 2008 special cluster issue of the *NWSA Journal,* "Women and Criminal Justice: Policing, Prosecution, and Incarceration," for more about

women and prison and Ross's *Inventing the Savage* for a detailed examination of Native women's experiences with the penal system. Ross shows how the social constructions of race, ethnicity, gender, and class are linked to representations of criminality and incarceration rates.

39. Miranda, "Dildos, Hummingbirds, and Driving Her Crazy," 146. While Miranda addresses the United States rather than Canada here, the argument works for both American Indian and Aboriginal women.

40. Driskill, "Stolen from Our Bodies," 52.

41. Ibid., 51.

42. Warrior, "Your Skin Is the Map," 340.

43. Woods, *A History of Gay Literature,* 275.

44. Gould, "Disobedience (in Language) in Text by Lesbian Native Americans," 32.

45. Gilley, *Becoming Two-Spirit,* 73.

46. Nagel, "Ethnicity and Sexuality," 108.

47. Weinmann, "Hold Me Closer, Fancydancer."

48. Alexie, *The Business of Fancydancing*. All subsequent quotes from the film are from this DVD.

49. Alexie, "Agnes Roth."

50. Womack, *Red on Red,* 280.

51. Quentin Youngberg suggests that "ethnohistorical conflicts are . . . manifested in the relationship between Steven and Seymour. Alexie uses Seymour and Steven as mechanisms for bringing to light the charged political and social relationships between Indian and white cultures. The history of violence shared between whites and Indians is superimposed onto the love relationship shared between these two men." Youngberg goes on to suggest that "the film treats the love relationship between Steven and Seymour in such a way that it formulates a link between politics and desire and, in doing so, demonstrates the complexity of identities (sexual, racial, social, and political) in lived experience." See Youngberg, "Interpenetrations," 67–68, 69. While I think Youngberg's reading of the film is insightful, I differ with him on this point. I agree that Seymour and Steven's relationship demonstrates the layered and multiple nature of identities, but I think rather than serving as a "link," their interactions form a discrete barrier between those identities.

52. Nealon, *Foundlings,* 1, 8.

53. Ibid., 1–2.

54. Weston, *Long Slow Burn,* 38.

55. See, for example, Gilley's chapter, "Adapting to Homophobia among Indians," in *Becoming Two-Spirit,* 53–85, and Anderson-Minshall, "Without Reservations."

56. Weston, *Long Slow Burn,* 45.

57. Erdrich, *The Plague of Doves,* 235.

58. Sedgwick, *Between Men.*

59. Alexie, *The Business of Fancydancing: The Screenplay,* 134.

60. In a fascinating parallel with the conclusion of *Johnny Greyeyes,* Seymour's last scene of dancing before he begins stripping off his regalia is set to the Christian anthem "Amazing Grace." As my chapter suggests, there is much to say about whom or what is "lost" and "found" in the final scenes of both films. See Youngberg for an excellent discussion of how the Shawl Dance functions as a cultural code earlier in the film "Interpenetrations: Re-encoding the Queer Indian," 63–64. And, finally, each time I see this scene I am reminded of Gerald Vizenor's exploration of the striptease in which he argues, "Tribal cultures are colonized in a reversal of the striptease. . . . Plains tepees, and the signs of moccasins, canoes, feathers, leathers, arrowheads, numerous museum artifacts, conjure the cultural rituals of the traditional tribal past," See Vizenor, "Socioacupuncture," 181.

61. Alexie, *The Business of Fancydancing,* 80.

62. Raheja, *Reservation Reelism,* xi. While Raheja discusses Indigenous representations more generally here, she provides an apt description of the realities of queer Indigenous representations in film.

63. Estrada, "Two-Spirit Film Criticism," 106.

5. Indigenous Assemblage and Queer Diasporas in the Work of Janice Gould

1. McCall, "The Complexity of Intersectionality," 1774.

2. The spelling of Koyoonk'auwi varies; thus Gould's tribe has been termed Concow, Konkow, Konkau, and Koyangk'auwi. Based on discussion with Gould, I alternate here between Koyoonk'auwi and Konkow. In terms of family history, Gould's maternal grandmother, Helen (Nellie Orcier), and grandfather, Harry B. Beatty, were both from Belden. Their mothers, Mary Beatty (Harry's) and Catherine Orcier (Nellie's), were Konkow women from Plumas County, the north fork area of the Feather River (Konkow territory). Mary's parents, Gould's great-great-grandparents, Dr. Charley and Emma Charley, were also Konkow people who lived in Konkow territory. The town of Belden itself is named after the family to whom Gould's mother was related.

Gould's family lived in the wake of and through California Indian genocide. The subsequent fragmentation of Indigenous kinship systems and the ensuing poverty of dispossessed California Indian peoples are key factors behind the adoption of Gould's mother into a non-Native family. Besides remaining extant in oral histories, these events have also been chronicled in texts such as Forbes, *Native Americans of California and Nevada;* Heizer, *"They Were Only Diggers"* and *The Destruction of California Indians;* Norton, *When Our Worlds Cried;* Costo and Costo, *The Missions of California;* Hurtado, *Indian Survival on the California Frontier;*

and Trafzer and Hyer, *"Exterminate Them!"* Most recently, Brendan C. Lindsay has documented "the creation, through the democratic processes and institutions of the people of the United States, of a culture organized around the dispossession and murder of California Indians." See Lindsay, *Murder State,* 2.

3. Gould, *Earthquake Weather,* ix.

4. The parallels between U.S. and Canadian policies toward Indigenous peoples are stark but by no means exact. In both cases, the relocation of children to government- and church-run boarding (United States) and residential (Canada) schools and cultural genocide vis-à-vis assimilation and psychic and geographical separations preceded adoption policies. Large-scale adoption functioned as yet another set of nation-state policies that threatened Indigenous nationhood and cultural continuity by directly targeting Indigenous children. Under practices that non-Native social workers characterized as for the "good of the children," Indigenous children were taken from their families and/or tribal communities, put into the foster care system, and disproportionately placed into non-Indigenous households. In most cases, adoption records were sealed and, where records were available, tribal affiliation, Aboriginal status, and band names were often omitted. Prior to the Indian Child Welfare Act in the United States, "placement of Indian children out of their homes [was] . . . disproportionately high when compared to their non-Indian counterparts. For example, in 1974, South Dakota had 16 times as many Indian as non-Indian children in foster care. In Minnesota, the ratio of Indian to non-Indian children in placement was five to one. Indian children in North Dakota, South Dakota, and Nebraska were placed outside their homes as more than twenty times the national average. In Wisconsin, Indian children were placed in either foster care or adoptive homes at a rate of 15 to 17 times higher than other children." See Garner, "The Indian Child Welfare Act," 47–48. In Canada, according to a Native Child and Family Services of Toronto report, "Many Aboriginal children were taken from their birth parents during the 'Sixties Scoop' which occurred during the 1960s, 1970s and early 1980s. It was initiated in 1965 when the Federal-Provincial Child Welfare Agreement was struck which gave the Province of Ontario the power and authority to administer child welfare services under the Ontario *Child Welfare Act* for status Indians on Reserve." The alarming numbers of Aboriginal adoptees slowly began to decrease after "December 1981 when the all Ontario Chiefs Conference (AOCC) Resolution 81/19 was passed." See Budgell, *Repatriation of Aboriginal Families,* 11.

There is a significant body of boarding/residential school literature. To offer just a few examples, see Adams, *Education for Extinction;* Archuleta, Child, and Lomawaima, *Away from Home;* Briggs and Dubinsky, "Native Adoption in Canada, the United States, New Zealand, and Australia"; Castellano, Davis, and Lahache, *Aboriginal Education;* Child, *Boarding School Seasons;* Reyhner and Eder, *American Indian Education.*

Lastly, despite the gains that followed in the wake of Indian Child Welfare Act, in the United States, recent work has shown a gradual return to the practice of out-adoption. See, for example, a well-documented three-part NPR investigation, "Native Foster Care: Lost Children, Shattered Families," by Laura Sullivan and Amy Walters, and the June 25, 2013, U.S. Supreme Court decision in *Adoptive Couple v. Baby Girl.*

5. See Vizenor, *Fugitive Poses.*

6. Garroutte, *Real Indians,* 4.

7. Lyons, *X-Marks,* 59.

8. Puar, *Terrorist Assemblages,* 192.

9. Eng, *The Feeling of Kinship,* 67.

10. Puar, *Terrorist Assemblages,* 195. Like Puar, I extend one of Deleuze and Guattari's key theoretical frames from *A Thousand Plateaus.* At the same time, I acknowledge the deficiencies of the text as a whole in its deployment of the rhetoric of difference/otherness. A strong strain of Orientalism runs throughout the text, as do unmoored and decontextualized references to American Indian and Indigenous people more generally. See Miller, "The Postidentitarian Predicament," for an excellent discussion of these textual gaps. See Jardine, "Woman in Limbo," for a feminist critique of *A Thousand Plateaus* in which she concludes, "It would seem that the most radical promises offered by D + G's theory . . . are not to be kept—at least for now. For when enacted, when performed, they are promises to be kept only between bodies gendered male" (59). Most recently, Chickasaw scholar Jodi A. Byrd offers both a critique and Indigenous (re)deployment of Deleuze and Guattari's theory in *The Transit of Empire,* especially 11–21.

11. Puar, *Terrorist Assemblages,* 204.

12. By forwarding Indigenous assemblage, I do not suggest we dismiss intersectional methodologies or the concept of tribally grounded Indigenous identities. Such strategies and subjectivities not only are often necessary but can, especially in the context of American Indian and Aboriginal politics, be politically, collectively, and personally empowering. The argument here, then, is not for the primacy of one theoretical lens over another—that assemblage negates the work of intersectionality—but is instead that, in the case of Gould's work, assemblage better recognizes the ever-shifting space of cultural and sexual recognitions represented in her texts. See Eng, *The Feeling of Kinship,* for an excellent analysis of the dangers in "the forgetting of race and the denial of racial difference" within the United States and Womack, "Theorizing American Indian Experience," for a discussion of realism, essentialism, and postmodernism in Native American studies.

13. See the preface to *Earthquake Weather* and Gould, "Singing, Speaking, and Seeing a World," for more on her family history.

14. Ramirez, *Native Hubs,* 11.

15. See Hedge Coke, *Blood Run;* Allen, "Serpentine Figures, Sinuous Relations."

16. Gould, *Earthquake Weather,* ix.

17. Ibid., ix, xi.

18. Puar, *Terrorist Assemblages,* 211.

19. Goeman, "Notes toward a Native Feminism's Spatial Practice," 173.

20. The utility of assemblage in considering processes of cultural recovery is situated precisely in its privileging of the potential for such change. When deployed to discuss identity, then, assemblage is "a multiplicity that necessarily changes in nature" (8). As discussed later in this chapter, Deleuze and Guattari use the metaphor of ants: their straight-line structure "may be broken, shattered at a given spot, but it will start up again on one of its old lines or on new lines. You can never get rid of ants because they form an animal rhizome that can rebound time and again after most of it has been destroyed." See Deleuze and Guattari, *A Thousand Plateaus,* 9. This fluid tenacity, which emphasizes resilient processes of reconstruction, is useful in discussing Gould's articulation of her relationship to her Koyoonk'auwi ancestry.

21. Eng, *The Feeling of Kinship,* 58–59.

22. See Dugan, *The Twilight of Equality?;* Puar, *Terrorist Assemblages.*

23. Eng, *The Feeling of Kinship,* 58–59.

24. Gould, "Autobiography," 19–20.

25. This is an especially poignant metaphor in a nation where the remains of an estimated 600,000 Native people are scattered in drawers and boxes across the country.

26. Brant, *Writing as Witness,* 20.

27. Gould subsequently smiled and said some of the dates changed throughout the texts—one example being the year of her mother's birth. She also noted "Autobiography" was inspired by a poem of the same title by Spanish writer Gloria Fuertes and spoke, as well, to the importance of music and rhythm to her thought process and artistic vision. Thus while it's "all autobiography," the idea of artistic production functioning as a mimetic window to a singular vision of a personal or tribal past is destabilized.

28. Gould, "Coyotismo," 11.

29. Like afterbirth, which is profane/perceived as waste in some contexts while seen as sacred/powerful and ritually buried or preserved in others, Coyote is read differently as cultural contexts change.

30. Miranda, "Dildos, Hummingbirds, and Driving Her Crazy," 138.

31. Allen, *The Sacred Hoop,* 25. See the introduction for a further discussion of Allen and the Indigenous erotic.

32. Million, "Felt Theory," 54. Million's essay focuses on the repercussions of the Indian Act and the movement of First Nations women to "bear witness" to the

colonial violence of residential schools, citing key autobiographical and literary texts in such testimony: Maria Campbell's *Half-Breed* (1973), Lee Maracle's *Indian Rebel* (originally published in 1975 as an as-told-to narrative under the pseudonym Bobbi Lee), Beatrice Culleton's *In Search of April Raintree* (1983), Jeannette Armstrong's *Slash* (1985), and Ruby Slipperjack's *Honour the Sun* (1987). Million's argument about the function of affect within these testimonies is particularly useful here.

33. Million, "Felt Theory," 56.

34. Ibid., 58.

35. See Edelman, *No Future*. For an Indigenous studies critique of Edelman, see Smith, "Queer Theory and Native Studies."

36. Chickasaw scholar Jodi Byrd would call these "transits." Byrd explains, "To be in transit is to be in active presence in a world of relational movements and countermovements. To be in transit is to exist relationally, multiply." See Byrd, *The Transit of Empire*, xvi–xvii.

37. Eng, *The Feeling of Kinship*, 59.

38. Gould, *Earthquake Weather*, viii.

39. Million, "Felt Theory," 58.

40. Gould, *Earthquake Weather*, x.

41. Gould, *Earthquake Weather*, xi.

42. Buckley and Young, "Janice Gould," 85.

43. Byrd, *The Transit of Empire*, 118.

44. Goeman, "Notes toward a Native Feminism's Spatial Practice," 173.

45. See Brant, *Writing as Witness*, 39–40.

46. See Brant, "Coyote Learns a New Trick"; Highway, *The Rez Sisters* and *Dry Lips Oughta Move to Kapuskasing*; Miguel, *Hot 'n' Soft;* Steward, "Coyote and Tehoma."

47. Deleuze and Guattari, *A Thousand Plateaus*, 88.

48. Papastergiadis, *The Turbulence of Migration*, 118.

49. This distance Gould depicts between her and her mother's perspectives functions as what Byrd might term a "subversive core." Byrd builds on the work of Slavoj Žižek, employing the astronomical concept of "parallax—a shift in an observer's perspective of a distant object based on a change in a vantage point" to discuss contrasting points of perceptual vision. Byrd argues, "The gap between two sides of the same phenomenon 'allows us to discern its subversive core' that cuts across the cosmopolitan hybrid/nomad and acknowledges the lived conditions of violence, class, and oppression." We see exactly this sort of gap in Gould's poem. See Byrd, *The Transit of Empire*, 30.

50. Gould, "Waiting for a Miracle," 21.

51. Deleuze and Guattari, *A Thousand Plateaus*, 88.

52. Ibid., 9.

53. Gould, "Foster Family," 39.

54. Muñoz, *Cruising Utopia,* 65.

55. Ibid.

56. Ibid., 49.

57. Brant, *Writing as Witness,* 8.

58. Ibid., 16.

59. Gould, "Disobedience (in Language) in Texts by Lesbian Native Americans," 41.

60. Miranda, *The Zen of La Llorona,* 4.

61. Gould, "The Woman I Love Most," 46.

62. Gould, "To Speak Your Name," 48.

63. Miranda, "Dildos, Hummingbirds and Driving Her Crazy," 141, 143–44.

64. Gould, "Autobiography," 19.

65. Gould, "Thursdays," 31.

66. Deleuze and Guattari, *A Thousand Plateaus,* 8.

67. Muñoz, *Cruising Utopia,* 65.

68. Halberstam's claims about the power of forgetting and the possibilities of failure resonate here, especially her argument that "queer culture, with its emphasis on repetition (Butler), horizontality (Muñoz, Stockton), immaturity and a refusal of adulthood (me) where adulthood rhymes with heterosexual parenting, resists a developmental model of substitution and instead invests in what Stockton calls 'sideways' relations, relations that grow along parallel lines rather than upward and onward. This queer form of antidevelopment requires healthy doses of forgetting and disavowal and proceeds by way of a series of substitutions." See Halberstam, *The Queer Art of Failure,* 73. The power of "forgetting," the efficacy of substitutions, and Gould's sideways relations with her father can be seen throughout this section.

69. Muñoz, *Cruising Utopia,* 65.

70. Womack, "Suspicioning," 133.

71. Deleuze and Guattari, *A Thousand Plateaus,* 9.

72. Ibid., 8.

73. Puar, *Terrorist Assemblages,* 211.

74. Muñoz, *Cruising Utopia,* 65.

75. Gould, "Autobiography," 19.

76. Gould, "My Father," 43.

77. Moraga configures a similar parallel, "a 'queer' inheritance, or a line of descent in which same sex desire 'runs' from father to daughter." See Tatonetti, "'A Kind of Queer Balance,'" 231.

78. Eng, *The Feeling of Kinship,* 58.

79. Ibid., 59.

80. Gould, "Feather River Sonnets," 10.

81. Gould, "My Father, Cynthia Conroy," 95.

82. Ibid., 100.

83. Ibid., 93, 101.

84. Gopinath, *Impossible Desires,* 28.

85. Berlant and Warner, "Sex in Public," 549.

86. Speaking of the difference between female-to-male (FTM) transsexuals and butch lesbian identities, Halberstam points out that "at present, the moniker 'FTM' names a radical shift in both identity and body base within the context of transsexuality that by comparison makes 'butch' look like a stable signifier. But the shifts and accommodations made in most cross-gender identifications, whether aided by surgery or hormones or not, involve a great deal of instability and transitivity." See *Female Masculinity,* 146. The interplay between Gould's own butch identity and Cynthia's male-to-female (MTF) transsexual subjectivity highlights this intransitivity, pointing to how the multiplicative and malleable nature of bodies and desires can unmoor grounding master narratives of family, nature, body, and self.

87. Halberstam, "The Pregnant Man," 78.

88. Deleuze and Guattari, *A Thousand Plateaus,* 9.

89. Gould, "My Father, Cynthia Conroy," 94.

90. Ibid., 44.

91. Deleuze and Guattari, *A Thousand Plateaus,* 9.

92. Gould, "My Father, Cynthia Conroy," 103.

93. Lyons, *X-Marks,* 59.

94. Rifkin, *When Did Indians Become Straight?,* 5.

95. Deleuze and Guattari, *A Thousand Plateaus,* 25.

96. Eng, *The Feeling of Kinship,* 59.

97. Gould, "Renegade," 3–4.

98. Miranda, *Indian Cartography,* x. Miranda returns to this topic in *Bad Indians,* explaining, "The Mission Unit is all too often a lesson in imperialism, racism, and Manifest Destiny rather than actually educational or a jumping off point for critical thinking or accurate history." See Miranda, *Bad Indians,* xvii.

99. Gould, "Indian Mascot, 1959," 1.

100. Morgensen, *Spaces between Us,* 225.

101. Ibid., 26.

102. Golla, *California Indian Languages,* 138.

103. Gould, "Renegade," 3.

104. "Wee-mo-way," better known as "The Lion Sleeps Tonight," was written in the 1920s by Zulu musician Solomon Linda, who received no royalties for the international hit. The Emmy-winning 2005 documentary *A Lion's Trail* by Francois Verster details this history. "Kumbaya," likewise, is mired in a history of capitalist appropriation: though Rev. Martin V. Frey claims to have penned the

song around 1936 and copyrighted sheet music for it in 1939, previous collected recordings of African American spirituals stemming from Gullah traditions exist at least as far back as the 1920s according to the American Folklife Center Archive at the Library of Congress (Winick).

105. Garroutte, *Real Indians,* 68–69.

106. Gopinath, *Impossible Desires,* 5; Eng, *The Feeling of Kinship,* 13.

107. Gopinath, *Impossible Desires,* 187.

108. Gould, *Earthquake Weather,* 22.

Conclusion

1. Muñoz, *Cruising Utopia,* 189.

2. Medicine, "Changing Native American Sex Roles," 150.

3. The rich work of rereading canonical texts is becoming increasingly important in queer Native literary studies. See Snyder's rereading of John Joseph Mathews, Rifkin's work with Zitkala-Sa, Leah Sneider's work on Sarah Winnemucca, and the recovery and queer reading of lesser-known texts as recently undertaken in Alicia Cox's analysis of Polingaysi Qoyawayma's autobiography, *No Turning Back.* These queer-framed inquiries deploy queerness as a reading practice rather than an identity and reinforce this book's mantra that Native American and Indigenous literatures were always already queer. See Snyder, "'He Certainly Didn't Want Anyone to Know That He Was Queer'"; Rifkin, *When Did Indians Become Straight?*; Sneider, "Queering Indigenous Feminisms"; Cox, "Remembering Polingaysi."

4. Raheja, *Reservation Reelism,* x.

5. Allen, *The Sacred Hoop,* 192.

6. Million, "Felt Theory," 58.

7. Eng, *The Feeling of Kinship,* 58–59.

8. Ibid., 12.

9. Miranda, *Bad Indians,* xix.

10. Ibid., 136.

11. Ibid.

12. I'm thinking here, for example, of work like Cox's "Remembering Polinaysi."

13. Brant, *Writing as Witness,* 64. Thanks to Scott Lauria Morgensen for an e-mail conversation about these groups.

14. I'm thinking particularly of work on North America; such analyses are under way in Gabriel S. Estrada's and James H. Cox's research. Estrada's essay "Two-Spirit Histories in Southwestern and Mesoamerican Literatures" traces queer Native literary histories across what is now the U.S.–Mexico border, while

Cox analyzes Riggs depictions of Indigeneity in Mexico in *The Red Land to the South,* an important book that examines Native American writers during the understudied period of the mid-twentieth century.

15. Chadwick Allen defines such comparative, collaborative, Indigenous–Indigenous relationships not simply as events but as a critical methodology for global Indigenous studies. See Allen, *Trans-Indigenous.*

16. Brant, *Writing as Witness,* 18.

Bibliography

"204: 81 Words." *This American Life*. Public Radio International. Chicago Public Media. January 18, 2002.

Abott, Larry. "Spiderwoman Theater and the Tapestry of Story." *Canadian Journal of Native Studies* 16, no. 1 (1996): 165–80.

Adams, David Wallace. *Education for Extinction: American Indians and the Boarding School Experience, 1875–1928*. Lawrence: University Press of Kansas, 1995.

Akiwenzie-Damm, Kateri. "Erotica, Indigenous Style." In *Without Reservation: Indigenous Erotica,* edited by Kateri Akiwenzie-Damm, xi–xii. Wharton, Ontario: Kegedonce, 2003.

———, ed. *Without Reservation: Indigenous Erotica.* Wharton, Ontario: Kegedonce, 2003.

"Akwesasne We Are Not the Enemy." *RFD* 14 (winter 1977): 51.

Alexie, Sherman. *The Business of Fancydancing: The Screenplay.* Brooklyn: Hanging Loose, 2003.

———. "Characters: Agnes Roth." The Business of Fancydancing. http://www.fallsapart.com/fancydancing.

———. *The Toughest Indian in the World.* New York: Atlantic, 2000.

Allen, Chadwick. "Serpentine Figures, Sinuous Relations: Thematic Geometry in Allison Hedge Coke's *Blood Run.*" *American Literature* 82, no. 4 (2010): 807–34.

———. *Trans-Indigenous: Methodologies for Global Native Literary Studies.* Minneapolis: University of Minnesota Press, 2012.

Allen, Paula Gunn. "Going Home, December 1992." In *Reinventing the Enemy's Language: Contemporary Native Women's Writing of North America,* edited by Joy Harjo and Gloria Bird, 151–56. New York: W. W. Norton, 1997.

———. "Lesbians in American Indian Cultures." *Conditions* 7 (1981): 67–87.

———. *The Sacred Hoop: Recovering the Feminine in American Indian Traditions.* Boston: Beacon, 1986.

———, ed. *Spider Woman's Granddaughters: Traditional Tales and Contemporary Writing by Native American Women.* New York: Random House, 1989.

———, ed. *Studies in American Indian Literature: Critical Essays and Course Designs.* New York: Modern Language Association of America, 1983.

———. *The Woman Who Owned the Shadows.* San Francisco: Spinsters, 1983.

Amnesty International. *Stolen Sisters: Discrimination and Violence against Indigenous Women in Canada: A Summary of Amnesty International's Concerns.* October 4, 2004, Report Index: AMR 20/001/2004. http://web.amnesty.org/library.

Anderson-Minshall, Diana. "Without Reservations: Native American Lesbians Struggle to Find Their Way." *Curve* 13, no. 2 (2003): 34–37.

Anhedonia. Written and directed by Thirza Cuthand. Toronto: V-Tape, 2001.

Anzaldúa, Gloria. *Borderlands/La Frontera: The New Mestiza.* San Francisco: Aunt Lute Books, 1987.

———. "Haciendo Caras, Una Etrada: An Introduction by Gloria Anzaldúa." In *Making Face, Making Soul Haciendo Caras: Creative and Critical Perspectives by Women of Color,* edited by Gloria Anzaldúa, xv–xxviii. San Francisco: Aunt Lute Foundation Books, 1990.

———, ed. *Making Face, Making Soul Haciendo Caras: Creative and Critical Perspectives by Women of Color.* San Francisco: Aunt Lute Foundation Books, 1990.

———. "To(o) Queer the Writer." In *The Gloria Anzaldúa Reader,* edited by AnaLouise Keating, 163–75. Durham, N.C.: Duke University Press, 2009.

Anzaldúa, Gloria, and AnaLouise Keating, eds. *This Bridge We Call Home: Radical Visions for Transformation.* New York: Routledge, 2002.

Anzaldúa, Gloria, and Cherríe Moraga, eds. *This Bridge Called My Back: Writings by Radical Women of Color.* Watertown, Mass.: Persephone, 1981.

Archuleta, Margaret L., Brenda J. Child, and K. Tsianina Lomawaima, eds. *Away from Home: American Indian Boarding School Experiences, 1879–2000.* Phoenix: Heard Museum, 2000.

Asals, Katharine. "Memoriam for Clint." Katharine Asals. http://www.katharineasals.com.

Bachrach, Susan. "Deadly Medicine." *Public Historian* 29, no. 3 (summer 2007): 19–32.

Badia, Janet. *Sylvia Plath and the Mythology of Women Readers.* Amherst: University of Massachusetts Press, 2011.

Barak, Julie. "Blurs, Blends, Berdaches: Gender Mixing in the Novels of Louise Erdrich." *Studies in American Indian Literatures* 8, no. 3 (fall 1996): 49–62.

Baringer, Sandra. "'Captive Woman?': The Rewriting of Pocahontas in Three Contemporary Native American Novels." *Studies in American Indian Literatures* 11, no. 3 (1999): 42–63.

Barker, Joanne. "Gender, Sovereignty, Rights: Native Women's Activism against Social Inequality and Violence in Canada." *American Quarterly* 60, no. 2 (2008): 259–66.

Barnard, Ian. *Queer Race: Cultural Interventions in the Racial Politics of Queer Theory.* New York: Peter Lang, 2004.

Bayer, Ronald. *Homosexuality and American Psychiatry: The Politics of Diagnosis.* 2nd ed. Princeton, N.J.: Princeton University Press, 1987.

Beemyn, Brett, ed. *Creating a Place for Ourselves: Lesbian, Gay, Bisexual, and Community Histories.* New York: Routledge, 1997.

Beidler, Peter G. "Mauser's Illness: Medical Humor in Erdrich's Four Souls." In *Studies in the Literary Achievement of Louise Erdrich, Native American Writer: Fifteen Critical Essays,* edited by Brajesh Sawhney, 11–28. Lewiston, N.Y.: Edwin Mellen, 2008.

Beidler, Peter G., and Gay Barton, eds. *A Reader's Guide to the Novels of Louise Erdrich.* Revised and expanded ed. Columbia: University of Missouri Press, 2006.

Bell, David. "Eroticizing the Rural." In *De-Centering Sexualities: Politics and Representations beyond the Metropolis,* edited by Richard Phillips, Diane Watt, and David Shuttleton, 83–101. London: Routledge, 2000.

Berger, Thomas. *Little Big Man.* Dial Press Trade Paperback ed. New York: Bantam Dell, 2011.

Berkhofer, Robert F. *The White Man's Indian: Images of the American Indian from Columbus to the Present.* New York: Vintage, 1979.

Berlant, Lauren, and Michael Warner. "Sex in Public." *Critical Inquiry* 24, no. 2 (winter 1998): 547–66.

Big Eden. Directed by Thomas Bezucha. San Francisco: Chaiken Films, 2000.

Bobbi the Social Worker Slayer. Written and directed by Ghastant'Aucoin. Toronto: V-Tape, 2003.

Bode, Carl. "Columbia's Carnal Bed." *American Quarterly* 15, no. 1 (spring 1963): 52–64.

Bodhrán, Ahimsa Timoteo, ed. "The Ancestors We Were Looking for, We Have Become: International Queer Indigenous Issue." Special issue, *Yellow Medicine River: A Journal of Indigenous Literature, Art, and Thought* 9 (fall 2010).

Brant, Beth. "Coyote Learns a New Trick." In *Mohawk Trail,* 31-51. Ithaca, N.Y.: Firebrand Books, 1985.

———. *Food & Spirits.* Ithaca, N.Y.: Firebrand Books, 1991.

———, ed. *A Gathering of Spirit: A Collection by North American Indian Women.* 1984. Reprint, New York: Firebrand Books, 1988.

———, ed. "A Gathering of Spirit: North American Indian Women's Issue." Special issue, *Sinister Wisdom* 22/23 (1983).

———. "Home Coming." In *Piece of My Heart: A Lesbian of Colour Anthology,* anthologized by Makeda Silvera, 249–55. Toronto: Sister Vision Press, 1991.

———. "Introduction: A Gathering of Spirit." In *A Gathering of Spirit: A Collection by North American Indian Women,* 8–14. 1984. Reprint, New York: Firebrand Books, 1988.

———. *Mohawk Trail.* Ithaca, N.Y.: Firebrand Books, 1985.

———. *Writing as Witness: Essay and Talk*. Toronto: Women's Press, 1994.

Brehm, Victoria. "The Metamorphoses of an Ojibwe Manido." *American Literature* 68 (1996): 677–706.

Briere, John N., and Diane M. Elliott. "Immediate and Long-Term Impacts of Child Sexual Abuse." Sexual Abuse of Children. Special issue, *The Future of Children* 4, no. 2 (summer/fall 1994): 54–69.

Briggs, Laura, and Karen Dubinsky, eds. "Native Adoption in Canada, the United States, New Zealand, and Australia." Special issue, *American Indian Quarterly* 37, no. 2 (spring 2013).

Brown, Michael. *Closet Space: Geographies of Metaphor from the Body to the Globe*. New York: Routledge, 2000.

Bruchac, Joseph. "New Leaves on the Trees of Our Nations: Five Native American Chapbooks." *American Indian Quarterly* 9, no. 4 (fall 1985): 473–76.

———, ed. *Songs from This Earth on Turtle's Back: Contemporary American Indian Poetry*. Greenfield Center, N.Y.: Greenfield Review, 1983.

Buckley, Christopher, and Gary Young. "Janice Gould." In *The Geography of Home: California's Poetry of Place*, 85–90. Berkeley: Heyday Books, 1999.

Budgell, Janet, and Native Child and Family Services of Toronto. *Repatriation of Aboriginal Families—Issues, Models and a Workplan*. March 1999. http://www.turtleisland.org/healing/repatriation.pdf.

Burdick, Debra A. "Louise Erdrich's *Love Medicine, The Beet Queen,* and *Tracks:* An Annotated Survey of Criticism through 1994." *American Indian Culture and Research Journal* 20, no. 3 (1996): 137–66.

Burns, Randy. "Preface." In *Living the Spirit: A Gay American Indian Anthology*, edited by Gay American Indians and Will Roscoe, 1–5. New York: St. Martin's, 1988.

The Business of Fancydancing. Written and directed by Sherman Alexie. New York: FallsApart/Wellspring Media, 2003.

Butler, Judith. *Gender Trouble: Feminism and the Subversion of Identity*. New York: Routledge, 1990.

———. "Melancholy Gender—Refused Identification." *Psychoanalytic Dialogues: The International Journal of Relational Perspectives* 5, no. 2 (1995): 165–80.

Byrd, Jodi A. *The Transit of Empire: Indigenous Critiques of Colonialism*. Minneapolis: University of Minnesota Press, 2011.

Cameron, Barbara. "Gee, You Don't Seem Like an Indian from the Reservation." In *This Bridge Called My Back: Writings by Radical Women of Color*, edited by Cherríe Moraga and Gloria Anzaldúa, 46–52. 1981. Reprint, New York: Women of Color Press, 1983.

Canning, Charlotte. *Feminist Theaters in the U.S.A.: Staging Women's Experiences*. London: Routledge, 1996.

Case, Sue-Ellen. "Introduction." In *Split Britches: Lesbian Practice/Feminist Performance,* edited by Sue-Ellen Case, 1–34. London: Routledge, 1996.

———, ed. *Split Britches: Lesbian Practice/Feminist Performance.* London: Routledge, 1996.

Cassedy, Ellen. "We Are All Here: Facing History in Lithuania." *Bridges* 12, no. 2 (fall 2007): 77–85.

Castellano, Marlene Brant, Lynne Davis, and Louise Lahache. *Aboriginal Education: Fulfilling the Promise.* Vancouver: University of British Columbia Press, 2000.

Castillo, Susan Perez. "The Construction of Gender and Ethnicity in the Texts of Louise Silko and Louise Erdrich." *Yearbook of English Studies* 24 (1994): 228–36.

———. "Women Aging into Power: Fictional Representations of Power and Authority in Louise Erdrich's Female Characters." *Studies in American Indian Literatures* 8, no. 4 (winter 1996): 13–20.

Chadwick, Jerry. "Poem after Le Roi's TOILET, after My Best Friend Got Beaten Up, after Richard Heakin Got Killed *To All the Fags Who Did Nothing.*" *Fag Rag* 18 (fall/winter 1976): 8.

Chaske, Ivy, Connie Fife, Jan Champagne, Edna King, and Midnight Sun, eds. "Native Women." Special issue, *Fireweed: A Feminist Quarterly* 22 (winter 1986).

Chauncey, George. "From Sexual Inversion to Homosexuality: Medicine and the Changing Conceptualization of Female Deviance." In *Passion and Power: Sexuality in History,* edited by Kathy Piess and Christina Simmons, 87–117. Philadelphia: Temple University Press, 1989.

———. *Gay New York: Gender, Urban Culture and the Making of the Gay Male World 1890–1940.* New York: Basic Books, 1994.

Chief Eagle, Dallas. *Winter Count.* Edited by Chadwick Allen. 1967. Reprint, Lincoln: University of Nebraska Press, 2003.

Child, Brenda J. *Boarding School Seasons: American Indian Families, 1900–1940.* Lincoln: University of Nebraska Press, 1993.

Chrystos. *Dream On.* Vancouver: Press Gang, 1991.

———. *Fire Power.* Vancouver: Press Gang, 1995.

———. *Fugitive Colors.* Cleveland: Cleveland State University Press, 1995.

———. *In Her I Am.* Vancouver: Press Gang, 1993.

———. "I Walk in the History of My People." In *This Bridge Called My Back: Writings by Radical Women of Color,* edited by Cherríe Moraga and Gloria Anzaldúa, 57. 1981. Reprint, New York: Women of Color Press, 1983.

———. *Not Vanishing.* Vancouver: Press Gang, 1988.

Cloudmaker. Written and directed by Adam Garnet Jones. Toronto: V-Tape, 2006.

"Cocksucking as an Act of Revolution." *Fag Rag* 3 (summer 1972): 8, 20.

Cohen, Cathy J. "Punks, Bulldaggers, and Welfare Queens: The Radical Potential of Queer Politics?" In *Black Queer Studies: A Critical Anthology*, edited by E. Patrick Johnson and Mea G. Henderson, 21–51. Durham, N.C.: Duke University Press, 2003.

Columpar, Corinn. *Unsettling Sights: The Fourth World on Film*. Carbondale: Southern Illinois University Press, 2010.

Corinne, Tee, ed. *Riding Desire: An Anthology of Erotic Writing*. Austin: Banned Books, 1991.

Cornelia, Marie. "Shifting Boundaries: Reflections on Ethnic Identity in Louise Erdrich's *The Master Butchers Singing Club*." *Glossen* 19 (2004). http://www2.dickinson.edu/glossen/heft19/cornelia.html.

Cornell, Daniel. "Woman Looking: Revis(ion)ing Pauline's Subject Position in Louise Erdrich's *Tracks*." *Studies in American Indian Literatures* 4, no. 1 (spring 1992): 49–64.

Costo, Rupert, and Jeannette Henry Costo, eds. *The Missions of California: A Legacy of Genocide*. San Francisco: Indian Historian, 1987.

Cox, Alicia. "Remembering Polingaysi: A Queer Recovery of *No Turning Back* as a Decolonial Text." *Studies in American Indian Literatures* 26, no. 1 (spring 2014): 54–80.

Cox, James H. *Muting White Noise: Native American and European American Novel Traditions*. Norman: University of Oklahoma Press, 2006.

———. *The Red Land to the South: American Indian Writers and Indigenous Mexico*. Minneapolis: University of Minnesota Press, 2012.

Crenshaw, Kimberlé. "Demarginalizing the Intersection of Race and Sex: A Black Feminist Critique of Antidiscrimination Doctrine, Feminist Theory and Antiracist Politics." *University of Chicago Legal Forum* 140 (1989): 139–67.

———. "Mapping the Margins: Intersectionality, Identity Politics, and Violence against Women of Color." *Stanford Law Review* 43 (July 1991): 1241–99.

Cummings, Denise K. *Visualities: Perspectives on Contemporary American Indian Film and Art*. East Lansing: Michigan State University Press, 2011.

Dance to the Berdashe. Written and directed by Kent Monkman. Toronto: Urban Nation, 2008.

Deep Inside Clint Star. Written and directed by Clint Alberta. Montreal: National Film Board of Canada, 2000.

Deloria, Ella Cara. *Speaking of Indians*. 1944. Reprint, Vermillion: University of South Dakota Press, 1983.

Deloria, Vine, Jr. "Foreword." In *New and Old Voices of Wah'Kon-Tah*, edited by Robert K. Dodge and Joseph B. McCullough, ix–x. New York: New York International, 1985.

DeMallie, Raymond J., ed. *The Sixth Grandfather: Black Elk's Teaching Given to John G. Neihardt.* Lincoln: University of Nebraska Press, 1985.

DeMallie, Raymond J., and Alfonso Ortiz, eds. *North American Indian Anthropology: Essays on Society and Culture.* Norman: University of Nebraska Press, 1994.

de Man, Paul. "Epistemology of Metaphor." *Critical Inquiry* 5, no. 1 (fall 1978): 13–30.

Demonstrations of Indianness #31. Written and directed by Adam Garnet Jones. Toronto: V-Tape, 2006.

Denetdale, Jennifer Nez. "Carving Navajo National Boundaries: Patriotism, Tradition, and the Diné Marriage Act of 2005." *American Quarterly* 60, no. 2 (June 2008): 289–94.

———. "Securing Navajo National Boundaries: War, Patriotism, Tradition, and the Diné Marriage Act of 2005." *Wicazo Sa Review* 24, no. 2 (fall 2009): 131–48.

DePastino, Todd. *Citizen Hobo: How A Century of Homelessness Shaped America.* Chicago: University of Chicago Press, 2003.

Derrida, Jacques. "White Mythology: Metaphor in the Text of Philosophy." Translated by F. C. T. Moore. *New Literary History* 6, no. 1 (fall 1974): 5–74.

Dolan, Jill. *The Feminist Spectator as Critic.* Ann Arbor: UMI Research, 1988.

Doty, Mark. *Atlantis.* New York: HarperCollins, 1995.

———. *My Alexandria.* Urbana: University of Illinois Press, 1993.

Driskill, Qwo-Li. "Doubleweaving Two-Spirit Critiques: Building Alliances between Native and Queer Studies." *GLQ: A Journal of Lesbian and Gay Studies* 16, nos. 1–2 (2010): 69–92.

———. "Shaking Our Shells: Cherokee Two-Spirits Rebalancing the World." In *Beyond Masculinity: Essays by Queer Men on Gender and Politics,* edited by Trevor Hoppe, 120–41. 2008. http://www.beyondmasculinity.com.

———. "Stolen from Our Bodies: First Nations Two-Spirits/Queers and the Journey to a Sovereign Erotic." *Studies in American Indian Literatures* 16, no. 2 (spring 2004): 50–64.

———. *Walking with Ghosts: Poems.* Cambridge, U.K.: Salt Publishing, 2005.

Driskill, Qwo-Li, Chris Finley, Brian Joseph Gilley, and Scott Lauria Morgensen. "Introduction." In *Queer Indigenous Studies: Critical Interventions in Theory, Politics, and Literature,* 1–28. Tucson: University of Arizona Press, 2011.

———, eds. *Queer Indigenous Studies: Critical Interventions in Theory, Politics, and Literature.* Tucson: University of Arizona Press, 2011.

Driskill, Qwo-Li, Daniel Heath Justice, Deborah Miranda, and Lisa Tatonetti. "Introduction: Writing in the Present." In *Sovereign Erotics: A Collection of Contemporary Two-Spirit Literature,* 1–17. Tucson: University of Arizona Press, 2011.

———, eds. *Sovereign Erotics: A Collection of Contemporary Two-Spirit Literature.* Tucson: University of Arizona Press, 2011.

Duggan, Lisa. *The Twilight of Equality? Neoliberalism, Cultural Politics, and the Attack on Democracy.* Boston: Beacon, 2003.

Edelman, Lee. *No Future: Queer Theory and the Death Drive.* Durham, N.C.: Duke University Press, 2004.

"Editor's Note." *Gay Sunshine: A Journal of Gay Liberation* 26/27 (winter 1965–1976): 1.

Embry, Marcus. "Ethnic Nostalgia: Ethnicity as Cultural Practice in the Twenty-First Century." In *Aesthetic Practices and Politics in Media, Music, and Art: Performing Migration,* edited by Rocio G. Davic, Dorothea Fischer-Hornung, and Johanna C. Kardux, 201–11. New York: Routledge, 2011.

Eng, David L. *The Feeling of Kinship: Queer Liberalism and the Racialization of Intimacy.* Durham, N.C.: Duke University Press, 2010.

Epple, Carolyn. "Coming to Terms with Navajo Nádleehí: A Critique of Berdache, 'Gay,' 'Alternate Gender,' and 'Two-Spirit.'" *American Ethnologist* 25, no. 2 (May 1998): 267–90.

Erdrich, Louise. *The Antelope Wife.* New York: HarperCollins, 1998.

———. *The Beet Queen.* New York: Bantam, 1986.

———. *The Bingo Palace.* New York: HarperCollins, 1994.

———. *Four Souls.* New York: HarperCollins, 2004.

———. *The Last Report on the Miracles of Little No Horse.* New York: HarperCollins, 2001.

———. *Love Medicine.* 1984. Expanded ed. New York: Harper, 1993.

———. *The Master Butchers Singing Club.* New York: HarperCollins, 2003.

———. *The Painted Drum.* New York: HarperCollins, 2005.

———. *The Plague of Doves.* New York: HarperCollins, 2008.

———. *Tales of Burning Love.* New York: HarperCollins, 1996.

———. *Tracks.* New York: Harper and Row, 1988.

Estrada, Gabriel S. "Two-Spirit Film Criticism: *Fancydancing* with Imitates Dog, Desjarlais and Alexie." *Post Script: Essays on Film and the Humanities* 29, no. 3 (2010): 106–18.

———. "Two-Spirit Histories in Southwestern and Mesoamerican Literatures." In *Gender and Sexuality in Indigenous North America, 1400–1850,* edited by Sandra Slater and Fay A. Yarbrough. Columbia: University of South Carolina Press, 2011.

Evans, Arthur. *Witchcraft: The Gay Counterculture.* Boston: Fag Rag Books, 1978.

"*Fag Rag* Blues." *Fag Rag* 2 (fall 1971): 3, 17.

Feier, Johanna. *We Never Hunted Buffalo: The Emergence of Native American Cinema.* Piscataway, N.J.: Transaction, 2011.

Ferguson, Roderick A. *Aberrations in Black: Toward a Queer of Color Critique.* Minneapolis: University of Minnesota Press, 2004.

Fife, Connie. *Beneath the Naked Sun.* Toronto: Sister Vision Press, 1992.

———, ed. *The Colour of Resistance: A Contemporary Collection of Writing by Aboriginal Women.* Toronto: Sister Vision Press, 1993.

———. "Peace Is Not Genocide." In *Poems for a New World,* 50–51. Vancouver: Ronsdale, 2001.

———. *Poems for a New World.* Vancouver: Ronsdale, 2001.

———. "The Revolution of Not Vanishing." In *Beneath the Naked Sun,* 49. Toronto: Sister Vision Press, 1992.

———. *Speaking through Jagged Rock.* Fredericton, New Brunswick: Broken Jaw, 1999.

First-Stories—Two-Spirited. Written and directed by Sharon A. Desjariais. Montreal: National Film Board of Canada, 2007.

Flavin, Louise. "Gender Construction amid Family Dissolution in Louise Erdrich's *The Beet Queen.*" *Studies in American Indian Literatures* 7, no. 2 (summer 1995): 17–24.

Forbes, Jack D. *Native Americans of California and Nevada.* Healdsburg, Calif.: Naturegraph, 1969.

Foster, Ken. "Bold, Sexy Stories from Alexie." Review of *The Toughest Indian in the World,* by Sherman Alexie. *San Francisco Chronicle,* May 21, 2000. http://www.sfgate.com/cgi-bin/article.cgi?file=/chronicle/archive/2000/05/21/RV25336.DTL.

Foucault, Michele. *Discipline and Punish: The Birth of the Prison.* Translated by Alan Sheridan. New York: Vintage, 1977.

Fraser, Joelle. "An Interview with Sherman Alexie." *Iowa Review* 30, no. 3 (winter 2000–2001): 59–70.

Future Nation. Written and directed by Kent Monkman. Toronto: V-Tape, 2005.

Gardner, Susan, ed. "Feminist and Postcolonial Approaches." Special issue, *Studies in American Indian Literatures* 6, no. 1 (spring 1994).

Garner, Suzanne. "The Indian Child Welfare Act: A Review." *Wicazo Sa Review* 9 no. 1 (spring 1993): 47–51.

Garroutte, Eva Marie. *Real Indians: Identity and the Survival of Native America.* Berkeley: University of California Press, 2003.

Gay American Indians and Will Roscoe, eds. *Living the Spirit: A Gay American Indian Anthology.* New York: St. Martin's, 1988.

Gengle, Dean. "Reclaiming the Old New World: Gay Was Good with Native Americans." *Advocate,* January 28, 1976, 40–41.

Georgi-Findlay, Brigitte. "Transatlantic Crossings: New Directions in the Contemporary Native American Novel." In *Transatlantic Voices: Interpretations of Native North American Literatures,* edited and intro by Elvira Pulitano, 89–107. Lincoln: University of Nebraska Press, 2007.

Gilley, Brian Joseph. *Becoming Two-Spirit: Gay Identity and Social Acceptance in Indian Country.* Lincoln: University of Nebraska Press, 2006.

Gilroy, Paul. *The Black Atlantic: Modernity and Double Consciousness.* Cambridge, Mass.: Harvard University Press, 1992.

Gittings, Chris. *Canadian National Cinema: Ideology, Difference and Representation.* New York: Routledge, 2002.

Glick, Elisa. "The Dialectics of Dandyism." *Cultural Critique* 48 (spring 2001): 129–63.

Goeman, Mishuana R. "Notes toward a Native Feminism's Spatial Practice." *Wicazo Sa Review* 24, no. 2 (fall 2009): 169–87.

Golla, Victor. *California Indian Languages.* Berkeley: University of California Press, 2011.

Gonzales, Angela, Judy Kertész, and Gabrielle Tayac. "Eugenics as Indian Removal: Sociohistorical Processes and the De(con)struction of American Indians in the Southeast." *Public Historian* 29, no. 3 (summer 2007): 53–67.

Gopinath, Gayatri. *Impossible Desires: Queer Diasporas and South Asian Public Cultures.* Durham, N.C.: Duke University Press, 2005.

Gordon, Linda. "Voluntary Motherhood: The Beginnings of Feminist Birth Control Ideas in the United States." Special double issue: Women's History, *Feminist Studies* 1, nos. 3–4 (winter/spring 1973): 5–22.

Gossett, Polly Paddock. "Tribal Past Is a Strong Presence in Alexie's Toughest Indian." Review of *The Toughest Indian in the World,* by Sherman Alexie. *Charlotte Observer,* July 2, 2000, 6F.

Gould, Janice. "Autobiography." In *Beneath My Heart: Poetry,* 19–20. Ithaca, N.Y.: Firebrand Books, 1990.

———. "The Beaver Woman." In *Beneath My Heart: Poetry,* 13. Ithaca, N.Y.: Firebrand Books, 1990.

———. *Beneath My Heart.* New York: Firebrand Books, 1990.

———. "Black Bear." In *Beneath My Heart: Poetry,* 14. Ithaca, N.Y.: Firebrand Books, 1990.

———. "Blood Sisters." In *Earthquake Weather,* 7. Tucson: University of Arizona Press, 1996.

———. "Coyotismo." In *Beneath My Heart: Poetry,* 11–12. Ithaca, N.Y.: Firebrand Books, 1990.

———. "Disobedience (in Language) in Text by Lesbian Native Americans." *ARIEL: A Review of International English Literature* 25, no. 1 (January 1994): 32–44.

———. *Doubters and Dreamers.* Tucson: University of Arizona Press, 2011.

———. *Earthquake Weather.* Tucson: University of Arizona Press, 1996.

———. "Easter Sunday." In *Earthquake Weather,* 41–42. Tucson: University of Arizona Press, 1996.

———. "Foster Family." In *Beneath My Heart: Poetry*, 39–40. Ithaca, N.Y.: Firebrand Books, 1990.

———. "History Lesson." In *Beneath My Heart: Poetry*, 28–32. Ithaca, N.Y.: Firebrand Books, 1990.

———. "Indian Mascot, 1959." In *Doubters and Dreamers*, 1–2. Tucson: University of Arizona Press, 2011.

———. "A Maidu in the City of Gold: Some Thoughts on Censorship and American Indian Poetry." In *The Colour of Resistance: A Contemporary Collection of Writing by Aboriginal Women*, edited by Connie Fife, 230–43. Toronto: Sister Vision Press, 1993.

———. "A Married Woman." In *Beneath My Heart: Poetry*, 56. Ithaca, N.Y.: Firebrand Books, 1990.

———. "My Crush on the Yakima Woman." In *Beneath My Heart: Poetry*, 41–42. Ithaca, N.Y.: Firebrand Books, 1990.

———. "My Father." In *Earthquake Weather*, 43–46. Tucson: University of Arizona Press, 1996.

———. "My Father, Cynthia Conroy." *GLQ: A Journal of Lesbian and Gay Studies* 16, nos. 1–2 (2010): 93–103.

———. "New Year's Day." In *Doubters and Dreamers*, 1–2. Tucson: University of Arizona Press, 2011.

———. "Our Bodies in the Half-Light." In *Beneath My Heart: Poetry*, 63. Ithaca, N.Y.: Firebrand Books, 1990.

———. "Renegade." In *Doubters and Dreamers*, 3–4. Tucson: University of Arizona Press, 2011.

———. "Speaking, Singing, and Seeing a World." In *Placing the Academy: Essays on Landscape, Work, and Identity*, edited by Jennifer Sinor and Rona Kaufman, 254–68. Logan: Utah State University Press, 2007. http://digitalcommons.usu.edu/usupress_pubs/20.

———. "Thursdays." In *Earthquake Weather*, 31–33. Tucson: University of Arizona Press, 1996.

———. "To Speak Your Name." In *Beneath My Heart: Poetry*, 48. Ithaca, N.Y.: Firebrand Books, 1990.

———. "Tribal History." In *Doubters and Dreamers*, 5. Tucson: University of Arizona Press, 2011.

———. "Waiting for a Miracle." In *Beneath My Heart: Poetry*, 21. Ithaca, N.Y.: Firebrand Books, 1990.

———. "We Could Not Forget." In *Doubters and Dreamers*, 6–7. Tucson: University of Arizona Press, 2011.

———. "When We Return to Aztlán." In *Beneath My Heart: Poetry*, 64. Ithaca, N.Y.: Firebrand Books, 1990.

———. "The Woman I Love Most." In *Beneath My Heart: Poetry*, 46. Ithaca, N.Y.: Firebrand Books, 1990.

Green, Rayna. *That's What She Said: Contemporary Poetry and Fiction by Native American Women*. Bloomington: Indiana University Press, 1984.

Group of Seven Inches. Written and directed by Kent Monkman. Toronto: V-Tape, 2005.

Guattari, Felix, and Gilles Deleuze. *A Thousand Plateaus: Capitalism and Schizophrenia*. Minneapolis: University of Minnesota Press, 1987.

Hafsteinsson, Sigurjón Baldur, and Marian Bredin. *Indigenous Screen Cultures in Canada*. Winnipeg, Canada: University of Manitoba Press, 2010.

Halberstam, Judith. *Female Masculinity*. Durham, N.C.: Duke University Press, 1998.

———. "The Pregnant Man." *Velvet Light Trap* 65 (spring 2010): 77–78.

———. *The Queer Art of Failure*. Durham, N.C.: Duke University Press, 2011.

Hampton, John G. "Unsettling Sex." In *Aboriginal Digital Access Project*, 2–11. Toronto: V-Tape, 2012.

Hansen, Elaine Tuttle. "'What If Your Mother Never Meant To?': The Novels of Louise Erdrich and Michael Dorris." In *Mother without Child: Contemporary Fiction and the Crisis of Motherhood*, 115–57. Berkeley: University of California Press, 1997.

Haugo, Ann. "Weaving a Legacy: An Interview with Muriel Miguel of Spiderwoman Theater." In *The Color of Theater: Race, Culture, and Contemporary Performance*, edited by Roberta Uno and Lucy Mae San Pablo Burns, 219–34. London: Continuum, 2002.

Hearne, Joanna. *Native Recognition: Indigenous Cinema and the Western*. New York: SUNY Press, 2013.

———. *Smoke Signals: Native Cinema Rising*. Lincoln: University of Nebraska Press, 2012.

Hedge Coke, Allison. *Blood Run: Free Verse Play*. Cambridge, U.K.: Salt Publishing, 2006.

Heizer, Robert F., ed. *The Destruction of California Indians*. Introduction by Albert L. Hurtado. Lincoln: University of Nebraska Press, 1993.

———. *"They Were Only Diggers": A Collection of Articles from California Newspapers, 1851–1866, on Indian and White Relations*. Socorro, N. Mex.: Ballena, 1974.

Hemphill, Essex. *Ceremonies: Poetry and Prose*. New York: Penguin, 1992.

Herdt, Gilbert. "The Dilemmas of Desire: From 'Berdache' to 'Two-Spirit.'" In *Two-Spirit People: Native American Gender Identity, Sexuality, and Spirituality*, edited by Sue-Ellen Jacobs, Wesley Thomas, and Sabine Lang, 276–83. Urbana: University of Illinois Press, 1997.

Her Giveaway: A Spiritual Journey with AIDS. Directed by Mona Smith. New York: Women Make Movies, 1988.

Herrick, Robert. *The Complete Poetry of Robert Herrick, Volume I*. Edited by Tom Cain and Ruth Connolly. Oxford: Oxford University Press, 2013.

Herring, Scott. "Out of the Closets, into the Woods: *RFD*, Country Women, and the Post-Stonewall Emergence of Queer Antiurbanism." *American Quarterly* 59, no. 2 (June 2007): 341–72.

Highway, Tomson. *Comparing Mythologies*. Ottawa: University of Ottawa Press, 2003.

———. *Dry Lips Oughta Move to Kapuskasing*. Saskatoon, Canada: Fifth House, 1989.

———. *Ernestine Shuswap Gets Her Trout: A "String Quartet" for Four Female Actors*. Vancouver: Talonbooks, 2005.

———. *Iskooniguni Iskweewuk: Meetaweewin*. Markham, Ontario: Fifth House, 2010.

———. *Kiss of the Fur Queen*. Norman: University of Oklahoma Press, 1998.

———. *Paasteewitoon Kaapooskaysing Tageespichit: Meetaweewin*. Markham, Ontario: Fifth House, 2010.

———. *The Rez Sisters: A Play in Two Acts*. Saskatoon, Canada: Fifth House, 1988.

———. *Rose: A Play*. Vancouver: Talonbooks, 2003.

———. "Why Cree Is the Sexiest Language of All." In *Me Sexy: An Exploration of Native Sex and Sexuality*, edited by Drew Hayden Taylor, 33–40. Vancouver: Douglas & McIntyre, 2008.

Hobson, Geary. *The Remembered Earth: An Anthology of Contemporary Native American Literature*. Albuquerque: University of New Mexico Press, 1981.

Holland, Sharon Patricia. *The Erotic Life of Racism*. Durham, N.C.: Duke University Press, 2012.

Honey Moccasin. Written and directed by Shelly Niro. New York: Women Make Movies, 1998.

Honored by the Moon. Directed by Mona Smith. New York: Women Make Movies, 1990.

hooks, bell. *Black Looks: Race and Representation*. Boston: South End, 1992.

Housman, A. E. *A Shropshire Lad*. London: Keegan Paul, 1896.

Hurtado, Albert L. *Indian Survival on the California Frontier*. New Haven, Conn.: Yale University Press, 1988.

"I Am a Black Faggot." *Fag Rag* 3 (summer 1972): 20.

I Am the Art Scene Starring Woman Polanski. Written and directed by James Diamond. Toronto: V-Tape, 2010.

Iovannone, J. James. "'Mix-Ups, Messes, Confinements, and Double-Dealings': Transgendered Performances in Three Novels by Louise Erdrich." *Studies in American Indian Literatures* 21, no. 1 (spring 2009): 38–68.

Jackson, Stevi. "Gender, Sexuality and Heterosexuality: The Complexity (and Limits) of Heteronormativity." *Feminist Theory* 7 (April 2006): 105–21.

Jacobs, Sue-Ellen. "Berdache: A Brief Review of Literature." *Colorado Anthropologist* 1, no. 1 (1968): 25–40.

———. "Is the 'North American Berdache' Merely a Phantom in the Imagination of Western Social Scientists?" In *Two-Spirit People: Native American Gender Identity, Sexuality, and Spirituality,* edited by Sue-Ellen Jacobs, Wesley Thomas, and Sabine Lang, 21–43. Urbana: University of Illinois Press, 1997.

Jacobs, Sue-Ellen, and Jason Cromwell. "Visions and Revisions of Reality: Reflections on Sex, Sexuality, Gender, and Gender Variance." *Journal of Homosexuality* 23, no. 4 (1992): 43–49.

Jacobs, Sue-Ellen, Wesley Thomas, and Sabine Lang. "Introduction." In *Two-Spirit People: Native American Gender Identity, Sexuality, and Spirituality,* edited by Sue-Ellen Jacobs, Wesley Thomas, and Sabine Lang, 1–20. Urbana: University of Illinois Press, 1997.

———, eds. *Two-Spirit People: Native American Gender Identity, Sexuality, and Spirituality.* Urbana: University of Illinois Press, 1997.

Jaimes, M. Annette, with Theresa Halsey. "American Indian Women: At the Center of Indigenous Resistance in Contemporary North America." In *The State of Native America: Genocide, Colonization, and Resistance,* edited by Annette M. Jaimes and Theresa Halsey, 311–44. Boston: South End, 1992.

———, eds. *The State of Native America: Genocide, Colonization, and Resistance.* Boston: South End, 1992.

Jardine, Alice. "Woman in Limbo: Deleuze and His Br(others)." *SubStance* 13, nos. 3–4 (1984): 46–60.

Johansen, Bruce. "Reprise/Forced Sterilizations: Native Americans and the 'Last Gasp of Eugenics.'" *Native Americas* 15 (winter 1998): 44–47.

Johnny Greyeyes. Directed by Jorge Manuel Manzano. San Jose, Calif.: Wolfe Video, 2002.

Johnson, Troy. *The Occupation of Alcatraz Island: Indian Self-Determination and the Rise of Indian Activism.* Urbana: University of Illinois Press, 1996.

Johnstone, David. *An Introduction to Disability Studies.* London: David Fulton, 2001.

Justice, Daniel Heath. *Dreyd: The Way of Thorn and Thunder, Book 3.* Wharton, Ontario: Kegedonce, 2007.

———. "Introduction: Daniel's Take." *GLQ: A Journal of Lesbian and Gay Studies* 16, nos. 1–2 (2010): 7–12.

———. *Kynship: The Way of Thorn and Thunder.* Wharton, Ontario: Kegedonce, 2005.

———. "Notes toward a Theory of Anomaly." *GLQ: A Journal of Lesbian and Gay Studies* 16, nos. 1–2 (2010): 207–42.

———. *Our Fire Survives the Storm: A Cherokee Literary History.* Minneapolis: University of Minnesota Press, 2005.

———. *The Way of Thorn and Thunder: The Kynship Chronicles.* Albuquerque: University of New Mexico Press, 2011.

———. *Wyrwood: The Way of Thorn and Thunder, Book 2.* Wharton, Ontario: Kegedonce, 2006.

Justice, Daniel Heath, Mark Rifkin, and Bethany Schneider, eds. "Sexuality, Nationality, Indigeneity." Special issue, *GLQ: A Journal of Lesbian and Gay Studies* 16, nos. 1–2 (2010).

Kadsan, Margo, and Susan Tavernetti. "Native Americans in a Revisionist Western: *Little Big Man* (1970)." In *Hollywood's Indian: The Portrayal of the Native American in Film,* edited by Peter Rollins, 121–36. Lexington: University Press of Kentucky, 1998.

Keenan, Deirdre. "Unrestricted Territory: Gender, Two Spirits, and Louise Erdrich's *The Last Report on the Miracles at Little No Horse." American Indian Culture and Research Journal* 30, no. 2 (2006): 1–15.

Kelsey, Penelope Myrtle, ed. *Maurice Kenny: Celebrations of a Mohawk Writer.* New York: SUNY Press, 2011.

———. "Reading the Wampum: An Introduction to the Works of Maurice Kenny." In *Maurice Kenny: Celebrations of a Mohawk Writer,* edited by Penelope Myrtle Kelsey, 1–6. New York: SUNY Press, 2011.

Kenny, Maurice. "Adowe: We Return Thanks." In *The Remembered Earth: An Anthology of Contemporary Native American Literature,* edited by Geary Hobson, 13–16. Albuquerque: University of New Mexico Press, 1981.

———. *And Grieve, Lesbia: Poems.* New York: Aardvark, 1960.

———. "Apache." *Mouth of the Dragon* 5 (June 1975).

———. *Between Two Rivers: Selected Poems, 1956–1984.* New York: White Pine, 1987.

———. *Blackrobe: Isaac Jogues, b. March 11, 1604, d. October 18, 1646: Poems.* Saranac Lake, N.Y.: North Country Community College Press, 1982.

———. "A Change of Worlds." Foreword to *Interpreting the Indian: Twentieth-Century Poets and the Native American,* by Michael Castro, ix–xiii. Norman: University of Oklahoma Press, 1983.

———. *Connotations: Poems.* New York: White Pine, 2008.

———. *Dancing Back Strong the Nation.* 2nd ed. Buffalo, N.Y.: White Pine Press, 1981.

———. *Dead Letters Sent, and Other Poems.* New York: Troubadour, 1958.

———. "Greta Garbo." *Fag Rag* 10 (fall 1974): 27. Reprinted in *Only as Far as Brooklyn: Poems.* Boston: Good Gay Poets, 1979.

———. *Greyhounding This America: Poems and Dialog.* Chico, Calif.: Heidelberg Graphics, 1988.

———. "Growing Pains: Five Poems." *Fag Rag* 21/22 (February/March 1978): 24.

———. "Heading East." *Fag Rag* 21/22 (February/March 1978): 24.

———. *The Hopeless Kill, and Other Poems.* Watertown, N.Y.: Little, 1956.

———. "I Am the Sun." *The First Month at Wounded Knee*. Special issue, *Akwesasne Notes* 5, no. 2 (spring 1973): 48. Reprinted in *I Am the Sun*. Buffalo, N.Y.: White Pine, 1979.

———. "Introduction: A Memoir." In *On Second Thought: A Compilation*, 2–15. Norman: University of Oklahoma Press, 1995.

———. "I Was Tired of What's Happening: (In Memory of Pedro Bissonette)." *Many Smokes* 8, no. 1 (spring 1974): 9.

———. "'Kill Fag's': Graffiti on the 7th Ave. Subway, N.Y.C., June 1976." *Fag Rag* 18 (fall/winter 1976): 8.

———. "Long Distance Telephone Call." *Fag Rag* 21/22 (February/March 1978): 24.

———. "Love in Brooklyn Heights." *Fag Rag* 23/24 (1978): 26.

———. "Loves into Legend." *ManRoot* 11 (spring/summer 1977): 26.

———. "Maurice Kenny: Gay Native American Poet." Interview by Charles Shivley and Clover Chango. *Gay Community News* 7, no. 47 (1980).

———. "My Nation, Behold It." *Many Smokes* 8, no. 3 (winter 1975): 4.

———. "A Night, a Bridge, a River: (Beneath Brooklyn Bridge)." *Fag Rag* 10 (fall 1974): 8.

———. "No Name." *Fag Rag* 15 (February/March 1976): 11. Reprinted in *Only as Far as Brooklyn: Poems*. Boston: Good Gay Poets, 1979.

———. *North: Poems of Home*. Marvin, S. Dak.: Blue Cloud Quarterly, 1977.

———. "Oka Tanna." *Dreams and Drumbeats*. Special issue, *Indian Historian* 9, no. 2 (spring 1976): 17–20.

———. *Only as Far as Brooklyn: Poems*. Boston: Good Gay Poets, 1979.

———. *On Second Thought: A Compilation*. Norman: University of Oklahoma Press, 1995.

———. "Papago." *Fag Rag* 18 (fall/winter 1976): 19. Reprinted in "Papago II." In *Only as Far as Brooklyn: Poems*, 21. Boston: Good Gay Poets, 1979.

———. "Papago." *Gay Sunshine* 29/30 (summer/fall 1976): 23. Reprinted in "Papago I." In *Only as Far as Brooklyn: Poems*, 20. Boston: Good Gay Poets, 1979.

———. "Poem . . . Too Late." *Fag Rag* 23/24 (1978): 17.

———. "Recuerdo." *Fag Rag* 18 (fall/winter 1976): 21.

———. "Standing Strong." *Dreams and Drumbeats*. Special issue, *Indian Historian* 9, no. 2 (spring 1976): 22.

———. "Steps." *Akwesasne Notes* 9, no. 3 (July 1977): 36.

———. "Three Parodies: With Apologies to A. E. Houseman." *Fag Rag* 18 (fall/winter 1976): 9.

———. "Tinselled Bucks: An Historical Study in Indian Homosexuality." *Gay Sunshine* 26/27 (winter 1975/76): 16–17, 15.

———. "Tulsa by Greyhound." *Fag Rag* 21/22 (February/March 1978): 24.

———. "Two Humors: One—With Apology to Byron; Two—Masturbatory Haiku." *Fag Rag* 23/24 (1978): 8.

———. "Two Parodies: With Apologies to Wordsworth." *Fag Rag* 14 (November/December 1975): 12.

———. "United." *Gay Sunshine* 26/27 (winter 1975/76): 17.

———. "Waiting at the Edge: Words toward a Life." In *I Tell You Now: Autobiographical Essays by Native American Writers,* edited by Brian Swann and Arnold Krupat, 37–54. Lincoln: University of Nebraska Press, 1987.

———. "Winkte." *ManRoot* 11 (spring/summer 1977): 26. Reprinted in *Only as Far as Brooklyn: Poems.* Boston: Good Gay Poets, 1979.

———. *With Love to Lesbia: A Sheaf of Poems.* New York: Aardvark, 1958.

———. "Yemen Boy." *Fag Rag* 18 (fall/winter 1976): 9. Reprinted in *Only as Far as Brooklyn: Poems.* Boston: Good Gay Poets, 1979.

———. "Yonnondio." *Rebirth of the Spirit.* Special issue, *Many Smokes* 9, no. 3 (fall 1975): 14.

"Kichx Anagaat Yatx'I": Children of the Rainbow. Written and directed by Duane Ghastant'Aucoin. 2003.

Kim, Christine, Sophie McCall, and Melina Baum Singer. "Introduction." In *Cultural Grammars of Nation, Diaspora, and Indigeneity in Canada,* edited by Christine Kim, Sophie McCall, and Melina Baum Singer, 1–18. Waterloo, Ontario: Wilfred Laurier University Press, 2013.

Klopotek, Brian. "'I Guess Your Warrior Look Doesn't Work Every Time': Challenging Indian Masculinity in the Cinema." In *Across the Great Divide: Cultures of Manhood in the American West,* edited by Matthew Basso, Laura McCall, and Dee Garceau, 251–73. New York: Routledge, 2001.

Kranich, Kimberly, and Kimberlie A. Kranich. "A Bibliography of Periodicals by and about Women of Color." *Feminist Teacher* 5, no. 1 (spring 1990): 26–41.

Kronick, Joseph G. *Derrida and the Future of Literature.* Albany: SUNY Press, 1999.

Krupat, Arnold. *Ethnocentrism: Ethnography, History, Literature.* Berkeley: University of California Press, 1992.

laFavor, Carole. *Along the Journey River: A Mystery.* Ithaca, N.Y.: Firebrand Books, 1996.

———. *Evil Dead Center: A Mystery.* Ithaca, N.Y.: Firebrand Books, 1997.

Lang, Sabine. *Men as Women, Women as Men: Changing Gender in Native American Cultures.* Translated by John L. Vantine. Austin: University of Texas Press, 1998.

———. "Various Kinds of Two-Spirit People: Gender Variance and Homosexuality in Native American Communities." In *Two-Spirit People: Native American Gender Identity, Sexuality and Spirituality,* edited by Sue-Ellen Jacobs, Wesley Thomas, and Sabine Lang, 100–118. Urbana: University of Illinois Press, 1997.

LaRocque, Emma. *When the Other Is Me: Native Resistance Discourse 1850–1890.* Winnipeg, Canada: University of Manitoba Press, 2010.

Lawrence, Jane. "The Indian Health Service and the Sterilization of Native American Women." *American Indian Quarterly* 24, no. 3 (summer 2000): 400–419.

Lawston, Jodie Michelle. "Women, the Criminal Justice System, and Incarceration: Processes of Power, Silence, and Resistance." *NWSA Journal* 20, no. 2 (summer 2008): 1–18.

Lessons in Baby Dyke Theory. Written and directed by Thirza Cuthand. Toronto: V-Tape, 1995.

Leyland, Winston. "Introduction." In *Orgasms of Light: The Gay Sunshine Anthology,* edited by Winston Leyland, 7–10. San Francisco: Gay Sunshine, 1977.

Lincoln, Kenneth. *Native American Renaissance.* Berkeley: University of California Press, 1983.

Lindsay, Brendan C. *Murder State: California's Native American Genocide, 1846–1873.* Lincoln: University of Nebraska Press, 2012.

Lischke, Ute, and David T. McNab. "Storytelling and Identity: Louise Erdrich's Exploration of the German/American Connection in *The Master Butchers Singing Club.*" *European Journal of American Culture* 25, no. 3 (2006): 189–203.

Little Big Man. Directed by Arthur Penn. Los Angeles: Cinema Center Films, 1970.

Livingston, Chip. *Crow-Blue, Crow-Black.* New York: Quarterly Books, 2012.

———. *Museum of False Starts.* Arlington, Va.: Gival, 2010.

Lugones, Maria. "Heterosexualism and the Colonial/Modern Gender System." *Hypatia* 22, no. 1 (winter 2007): 186–209.

Lyons, Scott Richard. *X-Marks: Native Signatures of Assent.* Minneapolis: University of Minnesota Press, 2010.

MacDonald, Megan L. "Two-Spirit Organizing: Indigenous Two-Spirit Identity in the Twin Cities Regions." In *Queer Twin Cities: Twin Cities GLBT Oral History Project,* 150–70. Minneapolis: University of Minnesota Press, 2010.

Machiorlatti, Jennifer A. "Video as Community Ally and Dakota Sense of Place: An Interview with Mona Smith." In *Teaching Native Americans on Film: Conversations, Teaching and Theory,* edited by M. Elise Marubbio and Eric L. Buffalohead, 322–36. Lexington: University Press of Kentucky, 2013.

Macleod, William Christie. *The Indians of Brooklyn in the Days of the Dutch.* New York: U.S. WPA, Historical Records Survey, 1941.

Manalansan, Martin F., IV. "Queer Intersections: Sexuality and Gender in Migration Studies." *International Migration Review* 40, no. 1 (spring 2006): 224–49.

The Man from Venus. Written and directed by James Diamond. Toronto: V-Tape, 1999.

Manyarrows, Victoria Lena. "Artist Statement: Victoria Lena Manyarrows." In *Women Artists of the American West Past and Present,* codeveloped by Susan Ressler and Jerrold Maddox. 1998. http://www.cla.purdue.edu/WAAW.

———. "The Drum Beats." In *Piece of My Heart: A Lesbian of Colour Anthology*, edited by Connie Fife, 141. Toronto: Sister Vision Press, 1991.

———. *Songs from the Native Lands: Poetry*. San Francisco: Nopal, 1995.

———. "We Have No Borders." In *Songs from the Native Lands: Poetry*, 78–79. San Francisco: Nopal, 1995.

Mars-Womb-Man. Written and directed by James Diamond. Toronto: V-Tape, 2006.

Martin, Lee-Ann, and Morgan Wood, curators. *Exposed: Aesthetics of Aboriginal Erotic Art*. Regina: Mackenzie Art Gallery, 1999.

Marubbio, M. Elise, and Eric L. Buffalohead, eds. *Native Americans on Film: Conversations, Teaching, and Theory*. Lexington: University Press of Kentucky, 2013.

Mayer, Sophie. "This Bridge of Two Backs: Making the Two-Spirit Erotics of Community." *Studies in American Indian Literatures* 20, no. 1 (spring 2008): 1–26.

McAdams, Janet. *Feral*. Cambridge, U.K.: Salt Publishing, 2007.

———. *The Island of Lost Luggage*. Lincoln: University of Arizona Press, 2012.

———. *Red Weather*. Lincoln: University of Arizona Press, 2012.

McCall, Leslie. "The Complexity of Intersectionality." *Signs* 30, no. 3 (spring 2005): 1771–1800.

McGuffey, C. Shawn. "Engendering Trauma: Race, Class, and Gender Reaffirmation after Child Sexual Abuse." *Gender and Society* 19, no. 5 (October 2005): 621–43.

McLeod, Albert. "Empowering Two-Spirit People." *Outwords* 190 (February 2012). http://www.outwords.ca.

Medicine, Beatrice. "Changing Native American Roles in an Urban Context and Changing Native American Sex Roles in an Urban Context." In *Two-Spirit People: Native American Gender Identity, Sexuality, and Spirituality*, edited by Sue-Ellen Jacobs, Wesley Thomas, and Sabine Lang, 145–55. Urbana: University of Illinois Press, 1997.

Merasty, Billy, and Maggie Huculak. *Fireweed*. Native Earth Performing Archives. University of Guelph, Ontario: Conolly Theatre Archives, 1992.

———. *For Godly and Divinia/Godly's Divinia (A Love Story)*. Native Earth Performing Archives. University of Guelph, Ontario: Conolly Theatre Archives, 1990.

Meskanahk (My Path). Written and directed by Kevin Lee Burton. Vancouver: Indigenous Media Arts Group, 2005.

Miguel, Muriel. *Hot 'n' Soft*. New York: American Indian Community House, 1992.

Miguel, Muriel, with Spiderwoman Theater. *Cabaret: An Evening of Disgusting Songs and Pukey Images*. Native American Women's Playwright Archive, 1979.

———. *The Fittin' Room*. 1980.

Mihesuah, Devon Abbott. *Indigenous American Women: Decolonization, Empowerment, Activism.* Lincoln: University of Nebraska Press, 2003.

Millay, Edna St. Vincent. *The Selected Poetry of Edna St. Vincent Millay.* Introduction by Nancy Milford. New York: Random House, 2002.

Miller, Christopher L. "The Postidentitarian Predicament in the Footnotes of *A Thousand Plateaus:* Nomadology, Anthropology, and Authority." *Diacritics* 23, no. 3 (fall 1993): 6–35.

Million, Dian. "Felt Theory: An Indigenous Feminist Approach to Affect and History." *Wicazo Sa Review* 24, no. 2 (fall 2009): 53–76.

Minton, Henry L. *Departing from Deviance: The History of Homosexual Rights and Emancipatory Science in America.* Chicago: University of Chicago Press, 2002.

Miranda, Deborah A. *Bad Indians: A Tribal Memoir.* Berkeley: Heyday Books, 2013.

———. "Dildos, Hummingbirds, and Driving Her Crazy: Searching for American Indian Women's Love Poetry and Erotics." *Frontiers* 23, no. 2 (2002): 135–49.

———. *Indian Cartography.* Greenfield Center, N.Y.: Greenfield Review, 1999.

———. "'What's Wrong with a Little Fantasy?': Storytelling from the (Still) Ivory Tower." In *This Bridge We Call Home: Radical Visions for Transformation,* edited by Gloria Anzaldúa and AnaLouise Keating, 192–202. New York: Routledge, 2002.

———. *The Zen of La Llorona.* Cambridge, U.K.: Salt Publishing, 2005.

Missionary Association. "The Indians: An Indian Chief in New York City." *American Missionary* 39, no. 1 (January 1885): 114–15.

Momaday, N. Scott. *House Made of Dawn.* New York: Harper and Row, 1968.

Monette, Paul. *Borrowed Time: An AIDS Memoir.* San Diego: Harcourt Brace, 1988.

———. *Love Alone: Eighteen Elegies for Rog.* New York: St. Martin's, 1989.

Moraga, Cherríe. "*La Güera.*" In *This Bridge Called My Back: Writings by Radical Women of Color,* edited by Cherríe Moraga and Gloria Anzaldúa, 27–34. New York: Kitchen Table, 1981.

———. *Loving in the War Years: Lo que nunca pasó por sus labios.* Boston: South End, 1983.

Morgensen, Scott Lauria. "Settler Homonationalism: Theorizing Settler Colonialism within Queer Modernities." *GLQ: A Journal of Lesbian and Gay Studies* 16, nos. 1–2 (2010): 105–31.

———. *Spaces between Us: Queer Settler Colonialism and Indigenous Decolonization.* Minneapolis: University of Minnesota Press, 2011.

Moses, Daniel David. *Almighty Voice and His Wife: A Play in Two Acts.* Stratford, Canada: Williams-Wallace, 1992.

———. *Big Buck City: A Play in Two Acts.* Toronto: Playwrights Guild of Canada, 1991.

———. *Brebeuf's Ghost: A Tale of Horror in Three Acts.* Toronto: Playwrights Guild of Canada, 1996.

———. *City of Shadows: A Play in One Act.* Toronto: Playwrights Guild of Canada, 1995.

———. *Coyote City: A Play in Two Acts.* Toronto: Playwrights Union of Canada, 1988.

———. *Delicate Bodies.* Vancouver: blewointment, 1980.

———. *The Dreaming Beauty: A Play.* Toronto: Playwrights Union of Canada, 1988.

———. *The Indian Medicine Shows: Two One-Act Plays.* Toronto: Exile Editions, 1995.

———. *Kytopolis: A Play in Two Acts.* Holstein, Ontario: Exile Editions, 2008.

———. *Pursued by a Bear: Talks, Monologues and Tales.* Toronto: Exile Editions, 2005.

———. *Sixteen Jesuses.* Toronto: Exile Editions, 2000.

———. *A Small Essay on the Largeness of Light and Other Poems.* Toronto: Exile Editions, 2012.

———. *The White Line: Poems.* Saskatoon, Canada: Fifth House, 1990.

———. *The Witch of Niagara: A Confabulation in One Act.* Toronto: Playwrights Union of Canada, 1998.

Muñoz, José Esteban. *Cruising Utopia: The Then and There of Queer Futurity.* New York: New York University Press, 2009.

———. *Disidentifications: Queers of Color and the Performance of Politics.* Minneapolis: University of Minnesota Press, 1999.

Nagel, Joane. "Ethnicity and Sexuality." *Annual Review of Sociology* 26 (2000): 107–33.

A Nation Is Coming. Directed by Kent Monkman. Toronto: Urban Nation, 1996.

Native American LGBT Two Spirit. Portland: Basic Rights Oregon, 2012.

Natives. Written and directed by Jeremy Hersh. San Francisco: Frameline, 2013.

Nealon, Christopher Shaun. *Foundlings: Lesbian and Gay Historical Emotion before Stonewall.* Durham, N.C.: Duke University Press, 2001.

Neihardt, John G. *Black Elk Speaks: Being the Life Story of a Holy Man of the Oglala Sioux.* 1932. Reprint, Lincoln: University of Nebraska Press, 1979.

Nevaquaya, Joe Dale Tate. *Leaving Holes & Selected New Writings.* Norman, Okla.: Mongrel Empire, 2011.

Ng, Vivien. "Race Matters." In *Lesbian and Gay Studies: A Critical Introduction,* edited by Andy Medhurst and Sally Munt, 215–31. London: Cassell, 1997.

Nicholson, Heather Norris. "Visual Irony: Reflecting on the Work of Shelley Niro." In *Screening Culture: Constructing Image and Identity*, edited by Heather Norris Nicholson, 157–68. Lanham, Md.: Lexington Books, 2003.

Nikamowin (Song). Written and directed by Kevin Lee Burton. Vancouver: Indigenous Media Arts Group, 2007.

Norton, Jack. *When Our Worlds Cried: Genocide in Northwestern California*. San Francisco: Indian Historian, 1979.

O'Hara, Jean, ed. *Two-Spirit Acts: Queer Indigenous Performances*. Toronto: Playwrights Canadian Press, 2014.

Oliver, Stephanie. "Diffuse Connections: Smell and Diasporic Subjectivity in Larissa Lai's Salt Fish Girl." *Canadian Literature* 208 (spring 2011): 85–107.

Orbin, Maria, and Alan Velie. "Religion and Gender in *The Last Report on the Miracles at Little No Horse*." *European Review of Native American Studies* 17, no. 2 (2003): 27–34.

Ortiz, Simon. *Going for the Rain: Poems*. New York: Harper and Row, 1976.

Papastergiadis, Nikos. *The Turbulence of Migration: Globalization, Deterritorialization, and Hybridity*. Cambridge, U.K.: Polity, 2000.

Parker, Arthur C. *Seneca Myths and Folktales*. 1923. Reprint, Lincoln: University of Nebraska Press, 1989.

Pidduck, Julianne. "Queer Kinship and Ambivalence: Video Autoethnographies by Jean Carlomusto and Richard Fung." *GLQ: A Journal of Lesbian and Gay Studies* 15, no. 3 (2009): 441–68.

Pilling, Arnold R. "Cross-Dressing and Shamanism among Selected Western North American Tribes." In *Two-Spirit People: Native American Gender Identity, Sexuality, and Spirituality*, edited by Sue-Ellen Jacobs, Wesley Thomas, and Sabine Lang, 69–99. Urbana: University of Illinois Press, 1997.

Power, Susan. *The Grass Dancer*. New York: Putnam, 1994.

Prince-Hughes, Tara. "Worlds In and Out of Balance: Alternative Genders and Gayness in the *Almanac of the Dead* and *The Beet Queen*." In *Literature and Homosexuality*, edited by Michael J. Meyer, 1–21. Atlanta: Rodopi, 2000.

Prosser, Jay. "No Place Like Home: The Transgendered Narrative of Leslie Feinberg's *Stone Butch Blues*." *Modern Fiction Studies* 41, nos. 3–4 (1995): 483–514.

Proulx-Turner, Sharron. *She Is Reading with a Blanket in Her Hand*. Calgary, Canada: Frontenac House, 2008.

———. *She Walks for Days inside a Thousand Eyes: A Two-Spirit Story*. Winnipeg, Canada: Turnstone, 2008.

———. *The Trees Are Still Bending South*. Wharton, Ontario: Kegedonce, 2012.

———. *What the Auntys Say*. Toronto: McGilligan Books, 2002.

Puar, Jasbir. *Terrorist Assemblages: Homonationalism in Queer Times*. Durham, N.C.: Duke University Press, 2007.

Pulitano, Elvira. *Toward a Native American Critical Theory.* Lincoln: University of Nebraska Press, 2003.

Purdue, Theda. "Race and Culture: Writing the Ethnohistory of the Early South." *Ethnohistory* 51, no. 4 (fall 2004): 701–23.

Queer as Chief. Written and directed by Duane Ghastant'Aucoin. 2005.

Rader, Pamela J. "Disrobing the Priest: Gender and Spiritual Conversions in Louise Erdrich's *The Last Report on the Miracles at Little No Horse.*" In *The Catholic Church and Unruly Women Writers, Critical Essays,* edited by Jeana DelRosso, Leigh Eicke, and Ana Kothe, 221–35. New York: Palgrave Macmillan, 2008.

Raheja, Michelle H. *Reservation Reelism: Redfacing, Visual Sovereignty, and Representations of Native Americans in Film.* Lincoln: University of Nebraska Press, 2010.

Rainwater, Catherine. "Reading between Worlds: Narrativity in the Fiction of Louise Erdrich." In *Louise Erdrich's Love Medicine: A Casebook,* edited by Hertha D. Sweet Wong, 163–78. New York: Oxford University Press, 2000.

Rajan, Tilottama. *Deconstruction and the Remainders of Phenomenology: Sartre, Derrida, Foucault, Baudrillard.* Stanford: Stanford University Press, 2002.

Ramirez, Renya K. *Native Hubs: Culture, Community, and Belonging in Silicon Valley and Beyond.* Durham, N.C.: Duke University Press, 2007.

Reyhner, Jon, and Jeanne Eder. *American Indian Education: A History.* Norman: University of Oklahoma Press, 2004.

Rich, Adrienne. "Compulsory Heterosexuality and Lesbian Existence." *Signs* 5, no. 4 (summer 1980): 631–60.

Rifkin, Mark. *The Erotics of Sovereignty: Queer Native Writing in the Era of Self-Determination.* Minneapolis: University of Minnesota Press, 2012.

———. "Romancing Kinship: A Queer Reading of Indian Education and Zitkala-Sa's American Indian Stories." *GLQ: A Journal of Lesbian and Gay Studies* 12, no. 1 (2006): 27–59.

———. *When Did Indians Become Straight? Kinship, the History of Sexuality, and Native Sovereignty.* New York: Oxford University Press, 2011.

Riggs, Lynn. "Green Grow the Lilacs." In *The Cherokee Night and Other Plays,* edited by Jace Weaver. 1931. Reprint, Norman: University of Oklahoma Press, 2003.

Robbins, Michael W., and Wendy Palitz. *Brooklyn: A State of Mind.* New York: Workman Publishing, 2000.

Robin's Hood. Written and directed by Kent Monkman. Toronto: Urban Nation, 2007.

Roemer, Kenneth M. "They Talk, Who Listens: Audience in American Indian Literatures—The Erdrich Example." *Reception: Texts, Readers, Audiences, History* 3 (summer 2011): 1–34.

Roscoe, Will. *Changing Ones: Third and Fourth Genders in Native North America.* New York: St. Martin's, 1998.

———. "Native North American Literature." In *The Gay and Lesbian Literary Heritage: A Reader's Companion to the Writers and Their Works from Antiquity to the Present,* edited by Claude J. Summers, 513–17. New York: Henry Holt, 1995.

———. *The Zuni Man-Woman.* Albuquerque: University of New Mexico Press, 1991.

Ross, Luana. *Inventing the Savage: The Social Construction of Native American Criminality.* Austin: University of Texas Press, 1998.

Ross, Marlon B. "Beyond the Closet as Raceless Paradigm." In *Black Queer Studies: A Critical Anthology,* edited by E. Patrick Johnson and Mae G. Henderson, 161–89. Durham, N.C.: Duke University Press, 2005.

Rowe, John Carlos. "Buried Alive: The Native American Political Unconscious in Louise Erdrich's Fiction." *Postcolonial Studies* 7, no. 2 (July 2004): 197–210.

Ruppert, James. "Maurice Kenny." In *The Handbook of Native American Literature,* edited by Andrew Widget, 453–58. London: Taylor and Francis, 1996.

Sackman, Douglas Cazaux. *Wild Men: Ishi and Kroeber in the Wilderness of Modern America.* New York: Oxford University Press, 2010.

Sandoval, Chela. *Methodology of the Oppressed.* Minneapolis: University of Minnesota Press, 2000.

Sarris, Greg. *Grand Avenue.* New York: Hyperion, 1994.

———. *Mission Indians.* 2001.

———. *Watermelon Nights.* New York: Hyperion, 1998.

Savageau, Cheryl. *Dirt Road Home.* Willimantic, Conn.: Curbstone, 1995.

———. *Home Country.* Cambridge, Mass.: Alice James Books, 1992.

———. *Mother/Land.* Cambridge, U.K.: Salt Publishing, 2006.

Schneider, Rebecca. "See the Big Show: Spiderwoman Theater Doubling Back." In *Acting Out: Feminist Performances,* edited by Lynda Hart and Peggy Phelan, 227–55. Ann Arbor: University of Michigan Press, 1993.

Schweninger, Lee. *Imagic Moments: Indigenous North American Film.* Athens: University of Georgia Press, 2013.

Scofield, Gregory. *The Gathering: Stones for the Medicine Wheel.* Vancouver: Pole Star Books, 1993.

———. *I Knew Two Metis Women.* Victoria, British Columbia: Pole Star Books, 1999.

———. *Kipocihkân: Poems New and Selected.* Gibsons, British Columbia: Nightwood Editions, 2009.

———. *Louis: The Heretic Poems.* Gibsons, British Columbia: Nightwood Editions, 2011.

———. *Love Medicine and One Song.* Victoria, British Columbia: Pole Star Books, 1997.

———. *Native Canadiana/Songs from the Urban Rez.* Vancouver: Pole Star Books, 1996.

———. *Singing Home the Bones.* Vancouver: Raincoast Books, 2005.

———. "Survival Poetry." In *The Gathering: Stones for the Medicine Wheel,* 34. Vancouver: Pole Star Books, 1993.

———. *Thunder through My Veins: Memories of a Métis Childhood.* Toronto: Harper Flamingo Canada, 1999.

Sears, Vickie. *Simple Songs.* Ithaca, N.Y.: Firebrand Books, 1990.

Sedgwick, Eve Kosofsky. *Between Men: English Literature and Male Homosocial Desire.* New York: Columbia University Press, 1985.

———. *Epistemology of the Closet.* Los Angeles: University of California Press, 1990.

———. *Touching Feeling: Affect, Pedagogy, Performativity.* Durham, N.C.: Duke University Press, 2003.

Sedgwick, Eve Kosofsky, and Adam Frank. "Shame in the Cybernetic Fold: Reading Silvan Tomkins." *Critical Inquiry* 21, no. 2 (winter 1995): 496–522.

Seidman, Steven. "Are We All in the Closet? Notes toward a Sociological and Cultural Turn in Queer Theory." In *Matters of Culture: Cultural Sociology in Practice,* edited by Roger Friedland and John Mohr, 255–69. Cambridge, U.K.: Cambridge University Press, 2004.

———. *Beyond the Closet: The Transformation of Gay and Lesbian Life.* New York: Routledge, 1997.

———. *Difference Troubles.* Cambridge, U.K.: Cambridge University Press, 1997.

Seigworth, Gregory J., and Melissa Gregg. "An Inventory of Shimmers." In *The Affect Theory Reader,* edited by Melissa Gregg and Gregory J. Seigworth, 1–28. Durham, N.C.: Duke University Press, 2010.

Serlin, David. "Crippling Masculinity: Queerness and Disability in U.S. Military Culture, 1800–1945." *GLQ: A Journal of Lesbian and Gay Studies* 9, nos. 1–2 (2003): 149–79.

Sex and the Rez. Directed by Duane Ghastant'Aucoin. 2004.

Shooting Geronimo. Written and directed by Kent Monkman. Toronto: Urban Nation, 2007.

Signorile, Michelangelo. *Queer in America: Sex, the Media, and the Closets of Power.* Madison: University of Wisconsin Press, 2003.

Silko, Leslie Marmon. *Almanac of the Dead.* New York: Penguin Group, 1991.

———. *Ceremony.* New York: Viking, 1977.

Silva, Elda. "*Johnny Greyeyes* Looks at Women behind Bars." *San Antonio Express-News* (Texas), April 6, 2001.

Silvera, Makeda. "Introduction." In *Piece of My Heart: A Lesbian of Colour Anthology,* edited by Makeda Silvera, xiii–xix. Toronto: Sister Vision Press, 1991.

———, ed. *Piece of My Heart: A Lesbian of Colour Anthology.* Toronto: Sister Vision Press, 1991.

Simard, Rodney. "A Wilderness Unlittered by Academic Trash." *Studies in American Indian Literatures* 5, no. 2 (summer 1993): 1–6.

Simpson, Audra. "From White into Red: Captivity Narratives as Alchemies of Race and Citizenship." *American Quarterly* 60, no. 2 (2008): 251–57.

Skins. Directed by Chris Eyre. Century City, Calif.: First Look Pictures, 2002.

Slotkin, Richard. *Gunfighter Nation: The Myth of the Frontier in Twentieth-Century America.* Norman: University of Oklahoma Press, 1991.

Smith, Andrea. *Conquest: Sexual Violence and American Indian Genocide.* Cambridge, Mass.: South End, 2005.

———. "Queer Theory and Native Studies: The Heteronormativity of Settler Colonialism." *GLQ: A Journal of Lesbian and Gay Studies* 16, nos. 1–2 (2010): 42–68.

Sneider, Leah. "Queering Indigenous Feminism: Complementary and Reciprocal Relationships in Native Literature." *American Indian Culture and Research Journal* (forthcoming).

Snyder, Michael. "'He Certainly Didn't Want Anyone to Know That He Was Queer': Chal Windzer's Sexuality in John Joseph Mathews's *Sundown.*" *Studies in American Indian Literatures* 20, no. 1 (spring 2008): 27–54.

Somerville, Siobhan B. *Queering the Color Line: Race and the Invention of Homosexuality in American Culture.* Durham, N.C.: Duke University Press, 2000.

Spurr, David. *The Rhetoric of Empire: Colonial Discourse in Journalism, Travel Writing, and Imperial Administration.* Durham, N.C.: Duke University Press, 1993.

Standing Bear, Luther. *My People the Sioux.* 1928. Reprint, Lincoln: University of Nebraska Press, Bison Books, 2006.

Stevens, James Thomas. *A Bridge Dead in the Water.* Cambridge, U.K.: Salt Publishing, 2007.

———. *Bulle/Chimère.* Lawrence, Kans.: First Intensity, 2006.

———. *Combing the Snakes from His Hair.* East Lansing: Michigan State University Press, 2002.

———. *dis(Orient).* Long Beach, Calif.: Palm, 2005.

———. *Mohawk/Samoa: Transmigrations.* Oakland, Calif.: Subpress, 2005.

———. *The Mutual Life.* Alexandria, Va.: Plan B, 2006.

———. "Poetry and Sexuality: Running Twin Rails." *GLQ: A Journal of Lesbian and Gay Studies* 16, nos. 1–2 (2010): 183–89.

———. *Tokinish.* New York: Intensity, 1994.

Steward, Daniel-Harry. "Coyote and Tehoma." In *Living the Spirit: A Gay American Indian Anthology,* edited by Gay American Indians and Will Roscoe, 157–62. New York: St. Martin's, 1988.

Stokes, Karah. "What about the Sweetheart? The 'Different Shape' of Anishinabe Two Sisters Stories in Louise Erdrich's *Love Medicine* and *Tales of Burning Love*." *MELUS* 24, no. 2 (1999): 89–105.

Sullivan, Laura, and Amy Walters. "Native Foster Care: Lost Children, Shattered Families." *All Things Considered*. National Public Radio. October 25, 2011.

Sullivan, Nikki. *A Critical Introduction to Queer Theory*. New York: New York University Press, 2003.

Suppe, Frederick. "Classifying Sexual Disorders: The Diagnostic and Statistical Manual of the American Psychiatric Association." *Journal of Homosexuality* 9 (summer 1984): 9–28.

Swaminathan, Nikhil. "Strange but True: Males Can Lactate." *Scientific American*, September 6, 2007. http://www.scientificamerica.com.

Szaloky, Melinda. "'As You Desire Me': Reading 'The Divine Garbo' through Movement, Silence and the Sublime." *Film History* 18, no. 2 (2006): 196–208.

Szanto, Laura Furlan. "An Annotated Secondary Bibliography of Louise Erdrich's Recent Fiction: *The Bingo Palace, Tales of Burning Love,* and *The Antelope Wife*." *Studies in American Indian Literatures* 12, no. 2 (summer 2000): 61–90.

Tanrisal, Meldan. "Mother and Child Relationships in the Novels of Louise Erdrich." *American Studies International* 35, no. 5 (1997): 67–80.

Tatonetti, Lisa. "Behind the Shadows of Wounded Knee: The Slippage of Imagination in *Wynema: A Child of the Forest*." *Studies in American Indian Literatures* 16, no. 1 (spring 2004): 1–31.

———. "Catholics, Carlisle, and Casting Stones: Richard Henry Pratt and the 1890 Ghost Dance." *Nineteenth-Century Contexts: An Interdisciplinary Journal* 33, no. 3 (July 2011): 1–21.

———. "Dancing That Way, Things Began to Change: The Ghost Dance as Pantribal Metaphor in Sherman Alexie's Writing." In *Sherman Alexie: A Collection of Critical Essays*, edited by Jeff Berglund and Jan Roush, 1–24. Salt Lake City: University of Utah Press, 2010.

———. "Disrupting a Story of Loss: Charles Eastman and Nicholas Black Elk Narrate Survivance." *Western American Literature* 39, no. 3 (fall 2004): 279–311.

———. "The Emergence and Importance of Queer American Indian Literatures, or, 'Help and Stories' in Thirty Years of *SAIL*." *Studies in American Indian Literatures* 19, no. 4 (winter 2007): 143–70.

———. "Indigenous Fantasies and Sovereign Erotics: Outland Cherokees Write Two-Spirit Nations." In *Queer Indigenous Studies: Critical Interventions in Theory, Politics, and Literature,* edited by Qwo-Li Driskill, Chris Finley, Brian Joseph Gilley, and Scott Lauria Morgensen, 155–71. Tucson: University of Arizona Press, 2011.

———. "'A Kind of Queer Balance': Cherríe Moraga's Aztlán." *MELUS: Multi-Ethnic Literature of the United States* 29, no. 2 (summer 2004): 227–47.

———. "Two-Spirit Images in the Work of Maurice Kenny." In *Maurice Kenny: Celebrations of a Mohawk Writer,* edited by Penelope Myrtle Kelsey, 119–33. New York: SUNY Press, 2012.

Taylor, Drew Hayden, ed. *Me Sexy: An Exploration of Native Sex and Sexuality.* Vancouver: Douglas and McIntyre, 2008.

Taylor, Ula. "The Historical Evolution of Black Feminist Theory and Praxis." *Journal of Black Studies* 29, no. 2 (November 1998): 234–53.

Taylor, Verta, Elizabeth Kaminski, and Kimberly Dugan. "From Bowery to the Castro: Communities, Identities, and Movements." In *Handbook of Lesbian and Gay Studies,* edited by Diane Richardson and Steven Seidman, 99–114. London: Sage Publications, 2002.

Teuton, Sean Kicummah. *Red Land, Red Power: Grounding Knowledge in the American Indian Novel.* Durham, N.C.: Duke University Press, 2008.

Thirza Cuthand's Through the Looking Glass. Written and directed by Thirza Cuthand. Toronto: V-Tape, 1999.

Thomson, Rosemarie Garland. *Extraordinary Bodies: Figuring Disability in American Culture and Literature.* New York: Columbia University Press, 1997.

Thunderstorm. Directed by Adam Garnet Jones. Toronto: V-Tape, 2005.

To Brooklyn and Back: A Mohawk Journey. Directed by Reaghan Tarbell, Paul Rickard, and George Hargrove. Montreal: Mushkeg Media, 2009.

Toland, John. *Adolf Hitler.* New York: Doubleday, 1976.

Trachtenberg, Alan. *Shades of Hiawatha: Staging Indians, Making Americans, 1880–1930.* New York: Hill and Wang, 2005.

Traditional Indigenous Values. Directed by Ruth Villasenor. San Francisco: Frameline, 2009.

Trafzer, Clifford E., and Joel R. Hyer, eds. *"Exterminate Them!": Written Accounts of the Murder, Rape, and Enslavement of Native Americans during the California Gold Rush.* Foreword by Edward D. Castillo. East Lansing: University of Michigan Press, 1999.

Two-Embrace. Directed, produced, and edited by Carrie House. Vimeo, 2009. http://vimeo.com/60814579.

Two-Spirited: First Stories Volume III. Directed and written by Sharon A. Desjariais. Montreal: National Film Board of Canada, 2007.

Two-Spirit People. Directed by Michel Beauchemin, Lori Levy, and Gretchen Vogel. San Francisco: Frameline, 1992.

Two Spirits. Directed by Ruth Fertig. San Francisco: Frameline, 2007.

Two Spirits. Directed by Lydia Nibley. Los Angeles: Riding the Tiger, 2010.

Two-Spirits: Belonging. Directed by Rope Wolf. San Francisco: Frameline, 2005.

Two Spirits, One Journey. Written and produced by Shawn Imitates Dog. Directed by Arthur Allen Seidelan and Chad Richman. Southern California Indian Center: Inter Tribal Entertainment, 2007.

Valerio, Anita. "It's in My Blood, My Face—My Mother's Voice, the Way I Sweat." In *This Bridge Called My Back: Writings by Radical Women of Color,* edited by Cherríe Moraga and Gloria Anzaldúa, 41–45. New York: Women of Color Press, 1983.

Valerio, Max Wolf. "'Now That You're White Man': Changing Sex in a Postmodern World—Being, Becoming, and Borders." In *This Bridge We Call Home: Radical Visions for Transformation,* edited by Gloria Anzaldúa, 239–54. New York: Routledge, 2002.

———. *The Testosterone Files: My Hormonal and Social Transformation from Female to Male.* Emeryville, Calif.: Seal, 2006.

Van Dyke, Annette. "A Hope for Miracles: Shifting Perspectives in Louise Erdrich's *The Last Report on the Miracles at Little No Horse.*" In *Studies in the Literary Achievement of Louise Erdrich, Native American Writer: Fifteen Critical Essays,* edited by Brajesh Sawhney, 63–74. Lewiston, N.Y.: Edwin Mellen, 2008.

———. "Of Vision Quests and Spiritual Guardians: Female Power in the Novels of Louise Erdrich." In *The Chippewa Landscape of Louise Erdrich,* edited by Allan Chavkin, 130–43. Tuscaloosa: University of Alabama Press, 1999.

———. "A Tribute to Paula Gunn Allen (1939–2008)." *Studies in American Indian Literatures* 20, no. 4 (winter 2008): 68–75.

Vernon, Irene S. *Killing Us Quietly: Native Americans and HIV/AIDS.* Lincoln: University of Nebraska Press, 2001.

Verster, Francois. "A Lion's Tale." *Independent Lens.* PBS, 2005.

Vizenor, Gerald. *The Darkness in Saint Louis Bearheart.* St. Paul, Minn.: Truck, 1978.

———. *Fugitive Poses: Native American Indian Scenes of Absence and Presence.* Lincoln: University of Nebraska Press, 1998.

———. *Manifest Manners: Narratives on Postindian Survivance.* Lincoln: University of Nebraska Press, 1994.

———. *The People Named the Chippewa: Narrative Histories.* Minneapolis: University of Minnesota Press, 1984.

———. "Socioacupuncture: Mythic Reversals and the Striptease in Four Scenes." In *The American Indian and the Problem of History,* edited by Calvin Martin, 181–91. New York: Oxford University Press, 1987.

Warrior, Robert. *Tribal Secrets: Recovering American Indian Intellectual Traditions.* Minneapolis: University of Minnesota Press, 1994.

———. "Your Skin Is the Map: The Theoretical Challenge of Joy Harjo's Erotic Poetry." In *Reasoning Together: The Native Critics Collective,* edited by Craig Womack, Daniel Heath Justice, and Christopher Teuton, 340–52. Norman: University of Oklahoma Press, 2008.

Wave a Red Flag. Directed by Adam Garnet Jones. Toronto: National Film Board of Canada, 2009.

Weaver, Jace. "Foreword." In *The Cherokee Night and Other Plays,* edited by Jace Weaver, ix–xv. Norman: University of Oklahoma Press, 2003.

Weaver, Jace, Craig S. Womack, and Robert Warrior. *American Indian Literary Nationalism.* Albuquerque: University of New Mexico Press, 2005.

Weinmann, Aileo. "Hold Me Closer, Fancydancer: A Conversation with Sherman Alexie." 2002. http://www.filmcritic.com.

Welch, James. *Fools Crow.* New York: Penguin, 1987.

———. *The Heartsong of Charging Elk.* New York: Doubleday, 2000.

———. *Riding the Earthboy 40.* 1971. Reprint, New York: Penguin, 2004.

———. *Winter in the Blood.* New York: Penguin, 1974.

Weston, Kath. *Families We Choose: Lesbians, Gays, Kinship.* New York: Columbia University Press, 1991.

———. *Long Slow Burn: Sexuality and Social Science.* New York: Routledge, 1998.

White, Kevin. *Where Eagles Dare to Soar: Indians, Politics and AIDS.* Kahnawake, Quebec: Owera Books, 1993.

Williams, Walter. *The Spirit and the Flesh: Sexual Diversity in American Indian Culture.* 1986. Reprint, Boston: Beacon, 1992.

Wilson, Michael D. "Maurice Kenny." In *The Dictionary of Literary Biography.* Vol. 175, *Native American Writers of the United States,* edited by Kenneth M. Roemer, 137–42. Detroit: Gale, 1997.

Wilson, Norma. "America's Indigenous Poetry." In *The Cambridge Companion to Native American Literature,* edited by Joy Porter and Kenneth M. Roemer, 145–60. Cambridge, U.K.: Cambridge University Press, 2005.

Wilson, Trista. "Changed Embraces, Changes Embraced? Renouncing the Heterosexists Majority in Favor of a Return to Traditional Two-Spirit Culture." *American Indian Law Review* 36, no. 1 (2011–2012): 161–88.

Winick, Stephen. "The World's First 'Kumbaya' Moment: New Evidence about an Old Song." *American Folklife Center News* 32 (summer/fall 2010): 3–10.

Womack, Craig. *Art as Performance, Story as Criticism: Reflections on Native Literary Aesthetics.* Norman: University of Oklahoma Press, 2009.

———. *Drowning in Fire.* Tucson: University of Arizona Press, 2001.

———. "Howling at the Moon: The Queer but True Story of My Life as a Hank Williams Song." In *As We Are Now: Mixblood Essays on Race and Identity,* edited by William S. Penn, 28–49. Berkeley: University of California Press, 1997.

———. "Politicizing HIV in Indian Country." In *Native American Religious Identity: Unforgotten Gods,* edited by Jace Weaver, 199–216. Maryknoll, N.Y.: Orbis Books, 1998.

———. *Red on Red: Native American Literary Separatism.* Minneapolis: University of Minnesota Press, 1999.

———. "A Single Decade: Book-Length Native Literary Criticism between 1986 and 1997." In *Reasoning Together: The Native Critics Collective,* edited by Craig

Womack, Daniel Heath Justice, and Christopher Teuton, 3–104. Norman: University of Oklahoma Press, 2008.

———. "Suspicioning: Imagining a Debate between Those Who Get Confused, and Those Who Don't, When They Read Critical Responses to the Poems of Joy Harjo, or What's an Old-Timey Gay Boy Like Me To Do?" *GLQ: A Journal of Lesbian and Gay Studies* 16, nos. 1–2 (2010): 133–55.

———. "Theorizing American Indian Experience." In *Reasoning Together: The Native Critics Collective,* edited by Craig Womack, Daniel Heath Justice, and Christopher Teuton, 353–410. Norman: University of Oklahoma Press, 2008.

Women's Institute for Freedom of the Press. "Celebrating Our Diversity: Women of Color Periodicals: 1968–1988." http://www.wifp.org.

Woods, Gregory. *A History of Gay Literature: The Male Tradition.* New Haven, Conn.: Yale University Press, 1998.

Wordsworth, William. *Lyrical Ballads and Other Poems, 1797–1800.* Edited by James Butler and Karen Green. Ithaca, N.Y.: Cornell University Press, 1983.

You Are a Lesbian Vampire. Written and directed by Thirza Cuthand. Toronto: V-Tape, 2008.

Youngberg, Quentin. "Interpenetrations: Re-Encoding the Queer Indian in Sherman Alexie's *The Business of Fancydancing.*" *Studies in American Indian Literatures* 20, no. 1 (2008): 55–75.

Index

Figures and notes are indicated by *f* and n, respectively.

Lisa Tatonetti is associate professor of English at Kansas State University. She is coeditor of *Sovereign Erotics: A Collection of Two-Spirit Literature.*